KARL BARTH AND AMERICAN EVANGELICALISM

Karl Barth and American Evangelicalism

Edited by

Bruce L. McCormack & Clifford B. Anderson

WILLIAM B. EERDMANS PUBLISHING COMPANY
GRAND RAPIDS, MICHIGAN / CAMBRIDGE, U.K.

Published 2011 by

Wm. B. Eerdmans Publishing Co.

2140 Oak Industrial Drive N.E., Grand Rapids, Michigan 49505 /

P.O. Box 163, Cambridge CB3 9PU U.K.

www.eerdmans.com

Printed in the United States of America

17 16 15 14 13 12 11   7 6 5 4 3 2 1

Library of Congress Cataloging-in-Publication Data

Karl Barth and American evangelicalism /
edited by Bruce L. McCormack & Clifford B. Anderson.
     p.   cm.
   Papers presented at a conference held June 22-24, 2007 in Princeton, N.J.
   ISBN 978-0-8028-6656-1 (pbk.: alk. paper)
   1. Barth, Karl, 1886-1968 — Congresses. 2. Evangelicalism — United States —
Congresses. 3. Van Til, Cornelius, 1895-1987 — Congresses.
   I. McCormack, Bruce L.   II. Anderson, Clifford B.

   BR1642.U5K37   2011
   230′.044092 — dc22

                     2011005881

Jason Springs, "But Did It Really Happen?" chapter 4 of Springs, *Toward a Generous Orthodoxy* (2010), is reprinted by permission of Oxford University Press.

Quotations from Karl Barth, *Church Dogmatics,* are reprinted by permission of Continuum and TVZ Theologischer Verlag Zürich AG.

Contents

v

Contents

Abbreviations

CD   Karl Barth. *Church Dogmatics.* Edited by Geoffrey W. Bromiley and Thomas F. Torrance. 4 vols. in 13 parts. Edinburgh: T. & T. Clark, 1936-75.

KD   Karl Barth. *Die kirchliche Dogmatik.* 4 vols. in 13 parts. Zollikon: Verlag der Evangelischen Buchhandlung, 1932-70.

Introduction

Clifford B. Anderson

With one exception, the essays contained in this volume first saw life as papers presented at the second annual conference on Karl Barth's theology co-sponsored by the Center for Barth Studies at Princeton Theological Seminary and the Karl Barth Society of North America, which took place in Princeton on June 22-24, 2007. The theme of the conference was "Karl Barth and American Evangelicalism: Friends or Foes?" Our purpose in creating this conference was threefold: (1) to re-examine the critique of Barth's theology advanced in the mid-twentieth century by one of his most vocal opponents, Cornelius Van Til; (2) to lay some foundations for what we hope will be a new phase in evangelical engagement with Barth through reflection on "hot topics" like the relation between philosophy and theology, Christology and covenant theology, the nature of the church, and the limits of salvation in Christ; and (3) to examine how Barth's theology might help evangelicals in their efforts to come to grips with contemporary theological movements.

The results of our conference far exceeded our expectations. The papers sparkled with understanding and wisdom. The insights they offered had much to teach us about the current situation in theology and, even more important, they provided a basis for moving evangelical engagement with Barth to a new stage in its history. We are now placing them before a wider public in the belief that they will generate broader evangelical reappraisal of Karl Barth.

*   *   *

Clifford B. Anderson

The essays in this volume are divided into three parts. The essays in Part I address the historical context of Cornelius Van Til's critique of Karl Barth. Who was Cornelius Van Til, and what theological and historical factors contributed to his animosity toward Karl Barth? The essays in Part II address contemporary theological topics. As far as possible, we sought in this section to pair representatives of Barth's theology with evangelical theologians. We had hoped to stimulate discussion by juxtaposing opposing points of view. A surprise of the conference, however, was how difficult it is to find "Barthians" who do not consider themselves evangelicals and to identify contemporary evangelicals who have not been inspired by Barth! The essays in Part III deal with four movements of current interest (radical orthodoxy, postliberal theology, the political ethics of Stanley Hauerwas, and the emerging church movement). The goal of this section was to point beyond the consonances and conflicts between Barth and evangelicalism to show how contemporary "Barthians" and evangelical theologians might find common cause in their response to several prominent theological movements of the present day.

*   *   *

The first two essays in this volume deal directly with the legacy of Cornelius Van Til (1895-1987). Van Til was a Dutch-born theologian, an American mediator of a polemical form of Dutch Neo-Calvinism, and a man whose notoriety outside of conservative Presbyterian circles is due largely to the many critiques of Karl Barth's theology he published over the course of his life.[1] Van Til, a member of the Christian Reformed Church, received his graduate education from Princeton Theological Seminary and Princeton University in the late 1920s. He taught apologetics at Princeton Seminary during the academic year 1928-29, but declined to accept the conditions of his renewed appointment in the wake of the Seminary's controversial reorganization in 1929. Van Til subsequently became a professor at the newly founded Westminster Seminary in Philadelphia, Pennsylvania. Van Til's greatest influence,

---

1. Van Til's most significant writings on Barth are as follows: Cornelius Van Til, *The New Modernism: An Appraisal of the Theology of Barth and Brunner* (Philadelphia: Presbyterian and Reformed Publishing Company, 1946); idem, "Has Karl Barth Become Orthodox?" *Westminster Theological Journal* 16 (1954): 135-81; idem, "Karl Barth on Chalcedon," *Westminster Theological Journal* 22 (1959/1960): 147-66; idem, *Christianity and Barthianism* (Philadelphia: Presbyterian and Reformed Publishing Company, 1962); idem, *Karl Barth and Evangelicalism* (Philadelphia: Presbyterian and Reformed Publishing Company, 1964).

no doubt, was felt during the years before interest waned among evangelicals in confessional (denominational) theologies, before the "church growth" movement, before doctrinal theology became a tool adapted to the requirements of political activism and therapeutic approaches to pastoral care. In those days, his writings on apologetics were widely read and discussed. But even with all these changes, Van Til continues to exercise an influence on a significant segment of evangelicalism, largely through the graduates of the various campuses of Westminster Seminary where his works (including those on Barth) are still required reading.

George Harinck, Professor of the History of Neo-Calvinism at the Vrije Universiteit Amsterdam, uncovers the early Dutch reception of Barth and its impact on Van Til, focusing especially on the influence of Klaas Schilder. The great Dutch Neo-Calvinists in the generation after Herman Bavinck and Abraham Kuyper — Schilder, Herman Dooyeweerd, and D. H. T. Vollenhoven — advanced their arguments with an eye not simply to countering Barth's influence, but to addressing the situation of Christians in postwar Europe more generally. Harinck contends that Karl Barth and Klaas Schilder were shaped by a similar concern — the position of Christendom after the catastrophe of the First World War — even amid their sharp disagreements. He notes that both were constructive theologians who recognized the need to reformulate classic Reformed doctrines in light of the upheavals in modern society. Van Til, by contrast, articulated his apologetics from the relatively tranquil precincts of Philadelphia, where he sought through philosophical means to defend the theological traditions of Old Princeton and Old Amsterdam. Harinck laments that a secondary consequence of Van Til's apologetics has been the impedance of a fruitful encounter between Neo-Calvinism and Dialectical Theology to the present day.

D. G. Hart, well known in this country for his biography of J. Gresham Machen and a history of the evangelical movement in the twentieth century, looks at Van Til's critique in its American context in an effort to explain why leading lights in the evangelical movement in the 1950s charted a different course in engaging Barth than did conservative Presbyterians like Van Til. Hart contrasts the reception of Barth among Neo-Evangelicals writing for *Christianity Today* with conservative Presbyterians publishing in the *Presbyterian Guardian*. Whereas Neo-Evangelicals were cautiously optimistic about Barth's orthodoxy, conservative Presbyterians tended to regard him as a threat. Hart contends that the difference in opinion had much to do with the differences in social setting between Neo-Evangelicals and conservative Presbyterians. The latter group had inextricably linked the rise of "Barthianism" with the fundamentalist-modernist divide in the Presbyterian Church and, in particular, the controversies at Princeton Seminary that led to the formation of Westminster Seminary and the Orthodox Presbyterian Church. Reading Van Til in the light of such Presbyterian controversies helps to explain his motivation for erecting a philosophical barricade against the intrusion of "Barthianism" among confessional Presbyterians.

*   *   *

Analysis of the historical context for Van Til's animus toward the theology of Karl Barth should not be considered an end in itself, but a prelude toward renewed theological engagement. The polemical context obstructed critical evaluation of the substance of Van Til's theological critique of Karl Barth. His criticisms have not yet received the scrutiny which would allow them to be judged independently according to their merits rather than as a "take it or leave it" whole.[2] It is our view, however, that the time has come to take a more measured, dispassionate approach. Van Til did not get everything wrong. Many of his observations have something to them and contemporary evangelicals may discover that he anticipated certain of their concerns about Barth's theology. Evangelicals may likewise have questions about Barth's actualistic ontology, his "historicized" Christology, his understanding of the Church as *event,* and his tilt toward universalism (as a consequence of his doctrine of election). So a theological re-examination of Van Til is a timely exercise, well suited to promote not only greater understanding of Barth but also greater self-understanding on the part of evangelicals generally.

We did not ask the contributors to Part II of this volume to respond to Van Til directly, but to take up historical areas of disagreement between Barth and evangelicals and advance the state of the discussion. The first two essays broadly examine the philosophical underpinnings of Van Til's critique, namely, his depiction of the impact of Immanuel Kant on modern theology generally as a way of connecting Barth's "new modernism" to the old modernisms of Friedrich Schleiermacher and Albrecht Ritschl.

John E. Hare, Noah Porter Professor of Philosophical Theology at Yale Divinity School, asks whether the depiction of the harmful impact of Kant on modern theology (held in differing degrees by *both* Van Til and Barth!) is

2. See, however, Bruce L. McCormack's "Afterword" for just such a critical theological analysis of the most prominent of Van Til's criticisms of Barth's theology.

correct and what it would mean for Van Til's critique of Barth if it were not. He notes that interpretation of Kant's philosophical theology has undergone significant shifts since Cornelius Van Til, Gordon Clark, and Carl Henry expressed their critique of the role of God in his system. Fascinatingly, Hare points out that Barth shared some of the same misconceptions about Kant's intentions. By contrast, Hare contends that the new interpretation of Kant's philosophy of religion, which places greater weight on what he terms the "'vertical dimension' of Kant's thought," opens up an avenue to a modern, rationalist apologetic for faith in God.

Clifford B. Anderson, Curator of Special Collections at Princeton Theological Seminary, explores the philosophical context of Barth's rejection of "religious experience" as a source of theological knowledge. He traces the roots of this rejection back to a thought form Barth learned in his student days from Hermann Cohen and Paul Natorp, exponents of the so-called "Marburg Neo-Kantianism." Anderson demonstrates how Barth learned a modified form of the transcendental argument from them, which effectively stood Kant's transcendental argument on its head. Whereas Kant argued that the categories of understanding constitute the conditions of possibility for experience in general, Barth argued that Christian experience forms a condition of possibility for Christian preaching. Obviously, Barth's adaptation of the transcendental argument denudes it of its anti-skeptical purpose — at least for those outside the Christian community. But the thought form helped him to reconstruct the idea of "Christian experience" without making concessions to natural theology or "lived religious experience." Intriguingly, Van Til likewise adapted a form of the transcendental argument while jettisoning Kant's critical philosophy.[3] The presence of a version of the transcendental argument in both Karl Barth and Van Til suggests the topic of a future study analyzing how each adapted and made use of that form of argument.

The next set of chapters goes to the heart of the matter. Does Barth's reconstruction of central Christian doctrines constitute a simple "rejection" of "historic Christianity" (as Van Til frequently asserted)? Or does it represent a faithful re-articulation of the biblical testimony upon which "historic Christianity" also rested? Neither of our essayists sides completely with Barth or Van Til on this issue.

---

3. For a contemporary appraisal of the place of the transcendental argument in Van Til, see Don Collett, "Apologetics: Van Til and Transcendental Argument," *Westminster Theological Journal* 65 (2003): 289-306, and John M. Frame, "Reply to Don Collett on Transcendental Argument," *Westminster Theological Journal* 65 (2003): 307-9.

Clifford B. Anderson

Michael S. Horton, J. Gresham Machen Professor of Systematic Theology and Apologetics at Westminster Seminary, California, evaluates Karl Barth's Christology from the standpoint of Reformed Orthodoxy. Horton's essay will likely provoke debate on both sides of the aisle. On the one hand, Horton approaches Barth appreciatively — as a bona fide theologian, not as a philosopher outfitting his speculations in religious garb. On the other, he articulates a series of criticisms which still stand as roadblocks to the full reception of Barth among defenders of contemporary Reformed Orthodoxy. Horton finds that Barth's Christology generates problems for the doctrine of the Trinity and the treatment of covenantal history. He argues that by tending to absorb and synthesize all doctrines into Christology, Barth's theology winds up subverting his avowed Christocentric standpoint. Horton's contribution to the conference and the book is especially welcome because of his clear and careful articulation of a number of longstanding evangelical criticisms of Barth. Readers of his essay will find him drawing together lines of argument from appreciative critics like Hans Urs von Balthasar, G. C. Berkouwer, and Emil Brunner to present a formidable critique of Barth's fundamental theological moves. His critique also meshes nicely with Suzanne McDonald's analysis of the relationship between Barth's universalism and the work of the Holy Spirit.

Adam Neder, Associate Professor of Theology at Whitworth University, defends Barth's Christology against several points raised by Horton. He sets out a close examination of Barth's Christology in *Church Dogmatics* IV/1 and IV/2. Neder shows just how radically Barth reconstructed the doctrine of the hypostatic union by moving away from substantial categories to concepts like "event" and "history" in his description of the two natures of Christ. Barth's moves foster a new perspective on the sixteenth- and seventeenth-century debates between the Lutherans and the Reformed about the communication of attributes. However, Neder raises critical questions about Barth's reinterpretation. While Barth's reinterpretation of the Chalcedonian categories is "innovative," he sees "major and minor conceptual problems" in Barth's Christology. He calls on evangelical theologians to think with Barth beyond Barth in order to overcome these perceived inconsistencies in his Christology.

In the end, Van Til was right to see that Barth was not just setting out the church's classical theology. Barth was aiming higher — to reinterpret classical Christological categories without recourse to outworn metaphysical assumptions and with greater emphasis on the biblical narrative about Jesus Christ. But was Van Til right to warn us away from Barth for that reason? Horton and

Neder both suggest that contemporary evangelicals will benefit from grappling with Barth's interpretation of traditional Christological formulations, no matter where they ultimately come down on the issues at stake.

The third set of chapters in Part II turn our attention away from Van Til to contemporary issues in ecclesiology. In recent years, many evangelicals have come to regard their doctrine of the church as historically insufficient and doctrinally "thin." Does Barth's doctrine of the church have anything to offer?

In "The Church in Karl Barth and Evangelicalism: Conversations across the Aisle," Kimlyn J. Bender, Associate Professor of Theology and Philosophy at the University of Sioux Falls, explores why evangelicals have not developed a satisfactory ecclesiology. Conflicting dynamics within evangelicalism have led to "general neglect of ecclesiology as a theological topic." Bender suggests that though evangelicals have traditionally been wary of Barth, Barth's theology can serve both as a corrective and a guide to the development of a stronger evangelical doctrine of the church. Evangelicals may be surprised to discover, for instance, that Barth shared many of their central intuitions about the church, including the primacy of mission.

Keith L. Johnson, Assistant Professor of Theology at Wheaton College, defends Barth against a line of criticism that has become increasingly popular among younger evangelicals, namely, that Barth's doctrine of the church is abstract and does not provide a robust enough connection between divine and human action. Does participation in the church make any difference? Johnson contends that Barth's understanding of the *concursus Dei*, or the mysterious relationship between divine and human action, preserves the natural distinction between God and humanity while still providing for a gracious continuity of action. For Barth, mere participation in church practices does not guarantee continuity with divine action; continuity comes from participation in the being of the church, namely, "witness and proclamation." The contributions of Bender and Johnson both thus highlight Barth's commitment to evangelism. Barth may in fact provide encouragement to contemporary evangelicals who have become disheartened for sociological or theological reasons with evangelicalism's historic concentration on mission.

The final set of chapters in Part II treats the question of universalism. Evangelicals have regularly charged that Barth's doctrine of election leads ineluctably to universalism, despite his protestations. Evangelicals typically reject universalism as unbiblical and as an impediment to mission.

In "So That He May Be Merciful to All: Karl Barth and the Problem of

Universalism," Bruce L. McCormack, Charles Hodge Professor of Systematic Theology at Princeton Theological Seminary, takes on the charge that universalism lacks any biblical warrant. He notes that Barth's leaning toward universal salvation is a "deal breaker for evangelicals," but asks whether "the possibility of a universal salvation [is] really so unthinkable in light of the [New Testament] witness?" McCormack argues that a tension between limited atonement and universalism pervades the New Testament. He contends that the church lacks the biblical warrant resolutely to decide in favor of one view or the other. As a theologian of the church, Barth grappled with that tension throughout his career, finally endorsing a view that implies universal salvation. But as a biblical theologian, he refused to endorse *apokatastasis* since, as McCormack remarks, "even the best theology can only be a witness to the truth, not the thing itself." Barth humbly recognized that only Jesus in his Second Coming can resolve the tension between limited atonement and universal salvation in the New Testament.

Suzanne McDonald, Assistant Professor of Theology at Calvin College, takes a different tack in "Evangelical Questioning of Election in Barth: A Pneumatological Perspective from the Reformed Heritage." She argues that the debate over the purportedly universalistic horizon of Barth's doctrine of election tacitly presupposes a more fundamental pneumatological consideration, namely, "how are we found to be 'in Christ'"? How does the Spirit unite believers to Christ? Is Barth's pneumatology consistent with his doctrine of election? McDonald raises fresh questions about Barth's doctrine of election, which may channel the debate over his "universalism" into more fruitful theological territory.

*   *   *

The theological world has not stood still since Van Til penned his criticisms of Karl Barth, of course. While the majority of the conference papers dealt with concerns raised by Neo-Evangelicals such as Carl Henry and conservative Presbyterians like Cornelius Van Til, we also commissioned four papers to address new theological movements that have elicited significant comment in evangelical circles. In Part III of this volume, four scholars explore Barth's relevance to these contemporary theological movements.

In "But Did It *Really* Happen?" Jason A. Springs, Assistant Professor of Religion, Ethics and Peace Studies at the University of Notre Dame's Kroc Institute of International Peace Studies, re-examines the Carl Henry-Hans Frei debate on biblical authority. According to Springs's reading, Barth may serve to mediate that debate, warding off as he did naïve biblical realism by emphasizing the dialectic between revelation and history, on the one hand, and guarding against all too sophisticated religious idealisms with his doctrine of analogy, on the other. Springs contends that Barth left a more enduring influence on Frei than many have presupposed and that Frei's reading of Barth helped (in part) to preserve him from adopting a purely idealistic (or antirealist) interpretation of biblical narrative.

The "emerging church" movement has generated much discussion among evangelicals during the past few years. John R. Franke, Theologian in Residence, First Presbyterian Church (Allentown, PA), contends that Barth helped to inspire the movement by exposing putative theological knowledge to an unceasing dialectic of negation and affirmation, by maintaining the irreducible plurality of the biblical witness, and by stressing the provisional and open-ended nature of doctrinal formulations. Barth's dialectical theology thus helped to open the theological space required for the emerging church conversation to begin. While many in the emerging church movement would resist being labeled "Barthian," Franke argues that "the open-ended plurality of its ecclesiological intuitions is consonant with the implications of Barth's open-ended dogmatics." He suggests that the health of the movement depends on its ability to become more self-critical about pluralism — or, dare we say, more "dialectical" in its approach to doctrinal diversity?

In "Ontological Violence and the Covenant of Grace," Kevin W. Hector, Assistant Professor of Theology and of the Philosophy of Religions at the University of Chicago, puts Karl Barth into dialogue with John Milbank and the "Radical Orthodoxy" movement. Hector contends that Barth provides a superior basis for "ontological peace" in his covenant of grace. Whereas representatives of Radical Orthodoxy connect their notion of ontological peace with a hierarchical doctrine of the church, Barth refuses to make the church into the visible mediator between God and humanity. In Barth's view, non-Christians may be unwitting witnesses to Jesus Christ whatever their relation to the church. In a way, Hector's essay underscores the central themes of Bender's and Johnson's contributions and exhibits the convergence of evangelical concerns with significant strands in Barth's doctrine of the church.

The relationship between the church and the secular world comes to the fore again in the final essay in this section. Todd V. Cioffi, Assistant Professor of Congregational and Ministry Studies at Calvin College, contends that while many evangelicals have developed renewed appreciation for the centrality of the church from Stanley Hauerwas, his writings have also fostered a kind of "us-them" relationship toward the state and the secular world more generally. Moreover, Hauerwas's influential interpretation of Karl Barth in *With the Grain of the Universe* gives the impression that his views on the church and the secular stand in close continuity with Barth's. Cioffi argues that Barth actually offers a compelling alternative to Hauerwas by upholding the integrity of the church while avoiding any dualism between the church and the secular world. Again, the key is the lordship of Christ over the church — Christ is "Lord" even over church practices.

*   *   *

An "Afterword" by Bruce L. McCormack rounds off the essays, providing a critical but friendly assessment of the central elements in Van Til's critique of Barth.

We hope that readers of this volume will experience the same recognition of spiritual friendship in Christ we discovered during the conference. The convergence between "Barthian" and evangelical theology has made it increasingly difficult to draw a clean line of demarcation. Clearly, contemporary evangelicals and "Barthians" have become more "friends" than "foes." While still admitting large swathes of disagreement, we expect our sense of common cause to continue to grow as we face together the challenge of doing theology in a society increasingly forgetful of God.

We would be remiss if we did not thank in conclusion the many people who made the conference and this publication possible. We would like particularly to thank Sharon Kozlowski and Amy Ehlin for their assistance with the organizational details of the event. We would also like to thank Travis McMaken for his help with the planning and orchestration of events. Sarah Seraphin likewise deserves our thanks for assisting with registration (and designing an excellent tote bag). This volume has benefited greatly from the careful and diligent editorial work of Keith L. Johnson and especially David Congdon. The editors are deeply grateful to David for assisting with the final production of the volume, including the composition of the index.

PART I

HISTORICAL CONTEXT

"How Can an Elephant Understand a Whale and Vice Versa?" The Dutch Origins of Cornelius Van Til's Appraisal of Karl Barth

George Harinck

Introduction

It may be true that the Barthians for a long time have neglected the evangelicals, but they knew at least one of them by name: Cornelius Van Til (1895-1987). This Dutch-American theologian and professor of apologetics and systematic theology at Westminster Theological Seminary in Philadelphia was about ten years younger than Karl Barth (1886-1968). He entered the world of Barth and the Barthians with a bang in 1946, when he published his first book, *The New Modernism: An Appraisal of the Theology of Barth and Brunner.*[1] In this book of close to four hundred pages — one of the first major publications of the Westminster faculty — Van Til offered a full-scale analysis of the theology of Barth and Emil Brunner (1889-1966), especially of its philosophical presuppositions. In the 1940s Van Til had read Barth's volumes of the *Kirchliche Dogmatik* thoroughly, and in his book he presented many arguments for his initial suspicion that Karl Barth's theology was not a corrective to Protestant liberalism, but a "heresy," "deeply and ultimately destructive of the gospel."[2] "Barth's theology, for all its historical

1. Cornelius Van Til, *The New Modernism: An Appraisal of the Theology of Barth and Brunner* (Philadelphia/London: Presbyterian and Reformed Publishing Co., 1946; 2nd ed., 1947).
2. John R. Muether, *Cornelius Van Til: Reformed Apologist and Churchman* (Phillipsburg, NJ: P&R Publishing, 2008), 136. Quotation from C. Van Til, "Has Karl Barth Become Orthodox?" *Westminster Theological Journal* 16 (1954): 181. When in the spring of

theological vocabulary" was, according to Van Til's thesis, "nothing more than neomodernism."[3]

Van Til's book was not very favorably received among Barthians, to put it mildly, especially not in Europe. I think the Dutch theologian Klaas Schilder (1890-1952) was quite correct in 1952 when he wrote that *The New Modernism* was received among the Barthians with "howls of an Indian."[4] The Dutch theologian Theodoor L. Haitjema (1888-1972), who had hosted Barth on his first visit to the Netherlands in 1926 and had published the first book on him in Dutch in that same year,[5] labeled Van Til's analysis of Barth as a "horrible misunderstanding."[6] Barth's Catholic interpreter, Hans Urs von Balthasar, dismissed as "ridiculous" Van Til's attempt "to explain the whole theology of Barth and Brunner on the basis of their earlier positions and in terms of the philosophical principles that are supposedly at the root of their system."[7] But the main reason why Barthians know and remember Van Til's name is that the master himself took up his pen against the Westminster Seminary theologian. In his personal correspondence Barth complained about "the fundamentalist Cornelius Van Til": "I have read two books by Dr. van Til. In both of them, especially in the second one, he . . . accused me of being the worst heretic p. Chr. n. [*post Christum natum*]. It is a long time ago since I read them. But I remember my feelings."[8] But much

---

2007 I wrote the lecture that resulted in this article, John Muether's biography on Van Til had not yet been published. He graciously allowed me to use his manuscript.

3. Bernard Ramm, *After Fundamentalism: The Future of Evangelical Theology* (San Francisco: Harper & Row, 1983), 21.

4. K. Schilder, "The new modernism," *De Reformatie*, January 5, 1952: "Indertijd, toen prof. dr C. van Til (Philadelphia) een boek schreef over de theologie van Karl Barth, en daarvoor de zéér nuchtere en doodgewone titel koos: 'The new modernism' (Het nieuwe modernisme), ging er uit het barthiaanse kamp een indianengehuil op." ("In those days, when Prof. Dr. C. Van Til [Philadelphia] wrote a book on the theology of Karl Barth, and chose for it the very businesslike and quite common title: 'The New Modernism,' howls of an Indian rose from the Barthian camp.") See also Schilder's announcement of *The New Modernism* in *De Reformatie*, March 9, 1946.

5. Th. L. Haitjema, *Karl Barth* (Wageningen: Veenman, 1926).

6. See Th. L. Haitjema, "Een Amerikaansche aanval op de dialectische theologie," in *Pro Regno, Pro Sanctuario: Een bundel studies en bijdragen van vrienden en vereerders bij de zestigste verjaardag van prof. dr. G. van der Leeuw*, ed. W. J. Kooiman and J. M. Van Veen (Nijkerk: Callenbach, 1950), 211-27, where he calls Van Til's critique a "afschuwelijk misverstand" (217).

7. Muether, *Van Til*, 135. See H. U. von Balthasar, *Karl Barth: Darstellung und Deutung seiner Theologie* (Köln: Hegner, 1951).

8. K. Barth to E. R. Geehan, November 14, 1965, copy, *C. Van Til Papers*, Montgomery

more influential was what Barth wrote in his introduction to volume IV/2 of his *Kirchliche Dogmatik,* published in 1955. Van Til biographer John Muether stated: "Barth likely had Van Til in mind when he wrote [in this introduction] that while he could discuss his view with some fundamentalists, there were 'butchers and cannibals [who] are beyond the pale (e.g., the one who summarily described my theology as the worst heresy of any age).'"[9]

By the 1950s Barth was a world famous theologian who was unable to respond to the myriad of praise for and critique of his work — though silence and neglect had always been important weapons for Barth. There were many publications on Barth that were sent to him by its authors in the hopes of getting a substantial reply.[10] Understandably, the only thing he usually did was flip through the pages to determine if the author appreciated his theology or not, and then put the book on his shelves without ever responding to the author. But apparently in 1958 Barth could no longer abide Van Til. So we can safely conclude that with opinions like those expressed in his magnum opus *The New Modernism,* Van Til made himself a name in Barthian circles, though it was a very bad name indeed.

The New Modernism was not only read by Barthians but also by evangelicals. In these circles the book was well received and it is hard to overestimate the impact of Van Til's rejection of Barth's theology on the general attitude of the Evangelical movement toward Karl Barth's neo-orthodoxy. According to Bernard Ramm *The New Modernism* "became the official evangelical interpretation of neo-orthodoxy. . . . Hence Barth had a bad press among evangelicals long before his *Church Dogmatics* was translated volume by volume into English."[11] And Francis Schaeffer wrote to Van Til in 1970 on the

---

Library, Westminster Theological Seminary, Philadelphia. Quoted in Muether, *Van Til,* 136. See Karl Barth to Geoffrey Bromiley, June 1, 1961, quoted in Eberhard Busch, *Karl Barth: His Life from Letters and Autobiographical Texts* (Eugene, OR: Wipf & Stock, 2005), 380. Busch mentions a book by Van Til dating from 1953, but it is unclear to which publication he is referring. See also note 73.

9. Muether, *Van Til,* 136. Muether quotes the English edition: *CD* IV/2, xii.

10. G. C. Berkouwer, K. H. Miskotte, and K. Schilder never received an answer when they sent their dissertations to Karl Barth in 1932 and 1933 (I have checked the copies of these books in Barth's library in Basel — they were never read), and the only reaction Berkouwer got, after sending his monograph *Karl Barth* (Kampen: Kok, 1936) to the Swiss theologian, was some years later an amusing, disqualifying remark: *"Der Einband war schön."* See G. Puchinger, *Gesprekken over Rome-reformatie* (Delft: W. D. Meinema, 1965), 305.

11. Ramm, *After Fundamentalism,* 23. By the time of the publication of *The New Modernism* only the first volume of Barth's *Kirchliche Dogmatik* I/1 (1932) had been translated into English (1936).

occasion of his seventy-fifth birthday: "You have pointed out for all the world to read that Barth's theology [was] wrong at its core, and not just in the details."[12] *The New Modernism* may have been as influential as Ramm suggested, but the book was tough reading, its prose being tense and tedious, and George Marsden's observation that "few fundamentalists read the book, but many repeated the title" might very well be to the point.[13]

Seen from the perspective of Van Til's book and the consistent "small library of criticism of Barth"[14] he has written during his academic career, the answer to the question in the title of this conference is clear: Barth and the evangelicals were foes and not friends. Much attention has been paid to the theological and philosophical issues that made them into enemies. The issue I would like to address in this essay, however, is a historical one: how did Van Til become such a fierce opponent of Karl Barth? Where did his opinions originate? And how did he develop views on Barth that resulted in the ostracizing effects he experienced in the mid-1940s and 1950s? I hope the answers to these questions will help to clarify the historical context of the confrontation between the Barthians and the evangelicals and take us beyond the antagonism that dominates their relationship, sometimes up to the present day. I will address three issues: (1) the way Van Til came to his opinion on Barth, (2) the strong antithetical character of his opinion, and (3) the reason why Barth was such a serious opponent of Van Til.

1. The way Van Til came to his opinion on Barth

Van Til published *New Modernism* in 1946, but the first publication in which he dealt with Karl Barth was a review of Alvin S. Zerbe's (1847-1935) book *The Karl Barth Theology or the New Transcendentalism* (1930), dating from 1931.[15] At that time not much of Barth was known in the United States and hardly anything of Barth had been translated and published in English.[16] The 1922

---

12. Muether, *Van Til*, 125.

13. George Marsden, *Reforming Fundamentalism: Fuller Seminary and the New Evangelicalism* (Grand Rapids: Eerdmans, 1987), 101.

14. Ramm, *After Fundamentalism*, 204.

15. Cornelius Van Til, *Christianity Today* 1, no. 10 (February 1931): 13-14.

16. The first American books on Barth were Finley D. Jenkins, *Germany's new paradox theology* (Princeton: n.p., 1926) and Alvin Sylvester Zerbe, *The Karl Barth Theology or the New Transcendentalism* (Cleveland: Central Pub. House, 1930). One of the first American dissertations on Barth was Raymond E. Walker, *Crisis Theology* (Andover Newton Theologi-

edition of *Der Römerbrief*, the book that made Barth famous in Germany, was published in English in 1933, the first volume of the *Church Dogmatics* in 1936. The stream of books and articles in English on Barth started to appear from the mid-1930s on. So Van Til was an early bird with his 1931 article. A reason for this early recognition of Barth's importance certainly was Van Til's mastery of the German language. He did not have to wait for English translations. But his first acquaintance and his first impressions of Karl Barth were not received in the United States but in the Netherlands, and therein lies the main reason for his early recognition of Barth's importance.

To explain this, a bit of biography is needed. Cornelius — or, Americanized, Case — Van Til was born in 1895 in Grootegast, in the province of Groningen, the Netherlands. His parents were farmers and belonged to the Reformed Churches in the Netherlands, founded in 1892 by Abraham Kuyper (1837-1920) and Herman Bavinck (1854-1921) and representing the ecclesiastical branch of neo-Calvinism. He immigrated to the United States with his family in May 1905, a few days after his tenth birthday. The Van Tils settled in Hammond, Indiana, where they joined the Christian Reformed Church — a sister church of the Reformed Churches in the Netherlands and the home of many Reformed Dutch immigrants — and continued their life as farmers. But Case sensed a call to the ministry and in 1914, at nineteen years of age, he enrolled at Calvin Preparatory School in Grand Rapids, and later on at Calvin College and Calvin Theological Seminary. In these educational institutions of the Christian Reformed Church he devoured the works of Kuyper and Bavinck.[17] Because almost all the professors at Calvin College and Seminary during Van Til's years as a student had been born in the Netherlands and had been educated there, the content of Van Til's basic education was Dutch in character, and his thinking clearly had a Dutch bent. But the Dutch connection was not without problems. After 1914, Calvin College and Seminary went through years of transition. Partly this had to do with the growth of these educational institutions and with a process of Americanization within the Christian Reformed Church that accelerated during the First World War. But it also had to do with the Dutch theological tradition Van Til devoured. An

---

cal School, 1930). Martin Luther King, Jr. in 1952 wrote a paper for Dr. L. Harold De Wolf at Boston University's School of Theology on "Karl Barth's Conception of God" that was largely based on Zerbe's book.

17. C. Van Til to D. H. Th. Vollenhoven, February 14, 1936: "When I was a student I entered with great enthusiasm into the works of Kuyper and Bavinck etc.", *Archive-D. H. Th. Vollenhoven*, Historical Documentation Center for Dutch Protestantism since 1800, VU University, Amsterdam.

important issue in his student years was the question whether, in view of the recent anti-naturalist developments within Western culture, the tradition of Kuyper and Bavinck needed an update or not — especially with regards to its epistemology and engagement with culture.[18]

Interestingly, Van Til avoided this issue by enrolling at Princeton Seminary in 1922.[19] Despite the absence of Benjamin B. Warfield (1851-1921), who had died a year before, Van Til was able to get acquainted with the Old Princeton theology. In his four years at the seminary he mixed the tradition of what he called the "inimitable trio"[20] — Kuyper, Bavinck, and Warfield — into a new blend of Calvinist apologetics in which the foundational importance of creation and its intimate connection with covenant were the most characteristic ingredients. Muether, Van Til's biographer, argues that in bringing the Reformed tradition to a more consistent epistemological expression, Van Til stood on the shoulders of this trio, especially regarding the exclusion of a zone of neutrality or common epistemological ground.[21] I think this process of blending was more complicated than Muether presents. It is not fully clear which elements of these three theologians were rejected as being "scholastic," and it is also unresolved whether Van Til ever came to a balanced mix. Now and then this blending of the neo-Calvinist "Old Amsterdam" and Scottish-Presbyterian "Old Princeton" traditions by Van Til has been oversimplified. A decade after his study at Princeton Seminary he admitted in a private letter:

> For a long time I felt that there is really a breach between the theology of Warfield and the Apologetics of Warfield. In his theology Warfield is as sound as can be, for instance on the point of regeneration. In Apologetics, however, he says we can and must reason with the opponents by setting ourselves to begin with on common ground with them. Now this was seemingly quite the opposite of Kuyper's Encyclopaedie and Bavinck's Dogmatiek. With that difference I have struggled ever since.[22]

18. See George Harinck, "Twin Sisters with a Changing Character: How Neo-Calvinists Dealt with the Modern Discrepancy between Bible and Natural Sciences," in *Nature and Scripture in the Abrahamic Religions: 1700-Present*, vol. II, ed. Jitse M. van der Meer and Scott Mandelbrote (Leiden: Brill, 2008), 357-59.

19. Muether (*Van Til*, 49) suggests Van Til left Calvin Seminary in 1922 because he did not want "to shirk the difficult questions." But in this Van Til's move to Princeton is misinterpreted. Van Til had not taken part in the debates on the "difficult questions" at Calvin; he only commented upon the attitude of the debaters (48-49).

20. Muether, *Van Til*, 56.

21. Ibid.

22. Van Til to Vollenhoven, February 14, 1936.

After receiving his master's degree in 1926, he enrolled at Princeton University, because in engaging this "struggle" he experienced himself as having a lack of philosophical schooling. This university granted him a Ph.D. in philosophy in 1927 for a dissertation on God and the absolute.

After thirteen years of study and college life, Van Til was free of duties and made a vacation trip to his native country, to meet family and to learn about the present state of the vast Reformed community in the Netherlands. Van Til had not known anything about Karl Barth up until this point. But that would change soon. When he arrived in the Netherlands in the summer of 1927, Karl Barth had recently made two trips to the Netherlands, one in May and June of 1926 and another in March and April of 1927. These were the first foreign trips Barth undertook. He enjoyed the Netherlands and would return many times. Here Barth "discovered a quite independent form of Reformed Christianity," or as Barth himself put it in 1926, "unmistakably Calvinism, with the problem of ethics instead of the 'assurance of salvation.'"[23] "Barth found astonishing perception about his theological concerns." The atmosphere was "a bit dry and solemn, but still full of movement, like Rembrandt's 'The Syndics' and 'Night Watch.'"[24] When Van Til arrived three months later, Barth was in the air in Holland.

Van Til visited his uncle and aunt in the village of Oegstgeest and also called on their pastor, Klaas Schilder. Schilder was not at home, but later that year they corresponded. Schilder was a young minister in the Reformed Churches, and he was intrigued with Karl Barth. Barth had been known by the neo-Calvinists since his appointment as a professor of Reformed theology at Göttingen University in 1921. They had supported the young professor and co-financed a *Konvikt* (house and community) for Barth's students. The neo-Calvinists considered Barth an outsider who had discovered Calvinism and was now approaching their position. In order to foster this exclusive international relationship, they helped him in many ways, for instance, by presenting him publications by Abraham Kuyper and Herman Bavinck, "together with a Dutch-German dictionary."[25] This favorable attitude changed, however, when Dutch Barthians like the Groningen professor Haitjema in 1926 introduced Barth in the Netherlands and started to use his theology to criticize the neo-Calvinists by labeling their attempts to Christianize culture

23. Busch, *Karl Barth*, 170.
24. Ibid.
25. F. C. Meijster to Barth, April 7, 1923, *Karl Barth-Archiv*, Basel. The Reformed pastor Meijster of Rotterdam had visited Barth earlier that year. Barth referred only a few times to Kuyper and Bavinck in his *Kirchliche Dogmatik*, and not at all after volume III/2 (1948).

as haughty. After Barth's first visit to the Netherlands his popularity was on the rise, and neo-Calvinists lost their Dutch monopoly on Barth.[26]

Schilder was impressed by the secularization of society and culture after World War I. Like Barth he was influenced by Søren Kierkegaard and very skeptical of the civilized character of Christian religion and the concurrence of Christianity and culture. But he consistently stressed the intimate relationship between God and created reality, and wondered what made Karl Barth so attractive to many. He attended a lecture by Barth at Leiden University in the spring of 1927 and had a conversation with Barth the day after at the home of church historian Albertus Eekhof (1884-1933) at Oegstgeest, where Barth had spent the night. Schilder had read Barth's *Römerbrief* and several other publications, but he hesitated to call Barth a Reformed theologian. Was Barth a like-minded thinker after all? His overall impression was not favorable, as he wrote to Van Til:

> I found out that he does not know anything of the background of the Reformed [neo-Calvinist] tradition. His wrestling with the Calvinist tradition is not over yet. Considering his background and development I would say that he came to his conceptions by way of negation more than by careful, quiet study, descending to the roots of philosophical systems.[27]

Van Til was impressed by the vivid debates on Barth in the Netherlands and tried to visit him in the summer of 1927 in his hometown of Münster — situated close to the Dutch border — but he did not succeed. Barth was also the reason why Van Til wanted to meet Schilder. Schilder was the first neo-Calvinist to pay serious attention to Barth's theology, and his interpretation would dominate the neo-Calvinist appreciation of Barth for almost twenty years. He had published his first essay on Karl Barth half a year before Van Til arrived, titled "The Paradox in Religion," and published his next one, "In the Crisis," in September 1927. In these two essays Schilder analyzed the theology of Karl Barth and concluded that it would not stop secularization, but on the contrary would support it.

---

26. George Harinck, "The Early Reception of the Theology of Karl Barth in The Netherlands (1919-1926)," *Zeitschrift für Dialektische Theologie* 17, no. 2 (2001): 170-87.

27. K. Schilder to C. Van Til, Oegstgeest, January 19, 1928, *Van Til Papers:* "Het bleek me, dat hij ook van den achtergrond van onze gereformeerde denkwijze niets weet. . . . Gezien ook zijn afkomst en ontwikkelingsgang is er alles voor te zeggen, dat hij langs den weg der negatie gekomen is tot zijn opvattingen, meer dan langs dien der voorzichtige, rustige, tot den wortel van andere filosofische systemen afdalende kennisneming."

Schilder appreciated Barth's stress on the objectivity of the Word of God as a "delight,"[28] but he disqualified Barth's use of the paradox in religion as a revolution in theology. Barth, and Haitjema in his footsteps, seemed to have given up the classic aim to resolve discord in thinking. Instead, Barth labeled this aim as a sin. In his view belief does not fit in, but breaks through the logical laws of reasoning. According to Schilder, this view harmed Reformed theology. This theology presupposed the possibility of congruency of belief and reason in stating the *perspicuitas, efficacia, claritas,* and *sufficientia* of Scripture. Schilder therefore concluded: this difference implies a fundamental disagreement on the possibility of knowing God and His will. In Schilder's opinion, Calvinism does not accept and employ paradoxes as such. Barth, however, emphasized the paradox and declared God to be incognito in this world. To Schilder this either meant that Barth's philosophical commitments were leading him astray in his theology, or that it was indeed impossible for humans to serve God.

In Schilder's view, Reformed theology postulated a relationship between God and man. Barth rejected this possibility as being pretentious. Barth stressed the majesty of God over against the liberal theology of his teachers, but according to Schilder, by rejecting the possibility of God's immanence, Barth was diminishing the condescending love of God. Schilder relied on Calvin by stressing God's immanence and His accommodation to us:

> God doesn't just cause vertical lightning to strike in this horizontal world; He also goes with us in a pillar of cloud and a pillar of fire on our horizontal winding roads through deserts, and bears in mind the setting we live in, the strength of our soul and senses. He doesn't restrict Himself to incisions, but breaks new ground, where He *goes with us.*[29]

As far as the Netherlands was concerned, Barth was not the answer to secularizing tendencies. But Schilder rejected the opinion that later on Barth changed, and objected all his life that God's immanence, His presence in historic reality, was an impossibility in Barth's dialectical theology.[30]

There was no theologian within the neo-Calvinist movement like Schilder, who was so intrigued by Barth that he dealt with him all his life.

---

28. *De Reformatie,* April 15, 1927.

29. K. Schilder, "De paradox in de religie," in K. Schilder, *Bij dichters en schriftgeleerden* (Amsterdam: Uitgeversmaatschappij Holland, 1927), 109.

30. G. C. Berkouwer, *Zoeken en vinden: Herinneringen en ervaringen* (Kampen: Kok, 1989), 243.

Notwithstanding his strong resistance to Barth, he resembled him a lot. His protests against the Christian religion as a matter of course, his emphasis on the objectivity of revelation, his rejection of common grace, of natural theology, and of psychological exegesis makes it impossible to understand Schilder's theology without taking into account the impulses he received from the theology of Barth.[31]

After Van Til returned home in the fall of 1927 and was ordained in the Christian Reformed Church as a minister in Spring Lake, Michigan, he read several recent Dutch publications on the new developments in theology, like the book *Karl Barth* by Barth's most important representative in the Netherlands, the Groningen professor Haitjema. When, at the end of 1927, Schilder included one of his Barth essays in his book *Bij dichters en schriftgeleerden (Among Poets and Scribes)*, Van Til wrote him a letter with the request for an author-signed copy. Schilder sent him this book and others as well.[32] Van Til was taken by Schilder's view, modern neo-Calvinist mentality, and polemic style. He made it a lifelong habit to read Schilder's trilogy *Christus in Zijn lijden* (1930) during Lent, and when in 1936 Schilder sent him his dogmatics-in-miniature, *Wat is de hemel?*, Van Til confessed: "For me personally your books are of the utmost value for my work here at Westminster."[33] In the 1930s, Van Til translated and adapted parts of this trilogy, but he was disappointed by the publication of Henry Zijlstra's translation just before he finished his, and so he abandoned the project.[34]

31. See Koert van Bekkum, "De gereformeerde theologie van Klaas Schilder," *Radix* 23 (1997): 123-66; René Barkema, *Nee tegen Karl Barth? Een historisch-theologische terugblik* (Barneveld: De Vuurbaak, 2007).

32. Van Til referred to Schilder's dissertation *Zur Begriffsgeschichte des "Paradoxon": Mit besonderer Berücksichtigung Calvins und des nach-Kierkegaardischen "Paradoxon"* (Kampen: Kok, 1933) in "The Theology of Dr. Mackenzie: A Rejoinder by Dr. Van Til," *Christianity Today* 4 (April 1934): 12-16.

33. Van Til to K. Schilder, June 30, 1936, *Archive-K. Schilder*, Archive and Documentation Center of the Reformed Churches, Kampen.

34. Schilder's trilogy was published in Zijlstra's English translation in 1938 *(Christ in His Suffering)*, 1939 *(Christ on Trial)*, and 1940 *(Christ Crucified)* (Grand Rapids: Eerdmans). Van Til did not fully abandon the plan of publishing his adaptation of Schilder's book. After Schilder died in 1952 he contacted the Presbyterian and Reformed Publishing Company in Nutley, New Jersey, about a publication. In the preface he wrote: "In writing these meditations I am greatly indebted to a three-volume work entitled *Christ in His Suffering* by the late Dr. K. Schilder." The meditations were never published. In 1980 he handed them over to the Dutch journalist Wobbe Driebergen, and they are now at Westminster Theological Seminary. See Ruud ter Beek to Grace Mullen [Montgomery Library], July 7, 2005, *Van Til Papers*.

In 1946 he sent Schilder his first major book, *The New Modernism,* with a dedication: "Klaas Schilder. With great appreciation for your work. Cornelius Van Til."[35]

Van Til adopted Schilder's point of view regarding Barth.[36] However, he overlooked the cultural context in which Schilder dealt with Barth. This is not an easy case to make, since Van Til did not refer to Schilder in *The New Modernism,* and unlike Barth and Schilder, he was never influenced by or part of the European modernist struggle during the post-war years. And Schilder, too, did not seem to be aware of the different American cultural context and the different use of the word "modernist."[37] An important trait of American Protestant modernism was its identification of the progress of humanity with the progress of Christ's kingdom. When Emil Brunner visited the United States in 1928, he stressed that Europe had lost its belief in progress since World War I and that the dialectical theology addressed this new cultural situation.[38] Van Til's understanding of the modernists Barth and Schilder has to be situated within the context of Old Princeton and Old Amsterdam, that is, in the era before the First World War. An illustration of this disconnect is found in what Van Til wrote in 1932 about the way the Westminster Confession spoke about human knowledge:

> In this Confession God is thought of as the creator of the universe. Hence man's thought is derivative. It is primarily receptive. It is reconstructive of God's thought. This is the "organizing principle" under which the theolo-

35. For this information I am indebted to L. A. Valkema, Bedum, the Netherlands, the present owner of Schilder's copy of *The New Modernism.*

36. Schilder to Van Til, January 19, 1928, *Van Til Papers:* "Het verblijdt mij, dat u instemming betuigen kunt met de hoofdgedachte van wat ik schreef in De Reformatie." ("I am glad, that you could agree with the central idea of what I wrote in De Reformatie.") In September 1927 Schilder wrote three articles, "In de crisis" (In the crisis), in the weekly *De Reformatie,* about the meaning of "crisis" in Barth's thought.

37. Schilder to Van Til, May 13, 1935, copy, *Archive-Schilder:* "Een bijzondere redden die mijn blijdschap vergroot is deze, dat de strijd dien u in Amerika te voeren hebt, veelszins overeenkomt met wat in Nederland geschieden moet. Ook hier is de invloed van Barth en Kierkegaard helaas niet te miskennen, en daarom ben ik zoo bijzonder dankbaar, dat uit Amerika uw stem spreekt." ("A special reason that enlarges my gladness is that the battle you have to deliver in America in many ways resembles what has to happen in the Netherlands. Unfortunately the influence over here of Kierkegaard and Barth is undeniable too, and that is why I am very grateful that your voice speaks from America.")

38. Frank Jehle, *Emil Brunner: Theologe im 20. Jahrhundert* (Zürich: Theologischer Verlag, 2006), 246-49.

gians and philosophers of the church have sought constantly to "rethink" the Christian faith.[39]

This means that Barth's and Schilder's key concern regarding the crumbling of the values of Western culture and especially the doubt about the possibility of objective knowledge never was Van Til's problem. He opposed Barth in an American debate about how to maintain the influence of Christianity in American culture. Unlike Van Til, Barth and Schilder were involved in a debate about how to make sense of Christianity in a post-Christian culture. Van Til's reaction to Barth may have been inspired by the comments of Schilder on Barth's paradox, transcendentalism, and dependence on Kierkegaard, but he isolated this critique from its historical context and implanted it in his own project of a Christian apologetics that did not question the possibility of objective knowledge nor doubted cultural values.

Van Til's trip to the Netherlands taught him two things: first, that the theology of Karl Barth was on the rise in Europe and dominated the theological discussions in the Netherlands; second, that the Dutch neo-Calvinist tradition was highly involved in the debates about Barth's theology. They knew Barth's liberal background, but they also knew he was on the threshold of the Calvinist school and "was attempting to depict the sovereignty of God and the form of historical life to which it gives rise."[40] Schilder opened Van Til's eyes to the serious differences between Barth's theology and Calvinist theology, as well as to the way some theologians made improper use of Barth in order to attack the neo-Calvinists. Van Til realized that Reformed theology in the United States would have to deal with Karl Barth at some point as well. So when Barth's theology reached the borders of the United States around 1930, Van Til knew what was at stake. Just like in Europe, Karl Barth's theology in the United States would be "a bomb tossed onto the playground of the theologians."[41] His theology would require an answer from the Reformed traditions in America, whether they liked it or not. Barth would become unavoidable.

For this reason, Van Til paid attention to Barth as early as February 1931, when he published a review in *Christianity Today* of the first American book on the theology of Karl Barth. The book was titled *The Karl Barth Theology or the New Transcendentalism,* and it was written by a theologian from the conservative German Reformed tradition, Alvin Sylvester Zerbe, professor emer-

---

39. C. Van Til, "For What Are We Contending?" *Christianity Today* 3 (December 1932): 5.

40. John Webster, *Barth's Earlier Theology: Four Studies* (London: T. & T. Clark, 2005), 12.

41. A statement by Karl Adam, quoted in Eric D. Bristley, "A. S. Zerbe Defending the Faith Versus Darwin and Barth," *Leben* 1 (April-June 2005): 13.

itus at Central Theological Seminary in Dayton, Ohio. In this book the 83-year-old Zerbe presented Barthianism as "a theological upheaval in which scarcely one stone remains in its original place,"[42] and concluded: "Unless it be remedied, we fear that Barthianism is a poorly disguised agnosticism and unfitted to confront this God-defying age."[43] In his review, Van Til hardly dealt with the contents of Zerbe's book, but used the review to make clear his own position over against Barth. In line with what was written by Schilder, he did not concentrate on Barth's view of Scripture — as many American evangelicals later on would do — but stressed the theories of reality and knowledge on which Barth's system of doctrine was built. Where Schilder's arguments had been of a theological nature, Van Til's were philosophical.

As to the issue of reality, van Til wrote that Barth's "whole theology is heralded as a reaction against the modern emphasis upon God's immanence in the universe. And his reaction is extreme. He even denies the real significance of the temporal world. The whole of history is to be condemned as worthless. The eternal is said to be everything and the temporal is said to be nothing."[44] In regard to knowledge, Barth "basically denied the complete self-consciousness of God as absolute personality. He has no room for revelation."[45] Man was being placed with God above the temporal order, so that no revelation was needed. Instead, knowledge was made a cooperative enterprise between God and man. While Schilder's theological argument was that God was exalted in such a way that God's love was restricted, Van Til's argument in philosophical terms was that the exaltation of God above time in fact neutralized this exaltation. "Modern theology holds that both God and man are temporal. Barth holds that both God and man are eternal. The results are identical."[46]

Van Til's first — and in a way also his final — statement on Barth was that his theology was anti-theistic. He considered Barth's theology to be an overreaction against the prevalent emphasis upon God's immanence. Van Til did not accept Barth's emphasis on divine transcendence as either Christian or theistic. According to Van Til, Barth's system of doctrine presented some external similarities to the Reformed point of view, but never at any point did it agree with Reformed theology. And Van Til had no illusion of convincing

42. Zerbe, *Karl Barth*, 270.

43. Quoted by Van Til in his review of this book in *Christianity Today* (February 1931): 13.

44. Van Til, from his review in *Christianity Today*.

45. Ibid.

46. Ibid.

the Barthians. On the contrary, he ended his review with the prediction "that Barthianism may last a long time because it is really Modernism."[47]

In order to understand this fierce reaction to Karl Barth, we first have to understand the way Van Til dealt with opponents. Typically, he started his review with the statement that Karl Barth's theology was based upon an anti-theistic theory, and he ended by concluding that the author of the book under review agrees in general with his position. In Van Til's review of Zerbe's book, for example, there is no information about the structure of the book or about the author's thesis. There seemed to be a Van Tilian universe, and you were either in or out. Unlike neo-Calvinists such as Bavinck or G. C. Berkouwer (1903-96), you would never learn from Van Til's publications how his opponents reason, or what they are aiming at.

Another trait, which is not per se typical of neo-Calvinism, is that Van Til is not all that interested in the intellectual problem that Barth poses, or in a discussion about such a problem. He is not interested in Barth's motives or preoccupations. Rather, Van Til is interested in the battle itself, in overwhelming opponents with his arguments, and in showing them how the consequences of their ideas will undermine their own position. Contrary to Schilder, Van Til did not develop a neo-Calvinist theology in reaction to Barth. In general, Van Til displayed an attitude more common among conservative theologians on the defense, in which one takes refuge in the illusion that the choice is either saving all or losing all. For Van Til, Barth simply had to be rejected.

Having said this, it is clear that we would be wrong to define Van Til's reaction to the theology of Karl Barth solely as a peculiarity. Van Til and his reaction to Barth have to be considered, at least in certain respects, as a part of the neo-Calvinist tradition. Though he relied in his apologetics on the Old Princeton tradition, and especially on Warfield, there is always a Dutch woof to the American Presbyterian warp. The unease within American Presbyterianism over Van Til's employment of presuppositional reasoning in his apologetics, for example, is "owed to its unfamiliarity with the Reformed tradition, and especially unfamiliarity with Bavinck. Van Til imported much of his ideas from Bavinck, whose four-volume *Gereformeerde dogmatiek* was largely inaccessible to the English-speaking world."[48]

---

47. Ibid.

48. Muether, *Van Til*, 115. In the meantime Bavinck's dogmatics have been translated into English and published in four volumes. See Herman Bavinck, *Reformed Dogmatics*, vols. I-IV (Grand Rapids: Baker, 2003-8).

2. The strong antithetical character of his opinion

One of the strong points of dialectical theology as a school is that it has invested a lot of energy into translating its publications into English. Given the immense effect of translating Barth, theologian Richard A. Muller once mused about what might have happened if Kuyper's major works had been published in English by 1930.[49]

Translating Barth really took off after the Second World War, but for Van Til this delay did not cause a problem. The only handicap he experienced was caused by the war. By the time of the publication of the first edition of *The New Modernism* (a second was published in 1947, a third in 1972, and a Korean translation in 1990) volumes II.2 (1942) and III.1 (1945) of Barth's *Kirchliche Dogmatik* were still not available in the United States.[50] One of the advantages of Van Til over many of his American colleagues was that he could read German well and that he was familiar with the reception of Barth's theology in the Netherlands in the 1920s and 1930s.

Given this exceptional position, it is no surprise that Van Til's overall disqualification of Barth's theology and the strong language he used struck his contemporaries — as it still strikes us today. Americans did not know much about Barth and Brunner by 1946, and what is more, they had never considered these foreigners a direct threat to the American Church. Preliminary American Presbyterian remarks on Barth, for example by J. Gresham Machen (1881-1937),[51] were cautious and tentative. Machen called Brunner's book "die grösste Erfrischung seit vielen Jahren."[52] To put it frankly, it is no treat to read *The New Modernism*. Van Til's confession that his atten-

---

49. Richard Muller, "The Place and Importance of Karl Barth in the Twentieth Century," *Westminster Theological Journal* 50 (1988): 152. Muller observes that one of the main reasons for Barth's international popularity is the translation into English of the *Church Dogmatics* and then adds in a parenthesis: "(It is worth a moment of speculation to raise the question of the intrinsic merit of the equally prolific Abraham Kuyper and to wonder what his influence would have been had he written in German rather than the Dutch and had been blessed with a following of Scottish Kuyperians intent upon translating the *Dictaten dogmatiek* and the *E voto dordraceno!*)."

50. C. Van Til, "Preface to the Second Edition," in *The New Modernism: An Appraisal of the Theology of Barth and Brunner* (Philadelphia: Presbyterian and Reformed Publishing Company, 1947), x.

51. J. Gresham Machen, "Karl Barth and 'The Theology of Crisis,'" *Westminster Theological Journal* 53 (1991): 197-205; D. G. Hart, "Machen on Barth: Introduction to a Recently Uncovered Paper," *Westminster Theological Journal* 53 (1991): 189-96.

52. Jehle, *Brunner*, 245: "the largest refreshment in many years."

tion to Barth bordered on an obsession is telling. "His doctor told him in 1949 that he was suffering from battle fatigue not unlike a soldier, which brought to mind the struggles Nicholas Van Til, [a] nephew, was experiencing: 'Nick used to see Japanese in his dreams. I see Buswell and Barth: which is worse?'"[53] Van Til is all too present in his text, his judgments are hasty and strong, and his interpretations make you wonder time and again: did Barth really mean this? In short, to me as a historian, the argument of this book is cogent, but not convincing.[54] Berkouwer rightly remarked about Van Til: "He saw Barth in his *The New Modernism* (1946) from the point of view of the consequences and this did not change, though he noticed changes in Barth's thinking."[55] Judging Barth by the consequences he had drawn from his texts led Van Til to attribute to Barth positions he actually denied. Bavinck would label what Van Til does *Konsequenzmacherei:* keeping your opponents responsible for the consequences of their standpoint.[56]

Why was Van Til so obsessed with Barth? In the first place, Van Til was overworked more than once in his life, because all his work was done more or less obsessively. He was polemic by nature, like Schilder, who developed his own theology in confrontation with others. When invited in 1936 to edit the new Dutch academic journal *Philosophia Reformata*, Van Til reacted positively, but he stipulated "that I could not participate in any activity that would exclude the freedom to polemicize."[57]

Besides this personal attitude, one of the reasons for Van Til's obsession with Barth may have been that he feared a repetition of what had happened in the Netherlands, where the Barthians had been on the advance in the 1930s and were the most serious opponents of neo-Calvinism.[58] Thanks to his personal contacts and his subscription to Dutch periodicals, Van Til was

53. Muether, *Van Til*, 128. Letter of C. Van Til to Henry Van Til, December 20, 1949.

54. For an overview of Van Til's response to Barth, see Gregory G. Bolich, *Karl Barth & Evangelicalism* (Downers Grove, IL: InterVarsity Press, 1980), 66-73.

55. Berkouwer, *Zoeken en vinden*, 90: "Hij zag in zijn *The New Modernism* (1946) Barth vanuit de consequenties en dat bleef zo, ook toen hij kennis nam van veranderingen bij Barth."

56. Ibid.

57. Van Til to Schilder, June 30, 1936, *Archive-Schilder*. See Van Til to Vollenhoven, February 14, 1936, *Archive-Vollenhoven*: "One of the most deadening things we meet with is the desire to kill controversy itself."

58. See Martien E. Brinkman, *De theologie van Karl Barth: dynamiet of dynamo voor christelijk handelen. De politieke en theologische kontroverse tussen Nederlandse barthianen en neocalvinisten* (Baarn: Ten Have, 1983).

well acquainted with the theological and ecclesiastical situation in the Netherlands. He visited Europe for a second time in August and September of 1938. This time he met with Schilder at his home ("Van Til, a cigar and tea?"[59]), who had been a professor in dogmatics at Kampen Theological Seminary since 1934. He deliberately made a special trip to Basel to visit Barth, only to find that Barth was out of town.[60] He sent students to study with Schilder and Dirk H. Th. Vollenhoven (1892-1978), a philosophy professor at the Free University in Amsterdam. The war stagnated the communication with Europe, but when Van Til in 1941 started to study Barth systematically, he knew quite well that his theology hindered neo-Calvinism in the Netherlands. And he was right, for by the time Van Til published his *New Modernism,* almost all of the theology professors in the Netherlands Reformed Church — the largest Dutch Protestant denomination — sympathized in one way or another with Barth and opposed neo-Calvinism. Compared with a quarter of a century earlier, the situation in the Netherlands had been reversed.

A second reason for Van Til's obsession may be that he personally experienced more or less the same inversion at Princeton Theological Seminary. After a year of ministering, Van Til in August 1928 accepted a position at this seminary as an instructor in apologetics. But in 1929, only one year later, he left Princeton to join the newly founded Westminster Theological Seminary in Philadelphia. According to Van Til, the departure of orthodox Calvinists from Princeton Seminary was a protest against Princeton's decision to head in a modernist direction. In 1923, Machen, the founder of Westminster, had defined the battle lines between orthodoxy and modernism in his eloquently written book, *Christianity and Liberalism.* Van Til's departure from Princeton meant that he agreed with the lines drawn by Machen. Princeton no longer was the orthodox bulwark, and in order to stay orthodox Van Til was willing to pay the price of joining an institution that lacked the venerability of his alma mater.

Van Til's perception was not undisputed. Many Presbyterians, and many Christian Reformed people as well, judged the 1929 departure from Princeton by Machen, Van Til, and others as untimely and an excessive reaction. Many orthodox Christians — including Henry Beets (1869-1947) of the Christian Reformed Church and Valentijn Hepp (1879-1950) of the Free University in Amsterdam — moderated the differences between Princeton and

---

59. J. Van Bruggen, "An interview with Prof. C. Van Til," *The Outlook* 28 (July 1978): 17.
60. Van Til to K. Barth, December 21, 1965, copy, *Van Til Papers.*

Westminster.[61] The board of Princeton had been reorganized, but the character of the institution was not altered, they said. Ned B. Stonehouse (1902-62), who earned his Ph.D. at the Free University in 1929, and also joined the Westminster faculty, informed Vollenhoven a few months after his departure from Amsterdam: "Princeton, of course, will not become modernist all at once. There are a few modernists in the governing board. But the striking thing is that the orthodox members don't seem to care."[62] This public opinion hindered the cause of Westminster. It was important to Van Til to persuade these people that they were mistaken in their belief that nothing had changed at Princeton. He bashed one of the successors at Princeton, but his attack on this "modern Princetonianist"[63] returned to him like a boomerang, because it was interpreted as an illustration of the fact that the orthodox party's argument was overdone.

At that moment Barth came into the picture at Princeton Seminary. Emil Brunner had visited Princeton in the spring of 1928, but he had left no trace behind. Informed by the controversies between neo-Calvinists and Barthians in the Netherlands, Van Til realized that at Princeton the neo-Calvinist contacts would not coexist with Barthian relationships. From the 1890s on there had been a relationship between Princeton Seminary and the Free University in Amsterdam. Van Til's beloved teacher at Princeton, Geerhardus Vos (1862-1949), had been instrumental in building up this relationship.[64] He and Warfield forged an alliance between Old Princeton and Amsterdam in the battle against liberal theology. As a result of this alliance the subsequent dogmatic professors in Amsterdam — Kuyper, Bavinck, and Hepp — were all invited to deliver the Stone lectures at Princeton in 1898, 1908, and 1930, respectively, and neo-Calvinist professors and other visitors often made a stop at Princeton on their American trips. But in 1930, Hepp turned out to be the last representative of this tradition to be invited. With John Alexander Mackay's (1889-1983) presidency of the seminary from 1936 on, the Barthians came in. Princeton did not simply extend its international

61. See Van Til to Schilder, May 3, [1935], *Archive-Schilder.* Cf. the introduction by Henry Beets to A. Kuyper, *Lectures on Calvinism* (Grand Rapids: Eerdmans, 1931), 19: "From the side of the men in authority at Princeton, however, we are assured that the historic position will not be altered."

62. N. B. Stonehouse to Vollenhoven, November 16, 1929, *Archive-Vollenhoven.*

63. Muether, *Van Til,* 74.

64. George Harinck, "Geerhardus Vos as introducer of Kuyper in America," in Hans Krabbendam and Larry J. Wagenaar, *The Dutch-American Experience: Essays in Honor of Robert P. Swierenga* (Amsterdam: VU Uitgeverij, 2000), 242-62.

relationship with the new dialectical theology, but also at the same time tacitly severed its ties with the neo-Calvinists and the Free University. The Dutch neo-Calvinists contributed to this shift as well by immediately — that is, in 1929, years before Barth was introduced in Princeton — choosing sides with Westminster Seminary (with the exception of Hepp), where they knew Van Til and Stonehouse personally.[65]

By framing this change in relations at Princeton using Machen's dichotomy of orthodoxy and liberalism, Van Til came up with an illustration that supported his argument that the founding of Westminster was not the result of orthodoxy's inflexibility, but the result of a change at Princeton. Van Til's opposition to the theology of Barth at the same time became a rationale for the existence of Westminster Seminary. Barth was much more to Van Til than just a theological opponent. He became a paradigm for all that the Westminster tradition was opposed to within American Presbyterianism.

Whatever the reason and the order, the shift in relationships at Princeton was a fact. But this was somewhat hushed up by confusing labels. In a 1932 editorial in *The Expository Times*, the similarity of the theology of Warfield and Barth was stressed, and it concluded that "the name of a traditional Calvinist like Dr. Warfield may be associated with those of neo-Calvinists like Karl Barth and Brunner."[66] Others used the same framework Van Til had utilized by naming Barth's theology neo-orthodox — claiming that Barth was not a modern sequel of liberalism but a new orthodox answer to it. This was rather confusing, but helped to convince several orthodox Reformed people that Princeton was still on the right track. This policy clearly irritated Van Til and time and again made him stress in his articles well into the 1960s the shift at Princeton. He wanted Barthianism to be disowned as an offshoot of Reformed theology, as he wrote in 1931.[67]

When Van Til was asked in 1935 for contributions on a regular basis for Schilder's weekly, *De Reformatie*, quite a few of the twenty-four issues of a "Brief uit Amerika" (Letter from America) that he wrote until 1940 — when the outbreak of the war and the German circulation ban on *De Reformatie*

65. George Harinck, "'Give us an American Abraham Kuyper': Dutch Calvinist Reformed Responses to the Founding of Westminster Theological Seminary in Philadelphia," *Calvin Theological Journal* 33, no. 2 (November 1998): 299-319.

66. Cited in David B. Calhoun, *Princeton Seminary, Volume 2: The Majestic Testimony, 1869-1929* (Edinburgh/Carlisle: The Banner of Truth Trust, 1996), 521; Muether (*Van Til*, 122) recalls that Princeton's president, Mackay, in 1960 labeled the new Barthian phase at Princeton as "neo-Calvinism."

67. Review of Zerbe, *Karl Barth*, in *Christianity Today* (February 1931): 14.

ended this cooperation — dealt with the influence of Barthianism in Princeton. The appointment in 1937 of the Barthian theologian Elmer Homrighausen at Princeton provided Van Til with new ammunition. In 1939 Schilder visited the United States and lectured at Westminster — though I have to add that he and Van Til paid a visit to Princeton as well. Schilder had a gift for music and played the organ in Miller Chapel.[68] But he did not lecture in Princeton. Dutch theologians invited by Princeton were no longer neo-Calvinists, but Barthians.

Van Til's appraisal of Barth's theology in *The New Modernism* was the next phase in Van Til's ongoing battle between the orthodox and the modernist traditions. The word "new" in the title of Van Til's book, *The New Modernism,* was a reference to Machen's well known book, as he made clear on the closing pages of his book: "We should be doing scant justice to his [Machen's] memory if we did less today with respect to the new Modernism and Christianity."[69]

Van Til's insights into Barth's rise in the Netherlands and at Princeton partly explain his antithetical response to Barth's theology. But there is still another aspect, one that has often been overlooked. The power relations within neo-Calvinism in the Netherlands were changing in the interbellum era with the rise of a new generation. Van Til had made contact with Schilder in 1927, and in the 1930s he became acquainted with two neo-Calvinist philosophers at the Free University, Dirk Hendrik Theodoor Vollenhoven and Herman Dooyeweerd (1894-1977). These two professors of about Van Til's age had been appointed in 1926, and in the next decade they developed a new Calvinistic philosophy that attracted much attention. Central to their philosophy was the notion that religious neutrality did not exist. Dooyeweerd in particular did a lot of work on the so-called transcendental critique of theoretical knowledge. Vollenhoven, with whom Van Til had been in touch since 1936 before the Second World War, promoted a Calvinistic way of doing science. The renewal movement spearheaded by Vollenhoven, Dooyeweerd, and Schilder had radical opinions; the group was very active and also quite militant. For this reason it met with opposition within its own circles. Many neo-Calvinists were content with the theological and ecclesiastical position in academia and society that had been established by a former generation, and they preferred to neglect the uncertainties within

68. Van Bruggen, "Interview," 15.
69. Van Til, *New Modernism,* 376. See the title of Muether's chapter on Van Til and Barth: "The New Machen against the New Modernism."

modern culture that the renewal movement wanted to address. In attitude and intention this movement was similar to the Barthian movement in Germany, and Dooyeweerd, Vollenhoven, and Schilder were met with suspicion, both by many neo-Calvinists and by the Dutch Barthians.[70]

The very same elements in this renewal movement that caused suspicion among people in the Netherlands were attractive to Van Til. He felt attracted to a Calvinism that was independent, radical, and antithetical. When in 1936 he got the impression that Vollenhoven would avoid polemics with those who were sympathetic to the movement, he wrote to him: "Controversy with opponents is also, by implication at least, controversy with those who agree to a large extent with us. You will understand . . . I cannot compromise my own convictions on this matter. We are in the midst of intense controversies."[71] Vollenhoven replied that his more irenic attitude was a difference of style, not of opinion. He was afraid that openly criticizing neo-Calvinist leaders in the Netherlands — in the way Schilder did — would estrange the willing among the people from the critic, instead of from those under the critic's scrutiny.[72] Van Til had experienced this after 1929 with people like Henry Beets, but it is clear that he was nevertheless attracted by the militant aspect of the renewal movement in the Netherlands. He felt they were in the same battle against modernism, and the oppositional character of the renewal movement hardened him in his own polemical attitude.

3. Why Barth was such a serious opponent to Van Til

Van Til's critical appraisal of Barth was part of a more extensive confrontation of two different theological traditions. In the introduction to *Kirchliche Dogmatik* III/4, Barth in 1951 complained that the neo-Calvinists had communicated their disagreement with his conceptions all the way along. This time he could not resist addressing them directly and *in globo,* and he attacked them as unreasonable, coldhearted, and those to whom one need not listen.[73] This aggressive reaction reminds one of Van Til,

70. See George Harinck, *De Reformatie: Weekblad tot ontwikkeling van het gereformeerde leven* (Baarn: Ten Have, 1993), 278-358.

71. Van Til to Vollenhoven, February 14, 1936, *Archive-Vollenhoven.*

72. Vollenhoven to Van Til, March 24, 1936, copy, *Archive-Vollenhoven.*

73. *KD* III/4 (1951), x: ". . . dass sie Menschen unverständigen, kalten und harten Herzens sind, auf die man nicht zu hören braucht." Barth explicitly addressed a neo-Calvinist (it was Schilder) who had referred critically to Mozart. In *KD* IV/2 (1955), x, Barth

though Van Til himself never questioned Barth's integrity or attacked him in person.[74]

As for the reasons behind this sharp tension between Barth and Van Til, I have pointed to several personal and theological aspects as well as to the tradition of which Van Til was a part. I would like now to add one more aspect, and that is the cultural context of the interbellum era in which these traditions simultaneously developed.

In August 1914, World War I put an end to cultural optimism. Western civilization turned out to be cruel, bloodthirsty, and self-centered. What would prove to be safe and reliable, when not reason but irrationality drove peoples and nations? What remained of the social structures, of the higher and middle classes, when they were being crushed, as happened during the Russian revolution of 1917? Christianity was deemed bankrupt. From whence should the rules come now?

The new worldview that arose from this military and cultural inferno was one of skepticism and doubt. The doubt revolved around the question of the possibility of knowledge. The nineteenth-century intellectual had trusted that he was able to know, describe, explain, and control his world. The First World War showed that this trust was based on an illusion.

Within neo-Calvinist circles it was Herman Bavinck and his pupils — for example, Vollenhoven — who made room for a reorientation.[75] Bavinck sensed that the root of the matter was the opening up of the closed and objectivist world view of the Enlightenment, and that this required a rethinking of the meaning of revelation. The nature of this theological reorientation, which he started in the 1910s, bears resemblances to Barth's departure from his liberal tradition to a theology based on God's dialectical revelation.[76]

---

apologized for the "heftigen Ausfall, den ich im Vorwort zu Band III, 4 gegen die holländischen Neocalvinisten *in globo* erhoben habe."

74. Van Til to Barth, December 21, 1965, copy, *Van Til Papers:* "The fact that my views differed from your published writings and that I tried to say why, did not, in the least, detract from my esteem for your personality. And I *never did say* that you were the 'greatest heretic' of all time." Cf. Muether, *Van Til,* 191: the latter remark is hard "to reconcile with Van Til's acerbic characterization in the previous decade."

75. See H. Bavinck, *Modernisme en orthodoxie: Rede gehouden bij de overdracht van het rectoraat aan de Vrije Universiteit op 20 october 1911* (Kampen: Kok, n.d. [1911]).

76. See H. Bavinck, *The Philosophy of Revelation: The Stone Lectures for 1908-1909, Princeton Theological Seminary* (New York: Longmans, Green and Co., 1909). I use the word "dialectical" in the way defined by Bruce McCormack, not as a philosophical method but as a characteristic of God's revelation. Bruce Lindley McCormack, "Der theologiegeschicht-

Schilder was not a pupil of Bavinck, but his theology also contributed to a new development within the tradition of neo-Calvinism that would lead to a confrontation with the self-contented Kuyperian theologians who had dominated the scene in the 1910s and 1920s. "He [Schilder] has opposed any self-evidence. There was an element of alarm in his thinking about the church going astray," Berkouwer wrote. Schilder feared the church "could not stand up to the threats of the coming apocalyptic times after the First World War."[77] Together with Dooyeweerd and Vollenhoven, Schilder ignited a strong renewal movement that stressed the encompassing religious character of reality (covenant), the radical character of Reformed theology and philosophy (antithesis), and the dynamics of modern life (existentialism). This renewal movement criticized established Kuyperian opinions regarding ecclesiology and common grace. The movement was oriented toward current developments and engaged in debate with Barthianism and National Socialism. A younger generation of neo-Calvinists, having grown up with the harsh realities of war, economic crisis, and the moral implosion of Western culture, was attracted to this total, absolute, and activist world- and life-view. Van Til was influenced, too, and not only by Schilder. He kept himself informed on the publications of Dooyeweerd and Vollenhoven and ordered their books: "I get great comfort and help from both of you."[78] In 1935 he started contributing to Schilder's weekly *De Reformatie,* and in 1936 he became one of the editors of Dooyeweerd and Vollenhoven's journal, *Philosophia Reformata.* This journal was published by the newly founded Vereeniging voor Calvinistische Wijsbegeerte, and in 1937 Van Til founded its American branch, the Calvinistic Philosophy Club. Its aim was "to study the problems of philosophy on the presuppositions of the Reformed Faith."[79] He became more closely attached to this Dutch movement than any other foreigner at that time.

But neither Vollenhoven nor Schilder ever wrote a four hundred-page

---

liche Ort Karl Barths," in *Karl Barth in Deutschland (1921-1935): Aufbruch-Klärung-Widerstand,* ed. Michael Beintker, Christian Link, and Michael Trowitzsch (Zürich: Theologischer Verlag, 2005), 15-40.

77. Berkouwer, *Zoeken en vinden,* 246, 247: "Hij heeft geopponeerd tegen alle zelfsprekendheid. Er lag een element van diepe verontrusting in [zijn denken], dat het niet goed ging met de kerk . . . hij meende dat de kerk niet . . . was opgewassen tegen de dreigingen van de komende apocalyptische tijd na de Eerste Wereldoorlog."

78. Van Til to Vollenhoven, February 14, 1936.

79. Marcel E. Verburg, *Herman Dooyeweerd: Leven en werk van een Nederlandse christen-wijsgeer* (Baarn: Ten Have, 1989), 246.

book against Karl Barth. Schilder gave in to his polemical impulse, but when it came to doing theology, he, like Vollenhoven and Dooyeweerd, was constructive, developed different theological themes, and as a result inspired many students and lay people to renew neo-Calvinism. As Van Til's student H. Evan Runner stated, when he wrote to his professor in 1939 about a class he took with Schilder in Kampen:

> As for me, we *must* have him give a series of lectures to the students later — and perhaps on the subject of *De Deo*. What beautiful lines he can draw from all shades of human thought. He has read almost everything — I don't know how! And also in general literature. . . . I count it a rare privilege to study under him.[80]

Again, just as Van Til only recognized the militant aspect of the renewal movement, it seems he got hold of only one side of its intellectual activity: its critique of Barth. And he fit that critique into the American religious dichotomy of the 1920s and 1930s when he wrote:

> [W]e do not wonder that Barth himself speaks of mutual hostility between the followers of the later Abraham Kuyper and himself. The followers of Kuyper hold fast to simple historic Christianity as expressed in the Reformed Faith. They believe in the facts of the virgin birth, the resurrection and the return of Christ as events that have taken place or will take place in "our" time. They do not play fast and loose with the calendar.[81]

While the theology of Schilder developed in the same cultural context as Barth's, and was inspired by, and not understandable without, the theology of Barth, Van Til's writings never came that close to Barth. To Van Til he was the outward enemy — one who started with different problems and proposed only wrong solutions. Consequently, what was lacking in Van Til's appraisal of Barth was the slightest bit of empathy. Schilder may have misinterpreted Barth, but he did not reject his theology just because it threatened his. He, too, felt the need to start anew after the cultural divide of the First World War and realized that he had to do more than simply hold "fast to simple historic Christianity as expressed in the Reformed Faith." In 1935 Schilder said that it was Barth's theology that situated its readers "in the midst of the

---

80. H. Evan Runner to Van Til, December 19, 1939, *Van Til Papers*.

81. C. Van Til, "Changes in Barth's Theology," *Presbyterian Guardian* 5 (December 1938): 221-22, 232.

issues of our time," and in 1941 he stated that "Barthianism has taught us that we in our confession are severely outdated."[82] Vollenhoven was also of the opinion that Barth and the renewal movement had a lot in common when it came to the analysis of the present cultural situation. But they differed with Barth on the basic assumptions when it came to solutions.[83] In 1920 the weekly *De Reformatie* voiced their generation's attitude to life when the first issue opened with the words: "Through gradual transitions and catastrophic events we have ended up in a totally different world."[84] Kuyper's epistemology was no longer sufficient, and Bavinck's rethinking of neo-Calvinist theology in relation to modern culture had just begun when he passed away in 1921. At this point, too, Van Til differed from his fellow Calvinists in the Netherlands. To him the epistemology of Bavinck, Kuyper, and Warfield stood unshaken. He was not searching for different answers, but wanted to preserve the old ones.

According to Schilder and Vollenhoven, Barth and the neo-Calvinists mainly differed on revelation. Barth did not know the renewal movement, and he did not know much of neo-Calvinism either, though he appreciatively referred to Bavinck's *Gereformeerde dogmatiek* in the *Göttingen Dogmatics* and the *Kirchliche Dogmatik*. Kuyper, however, was less appreciated. Most of what Barth knew about the present state of neo-Calvinism he would have learned from his Dutch representative, Haitjema, the self-declared "opponent of Kuyper,"[85] who regularly polemicized with Schilder on the interpretation of Barth. Haitjema explained neo-Calvinism as a contemporary

82. "Dictaat 'Credo': Behandeling der 12 artikelen in verband met 'Credo' van Karl Barth, van K. Schilder" (n.p., 1946), 55; G. Puchinger, ed., *Ontmoetingen met Schilder* (Kampen: Kok, 1990), 33.

83. "In het negatieve kan men het op verschillende punten met Barth eens zijn. Het gaat om het positieve. . . . Het gaat er om, is er na den zondeval een rechtsleven mogelijk, een tweede omslag waarbij de mensch weer naar God toegaat." ("As to the negative, several points can be agreed with Barth. But here we are concerned with the positive. The issue is whether righteous life is possible after the fall, a second conversion that makes man turn to God again.") Lecture by Vollenhoven on "The background of the intellectual confusion in the present times," *De Standaard*, September 11, 1935.

84. "Door geleidelijke overgangen en catastrofale gebeurtenissen zijn wij gekomen in een veelszins andere wereld." My translation. See for the cultural and religious context of this new weekly George Harinck, *De Reformatie, weekblad tot ontwikkeling van het gereformeerde leven, 1920-1940* (Baarn: Ten Have, 1993), 11-67.

85. Th. L. Haitjema, "Abraham Kuyper und die Theologie des höllandischen Neucalvinismus. Vortrag gehalten am 9. April 1931 auf dem Ferienkurse an der Universität Bonn," *Zwischen den Zeiten* 9 (1931) 353: "Ein Gegner Kuypers."

form of the eighteenth-century natural theology that Barth was seeking to uproot. As a result neo-Calvinism had a bad name for many Barthians in both the Netherlands and abroad and was considered the opposite of Barth's theology.

There was the rare possibility of an encounter between Barth and a neo-Calvinist in 1931. On April 9 of that year, Haitjema lectured at the University of Bonn on Abraham Kuyper and the theology of Dutch neo-Calvinism. Barth appreciated this lecture and published Haitjema's text that same year in *Zwichen den Zeiten*.[86] When he learned that Vollenhoven would lecture in Elberfeld in early 1932, he invited him to visit Bonn as well, to lecture in a seminar for him and his students. The topic of Barth's lectures that semester was natural theology. Haitjema's identification in his *Zwischen den Zeiten* article of the neo-Calvinist view of regeneration with *gratia infusa*, and its qualification as "more or less Roman Catholic" and a "humanism of the born again personality,"[87] was reflected in Barth's request to speak on the relation between neo-Calvinism and natural theology. Barth wrote to Vollenhoven:

> It would be very interesting for my students and for me to be instructed in our midst about the distinctive interpretation of Calvin's teachings through the school of A. Kuyper by a person who represents this school . . . and to speak about your own teaching on the possibility of knowledge of God that precedes revelation. . . . It would especially interest us to experience if and to what extent a positive position here is possible in the field of Protestantism and in clear distinction and opposition to the Augustinian-Thomistic concept. I don't have to tell you that I am inclined to deny this possibility.[88]

86. See note 85.

87. Haitjema, "Abraham Kuyper," 352: "ein gewisser Humanismus des wiedergeborenen Menschen." The neo-Calvinists indeed defended a *gratia infusa*, but Christ and not this infusion is the reason for justification — and thus religion is not founded on morality. See H. Bavinck, *Gereformeerde dogmatiek* IV (Kampen: Kok, 1918), 267 (par. 480).

88. K. Barth to Vollenhoven, December 9, 1931, *Archive-Vollenhoven:* "Es würde nun sowohl für meine Studenten wie für mich selber von hohem Interesse sein, wen wir die eigenartige Interpretation gerade der calvinischen Lehre durch die Schule von A. Kuyper in der Person eines Vertreters dieser Richtung in unserer Mitte direct kennen lernen dürften . . . [und über] Ihrer eigenen Lehre von der Möglichkeit einer der Offenbarung vorausgehenden Erkenntnis Gottes zu sprechen . . . es würde uns ganz besonders interessieren, zu erfahren, ob und inwiefern hier auf dem Boden des Protestantismus und in klarem Unterschied und Gegensatz zu der augustinisch-thomistischen Konzeption eine positieve Einstellung möglich ist. Ich brauche Ihnen nicht zu sagen, dass ich geneigt bin, dies zu verneinen."

Vollenhoven accepted the invitation, but immediately explained to him that he had misinterpreted the position of neo-Calvinism:

> I would also like to visit Bonn . . . and give a lecture to the people in your seminar on the key issues of Dutch neo-Calvinism (as seen by one of its adherents). . . . As you see, I have formulated the title of my Bonn lecture slightly different than you did. The point is that I too deny the possibility of a human knowledge of God that precedes (Word) revelation. We do not differ on this point, as far as I can see, but on our interpretations of (Word) revelation.[89]

There have been many public confrontations between Barthians and neo-Calvinists,[90] but this would have been one of the few personal encounters between Barth and a neo-Calvinist since Schilder's meeting with Barth at Eekhof's home in 1927 and before Berkouwer broke through the lines with his second book on Barth, *De triomf der genade in de theologie van Karl Barth* (1954).[91] Unfortunately, Vollenhoven was unable to make the visit to Elberfeld and Bonn, and Haitjema's interpretation of neo-Calvinism was never corrected within Barthian circles.

Given this lack of knowledge of the character of neo-Calvinism and of the actual developments within this tradition in the 1930s, the Barthians could not know that Van Til's radicalism had been inspired by Dutch academics who reacted to the same cultural and theological conditions and stressed the same theological themes as they did. The Barthians accepted Barth's radicalism as necessary and liberating, while they took Van Til's as *rabies theologiae*. The similar themes combined with the frictions between

89. Vollenhoven to Barth, December 18, 1931, *Karl Barth-Archiv:* "Werde ich gerne auch nach Bonn kommen, . . . und in Kreise Ihres Seminars einen Vortrag zu liefern über die entscheidende Pünkte des holländischen Neu-Calvinismus (wie ein seiner Anhänger diese sieht). . . . Wie Sie sehen, habe ich der Titel des eventuellen Bonner Vortrag etwas anders formuliert als Sie. Auch ich verneine nl. Die Möglichkeit einer der (Wort-) offebarung vorausgehenden menschlichen Erkenntnis Gottes. Die Controverse zwischen uns liegt nicht hier, so weit ich sehe, aber in der Auffassung von der (Wort) offenbarung."

90. Two notable contemporary discussions of neo-Calvinist themes by Barthians are Th. L. Haitjema, "Der Kampf des holländischen Neu-Calvinismus gegen die dialektische Theologie," in *Theologische Aufsätze: Karl Barth zum fünfzigsten Geburtstag* (München: Kaiser Verlag, 1936), 571-89; and the review of K. H. Miskotte by H. L. Both et al., *Jezus Chritus en het menschenleven* (Culemborg: De Pauw, 1932), especially of the contributions of H. Colijn and K. Schilder, in *Onder Eigen Vaandel* 8 (1933): 162-69.

91. Translated as *The Triumph of Grace in the Theology of Karl Barth* (Grand Rapids, MI: Eerdmans, 1956). For Barth's appreciation of Berkouwer's book, see *KD* IV/2, x.

both traditions made a Dutch theologian conclude: "Derailments like these seem to be unavoidable if you don't answer each other's letters, if you time and again let yourselves be informed about each other via third persons, and never visit each other."[92] The result was that neo-Calvinism and Barthianism were like ships that pass each other in the night.[93]

The style of *The New Modernism* confirmed this situation. In the context of this estrangement, Van Til's obsession with the rising tide of Barthianism was not really surprising, and the cold Barthian shoulder to Van Til's book was almost predictable.

Conclusion

Because most Barthians hardly ever knew other neo-Calvinists besides Van Til, his antithetical and non-empathetic appraisal was easily identified with neo-Calvinism in general. The sympathizers with neo-Calvinism in North America in the 1950s identified this tradition with Van Til; there was hardly anyone in the academic world that knew the Dutch renewal movement of the 1930s. Schilder escaped from a full dependency on American interpreters thanks to the early translation of *Christ in His Suffering* by Zijlstra. But until the 1950s Americans familiar with Dooyeweerd only knew of him through Van Til's publications. "Many Americans may not have understood the philosophical differences between Van Til and Dooyeweerd," according to Paul Otto, "until after the Dutch philosopher's 1958 lecture tour and the publication of [Dooyeweerd's] *In the Twilight of Western Thought*" in 1960.[94]

---

92. M. E. Brinkman, "Schilder en Barth: Gebrekkige communicatie," in *Geen duimbreed! Facetten van leven en werk van prof. dr. K. Schilder (1890-1952)*, ed. J. De Bruijn and G. Harinck (Baarn: Ten Have, 1990), 70: "Als je elkaars brieven niet fatsoenlijk wenst te beantwoorden, als je je veelvuldig slechts via derden over elkaar laat informeren en elkaar nooit persoonlijk opzoekt, ja dan lijken zulke deraillementen . . . onontkoombaar."

93. See Barth's assessment in Barth to Geehan, November 14, 1965, copy, *Van Til Papers*: "The author [Van Til] seems to have understood *not a single word* of all I have written. And certainly I myself have *not* understood *a single word* of his critique. Indeed: how can an elephant understand a whale (let's say, Moby Dick) and vice versa?" Barth used the same comparison in 1961 to describe his relation with Brunner: "Both are God's creatures, but they simply cannot come to an understanding." See Busch, *Karl Barth,* 449.

94. Paul Otto, "In the Twilight of Dooyeweerd's Corpus. The Publishing History of *In The Twilight of Western Thought* and the Future of Dooyeweerd Studies," *Philosophia Reformata* 70 (2005): 26.

Familiarity with Vollenhoven in North America continues to depend upon Van Til even to the present day.

Leaving Van Til's intermediary role aside, little historical study has been done on the complex relationship of Barthianism and neo-Calvinism. Our distance in time may help us to see both traditions in their historical contexts. Instead of asking whether we agree with one of the traditions (to the exclusion of the other), we might ask instead whether we are able to understand both positions. In choosing this approach we may overcome some of the inaccurate impressions from earlier days. My hope is that historical and theological research by both Barthians and neo-Calvinists in the future will be carried out *sine ira et studio,* and without the antagonism that has obstructed their relationship and prevented a fair view of each other in the past.

In wishing this, I am in good company. As is well known, Barth was rude towards Van Til, but it is less widely known that he also made an elegant gesture toward Van Til, which embarrassed him. They did not meet in Münster in 1927, and they missed each other in Basel in 1938, but they met each other in the end in Princeton in 1962. Here is what Van Til wrote to Barth afterward:

> When you came to Princeton I called up the Seminary and asked whether I could see you but was discouraged from doing so. When I looked for an opportunity to shake hands with you after your Princeton lectures [the Warfield lectures] you were hurried away. When at last I did come near to you in the hallway and somebody called your attention to my presence and you graciously shook hands with me, saying: 'You said some bad things about me but I forgive you, I forgive you,' I was too overwhelmed to reply. . . .
>
> > *Cordially yours,*
> > *C. Van Til*
> > *Ein Menschenfresser*[95]

95. Van Til to Barth, December 21, 1965, copy, *Van Til Papers.* See also Muether, *Van Til,* 191. Muether situates the meeting in the Princeton University Chapel. Van Til's signing himself as a *Menschenfresser* is a reference to *KD* IV/2, x. Dealing with neo-Calvinists, Barth wrote about Berkouwer: "Es gibt offenbar auch 'Fundamentalisten,' mit denen sich reden lässt." And then he continued: "'Die Menschenfresser ganz allein, die sollten ausgenommen sein'- z.B. jener Mann, der meine Theologie noch vor kurzem die schlimmste Häresie aller Zeiten genannt hat! — aber auch sie nur vorläufig, weil ja eines Tages auch sie noch zu humaneren Gesinnungen und Stellungnahmen vordringen könnten."

Beyond the Battle for the Bible: What Evangelicals Missed in Van Til's Critique of Barth

D. G. Hart

To say that the battle for the Bible of the late 1970s and early 1980s was primarily a referendum on the views of Cornelius Van Til and Karl Barth would be simplistic. Even so, that the controversy over inerrancy coincided with born-again Protestant ambivalence over the Old Princeton doctrine of Scripture and growing openness to Barth's theology was more than coincidental. In fact, the debates among American evangelicals over the infallibility and authority of Scripture were signs of theological transition among conservative Protestants. This shift involved a rise and decline respectively of the theological fortunes of Barth and Van Til, with the Westminster professor's value falling seemingly in proportion to the European dogmatician's increasing worth.

In what now seems like distant evangelical history, Harold Lindsell, formerly registrar and church historian at Fuller Seminary and then an editor at *Christianity Today,* instigated as much as he called attention to born-again Protestant discomfort with inerrancy in two books, *The Battle for the Bible* (1976) and *The Bible in the Balance* (1979). For roughly a decade after 1976, evangelicals debated the Old Princeton doctrine of Scripture with the older generation of neo-evangelical leaders defending the Hodge-Warfield position as crucial to the identity and health of evangelicalism and a younger generation of conservative Protestants faulting inerrancy for a wooden rationalism or for harboring a tired and predictable attachment to the Enlightenment.[1]

1. For some of the literature on inerrancy, see *Inerrancy,* ed. Norman L. Geisler (Grand Rapids: Zondervan, 1979); *Biblical Errancy: An Analysis of Its Philosophical Roots,* ed. Nor-

Barth played a minor role in the debates and Van Til was practically invisible thanks to the scrutiny that Warfield's writing received. Even so, when Jack B. Rogers and Donald K. McKim entered the fray in 1979 with *The Authority and Interpretation of the Bible,* Barth's usefulness for those who desired a paradigm different from inerrancy was readily apparent. They devoted the final chapter of their book to Barth and G. C. Berkhower after having submitted paleo- and neo-Protestant scholasticism to a substantial critique.[2] Because Rogers and McKim inhabited the world of mainline Protestantism, their book was not obviously an expression of the younger evangelical rejection of Princeton's doctrine of inerrancy. But because Rogers was on the faculty at the neo-evangelical bastion, Fuller Seminary, the shift to Barth and away from Hodge and Warfield also left a significant impression on evangelical discussion of the doctrine of Scripture. It also signaled the repudiation of the sort of critique that Van Til had registered against Barthianism and paved the way for the warm embrace of Barth in Donald Bloesch's *Jesus is Victor: Karl Barth's Doctrine of Salvation* (1976), Geoffrey Bromiley's *Introduction to the Theology of Karl Barth* (1979), Gregory C. Bolich's *Karl Barth and Evangelicalism* (1980), and Bernard Ramm's *After Fundamentalism: The Future of Evangelical Theology* (1983).

Although the growing evangelical esteem for Barth marked a transition

---

man L. Geisler (Grand Rapids: Zondervan, 1981); *Challenges to Inerrancy: A Theological Response,* ed. Gordon Lewis and Bruce Demarest (Chicago: Moody Press, 1984); *Inerrancy and the Church,* ed. John Hannah (Chicago: Moody Press, 1984); *Hermeneutics, Inerrancy, and the Bible,* ed. Earl Radmacher and Robert Preus (Grand Rapids: Academie Books, 1984); *The Foundations of Biblical Authority,* ed. James Montgomery Boice (Grand Rapids: Zondervan, 1978); Robert K. Johnston, *Evangelicals at an Impasse: Biblical Authority in Practice* (Atlanta: John Knox Press, 1979); William J. Abraham, *Divine Revelation and the Limits of Historical Criticism* (New York: Oxford University Press, 1982); idem, *The Coming Great Revival: Recovering the Full Evangelical Tradition* (San Francisco: Harper & Row, 1984); John D. Woodbridge, *Biblical Authority: A Critique of the Rogers/McKim Proposal* (Grand Rapids: Zondervan, 1982); George M. Marsden, *Fundamentalism and American Culture: The Shaping of Twentieth-Century Evangelicalism, 1870-1925* (New York: Oxford University Press, 1980), especially chs. 12-14 and 24; Ernest R. Sandeen, *The Roots of Fundamentalism: British and American Millenarianism, 1800-1930* (Chicago: University of Chicago Press, 1970), especially ch. 5; and George M. Marsden, "Everyone One's Own Interpreter?: The Bible, Science, and Authority in Mid-Nineteenth-Century America," Timothy P. Weber, "The Two-Edged Sword: The Fundamentalist Use of the Bible," and Grant Wacker, "The Demise of Biblical Civilization," in *The Bible in America: Essays in Cultural History,* ed. Nathan O. Hatch and Mark A. Noll (New York: Oxford University Press, 1982), 79-100, 101-20, and 121-38, respectively.

2. Jack B. Rogers and Donald K. McKim, *The Authority and Interpretation of the Bible* (San Francisco: Harper & Row, 1979).

in born-again Protestant theology — one could even call it the beginning of post–World War II evangelicalism's loss of a theological consensus — the rising importance of Barth for a younger generation of born-again Protestants was also part of a battle for American Presbyterianism in which Barth emerged as the victor over Van Til. For all of twentieth-century evangelicalism's non-denominational character, Presbyterianism had been an important resource for the neo-evangelical leaders who carved out an identity for conservative Protestantism that was distinct from fundamentalism. Several neo-evangelical intellectuals such as Harold John Ockenga, Edward J. Carnell, and Carl Henry had either studied with Machen and/or Van Til, or had been students of Orthodox Presbyterians who taught at Wheaton College. Fuller Seminary had been established to be a rival to Princeton Seminary and to carry out its mission in a fashion better than Westminster Seminary.[3] Furthermore, *Christianity Today* (not to be confused with the conservative Presbyterian magazine of the same title begun in 1930), the evangelical periodical of record, used many Westminster faculty as contributing editors. As such, the battle for American Presbyterianism between Barthians at Princeton Seminary and anti-Barthians at Westminster Seminary had reverberations in the evangelical battle for the Bible. Consequently, when young evangelicals adopted Barth they also implicitly rejected Van Til. The subtext of this verdict was to regard Van Til as a fundamentalist and Barth as genuinely evangelical.

Although Van Til's critique of Barth was so unrelenting and acerbic that it plausibly struck evangelicals as fundamentalist, this dismissal missed the deeper significance of the conservative Presbyterian assault on Barthianism. As already suggested, that deeper import involved a battle among American Presbyterians, specifically at Princeton and Westminster seminaries, over the health of Reformed Christianity in the United States. In fact, the debates between Van Til and Barth look significantly different and make more sense as a chapter in American Presbyterian history than as a current within American evangelicalism's theological evolution. What follows is an overview of the reception of Barth first by evangelicals and then by Orthodox Presbyterians that culminated in the evaluations by each group of the Presbyterian Church (U.S.A.) Confession of 1967. While born-again Protestants either enlisted or rejected Barth to suit the theological needs of the neo-evangelical movement, Van Til and other confessional Reformed critics of

3. On the Princeton-Westminster-Fuller links, see George M. Marsden, *Reforming Fundamentalism: Fuller Seminary and the New Evangelicals* (Grand Rapids: Eerdmans, 1987), 22-52.

Barth viewed the rise of Barthianism in the Presbyterian Church as another indication of the enfeebled witness of the mainline church. Although the ecclesial dimension of Van Til's critique will not endear his arguments to Barthians, it does explain why Van Til found the Swiss theologian to be much more threatening than evangelicals did.

A Kinder, Gentler Reception

Neo-evangelicals (synonymous here with evangelicals)[4] were latecomers in the American reception of Barth. This intellectual tardiness was not as much an indication of what some feared as obscurantism as it was of the relative youth of the Protestant identity now known as evangelical. Not until a decade or so after Wilhelm Pauck wrote *Karl Barth: Prophet of a New Christianity* (1931) and John McConnachie followed with *The Significance of Karl Barth* (1933) did progressive fundamentalists who cornered the label "evangelical" found a new interdenominational agency, the National Association of Evangelicals, launched in 1942.[5] The think-tank for the new evangelicals, Fuller Seminary, had to wait another five years, while the creation of an organ for evangelical ideas and opinion did not muster sufficient support until 1956 with the founding of *Christianity Today*.[6] Only with such institutional resources in place could evangelicals begin to devote sustained attention to Barth. By that point, Barthianism was no longer a novelty but was sufficiently mainstream for *Time* magazine to devote one of its 1962 covers to the man dubbed during his pre–World War I years as "the Red pastor."

4. One of the problems with the literature on Barth and evangelicals, like most of the recent scholarship on evangelicalism, is that it suffers from a squishy consensus that puts every Protestant who is outside the mainline into the evangelical camp. Of course, sometimes the mean fundamentalists need to be distinguished from the nice evangelicals! But rare is the study that considers whether a Pentecostal is actually the same as a Presbyterian, not to mention that many so-called evangelicals, like Van Til, were members of communions such as the OPC that refused to join the neo-evangelical cooperative agency, founded in 1942, the National Association of Evangelicals. For a longer version of my reservations about the scholarship and identity of American evangelicalism, see D. G. Hart, *Deconstructing Evangelicalism: Conservative Protestantism in the Age of Billy Graham* (Grand Rapids: Baker, 2005).

5. On the early American reception of Barth, see Dennis Voskuil, "America Encounters Karl Barth, 1919-1939," *Fides et Historia* 12 (1980): 61-74.

6. In addition to Marsden, *Reforming Fundamentalism,* on the rise of neo-evangelicalism, Joel A. Carpenter, *Revive Us Again: The Reawakening of American Fundamentalism* (New York: Oxford University Press, 1997) is essential reading.

Between 1956, *Christianity Today's* first year, and 1986, the centennial of Barth's birth, the magazine ran roughly thirty different pieces on the Basel theologian. This coverage ran the gamut from news stories that reported on his visit to the United States in 1962, pieces of theological opinion that assessed Barth's teaching and possible usefulness for evangelical Protestantism, and then after his death a series of reviews of books about Barth or retrospective essays that evaluated the sweep of the theologian's career. The pieces that evangelicalism's journal of record deemed fit to print veered between hostile critics and appreciative interpreters. In the former category fell a variety of confessional Protestants, Lutheran and Reformed, who thought Barth's appropriation of Reformation theology to be inauthentic. Among those who appreciated Barth were those most deeply invested in neo-evangelical institutions such as Fuller Seminary and *Christianity Today* itself. What neo-evangelicals found attractive in Barth was his repudiation of liberalism. Here was a prominent and learned theologian from one of the centers of European learning saying what conservative Protestants in the United States had long been saying but who had been dismissed as fundamentalist for saying it. Barth appeared to give gravity to being a conservative Protestant and resisting the influence of mainline Protestantism. At the same time, Barth's wobbly views about the Bible and the historicity of the New Testament prevented neo-evangelicals from embracing the neo-orthodox theologian fully.

Although Van Til would eventually step in for a few at-bats against neo-orthodoxy's most influential dogmatician in *Christianity Today's* pages, the first confessional Protestant critic to take aim at Barth was J. Theodore Mueller, then a retired professor of systematics from the Lutheran Church Missouri Synod's Concordia Seminary. In his 1957 article, Mueller rendered a verdict that echoed what Van Til had been saying for close to a quarter of a century. Barth could not, according to the Lutheran theologian, escape the past of his dialectical philosophy. Barth's very method turned theology into a "religious philosophy" and directed neo-orthodoxy "back again into the old rationalizing liberal channels of which the world long before had become weary." For Mueller, Barth gave the appearance of breathing new life into Protestantism by recovering the insights of the Reformers. But the new message of the necessity of the "reality and necessity of divine grace" became little more than a "repetition . . . of what Schleiermacher, Ritschl, and Herrmann, together with many others had said before."[7] In sum, neo-orthodoxy "has neither a sure, divine foundation on which the Christian be-

---

7. J. Theodore Mueller, "Back to the Reformers," *Christianity Today* 2 (Oct. 28, 1957): 7.

liever may rest his faith, nor has it the infallible Biblical redemptive message on which the distressed penitent soul may firmly fix its hope of a sure salvation." Like liberalism before it, Barth's theology only had words, "learned words" to be sure, but also "unintelligible words, confusing words — with no clear and unmistakable meaning for those desiring assurance of salvation." Mueller even took a page from H. L. Mencken when he wrote that "Barthianism is a bit of a theological Barnum."[8]

Two years later Van Til wrote a piece for *Christianity Today* about half the length of Mueller's and with half the bark — even if the bite was still evident. Van Til's comments centered on the allegations of a new Barth, the one who had repudiated Bultmannian subjectivism for a theocentric objectivism. It was hardly a surprise that Van Til was unconvinced that this version of Barth was any better than the older one. The problem still had much to do with Barth's doctrine of revelation, which had enormous implications for the resurrection. Because of Barth's repudiation of Bultmann, Van Til wrote, "evangelicals might assume that . . . Barth defends Christ's resurrection and believes in the resurrection because he submits himself to the teaching of the Scriptures." But Barth did not believe Scripture was a direct revelation from God any more than he thought of Jesus Christ as a direct revelation of God in history. Barth "is still devoted to his basic principle," Van Til explained, "that, while revelation is historical, history is not revelational."[9] The Westminster professor conceded that Barth gave the appearance of affirming the resurrection. But Barth "finds the resurrection in a Scripture which he asserts to be 'full of obscurities and indissoluble contradictions.'" Barth compounded confusion by finding the resurrection to be "an actual event in history even though in all history God is said to be wholly hidden as well as wholly revealed." Van Til concluded that this was a strange sort of repudiation of subjectivism: to escape it "we must avoid an objective resurrection. To avoid relativism in history, we must avoid history!"[10] Before closing the article Van Til, perhaps sensing that he was famous for criticizing Barth, explained that his comments did not involve judgment of the "personal faith of Barth." Van Til credited Barth and Bultmann each with a desire to bring the gospel to modern men and women. The problem was that neither man had "any Gospel in the evangelical sense of the term."[11]

8. Ibid., 8.

9. Cornelius Van Til, "What of the New Barth?" *Christianity Today* 3 (June 8, 1959): 5.

10. Ibid., 5-6.

11. Ibid., 7.

At the other end of the spectrum from the confessional Protestant reaction was G. W. Bromiley who wrote *Christianity Today*'s very first article on Barth. At the time a rector of St. Thomas's English Episcopal Church in Edinburgh, Bromiley would eventually become one of Barth's most sympathetic evangelical interpreters while teaching historical theology at Fuller Seminary by producing a one-volume condensation of the *Church Dogmatics*. His first article of many was not without critical comments. In fact, Bromiley recognized the same problems in Barth that Mueller and Van Til had. He noted that Barth's view of Scripture, though generally conservative on the canon, was less than satisfactory on the Bible's historical reliability. Bromiley judged that Barth rendered "sweeping and categorical judgments" designed "to clear him from a possible charge of Fundamentalism." Yet, by attributing the unreliable parts to the human element of Scripture and preserving its authority through its divine status, Barth only raised another problem, namely, whether the "christological analogy" would work in the same way for the two natures of the inscripturated Word as it did for the Word incarnate.[12] Bromiley also detected in Barth's doctrine of inspiration a form of subjectivism, but he took the Swiss theologian at his word that his intention was to avoid the experientialism that characterized Protestant liberalism. In a subsequent appraisal of Barth in 1959, Bromiley noted a "dangerous subjectivizing in much that passes for evangelical theology today." Then he asked whether Barth himself fell "into much the same error in his doctrine of inspiration by making the real inspiration the work of the Holy Ghost in the readers rather than a given and objective work in and through the authors."[13] Bromiley even faulted Barth for bad exegesis in his handling of the Pauline epistles on the inspiration of Scripture. Barth's attempt to "read into passages on inspiration a movement from recollection to expectation . . . are not a very convincing exposition."[14] Bromiley was forced to conclude, reluctantly to be sure, that on this point Barth was teaching something different if not at odds with the Reformers.

Yet, for all of these tough questions that Bromiley put to Barth, the Anglican's overarching assessment was upbeat. Bromiley could not contain some of his admiration for Barth when he introduced his first article by observing the "most happy coincidence" of the theologian's seventieth birthday

12. G. W. Bromiley, "Barth's Doctrine of the Bible," *Christianity Today* 1 (Dec. 24, 1956): 15.

13. G. W. Bromiley, "Barth: A Contemporary Appraisal," *Christianity Today* 3 (Feb. 2, 1959): 10.

14. Bromiley, "Barth's Doctrine of the Bible," 16.

and the completion of the English translation of volume one, part two of the *Dogmatics*.[15] This gave Bromiley's analysis the ring of a tribute. This celebratory tone also came through in Bromiley's ability to overlook Barth's problems and recommend his work to the evangelical readership of *Christianity Today*. Again, even as he observed difficulties that Mueller and Van Til pointed out, Bromiley essentially gave Barth the stamp of approval. Barth stood in line, Bromiley wrote in 1959, "with three great emphases of evangelicalism: the historicity of God's saving action; the supremacy of the Bible; and the objectivity of God's work, particularly in the atonement."[16] Bromiley also detected in Barth a theologian of genuine devotion, especially in his reliance on Scripture. By demanding that the Bible be read on the basis of biblical presuppositions rather than historical-critical ones, Barth "reminds us that genuine reading of the Bible is possible only in obedient humility, and therefore with prayer."[17] Whether or not Bromiley's judgments were naive, they did suggest the degree to which evangelical theological analysis, in contrast to confessional Protestant strictness, was prone to indulge views not entirely on target.

Bromiley's view did not necessarily prevail in the editorial offices at *Christianity Today* even if it helped to secure him an appointment in 1959 at Fuller Seminary. But if those responsible for evangelical Protestantism's chief theological organ had been forced to choose between Bromiley's winsome appraisal and Mueller and Van Til's vinegary report card, the proponents of a kinder and gentler conservative Protestantism did not face a significant dilemma. As much as Barth's theology, especially his doctrine of Scripture, raised a host of problems for American evangelicals, evangelicalism's intelligentsia did not have the constitution for condemnation. As such, the evangelical response to Barth from roughly 1960 on was in effect, "he may be wrong but we need to listen."

In several unsigned editorials during the early to mid-1960s, likely penned by either Carl Henry or Harold Lindsell, the readers of *Christianity Today* learned several reasons for holding Barth at arm's length. The problem with the leading source of neo-orthodox theology was that it led in seemingly mutually contradictory directions, thus rendering Barth an "enigma." On the one hand, for those interested in defending the verbal and plenary inspiration of the Bible, "Barth's emphasis on biblical authority"

---

15. Ibid., 14.
16. Bromiley, "Barth: A Contemporary Appraisal," 10.
17. Bromiley, "Barth's Doctrine of the Bible," 15.

seemed "amazing." On the other hand, he was inconsistent or less than thorough in carrying out the effort to establish theology independent of "philosophical, sociological, or other presuppositions."[18] If Barth truly believed that we cannot correct the Bible but that it corrects us, then how could he render the judgment that Scripture contains errors? Would not such a determination require Barth to sit in judgment of God's word, and make the Bible dependent on its interpreters? "Unwittingly, he operates on liberal presuppositions," one editorial declared. "There is still some Schleiermacher and Herrmann in his blood, and this leads to Feuerbach and humanism."[19] A year later another editorial put the inconsistency this way: "Barth does precisely what he has just said should not be done: he looks over the prophets' shoulders and gives them bad marks." As such he failed to answer the question of how to maintain the "categorical authority of the Bible as an external canon and also declare the prophets and apostles guilty of error."[20] As critical as these editorials were, they would not go as far as the confessionalists who concluded Barth was a wolf in sheep's clothing. For the editors at *Christianity Today* the worst they could assert was that Barth was an enigma, a category that captures something of the problem of wolves dressing up as sheep but fails to recognize the danger of being enigmatic.

Yet, when Barth died in 1968, the tone of evangelicals' assessments warmed considerably. In fact, the editorial obituary that appeared on January 3, 1969, did not register a single complaint against the man who defined an epoch of theological development. Four contributions were notable. First, Barth brought "into fashion again, not merely the Scriptures in terms of content . . . but the Reformers and many other thinkers whose writing had been neglected or disparaged in the age of liberal ascendancy."[21] His second positive contribution was his theological rejoinder to totalitarianism, a point that may have caught some readers by surprise since the writers for *Christianity Today* had not seen fit to comment on Barth's politics in any specific manner. The third notable achievement was Barth's sheer strength and perseverance to write a multi-volume dogmatics. "The *Church Dogmatics*," *Christianity Today* opined, "is a book of real theology that takes time to digest and could well play its biggest role long after its first appearance."[22] Its lasting value was its posing the challenge that "theology has to be an objective presentation of

18. "Enigma in Barth" (editorial), *Christianity Today* 6 (June 8, 1962): 24.
19. Ibid., 24-25.
20. Carl F. H. Henry, "Dilemma Facing Barth," *Christianity Today* 7 (Jan. 4, 1963): 27.
21. "Karl Barth" (editorial), *Christianity Today* 13 (Jan. 3, 1969): 22.
22. Ibid.

God according to his self-revelation and its attestation in Holy Scripture."[23] Aside from these contributions, Barth finally exuded in his writing and demeanor a spirit of religious devotion that gave his at times difficult statements a "doxological orientation."[24] The editor admitted that Barth's project may not have finally come round to the views of the Protestant Reformers, but concluded, "we are grateful he came back as far as he did."[25]

By the time the debates were heating up over the battle for the Bible, *Christianity Today* was still concerned about inerrancy but hoping to moderate the war between the inerrantists and inerrancy's critics. In that context, Barth proved to be a useful source of moderation. According to one of the magazine's editors who had taken three courses with Barth, Kenneth Kantzer, fundamentalists and neo-evangelicals both needed to learn from the Swiss theologian. The most important lesson was that the Bible still possessed authority even if it came clothed in the swaddling clothes of human authors and ancient cultures. "Evangelicals are grateful for Barth's radical insistence on the humanity of Scripture," Kantzer asserted, because "fundamentalists so stressed the divine authority of Scripture that the reality and importance of its humanity was lost."[26] Barth's problem, however, was that in affirming the humanity of Scripture he also believed the Bible contained errors. Yet Kantzer believed he knew what Barth really meant. In his lectures, Kantzer explained, Barth would contrast the truth of his own position with the falsity of Bultmann's. What Barth failed to recognize was that evangelicals believe "the Bible contains only the kind of statements Barth thought he was making — the kind we ordinarily call true." Although Barth maintained throughout his career that the Bible contained errors, it was "exceedingly difficult to locate any instances . . . where he sets forth any particular error in Scripture."[27] Kantzer seemed to believe that Barth came out essentially where evangelicals always were — affirming "the radical humanity of Scripture, and at the same time, [the] complete trustworthiness of Scripture."[28]

One last editorial on Barth appeared on the centennial of Barth's birth, again written by Kantzer. "Thank God for Karl Barth, But . . . We Need to Read Him with Our Eyes Open" was the title of the editorial, and it essentially

23. Ibid.
24. Ibid., 23.
25. Ibid., 22.
26. Kenneth S. Kantzer, "Biblical Authority: Where Both Fundamentalists and Neoevangelicals Are Right," *Christianity Today* 27 (Oct. 7, 1983): 11.
27. Ibid., 12.
28. Ibid.

summarized the view that took root among neo-evangelicals. The most poignant piece of the editorial came when, after pointing out several weaknesses and deficiencies in Barth's theology, Kantzer asked, "can his theology be of any value to us?" His answer was a decisive "yes" because Barth drew on a "broad stream of solid biblical and Reformation theology," and always drew his teaching from the Bible. For these reasons, according to Kantzer, "God used [Barth] to break the backbone of liberal neo-Christianity."[29] In sum, "Barth was neither an angel of light in defense of orthodox faith once delivered to the saints, nor was he a sneaky wolf in sheep's clothing seeking to destroy the true church."[30] This verdict did not determine whether Barth was an ally but it surely indicated he was not an enemy of evangelicals. For an assessment that was colder than the warmer-than-luke-warm estimate of *Christianity Today,* conservative Protestants would need to look elsewhere.

The Battle for American Presbyterianism

If the conservative Presbyterians who supported J. Gresham Machen in his critique of liberalism and opposition to the broadening ways of the Presbyterian Church (U.S.A.) leadership had not lost Princeton Seminary as their institutional home and if Barthianism had not become the way to rescue the mainline church from the extremes of liberalism, the sectarian Presbyterian critique of Barth might have turned out differently. This is not idle speculation.[31] In the spring of 1928, well before the works of Barth and Brunner became accessible in the United States, Machen wrote an essay, "Karl Barth and 'The Theology of Crisis,'" for presentation at the Adelphi Club, a group of Presbyterian ministers in the Philadelphia vicinity who gathered for edification and intellectual enrichment. Asked to publish the piece, Machen was unsure of his ability to understand neo-orthodoxy. "I really ought to learn far more about a subject before I try to write about it," Machen wrote to one editor. "Blind leaders of the blind may get into serious trouble."[32] Even so,

29. Kenneth S. Kantzer, "Thank God for Karl Barth, But . . ." *Christianity Today* 30 (Oct. 3, 1986): 15.

30. Ibid., 14-15.

31. This and the next two paragraphs are slightly adapted from D. G. Hart, "Machen on Barth: Introduction to a Recently Discovered Paper," *Westminster Theological Journal* 53 (Fall 1991): 191-92.

32. J. Gresham Machen to Paul Woolley, July 16, 1928, Machen Archives, Westminster Theological Seminary, Glenside, Pennsylvania.

Machen's initial response to neo-orthodoxy was generally positive. The teaching of Barth, he wrote, sounds like "a return to evangelical Christianity." "The living and Holy God, man lost in sin, God's grace in the gift of Jesus Christ His Son, faith as itself the gift of God — it sounds like John Bunyan and John Calvin and the Shorter Catechism and the Reformed Faith." No wonder, Machen added, that some had uttered against Barth the insulting charge that his teaching is nothing but "'orthodoxy' after all."[33] Not only did Barth sound orthodox, but he had restored theology to its "rightful place."[34] To be sure, Barth had problems. His view of biblical history suggested that "we can hear the Word of God in the New Testament, addressed to our own soul, no matter what the facts about Jesus of Nazareth were." A consistent Barthian might not be "disturbed if scientific history should prove that Jesus of Nazareth had committed, for example, positively immoral acts." Even if Barth had rejected the "immanence philosophy" upon which modern theology was based, he had not broken with "the application of the immanence philosophy to the historical problem that the New Testament represents." Machen conceded that Barthianism was "bringing us to the Word of God" but did so on terms that departed from historic Protestantism.[35]

Another Princeton Seminary faculty member, Caspar Wistar Hodge, with whom Machen corresponded about this essay and neo-orthodoxy more generally, was also receptive to the dialectical theology of Barth. This grandson of Charles Hodge was more concerned with Barth's philosophical starting point than Machen. Hodge's "fundamental criticism" was that Barth's "acceptance of Kierkegaard's assertion of the infinite qualitative difference between God and man" led to "a dialectic of a logical and metaphysical kind" that resulted in skepticism.[36] Even so, Hodge continued to study neo-orthodoxy during the 1930s and admitted that Barth was the only contemporary theologian who interested him. In 1932, Hodge wrote that Barth had helped convince him that the "chief elements" in Christian theology were "Revelation and Faith" and that revelation was "super-rational as well as supernatural." At one point in correspondence with Machen, Hodge sensed a need to deny that he had become a Barthian. He faulted Barth for disparaging

33. Machen, "Karl Barth and the 'Theology of Crisis,'" paper delivered in Philadelphia, April 23, 1928, Machen Archives, 9. This paper was also published under the same title in *Westminster Theological Journal* 53 (1991): 197-205.

34. Ibid., 10.

35. Ibid., 14-16.

36. Hodge to Machen, July 14, 1928, Machen Archives; and Hodge, "The Reformed Faith," *Evangelical Quarterly* 1 (1930): 3-24, quotation from 13.

apologetics as "the Trojan horse which let Rationalism into the Church." Still, Hodge came away impressed with Barth's positive affirmations.[37]

From the perspective of Reformed theology prior to 1935, Barth may not have looked as bad as he did to those like Machen's students who taught at Westminster and became leaders of the Orthodox Presbyterian Church (OPC). Indeed, after leaving Princeton for Westminster in 1929, and seeing Princeton embrace Barth as the alternative conservatism to Old Princeton's brand of Reformed orthodoxy, conservative Presbyterians were not inclined to be as generous as Hodge and even Machen had been before the Presbyterian controversy of the 1920s and 1930s turned ugly with a highly partisan trial of Machen and what appeared to be a petty civil suit brought by the PCUSA against the OPC over the name of the new denomination (it was originally the Presbyterian Church in America).[38] Certainly, Van Til and his colleagues at Westminster had sufficient targets in American Protestantism about which to warn their students and fellow Orthodox Presbyterians. Reinhold Niebuhr, Paul Tillich, and Henry Pitney Van Dusen at Union Seminary, as well as the entire Biblical Theology movement of the middle decades of the twentieth century, were arguably more influential threats to the American church than Barthianism, a system of teaching that came in a form, namely, dogmatics, inherently repulsive to the average American Christian. Yet Westminster's faculty and Orthodox Presbyterian ministers maintained a steady barrage of criticism of Barthianism and aimed their guns primarily at Princeton Seminary and its influence on the mainline Presbyterian Church.

Between 1937 and 1967, the *Presbyterian Guardian,* the unofficial magazine of the OPC, ran twenty different pieces on changes and defections at Princeton Seminary and the overwhelming theme was the Barthian captivity of the school once dominated by the Alexanders, the Hodges, and Warfield.[39] This was not a refrain sung exclusively by Van Til, who wrote close to

37. Hodge to Machen, Feb. 17, 1932, Machen Archives.

38. See Edwin H. Rian, *The Presbyterian Conflict* (Grand Rapids, MI: Eerdmans, 1940), chs. 7-9; and Presbyterian Church in the U.S.A., "Presbyterian Church in the United States of America, Complainant, vs. J. Gresham Machen, Accused" (Transcript of Proceedings, February 14th, 1935, First Presbyterian Church, Trenton, New Jersey).

39. Even before 1937, Cornelius Van Til had sparred in the pages of the original *Christianity Today* with John E. Kuizenga and Donald Mackenzie, two new appointments at the reorganized Princeton, but Van Til did not count Barthianism among their offenses. Kuizenga had erred in adopting modern psychology in his method of apologetics, according to Van Til, and Mackenzie, who responded twice in *Christianity Today,* was guilty of substituting synergism for monergism in his soteriology. That Van Til, other Westminster faculty, and *Guardian* editors did not begin to accuse Princeton of Barthianism until after the

a dozen articles against Barth specifically.[40] The rest of the Westminster faculty and editors of the *Guardian* also joined the chorus. Their song sounded a singular counterpoint to the generally upbeat tune that evangelicals would eventually hum in the presence of Barth.

The first indication that Barthianism had become the conservative alternative to Old Princeton's Calvinism was the appointment of John A. Mackay in 1937 as the president to succeed J. Ross Stevenson. Ned B. Stonehouse, who taught New Testament at Westminster, took the first shot by stating the oft-repeated conservative objection that Princeton's reorganization was not administrative but part of the "broadening" of the seminary and church. The evidence always used to substantiate this claim was the presence of signers of the Auburn Affirmation on the Board of Trustees, a statement issued by liberal Presbyterians in 1923 to argue for confessional tolerance in the church.[41] In addition, Mackay had served on the controversial Board of Foreign Missions in the Presbyterian Church, and had participated in various ecumenical activities spearheaded by the Federal Council of Churches. All of these were telltale signs that Mackay was simply continuing the Stevenson administration. But Stonehouse did not stop there. The third strike against Mackay was a recent article he had written for the *Journal of Religion* in which he "blossom[ed] as a Barthian."[42] In it, according to

---

founding of the OPC suggests at least that only after the Presbyterian controversy was completely lost were conservative Presbyterians willing to bring out the heavy artillery. See Cornelius Van Til, "A New Princeton Apologetic" (Part I), *Christianity Today* 3 (Jan. 1933): 4, 12-13; idem, "A New Princeton Apologetic" (Part II), *Christianity Today* 3 (Feb. 1933): 5-6; idem, "Christianity — The Paradox of God," *Christianity Today* 4 (Feb. 1934): 9-11; and idem, "Mackenzie v. Van Til," *Christianity Today* 4 (May 1934): 13-15.

40. In addition to the articles cited below, Van Til contributed the following: "Karl Barth on Scripture," *Presbyterian Guardian* 3 (Jan. 9, 1937): 137-38; "Karl Barth on Creation," *Presbyterian Guardian* 3 (Feb. 27, 1937): 204-5; "Karl Barth and Historic Christianity," *Presbyterian Guardian* 3 (July 1937): 108-9; "Changes in Barth's Theology," *Presbyterian Guardian* 4 (Dec. 1938): 221-22, 232; and *"Umdeutung,"* *Presbyterian Guardian* 25 (Feb. 25, 1959): 51-53.

41. On the controversies among northern Presbyterians during the 1920s, see Lefferts A. Loetscher, *The Broadening Church: A Study of Theological Issues in the Presbyterian Church Since 1869* (Philadelphia: University of Pennsylvania Press, 1954); Bradley J. Longfield, *The Presbyterian Controversy: Fundamentalists, Modernists, and Moderates* (New York: Oxford University Press, 1991); William J. Weston, *Presbyterian Pluralism: Competition in a Protestant House* (Knoxville: University of Tennessee Press, 1997); and D. G. Hart, *Defending the Faith: J. Gresham Machen and the Crisis of Conservative Protestantism in Modern America* (Baltimore: Johns Hopkins University Press, 1994).

42. Ned B. Stonehouse, "Princeton's New President," *Presbyterian Guardian* 3 (Feb. 13, 1937): 182.

Stonehouse, Mackay expressed a weak view of Scripture that departed from the old view of biblical authority in which a reader's aim was "to get the message of the Bible straight" and replaced it with the goal of arriving "at an attitude of mind like that of the various writers, and especially like the 'mind of Christ.'" "Dr. Mackay may not draw all of the conclusions that Barth draws," Stonehouse concluded, "but of the observation that he espouses Barthianism in its main outlines there can be no question."[43]

A year later Van Til echoed Stonehouse on Mackay's Barthianism before going on to cite the influence of Barth on Otto Piper and Emil Brunner, two visiting professors who indicated where Princeton was headed. As late as 1939 the view from the *Guardian* was that Mackay was the source of a Barthian turn at Princeton. According to Edwin H. Rian, who wrote an editorial entitled "The New Modernism at Princeton Seminary," "So-called Barthianism is the prevailing philosophy taught at Princeton Seminary by Dr. Mackay and others." In Rian's judgment Barthianism "flatly contradict[ed] historic Christianity" by putting the events of redemption into a "supra-historical" category and by denying the truthfulness of Scripture. Only one conclusion was possible, namely, that "Barthianism is the 'new Modernism' and Princeton Seminary has adopted it as a shibboleth."[44] This was an arresting conclusion for a man who a decade later would leave the OPC and re-enter the PCUSA to work in the administration of Trinity University in San Antonio, Texas.[45]

The *Guardian*'s reaction to Mackay's appointment was simply the appetizer for a four-course meal served up in a series of articles in 1942 by Westminster faculty. Here the portions were larger even if the ingredients were basically the same as those already used to object to the new president. Stonehouse had the assignment of examining in greater detail the views of Otto Piper. Among the many compliments he paid to Piper was a recognition of the Princeton professor's learning which he wore "naturally and

---

43. Ibid., 183.

44. Edwin H. Rian, "The New Modernism at Princeton Theological Seminary," *Presbyterian Guardian* 6 (April 1939): 69.

45. On Rian's decision in 1947 to leave the OPC and rejoin the PCUSA, see "Grist for the Modernist Mill," *Presbyterian Guardian* 14 (July 25, 1947): 215-16; and "Rian Reunites with the Presbyterian Church," *Christian Century* 64 (June 25, 1947): 788-89. The *Century* reported that Rian had rediscovered Calvin's doctrine of the church and consequently repudiated sectarianism, "that abiding scandal of Western Christianity." In its editorial, the *Guardian* opined that Rian did not "really stand on the ground of Calvin" any more than the *Century* did. In fact, "on the inclusivist position" of the mainline churches that Rian joined, not even the Protestant Reformation could find an "adequate" justification.

modestly" in his scholarship. Stonehouse even detected that Piper stood to the right of Barth. But this was still not sufficiently conservative. The problem was that Piper had embraced Barth's doctrine of the Word — that the Bible becomes the Word of God — a conception that placed Piper basically with Charles Briggs, who "subordinated the authority of the Bible to the interior witness of the Spirit to the individual."[46] To be sure, Piper exhibited other deficiencies, such as an aversion to a "system of doctrine" and an "inadequate view of sin." But the basic error was in following Barth rather than the historic Protestant position. "Superficially considered," Stonehouse admitted, Piper's view of Christianity "resembles the Biblical perspective to a remarkable degree."[47] But it rested on the "philosophical presuppositions of the Barthian school." As such, Piper could not unequivocally escape the "immanentism of modern thought" and affirm "the independence of the Almighty from the universe of spiritual and material realities."[48]

Not surprisingly, Van Til contributed to this series. His target was Elmer George Homrighausen, professor of Christian education. Van Til began by reporting on some of the difficulties that Homrighausen had in clearing hurdles in the Presbyterian Church, since his appointment needed to be ratified by the General Assembly. The new professor needed to reassure various critics that his views were sound even while he affirmed "the main tenets of Barthianism."[49] From here Van Til went on to criticize Homrighausen's personalist conception of Christianity and found numerous quotations that reflected a capacious understanding of mystery. At one point, Van Til registered what may have been the cruelest cut when he wrote, "We are now in 'the house of personality' with Dr. Harry Emerson Fosdick."[50] But because Van Til regarded Barthianism as simply a higher-octane version of liberalism, the differences between America's most popular liberal preacher and Europe's neo-orthodox authority were not substantial. As Van Til observed in conclusion about Homrighausen, "[w]hen he speaks about the Bible as the infallible rule of faith and practice, and when he speaks of revelation as historical, he together with the Modernist and the Barthian, merely uses a figure of speech."[51]

46. Ned B. Stonehouse, "Princeton's New Professor of New Testament," *Presbyterian Guardian* 12 (Feb. 25, 1943): 59.

47. Ibid., 60, 61.

48. Ibid., 61.

49. Cornelius Van Til, "A Substitute for Christianity," *Presbyterian Guardian* 12 (Feb. 10, 1943): 35.

50. Ibid., 37.

51. Ibid.

The newcomer to the series was Leslie W. Sloat, the librarian at Westminster, who piled on by holding up Mackay for further inspection. Sloat did not introduce much that was new. He faulted Mackay again for a defective view of revelation. The Bible for Mackay is not "a deposit of divine truth communicated to man by God." Mackay held instead that "before we can hear God speaking to us — before the Bible actually becomes revelation — it must . . . 'be read with the same spirit with which it was written.'"[52] Here Sloat observed how such an encounter with revelation was closely related to a personalist conception of Christianity like Homrighausen's. But while repeating objections to Mackay, Sloat explained why this topic was important. "When we recall that these are the remarks of the man who now heads an institution formerly known throughout the world as the bulwark of the Reformed Faith," Sloat lamented, "it becomes apparent what a change has come over this school." No longer the institution of the Alexanders, the Hodges, Warfield, and Machen, Princeton had become a seminary "dedicated to the memory of Søren Kierkegaard, Karl Barth, and — Ichabod!"[53]

Sloat's rhetorical flourish pointed back to the main reason for the series, a point that had been amplified significantly in the first article written by Paul Woolley, who taught church history at Westminster. In his estimate of Princeton, Woolley started with Calvin's Geneva Academy and traced the training of Reformed pastors down to the establishment of the Presbyterian Church's first seminary in North America. From there Woolley looked at the changes in curriculum at Princeton since 1912, when Warfield had opposed revisions that he believed dumbed down the seminary's high academic and theological standards. The subsequent diminution of systematic theology at Princeton was the Trojan horse that let in the invading forces of Barthianism. "For the Barthian," Woolley wrote, "any system of theology can be only an indication, a directional arrow pointing toward the truth. . . . There is no particular virtue therefore in insisting upon the presentation of a complete *system of theology*."[54] Woolley concluded that to "hold that the modern Princeton is pursuing the tradition of the Reformed theology, to hold that she is remaining faithful to her *Plan* . . . is to be blind indeed when the facts are so plain."[55]

The Van Til-and-company critique of Barth, as this series from the

---

52. Leslie W. Sloat, "Princeton's President," *Presbyterian Guardian* 12 (March 10, 1943): 68.

53. Ibid., 69.

54. Paul Woolley, "Downward Trends at Modern Princeton," *Presbyterian Guardian* 12 (Jan. 25, 1943): 28.

55. Ibid., 29.

Guardian suggests, was bound up with the Presbyterian controversy of the 1920s and 1930s that saw Princeton lose its reputation as the American beacon of Reformed orthodoxy. For the Orthodox Presbyterians at Westminster, the demise of Princeton still stung and they wanted everyone — at least the readers of the *Guardian* — not to be fooled by efforts to offer Barth as a sufficient corrective to Protestant modernism. In fact, the editorial that introduced the series noted that some American Calvinists were being duped by changes at Princeton. Clarence Bouma, managing editor of the Christian Reformed Church–related *Calvin Forum* in 1942 had opined that Brunner's departure from Princeton indicated that "the popularity of 'Barthianism' is definitely on the wane" at the seminary. Bouma added that it was wrong to categorize Princeton as either modernist or Barthian. But T. R. Birch, managing editor of the *Guardian,* was having none of such confidence in Princeton. The four-part series was designed to correct this erroneous impression. A thorough study of the situation "will convince even the most skeptical that Princeton Seminary is still totally unworthy of evangelical confidence."[56]

Yet these criticisms made almost no dent on neo-evangelicals. By the time *Christianity Today* was up and running Bromiley's winsome estimates of Barth, the Presbyterian controversy that had fueled Orthodox Presbyterian criticisms were part of a distant and fundamentalist past that the magazine's editors were trying to leave behind. To be sure, the Van Tilian critique of Barth's philosophical theology along with the Old Princeton doctrine of Scripture was plausible to the new evangelicals to a point. But the concerns for Presbyterianism in the United States and the institutions that had propagated Reformed Christianity were generally of no consequence to the pan-Protestant, parachurch-driven evangelicalism that informed *Christianity Today* and subsidiary institutions such as the National Association of Evangelicals, Fuller Seminary, and the Billy Graham Evangelistic Association. In other words, to do justice to Van Til's critique of Barth, evangelicals would have needed to identify with the ecclesiastical struggle in which Machen had played such a crucial role.

The Confession of 1967

The differences between Orthodox Presbyterian and neo-evangelical reactions to Barth were particularly evident in the debates surrounding the Pres-

---

56. T. R. Birch, "Whither Princeton," *Presbyterian Guardian* 12 (Jan. 25, 1943): 25.

byterian Church's adoption of the Confession of 1967. For the former, the Confession and the *Book of Confessions* that accompanied it signaled the complete victory of Barthianism in the mainline Presbyterian Church. For evangelicals, it was barely a passing distraction. In the process, the different wings of post–World War II conservative Protestantism — the proponents of either parachurch expansion or denominational mission — revealed that the evangelical hope for a united conservative front was unrealistic.

The Confession of 1967 was the fruit of the 1958 merger of the PCUSA and the United Presbyterian Church of North America, thus designating the mainline Presbyterian Church for a quarter of a century as the United Presbyterians or UPCUSA. The united denominations had considered a brief statement of the Reformed faith to reflect ecclesiastical union. But the committee assigned the task of preparing the brief statement, under the leadership of Princeton Seminary's Edward A. Dowey, soon received approval to expand its work to reconsider American Presbyterians' confessional heritage. By 1965 the committee had produced a *Book of Confessions,* which ran from the Apostles' Creed, different sixteenth- and seventeenth-century formulas, including the Westminster Standards, down to the Barmen Declaration and the controversial Confession of 1967. As James Moorhead has argued, the Confession of 1967 culminated the ascendancy of neo-orthodoxy within the northern Presbyterian Church.[57]

Without surprise, the conservative Presbyterians of the OPC were not slow to point out the errors of the mainline church. Westminster's Old Testament professor, Edward J. Young, took the lead in 1965 with two articles for the *Guardian.* Although he never mentioned Barthianism by name, Young's critique drew upon the same complaints registered by Van Til and others about Barth's version of modernism. For instance, Young asserted that the Confession of 1967 nowhere called the Bible the word of God but instead referred to it as "merely a normative witness to the Word of God, which is Jesus Christ."[58] He also noted that for all of the Confession's language of reconciliation through Jesus Christ, its rejection of theory and the ability of words to convey precise theological meaning rendered it a manifestation of "the irrationalism so prevalent in much of modern thought."[59]

---

57. For background on the Confession of 1967, see James H. Moorhead, "Redefining Confessionalism: American Presbyterians in the Twentieth Century," in *The Confessional Mosaic: Presbyterian and Twentieth-Century Theology,* ed. Milton J. Coalter, John M. Mulder, and Louis B. Weeks (Louisville: Westminster/John Knox, 1990), 59-83.

58. Edward J. Young, "Why We Are Sad," *Presbyterian Guardian* 34 (July-Aug. 1965): 91.

59. Edward J. Young, "Confession in a Fog," *Presbyterian Guardian* 34 (Sept. 1965): 103.

If Young failed to link the Confession of 1967 explicitly to Barth and neo-orthodoxy, Van Til was ready and eager to connect the dots. In a 127-page, privately published booklet, *The Confession of 1967: Its Theological Background and Ecumenical Significance,* distributed to conservatives in the UPCUSA courtesy of the den Dulk Foundation, Van Til culminated his critique of Barth. In this booklet, the Westminster professor of apologetics drew on many of his earlier criticisms of Barthianism. In one chapter he dissected the dimensionalist philosophy of men on the committee responsible for the Confession who also happened to be professors at Princeton: George S. Hendry, John Mackay, and Edward Dowey. In another chapter he singled out James I. McCord, the new president at Princeton, for a defective anthropology that assumed the Westminster Divines could not grasp the complexity of human existence the way that moderns could, thanks to Darwin and Freud. Another chapter involved a lengthy demolition of the idea of the "Christ-event" in Barth's dogmatics. Van Til even managed to offend Lutherans when he decided to analyze a favorable article by Martin Marty in the *Christian Century.* Marty would respond to Van Til by saying that the Dutch American was "either completely ignorant or demon possessed."[60]

Although Van Til probably lost many readers not simply because of his polemics but also owing to the intricacies of Immanuel Kant, he showed no signs of being either stupid or deranged. In the passage where he pummeled Marty, Van Til turned from the high-brow discourse of I-Thou to the simplicity of the *Peanuts* cartoon strip. "It is always a mean thing to take toys away from children," Van Til began:

> Linus must have his blanket. But when will Orthodoxy grow up? When will it learn to drive a modern car instead of cling to its Model T? How exhilarating it is to move with the greatest of ease from *Historie* to *Geschichte* and from *Geschichte* to *Historie!* The whole thing becomes a matter of reflexes. We have to pinch ourselves to think back to the time when it seemed strange to say that when God was wholly revealed in Jesus of Nazareth and in the words of the Bible, he is, for that very reason, at the same time also wholly hidden, and that there is no mystery in God but that is wholly revealed in Christ. Christ is both the electing God and the elected man; let us sing it as a "lyrical tribute" to Karl Barth.[61]

60. Martin E. Marty, quoted in John R. Muether, *Cornelius Van Til: Reformed Apologist and Churchman* (Phillipsburg: P&R Publishing, 2008), chap. 7, note 37.

61. Cornelius Van Til, *The Confession of 1967: Its Theological Background and Ecumenical Significance* (Philadelphia: Presbyterian & Reformed Publishing, 1967), 90.

But Van Til was on Linus's side and unwilling to give up his blanket. The particular blanket he had in mind was the first question and answer from the Heidelberg Catechism, from which he quoted the entire answer before explaining:

> You see that those of us who hold to the Christ of the orthodox faith do not hold to some abstract notion either of God or of man. We believe that, and only that, which Christ has told us about God, and our relation to him. Could there be anything more existential than this first question and answer of the Heidelberg Catechism?[62]

Citing a Reformed confessional norm outside the Westminster Standards may not have been the wisest strategy for countering the addition of other creeds to the Presbyterians' Confession and catechisms, but that did not deter Van Til from concluding, "This is my blanket. Without it I cannot sleep. Without it I cannot go anywhere. I do not want to be seen anywhere without it. And now, the new theology and the new creed are trying to take my blanket from me."[63]

While readers of the *Guardian* were learning why they should lament the ultimate broadening of the mainline Presbyterian Church, subscribers to *Christianity Today* received news of the proposed Confession with the strongest comments coming from former members of the UPCNA, who used the Confession to call into question the merger with mainline Presbyterians in the first place. Only two journalistic accounts covered the debates in the Presbyterian Church. The only neo-evangelical to comment on the Confession of 1967 was Geoffrey Bromiley, who argued that Barth's theology was better than the new creed's. "It would in fact be far stronger theologically," Bromiley wrote, "and more rather than less positive from the standpoint of orthodoxy, if [the Confession of 1967] were in many respects closer to *Church Dogmatics*."[64] The former United Presbyterians who weighed in for *Christianity Today* were John H. Gerstner, Abram Miller Long, and Harold H. Lytle. Both Gerstner and Long wrote two articles. Gerstner first opposed the Confession because of a defective view of Scripture but then reversed course by appealing to the meaning implied by those delegates to the Assembly who ratified creedal revision.[65] Long remained opposed in both of

---

62. Ibid.

63. Ibid., 93.

64. Geoffrey W. Bromiley, "1967 Confession and Karl Barth," *Christianity Today* 10 (March 4, 1966): 17.

65. John H. Gerstner, "Church Historian Warns: Presbyterians Are Demoting the Bi-

his articles, first objecting that the Confession made too many concessions to literary and historical criticism of the Bible, and second taking issue with the Social Gospel agenda implied in the Confession's attempt to address various social, political, and economic circumstances.[66] Lytle's article was the last in *Christianity Today*'s coverage and his title summarized his main contention, "They Are Taking My Church Away from Me." "The voice of the new confession," Lytle wrote, "speaks in words that almost obscure the startling fact that faith in the Bible has been turned to doubt, that belief has been changed into unbelief, and that reliance on the power of the Holy Spirit has been changed into reliance on the fallible interpretations of men."[67]

If Lytle's concerns elicited sparse support from the neo-evangelicals, they received a double portion from Orthodox Presbyterians. In fact, the OPC was so alarmed by the Confession of 1967 that it issued a rare declaration at its 1967 General Assembly, complete with four points. First, the new Confession "effectively" removed "the Bible from its position as the only infallible rule of faith and life." Second, it denied "doctrines essential to the system of faith" of the Westminster Standards. Third, the Presbyterian Church had "effectively" removed "any confessional foundation for [its] life and witness." Finally, by accommodating the gospel to contemporary culture, the Confession essentially undermined "the very reconciliation it purports to advance." With these warnings the OPC was trying to expose the mainline Presbyterian Church's departure "from the position of a catholic, evangelical, and reformed church."[68]

Whether or not the Confession of 1967 reflected the influence of Barth on the mainline church, debate about it was a fitting way to culminate the line of criticism that Van Til had initiated and that other Orthodox Presbyterians seconded. From the perspective of those Presbyterians who had left the mainline in 1936, the Confession of 1967 reflected the ultimate outworking of liberal Presbyterianism from the 1920s. In fact, for conservatives the new Confession bore remarkable similarities to the Auburn Affir-

---

ble," *Christianity Today* 10 (Dec. 3, 1965): 11-14; and idem, "New Light on the Confession of 1967," *Christianity Today* 11 (Dec. 9, 1966): 4-6.

66. Abram Miller Long, "Do Presbyterians Need a New Confession?" *Christianity Today* 10 (April 1, 1966): 10-14; and idem, "Does the New Confession Alter the Spiritual Mission of the Church," 10 (May 13, 1966): 16-20.

67. Harold H. Lytle, "They Are Taking My Church Away from Me," *Christianity Today* 11 (Aug. 18, 1967): 18.

68. "Orthodox Presbyterian Assembly Makes Declaration on the Confession of 1967," *Presbyterian Guardian* 36 (April 1967): 36, 55, 56.

mation of 1923.[69] Like liberal Presbyterians of the 1920s, those advocating the new Confession believed the Westminster Standards were outdated and that the church needed a creed to reflect contemporary understandings of people and society.[70] So too, like the Auburn Affirmation, the new Confession revealed an anti-theoretical cast of mind that doubted the ability of language to capture the significance of divine revelation in precise ways.[71] This may explain why E. J. Young could write that "in the Confession of 1967 there is present another gospel, which is not another. Historical Christianity is a religion of redemption, but the religion of the proposed Confession is something quite different." When he concluded that "[b]etween them we must make a choice," Young was clearly echoing J. Gresham Machen's *Christianity and Liberalism*, a book that not only questioned the affirmations of liberals but whose author also argued that the Auburn Affirmation effectively denied the constitutional status of the Westminster Confession and Catechisms.[72] No matter how distinct Barthianism may have been from the theology of the Confession of 1967, Van Til's battle over Barth was a major front in the older war between conservative and liberal Presbyterians in the northern church.

Evangelicals might have been forgiven for missing the Presbyterian politics behind Van Til's opposition to Barth, though Fuller Seminary's aspirations to be the new and improved Princeton and its large number of alumni and faculty in the Presbyterian Church should have improved evangelicals' perceptions of Barthianism's subtler significance. For many in the neo-evangelical movement, Barth simply represented an important theologian who repudiated liberalism and so bolstered the plausibility of evangelicalism's mild hostility to modernist Protestantism. But for conservative Presbyterians who were still smarting from the loss of the Presbyterian Church and its beloved Princeton Seminary, nothing, especially the Theology of Crisis, was ever so simple. Consequently, before Barth's reception by evangelicals ever instigated the "battle for the Bible," his appropriation by Princeton's faculty prolonged the conflict between the mainline and sideline Presbyterians that had first erupted at the 1920 General Assembly when Machen witnessed Princeton's president, J. Ross Stevenson, presenting a plan for the organic union of the largest Protestant denominations. From

69. Longfield, *Presbyterian Controversy,* ch. 4, provides a useful overview of the "Affirmation" and its place in the Presbyterian debates of the 1920s.

70. Young, "Why We Are Sad," 92.

71. Young, "Confession in a Fog," 102.

72. Ibid., 104.

1920 to 1967 the faculty of Princeton and its step-daughter, Westminster, carried on a battle over the character and limits of Reformed Christianity. Even though the formation of Westminster in 1929 and the founding of the OPC in 1936 would seem to have concluded the Presbyterian conflict, Barth's presence in American Protestantism prolonged that struggle. With the Confession of 1967 and the OPC's declaration in the same year, that battle finally came to an end.

Never Beyond Battle

The post-war leaders of neo-evangelicalism were not the only ones to miss the American Presbyterian overtones of Van Til's reaction to Barth. Most of those to evaluate Van Til's critique since the Barthian turn among evangelicals have looked at the battle simply from the perspective of an emerging evangelical consensus rather than as a struggle within Reformed Christianity. Gregory C. Bolich, for instance, asserts that under Van Til's influence, "the work of Barth was declared off limits to a generation of evangelicals," and that the Westminster professor's evaluation "became the primary response of the American conservative community to Karl Barth."[73] Bernard Ramm concluded that Van Til, along with Carl Henry and Francis Schaeffer, felt that "the older paradigm of evangelical theology still holds."[74] Phillip R. Thorne categorized Van Til as part of the "Fundamentalist Evangelical reception of Barth" which was characterized by interpreting departures from orthodoxy as "speculative distortions of biblical truth under the influence of post-Kantian philosophy."[75] Kevin Vanhoozer regards Van Til as the "first evangelical" to engage Barth critically and observes that Van Til's basic assumption was that "Barth uses orthodox terms in a non-orthodox way."[76] The one exception to this interpretation of Van Til was R. Albert Mohler's 1989 dissertation on evangelicals and Barth in which the future Southern

---

73. Gregory C. Bolich, *Karl Barth and Evangelicalism* (Downers Grove: InterVarsity Press, 1980), 66-67.

74. Bernard Ramm, *After Fundamentalism: The Future of Evangelical Theology* (San Francisco: Harper & Row, 1983), 26.

75. Phillip R. Thorne, *Evangelicalism and Karl Barth: His Reception and Influence in North American Evangelical Theology* (Pittsburgh, PA: Pickwick Publications, 1995), 31.

76. Kevin J. Vanhoozer, "A Person of the Book? Barth on Biblical Authority and Interpretation," in *Karl Barth and Evangelical Theology: Convergences and Divergences,* ed. Sung Wook Chung (Grand Rapids: Baker Books, 2006), 28.

Baptist Seminary president noted that Van Til was never comfortable with evangelicalism because of a prior commitment to Reformed orthodoxy.[77] Even so, Mohler concludes that Van Til's judgment became the "definitive judgment of conservative Protestantism prior to the emergence of the 'new evangelicals.'"[78] These estimates of Van Til fail to notice the denominational struggle between the PCUSA and the OPC or the seminary conflict between Princeton and Westminster. Even more revealing, they do not reflect that the reception of Barth by the neo-evangelical magazine of record, *Christianity Today,* was far more receptive than Van Til's and that this receptivity occurred well before Ramm's or Bolich's books.

The question that naturally arises, then, is why evangelicals missed the Presbyterian aspect of Van Til's critique of Barth. One obvious reason is that neo-evangelicals and the constituency they cultivated were not Presbyterian. Denominational struggles had little relevance to the larger and more pressing need for a pan-Protestant effort that would rival the liberal mainline churches and reclaim Protestantism's good name for America.[79] If Van Til and his conservative Presbyterian peers could contribute to that larger evangelical project, fine. But if Van Til and company were going to become bogged down in the fine points of Reformed orthodoxy, Presbyterian polity, or the bragging rights of theological seminaries, then they should take their squabble elsewhere. This is precisely what happened early on when the OPC determined it would not join the National Association of Evangelicals (NAE). When Orthodox Presbyterians decided that the neo-evangelical movement was not sufficiently Reformed to include their beliefs, evangelical leaders should have known that Van Til and like-minded critics of Barth were fighting a different battle. But so optimistic were neo-evangelicals in their search for a consensus of conservative Protestants that they overlooked Van Til's Reformed dogmatism in hopes that his philosophical skills could be appropriated for evangelical ends.

The flipside of this point about why evangelicals missed the Presbyterian dimension of Van Til's battle with Barth is that neo-evangelicals were by definition inclined to avoid polemics and to strive instead for a positive and united expression of conservative Protestantism. The Protestants who created the NAE, Fuller Seminary, and *Christianity Today* in the 1940s and

77. Richard Albert Mohler, Jr., "Evangelical Theology and Karl Barth: Representative Models of Response" (Ph.D. Dissertation, Southern Baptist Theological Seminary, 1989), 71.

78. Ibid., 106.

79. Marsden, *Reforming Fundamentalism,* and Carpenter, *Revive Us Again* remain the best treatments of the impulses that motivated neo-evangelicals.

1950s were intent on being conservative but not fundamentalist — which is why the word "evangelical" was so important. Fundamentalists had been guilty of fighting too many battles and of being insufficiently cooperative. In sum, fundamentalism was narrow and mean. Evangelicalism was designed to rescue conservatives from such sectarianism and nastiness by providing a kinder and gentler version of conservative Protestantism. This difference was certainly evident in the different responses to Barth in *Christianity Today* and the *Presbyterian Guardian*. The upside of neo-evangelical optimism was the ability to carve out an alternative American Protestant identity that by some estimates constitutes as much as forty percent of the U.S. population. The downside was that neo-evangelicals missed out on the value of ecclesiology and polemics, the very convictions that animated Van Til.[80]

The quest for Protestant unity in the United States has generally nurtured, whether among evangelicals or mainliners, the instinct to regard dissent as fundamentalist. Evangelicals may have had a longer list of essential articles — the NAE had nine points compared to the Federal Council of Churches' sole affirmation that Christ is Lord.[81] But like mainline Protestants, evangelicals tended to view vociferous defenses of a particular Protestant tradition as an unnecessary and unwelcome barrier to Protestant cooperation and unity. The goal and effects of united action, accordingly, far outweighed the strengths and vitality of a specific theological or ecclesial tradition, whether Lutheran or Reformed. Consequently, just as faculty at Old Princeton were adamant opponents of the cooperative Protestantism that led to the forming of the Federal Council of Churches in 1908 and that instigated the Presbyterian controversy in the early 1920s,[82] so their successors at Westminster were critical of neo-evangelical endeavors to create conservative pan-Protestant institutions.

For such Protestants as Van Til, being Reformed mattered more than being evangelical. The reason had much to do, ironically, with being broad

---

80. Muether, *Cornelius Van Til,* is especially valuable in placing Van Til's polemics in the context of his efforts as a churchman.

81. On the perceived differences between the sectarian NAE and the ecumenical Federal Council, see "Sectarianism Receives New Lease on Life," *Christian Century* 60 (May 19, 1943): 596; and "Why the Federal Council?" *Christian Century* 65 (Jan. 28, 1948): 104.

82. On conservative Presbyterian — largely at Princeton Seminary — opposition to late nineteenth-century American Protestant ecumenism, see D. G. Hart, "The Tie that Divides: Presbyterian Ecumenism, Fundamentalism, and the History of Twentieth-century American Protestantism," *Westminster Theological Journal* 60 (1998): 85-107.

rather than being narrow. For confessional Protestants, attention to the breadth of biblical teaching, rather than trying to condense it to a few terse affirmations of Christian truth, was crucial to the witness and ministry of the church. Even if the rhetoric of proclaiming "the whole counsel of God" sounded sanctimonious, holding to the Westminster Standards as a summary of biblical teaching was arguably a far richer understanding of Christianity than a nine-point doctrinal statement. What is more, the sort of Reformed orthodoxy that Van Til defended led, from one perspective, to a broader form of ecumenism than the one neo-evangelicals proposed. Van Til was part of a fraternal relationship with Reformed churches from around the world. Neo-evangelical cooperation focused almost exclusively on uniting Protestants in the United States.[83] Determining whether Reformed confessionalism or American neo-evangelicalism is broad or narrow is, admittedly, a complicated and contested question. But the verdict on Van Til's reaction to Barth has rarely considered other perspectives on sectarianism and ecumenicity other than the quest for unity as defined by both mainline and evangelical Protestantism. For both groups of Protestants, Van Til's critique was typical of fundamentalism — a judgment that almost takes one's breath away for its simplistic rendering of Van Til's Reformed orthodoxy and philosophical theology as the equivalent of the creationism, inerrancy, and dispensationalism characteristic of actual fundamentalism.

Also important to notice about the effort to unite Protestants, again whether mainline or evangelical, is the preference for subjective over objective measures of inclusion. Van Til was not the first American Presbyterian to be regarded as mean. His mentor, Machen, also bore that taunt. Of course, disagreement can be disagreeable. But simply evaluating a book or collection of writings and concluding that it falls outside the boundaries of the Westminster Standards or Reformed orthodoxy is not inherently uncharitable. But for American Protestants influenced more by pietism and religious experience than confessionalism and formal expressions of Christianity, the temptation has always been to consider disagreement as a sign of ungraciousness rather than as simply a legitimate part of theological evaluation or ecclesiastical discipline. To put this another way: pietists generally regard good intentions (orthopathy) as more important than right doctrines (orthodoxy).

---

83. On the different ways that ecumenism might be implemented by twentieth-century conservative Protestants, either national or international, see Hart, *Defending the Faith*, epilogue.

This difference surfaced clearly in the responses to Barth from neo-evangelicals and Reformed critics. Evangelicals were generally more receptive because they believed that Barth meant well and so they were willing to overlook infelicitous statements. Van Til and other Reformed thinkers, however, did not care as much about intentions but looked for doctrinal conformity. This helps to explain why evangelicals and Van Til noticed similar problems in Barth, but came to distinct conclusions. Evangelicals hoped they could work with Barth to a better formulation of the doctrine of Scripture. Van Til sensed that such work was futile given Barth's theological and philosophical baggage. Consequently, while Van Til needed to explain that his criticisms were not personal and did not necessarily involve a determination on Barth as a Christian, evangelicals repeatedly commented on Barth's personal warmth and visible devotion to justify their high regard for him even when troubled by Barthianism. Dr. Laura may be the best judge of which approach is better for evaluating a person. Still, it is worth remembering that as unattractive as Van Til's bearing may have looked while debating Barth, the evangelical approach may look less appealing when it generates favorable receptions of born-again government officials, like say, occupants of the White House.

Even so, in the final analysis, evangelicals could have realized that they themselves sounded narrow and mean in their own nice and affirming way. On the one hand, neo-evangelicals were part of a Protestant effort that was repudiating, no matter how positively, the existing Protestant ecumenical effort controlled by the mainline churches. To form the NAE to counter the Federal Council or to establish *Christianity Today* to rival the *Christian Century* was to take a narrower road than the one provided by mainstream Protestantism. On the other hand, to receive Barth more warmly than Van Til involved making a personal evaluation not only of the Swiss theologian but also of his vociferous Dutch-American critic. Why Edward John Carnell believed that his criticism of Van Til in the *Christian Century* in 1962, for instance, was generous or charitable is impossible to know. But when he wrote for mainline Protestant consumption that he was "utterly ashamed of the manner in which extreme fundamentalists in America continue to attack Barth," and followed with an admission of actually feeling pain upon reading in *Time* magazine that Van Til had said Barthianism was more hostile to the Reformation than Roman Catholicism, Carnell did not seem to consider that he may have also been causing pain in the Philadelphia suburbs where his former professor lived. Whether Carnell's subsequent proposal that Van Til needed to "ask God to forgive him for such an irresponsible judgment" was narrower or meaner than Van Til's own assessment of Barth is debatable.[84] Yet, Carnell's invective provides a worthwhile reminder about the danger of concluding that only Van Til was the ornery one in the reception of Barth. Evangelical niceness possessed its own variety of cussedness as Van Til himself knew.

84. Edward John Carnell, "Barth as Inconsistent Evangelical," *Christian Century* 79 (June 6, 1962): 714.

PART II

PHILOSOPHICAL AND THEOLOGICAL ANALYSIS

Karl Barth, American Evangelicals, and Kant

John E. Hare

This essay is an attempt to relate three things: Immanuel Kant, Karl Barth, and American evangelicalism. Of these three, I know the most about Kant. My knowledge of Barth comes from having moved to Yale Divinity School, where Barth is still, I think, the presiding genius. Because my students ask me constantly how what I am saying relates to Barth, I have found I have to read him, for which I am very grateful. My knowledge of American evangelicalism is not as a student of the movement, but as an adherent, at least in a very general sense (though I am uneasy with some current applications of the term). American evangelicalism is a many-splendored thing. I will speak mainly about Cornelius Van Til *(The New Modernism* and *Has Karl Barth Become Orthodox?)* and Carl Henry *(God, Revelation and Authority),* who depends heavily on Gordon Clark *(Karl Barth's Theological Method).* I will also briefly mention James Buswell *(A Systematic Theology of the Christian Religion).*[1] I could have chosen other more irenic evangelical voices, including some of the people at the conference at which I read this as a paper. But I wanted to get on the table one particular kind of critique of Barth.

In the first part of the essay I will lay out a critique of Barth to be found

---

1. Cornelius Van Til, *The New Modernism* (London: James Clarke, 1946); Van Til, *Has Karl Barth Become Orthodox?* (Philadelphia: Presbyterian and Reformed Pub. Co., 1954); Carl F. H. Henry, *God, Revelation and Authority,* vol. III (Waco, TX: Word Books, 1979); Gordon H. Clark, *Karl Barth's Theological Method* (Nutley, NJ: Presbyterian and Reformed Pub. Co., 1963); James Oliver Buswell, *A Systematic Theology of the Christian Religion* (Grand Rapids: Zondervan, 1962).

in these sources I am using, namely, that Barth is dependent on Kant to a degree that is inconsistent with faithfulness to the gospel. In spelling this out, I will need to describe and briefly evaluate how these authors are reading Kant. In the second part of the essay I will return in more detail to how I read Kant myself. Here I am on my home territory and will not feel the same need to be apologetic. In the third and final part of the essay I will talk about Barth, and I will focus especially on what he says about Kant. If I had more space, I would include a section on Søren Kierkegaard, because I think that Barth, in following Kierkegaard especially in his early work, is retracing a partial return that Kierkegaard makes back from G. W. F. Hegel to Kant. The degree to which Barth mentions Kierkegaard decreases in his later work, but in my tentative judgment the reliance on Kant is not affected by this and is a constant. In any case I will not be able to reflect here on the melancholy Dane.

(1) American Evangelicals

Cornelius Van Til holds that there is an inherent hostility between Kant's philosophy, which Van Til calls "Criticism," and the Christian religion. Here is a quotation to give the flavor: "There must of necessity be a death-struggle whenever Christianity and Criticism meet. And they meet at every front since the days when the Copernicus of philosophy took his regular walks in Königsberg. It is Criticism, too, which in the persons of Barth and Brunner meets and attacks the historic Christian faith under cover of an orthodox-sounding theology."[2] Van Til's starting point is that Kant teaches that things in themselves are ruled by Chance.[3] These brute facts then manifest themselves to human beings as phenomena, and human beings order them under the forms of intuition (space and time) and under categories that they create. Human beings are, in this process, wholly autonomous, which requires that they be uncreated, and have ultimate legislative powers, so that humans are the "ultimate determiners of reality."[4] What place does this leave for God? Van Til holds that Kant's limitation of our knowledge to phenomena reduces God to a limiting concept, a *regulative* as explicitly opposed to a *constitutive* notion.[5] These are indeed Kantian terms. A regulative principle is one that

2. Van Til, *New Modernism*, 27.
3. Ibid., 14.
4. Ibid., 23.
5. Ibid., 21; as applied to Kierkegaard, see ibid., 64.

helps us organize our experience, but does not claim the existence of anything; we are merely helped by thinking *as if* something existed. A constitutive principle makes an actual existence claim. And Kant does say, in the First Critique, that from within the theoretical use of reason, we can appeal to God as a regulative but not as a constitutive principle.[6] All of the sources I am using in this first section of the essay make note of this point. God is thereby denied antecedent being, Van Til says, and thereby what he calls "the ontological Trinity" is also denied, or any God-in-Himself as opposed to God-for-us. When Van Til comes to Kant's *Religion within the Boundaries of Mere Reason,* Van Til takes it that Kant means to *reduce* the Christian religion to fit within these bounds. This means, for example, that when Kant talks about Christ, we are to understand humanity in its moral perfection, and when Kant talks about Christ's suffering, he is denying the salvific significance of any historical event.[7]

Much of this strikes me as a wrong reading of Kant. Kant cannot say within the *theoretical* use of reason that things in themselves are under the rule of Chance, because he cannot say anything about things in themselves except that they appear to us in a certain way. Within the *practical* use of reason, his view is that things in themselves other than God are created by God's intellectual intuition and maintained by God's providence, so that God can bring about the proportioning of our happiness and our duty. Humans are not, as I read Kant, the ultimate determiners of reality. Nor is Kant's notion of autonomy equivalent to creating the moral law. Kant judges that this would be impossible because the law is necessary (like the proposition that a triangle has three angles); rather, autonomy means making the law our own law or appropriating it.[8]

I take Kant's Copernican Revolution to have three moments: he is an

---

6. Immanuel Kant, *Kritik der reinen Vernunft,* 1st ed., vol. 4, *Kants Werke: Akademie-Textausgabe* (9 vols.; Berlin: W. de Gruyter, 1968), 644 (hereafter *KrV* 4:A); Kant, *Kritik der reinen Vernunft,* 2nd ed., vol. 3, *Akademie-Textausgabe,* 672 (hereafter *KrV* 3:B). Translated as Immanuel Kant, *Critique of Pure Reason,* Cambridge Edition of the Works of Immanuel Kant, ed. Paul Guyer and Allen W. Wood (Cambridge: Cambridge University Press, 1998), 591. Future references to Kant will follow this format: the German reference to the Berlin Academy Edition, by volume and page number, and the reference to the English translation (ET), where applicable, from the Cambridge Edition.

7. Van Til, *New Modernism,* 85.

8. I have explained my views of Kant's notion of autonomy in more detail in *God and Morality: A Philosophical History* (Oxford: Blackwell, 2007), chapter 3. Karl Barth, in *Epistle to the Romans,* trans. E. C. Hoskyns (New York: Oxford University Press, 1933), 46, seems to understand autonomy this way, and if this is indeed so, he is here faithful to Kant's meaning.

empirical realist, a transcendental idealist, and a transcendent realist. This is the understanding of Kant that was proposed by his contemporary Karl Reinhold, and Kant endorsed it. Karl Ameriks has recently edited and republished this account.[9] It has been one traditional account ever since it was published.[10] This account stresses Kant's teaching, in the preface to the second edition of the First Critique, that we have "to deny knowledge *in order to* make room for faith."[11] That is the purpose of the whole project of the First Critique. Knowledge is confined within the limits of what we could possibly experience, which means that we cannot have knowledge of God in Kant's restricted sense. But once we have understood this limit, we can then have justified true belief in the existence of God, knowledge in that more ordinary sense, even though God cannot be perceived by the senses. Indeed Kant thinks we are required to have this belief if our practical lives are to be rationally stable.[12] So while our principles about God are merely regulative within theoretical reason, he says that they are *constitutive* within practical reason. "For all these Ideas [including God] are [to pure theoretical reason] transcendent and without objects. Here [within pure practical reason] they become immanent and constitutive, since they are the grounds of the possibility of realizing the necessary object of pure practical reason (the highest good); otherwise they are transcendent and merely regulative principles of speculative reason, which is charged with the task not of assuming a new object beyond experience but only of approaching perfection in its employment within experience."[13] Finally, in *Religion within the Boundaries of Mere Reason,* Kant's project is not reductive, though I will somewhat qualify this claim later. In the preface to the second edition he describes revelation in terms of two concentric circles, of which the outer area of the larger circle contains historical revelation, and the inner circle contains the revelation to reason. He means to leave biblical theology in the outer circle untouched.[14]

9. Karl Leonhard Reinhold, *Letters on the Kantian Philosophy,* ed. Karl Ameriks, trans. James Hebbeler (Cambridge: Cambridge University Press, 2005).

10. See, e.g., Heinz Heimsoeth, "Metaphysical Motives in the Development of Critical Idealism," in *Kant: Disputed Questions,* ed. M. S. Gram (Chicago: Quadrangle Books, 1967), 158-99.

11. *KrV* 3:Bxxx; ET, 117. Emphasis added.

12. The reference to "instability" comes in Volckmann's notes to Kant's *Lectures on Natural Theology,* 28.1151.

13. Immanuel Kant, *Kritik der praktischen Vernunft,* vol. 5, *Akademie-Textausgabe,* 135 (hereafter *KpV* 5); my translation. See Immanuel Kant, *Practical Philosophy,* ed. Mary J. Gregor (New York: Cambridge University Press, 1996), 249.

14. Immanuel Kant, *Die Religion innerhalb der Grenzen der blossen Vernunft,* vol. 6,

His own province, as what he calls a "philosophical theologian," is only what can be used by reason and hence does not include particular events occurring at particular times and places, which can be known only to particular people at particular times and places.[15]

The application of Van Til's views of Kant to his views of Barth is no doubt already apparent. Van Til thinks that Barth too starts from a view of history as brute fact organized by us under the forms of intuition and under concepts that we create, such that history becomes incapable of directly revealing God. "The question between Barth and historic Christianity is that of the reality of the identification of God's revelation in history. When Barth answers his question with a resounding NO, orthodox theology answers it with a resounding YES."[16] Van Til thinks that Barth, like Kant, makes humanity the ultimate determiner of reality, and so denies a self-sufficient God, or God as antecedent being, or an ontological Trinity. He thinks that for Barth, as for Kant, the salvific role of Christ is as the real man, beyond history, and so salvation is man's self-salvation, and the historical narratives in Scripture are merely pointers to a reality which is not itself within history,[17] a reality in which human being is transformed into divine being.[18] Time is swallowed up in eternity, and so is not given by Barth (as it is not by Kant) the reality given it by Scripture. Van Til also objects separately to the universalism that he takes to be implicit in Barth's Christology.[19]

Carl Henry reiterates many of Van Til's criticisms, though barely mentioning him, and follows him in locating Barth's original error in his allegiance to Kant. I have chosen to talk about Carl Henry partly because of his status as an elder statesman of American evangelicalism, and partly also because I am discharging a personal debt. He himself gave me copies of his books, and I said I would read them; I am ashamed to say that until the preparation for the conference at which I read this paper, I never did. Henry draws a connecting line between Barth and Bultmann and says, "Much of this modern theological development stood in witting or unwitting indebtedness to Kantian knowledge-theory, which sharply limited the reality perceptible by theoretical reason. Restriction of the content of knowledge to

---

Akademie-Textausgabe, 12 (hereafter *Religion 6*); *Religion and Rational Theology*, ed. Allen W. Wood and George di Giovanni (New York: Cambridge University Press, 1996), 64.

15. Ibid., 9-10; 12; ET, 61-62, 64.
16. Van Til, *Karl Barth*, 139.
17. Ibid., 142-44.
18. Ibid., 147.
19. Ibid., 149.

sensations of the phenomenal world in principle deprives man of cognitive knowledge of metaphysical realities. Divine revelation on this basis can neither be connected with cognitive reason nor can it have external and objective grounding, since Kant's view excludes revelation in nature and history, as well as in an objective scriptural revelation."[20] What place does this Kantian restriction leave for God? Henry continues, "God is for Kant only a transcendental postulate; he conceived metaphysical relationships in terms of ethical ideals for fully experiencing selfhood." The theological principles are thus, in Kant's terms, regulative and not constitutive. "Kant postulated God from the moral nature of man . . . not indeed as an object of rational knowledge but *projected* as an internal logical necessity."[21] Henry talks of "[Kant's] denial of the cognitive status of religious beliefs."[22]

Again, much of this strikes me as a wrong reading of Kant. I will focus on the terms "cognitive" and "objective," both of which are full of difficulty. Kant does not limit "cognition" to the theoretical use of reason, but he allows also what he calls "practical cognition."[23] In our thought about God or freedom or the soul, we will not have percepts or empirical concepts organizing them, and so we will not have knowledge in the restricted sense. But we will have cognition of ideas (or pure concepts), whose content is not empty, because it is grounded in practice and in what Kant calls the "fact of reason," namely, the fact that we are under the moral law.[24] The term "objective" has many senses, and Kant's usage does not stick to any one of them. But Kant says that these pure concepts, which are merely thinkable outside the practical use of reason, are within this practical use "described assertorically as actually having objects, because practical reason inexorably requires the existence of these objects for the possibility of its practically and absolutely necessary object, the highest good."[25] To go back to the phrase I quoted earlier from the First Critique, we deny knowledge in the restricted sense in order to make room for faith or belief in the actual existence of God, as well as the actual existence of freedom and of immortality. In a second sense, this faith is objective, in that it is required of every rational being,

20. Henry, *God, Revelation and Authority*, 3:278.

21. Ibid., 3:430; emphasis added.

22. Ibid., 3:463.

23. *KrV* 4:A633 = 3:B661; *KpV* 5:137; Kant, *Kritik der Urteilskraft*, vol. 5, *Akademie-Textausgabe*, 470, 475; Kant, *Logik*, vol. 9, *Akademie-Textausgabe*, 86-87.

24. *KpV* 5:31; ET, 164. For the extension to the real possibility of the highest good, see ibid., 135; ET, 249.

25. Ibid., 135; my translation. See ET, 248.

whether he or she recognizes this requirement or not. Duty is also objective for Kant in this sense.

Henry then applies his views of Kant to Barth, as Kant's heir. Barth is accused of "detaching divine revelation from the arenas of objective history and logical evidence and . . . correlating it only with internal response."[26] "Neoorthodoxy declared the incarnation and cross to be intellectual paradoxes that provide no objectively valid information and viewed the scriptural witness as merely a fallible index to a superhistorical Christ."[27] Henry quotes Gordon Clark's criticism of Barth, "If God has all truth and we have nothing that God has, then surely we have no truth at all."[28] But Henry, unlike Van Til, acknowledges that Barth sometimes agrees with evangelicals. Barth says that God somehow makes human words adequate, so that we can have real knowledge of God.[29] Barth also teaches that revelation is verbal and rational (though "ratio" includes more than merely intellect) and informational, and even, occasionally, propositional.[30] So Henry concludes not that Barth is consistently unfaithful, but that he is incoherent, that he "assumes a Jekyll and Hyde role."[31] Henry's verdict on Barth is that he is split between a Kantian, and so unfaithful, side and on the other hand an instinct to go on saying with the tradition that historical revelation gives us objective cognitive knowledge of God. In this way Henry is different from Van Til, who says that we either have to accept the whole of Barth, or reject the whole as infected with an unorthodox Christology.[32]

Now just a brief word about James Buswell. Buswell stresses that Kant makes God a regulative concept, not a being whose existence can be rationally established.[33] He reads Kant's *Religion* as reducing Christ to "the archetype lying in our reason" or "an etherealized savior,"[34] which thus transforms Christianity into a creed of self-salvation. He then attacks Barth for making the same mistakes. He tells the story of Barth's visit to Washington D.C., in 1962, when Carl Henry asked him at a public event attended by re-

---

26. Henry, *God, Revelation and Authority*, 3:100.

27. Ibid., 3:110.

28. Ibid., 3:225, 466.

29. *CD* II/1, 235.

30. "God reveals Himself in propositions by means of language, and human language at that." Ibid., 156.

31. Henry, *God, Revelation and Authority*, 3:227.

32. Van Til, *Karl Barth*, 161.

33. Buswell, *Systematic Theology*, 17.

34. Ibid., 351; see ibid., 29.

porters whether the saving events of the first century, particularly the bodily resurrection and virgin birth, were of such a nature that newspapers would have been responsible for reporting them as news — that is, whether they were events in the sense that the ordinary person understands the happenings of history.[35] Barth replied by asking whether the newspaper photographers would also have taken pictures of the virgin birth, and by pointing out that the bodily resurrection did not convince the soldiers who saw the empty tomb, but only had significance for Christ's disciples. "It takes the living Christ to reveal the living Christ," he said. Buswell quotes approvingly from the *Christianity Today* article that reported the story, which continued, "Barth refused to defend the facticity of the saving events independently of the prior faith of the observers," and Buswell triumphantly comments that Barth is here inconsistent because he does after all acknowledge the facticity of the empty tomb.[36] It is striking that Buswell and Henry are here taking history to require sensory verification, much as the logical positivists did. There is a curious alliance here. I remember at the interview for my present job at Yale I was asked by a liberal biblical scholar who will remain nameless, "Is Genesis history or fiction?" Those were the only two alternatives, and the preferred answer was clearly "fiction." This dichotomy in effect puts history under the same restraint under which Kant puts knowledge, but *not* true justified belief. Because these evangelicals make the same unnecessary dichotomy, they and Barth often end up talking past one another. He does not mean to deny what they mean to assert, but they do not have the common language to discover this fact.

There is much more that could be said here, but other papers in this volume will discuss the American evangelical critique of Barth with much greater knowledge. I do not want to give the impression that *only* American evangelicals held these sorts of views about Kant. Liberals, such as for exam-

---

35. Buswell, *Systematic Theology*, 219. See also Henry, *God, Revelation and Authority*, 253.

36. To give one more example, Millard Erickson similarly describes Kant as refuting the possibility of theoretical knowledge of objects transcendent to sense experience, and continues: "This of course disposed of the possibility of any real knowledge of or cognitive basis for religion as traditionally understood." Millard Erickson, *Christian Theology* (Grand Rapids: Baker, 1983), 19. Religion became, for Kant, a matter of ethics, he says, and Albrecht Ritschl then applied this view to Christian theology, saying that "religion is a matter of moral judgments." Erickson makes the critique of Barth that he does not ground knowledge of Jesus' divinity in any historically provable facts about his earthly life (ibid., 665), and that Barth does not allow the observation and detailed description of the man Jesus to give any revelation of his deity (ibid., 716-17).

ple Gordon Kaufman in *God the Problem,* said much the same.[37] The very same purported views of Kant that make him an enemy to the evangelicals make him a friend to the liberals. If we ask why both sides saw Kant this way, the answer is probably that they were reading the same *secondary* literature.[38]

(2) Kant

I want to go on now to the second section of the essay, which is about Kant directly. The picture I have been giving of Kant may be unfamiliar, though there has been a significant change in Kant scholarship over the past twenty years. I date the shift from the conference that produced the volume, *Kant's Philosophy of Religion Reconsidered,* which was published in 1991. A recent collection of papers in the new school of interpretation is *Kant and the New Philosophy of Religion,* edited by Chris Firestone and Stephen Palmquist.[39] Recent Kant scholarship has been much more ready to stress what I call "the vertical dimension" of Kant's thought, his thought about our relation to God, and the centrality of this relation. Why should evangelicals be interested in this interpretation of Kant? Because they should be interested in the spread of the gospel, and this new or recovered understanding of Kant gives us scope for what Charles Taylor calls "retrieval." Taylor says, at the end of *Sources of the Self,* "The intention of this work was one of retrieval, an attempt to uncover buried goods through rearticulation — and thereby to make these sources again empower, to bring the air back again into the half-collapsed lungs of the spirit."[40] We can have intellectual conversations that go like this. We say to someone whose moral view is heavily influenced by Kant, Did you realize that Kant says that the attempt to lead a morally good life without believing in

37. Gordon D. Kaufman, *God the Problem* (Cambridge, MA: Harvard University Press, 1972), 114 and 134-35.

38. Van Til mentions the work of Norman Kemp Smith (*New Modernism,* 12, 18, 23). But his first introduction to Kant was under Harry Jellema at Calvin. He was also taught by C. W. Hodge at Princeton Seminary and A. A. Bowman at Princeton University. George Harinck is the source of this information. I should also mention that Kemp Smith's view of Kant has been repeated in a recent volume, Peter Byrne's *Kant on God* (Aldershot: Ashgate, 2007). I have replied to Byrne in an extensive review in *Conversations in Religion and Theology* 7, no. 1 (2009): 71-79.

39. Chris Firestone and Stephen Palmquist, eds., *Kant and the New Philosophy of Religion* (Bloomington: University of Indiana Press, 2006).

40. Charles Taylor, *Sources of the Self: The Makings of the Modern Identity* (Cambridge, MA: Harvard University Press, 1989), 520.

God is rationally unstable?[41] If you want to do Kantian ethics without God, we ask, what substitute do you have to play the role that Kant gives to God? Now I know that most of those whose moral views are heavily influenced by Kant do not know about Kant, and have not even heard his name. They go cheerfully about their business using phrases like "human dignity" and "human rights," without acknowledging the Prussian professor whose work had such a crucial place in the intellectual lineage of these ideas. In the academy, Kant's influence is acknowledged, but the vertical dimension of his philosophy has in the past either been overlooked, attributed to clumsy editing, or dismissed as an insincere concealment of his *real* views in order to get past the censor or ingratiate himself to his pietist neighbors. This is what I call "cushion hermeneutics," and it should be adopted only as a last resort, when no other interpretation of the texts is possible.

There is another interpretation possible, however, namely, that Kant was quite sincere in denying knowledge *in order to* make room for faith, which includes belief in the existence of an omnipotent, omniscient, and omnibenevolent God. The close connection of Kant's moral system to the Christian theology he grew up with was seen clearly in the nineteenth century by Friedrich Nietzsche, who predicted that with the death of God would come the death of guilt, by which Nietzsche meant the sense of having failed by the standards of a Kantian morality, of having failed to do one's duty.[42] I think there is evidence that he was right, that in places where God is not acknowledged, the claims of Kantian morality have also come under question. In any case pointing to this close connection is the strategy of retrieval, retrieving the theological sources of the great classics of modern thought. I will try to retrieve one item of belief for which Kant makes room, namely, the appeal to God as the source of assistance in accomplishing a revolution of the human will.

First, though, I want to make a point about Kant's translation project. I mentioned that Kant sees revelation in terms of two concentric circles, historical revelation on the outside and the revelation to reason on the inside. His project in *Religion* is to see whether, by using moral concepts, he can translate items in the outer area into the language of the inner circle. In fact the structure of *Religion* is dictated by his translation of creation, fall, redemption, and second coming. Now we might see a danger in this translation project, and

---

41. I have defended the claim in "Kant on the Rational Instability of Atheism," in *God and the Ethics of Belief,* ed. Andrew Dole and Andrew Chignell (Cambridge: Cambridge University Press, 2005), 202-18.

42. Friedrich Nietzsche, *On the Genealogy of Morals,* trans. Walter Kaufmann (New York: Vintage Books, 1967), 90-91.

indeed not just the possibility but the actuality of its abuse in the reductive translations by Barth's immediate predecessors in the German theological schools. But here I think evangelicals should say that the translation project is not necessarily reductive; there is no necessity that a theologian's translation will end up denying the validity of that from which he or she translates. On the contrary, translation can be very useful in reaching people for whom the traditional theological language has become dead or associated with various forms of oppression. But we have to be careful when we do this, stressing, as Kant does, that we are doing philosophical theology and not biblical theology, and that we are leaving biblical theology as it is.

To understand Kant's views on grace, we have to start with what he says about the predisposition to good and the propensity to evil. These are, respectively, his translations of creation and fall, using the moral concepts. We are born with both, he says, but the predisposition to good is included in our definition as human, while the propensity to evil is not. This is a general point about the way Kant sets up species distinctions; he separates species in terms of their predispositions. But in our case, the predisposition to good, to love the moral law, is a seed of goodness that is prevented from reaching the fruit of a good life by the propensity to evil that lies over the top of it. We are born, he says, with the innate and imputable tendency to prefer our happiness to our duty.[43] Since this propensity is, from our birth, the fundamental maxim of our lives, we are unable by our own devices to accomplish a revolution of our will. We cannot occupy what Kierkegaard would call "the Archimedean point" from which to lift ourselves. Since we are, nonetheless, under the moral law, we have the obligation to put our duty above our happiness. We thus have to invoke some assistance *outside ourselves* in order to accomplish this revolution.[44] Here Kant is translating the doctrine of Augustine, repeated by Martin Luther, that God bids us do what we cannot, in order that we might learn our dependence upon God.[45] Throughout his published corpus, Kant says that we have to recognize our duties as God's commands.[46] "Grace" is Kant's own name for the assistance that reason requires us to believe God provides. We can try to understand this either negatively, as a removal of hindrances, or positively as an increase in power, but there is every reason, within Kant's system, to acknowledge that we will not in fact understand *how* God

43. *Religion* 6:32; ET, 79-80.
44. Ibid., 45; ET, 90.
45. Augustine, *On Grace and Free Will*, 16.32.
46. See, e.g., *KpV* 5:129.

accomplishes such a thing, given the limits of the human understanding.[47] When Kant discusses the effects of grace, in the general remark at the end of the first book of *Religion,* he says that we can "make room" for them as something incomprehensible, but we cannot incorporate them into our maxims for either theoretical or practical use.[48] The reason we cannot make use of them theoretically is that they deal with matters beyond the domain of possible sense experience. The reason we cannot make use of them practically is that the effects of grace are not things *we* bring about, and reason's practical use is to determine what we ought to do, or how we ought to live. Nonetheless, we can make room for belief in the effects of grace, and indeed we have to do so, because otherwise we will be stuck in the untenable position of having an obligation that it is impossible for us to fulfill. This belief or faith *(Glaube)* is not, Kant says, dogmatic, which would imply that it gives us knowledge, but it is reflective, belonging to the area which does not belong within the inner circle of rational religion, but is immediately adjacent to it.[49]

Here an objection might be made to my exegesis of Kant. How can he be said to make room for the effects of grace when he says at the beginning of the very same general remark, "The human being must make or have made himself into whatever he is or should become in a moral sense, good or evil"?[50] Van Til quotes this sentence at a key point in his argument to show that Kant's view is self-salvation. Van Til comments, "To be responsible for his deeds, Kant argues, man must be wholly original in what he does or leaves undone. As such he must have before him a field of pure possibility. He cannot be hampered by such ideas as creation and providence, if these are taken to mean what the church's confessions have taken them to mean."[51] In a similar way Nicholas Wolterstorff calls the principle I just quoted from Kant "the Stoic maxim," and he takes it to *contradict* what Kant says three sentences later, "Granted that some supernatural cooperation is also needed to man's becoming good or better."[52] But it is

---

47. *Religion* 6:44; ET, 89.

48. Ibid., 53; ET, 97. The word in German is *einräumen.* Note the statement in *KrV* 3:Bxxx about making room for faith (see fn. 11 above), though it is not the same phrase in German, *platz zu bekommen.*

49. *Religion* 6:52; ET, 96.

50. Ibid., 44; ET, 89.

51. Van Til, *New Modernism,* 82.

52. Nicholas Wolterstorff, "Conundrums in Kant's Rational Religion," in *Kant's Philosophy of Religion Reconsidered,* ed. Philip J. Rossi and Michael J. Wreen (Bloomington: Indiana University Press, 1991), 40-53, especially 48f. Wolterstorff was, like Van Til, Jellema's student at Calvin College.

better to make Kant consistent if we can, and here we can. What he means is that we are only to be called morally better to the extent that we are morally responsible for the improvement. If God does something in us, which Kant thinks we have to believe God in fact does, then this is not imputable to us and is therefore not strictly moral betterment, though it is betterment. He says that if "they [the good and evil] could not be imputed to him . . . he could be neither *morally* good nor evil."[53] Kant is saying, as I understand him, that we have to believe two things about God: first that God creates the predisposition to good, and second that God then provides a supplement because of our propensity to evil. This supplement is the effect of grace that enables the revolution of the will. There will still be something that we contribute, even if it is only the activity of the predisposition in us which lies under the propensity, and hates the evil under which we lie. We will not be able to contribute morally good *action*, because this requires that the revolution of the will has already taken place. Whether this account is consistent with Christian orthodoxy is a subtle question. Kant does not offer it, if I am right, as an account of the whole truth about regeneration, but as an account of what we can make room for as a prerequisite for religion within the bounds of mere reason, that is, for philosophical theology. Whether we think Kant's view orthodox will depend on what version of total depravity we think orthodoxy requires. Kant regards himself, I think, as translating the Lutheran catechism he learned as a boy. Luther himself accepted from the scholastics the survival in fallen humanity of the passive but not the active potency of good, and John Calvin allows the survival of a "seed of religion," but these are deep waters and I will not wade in any further.[54]

I said I would make one qualification to the claim that evangelicals should agree with Kant on the question of the legitimacy of the translation project. The qualification relates to what Kant says about Scripture as the vehicle of rational religion, and here I want to say that evangelicals should side with Barth against some things Kant says. Kant is, I believe, what he himself calls "a pure rationalist."[55] A pure rationalist is someone who allows special revelation, but does not think that it is necessarily necessary for religion.[56] Special revelation, for example Scripture, provides what Kant calls the "vehicle" of rational religion, and he accepts that we humans in our present state

53. *Religion* 6:44; ET, 89.

54. See Martin Luther, *Heidelberg Disputation*, thesis 14, in *Luther's Works*, vol. 31, ed. Harold J. Grimm (Philadelphia: Fortress Press, 1957), 49-50; John Calvin, *Institutes*, I.III.1.

55. Allen Wood denies this, but I will not try to reply to Wood here, as I have done so in *Faith and Philosophy* 11, no. 1 (1994): 138-44.

56. *Religion* 6:155; ET, 178.

require a vehicle. But he does not think the vehicle is necessarily necessary. The double modality is important here, and is repeated in other places. For example, in the *first* edition of *Religion* Kant says that the historical faith, which needs a holy book to guide human beings, will itself cease and pass over into a pure religious faith which illumines the whole world equally, and we should even now work for this, even though the shell *(Hülle)* is at this point still indispensable.[57] But then he adds a clarifying footnote in the *second* edition, "Not that 'it will cease' (for it might always be useful and necessary, perhaps, as vehicle) but that 'it can cease'; whereby is intended only the intrinsic firmness of pure moral faith."[58] So he corrects himself, making not a prediction that historical faith will cease but an affirmation that even though it *may* always be *necessary* (note the double modality) the pure religious faith has the intrinsic ability to exist without it. Much depends here on what conditions other than our present ones Kant is contemplating. If he is thinking just about the next life, in which we see Christ face to face, and no longer need a *book*, there is no need for evangelicals to be anxious. But if he means a future state of this world, an ethical commonwealth in which humans no longer need *historical faith*, evangelicals might worry. I myself think that Kant is not consistent about this. There are texts naturally supporting both the first conception (that we would not need the book) and the second (that we would not need the historical faith).[59] To the extent he is saying the second, I think Barth would disagree with him, and an evangelical should side with Barth. I will now move to the third and final section of this essay by directly engaging Barth's own interpretation of Kant.

(3) Barth

Barth is a sophisticated reader of Kant, and he assumes the correctness of Kant's basic epistemology throughout his own corpus. In particular he likes Kant's humility about the limits of human knowledge as human, and he shares Kant's view of its relation to time. But does Barth recapitulate the positive picture of Kant's *philosophical theology* that I have just been describing? I will be relying in my answer on his treatment of Kant in *Protestant Theology in the Nineteenth Century* (the first German edition was in 1947,

57. Ibid., 135; ET, 162.

58. Ibid.

59. I have discussed this briefly in *The Moral Gap: Kantian Ethics, Human Limits, and God's Assistance* (Oxford: Clarendon Press, 1996), 71-74.

though neither Van Til nor Henry refers to the work).[60] Barth's answer is, not surprisingly, NO and YES. On the one hand — this is the YES — Barth anticipates some of the recent development in Kant scholarship that I have referred to, forty years in advance of it, although these recent scholars did not read his treatment of Kant. However — and this is the NO — he puts these features in a picture of Kant that is dialectical, a picture that repeats the Barthian pattern of response to the world as a whole. I am going to claim that this picture is misleading in certain ways as he applies it to Kant. Its dialectical character complicates the final evaluation of the merit of the evangelical critique I started with, and I will say a few sentences about this by way of conclusion.

The key reason for Barth's NO, is, as we might expect, Kant's Christology. Kant translates within the boundaries of mere reason, using the moral concepts, so that all reference to particular persons is excluded. He is left with Christ as "humanity in its moral perfection." Barth concludes (as did Van Til) that in Kant's philosophy of religion "man is the measure of all things" (including God).[61] Barth sees in this the beginning of a straight line to Albrecht Ritschl. But he exaggerates Kant's position here, and I will give seven examples of this. I will not go into much detail with each example, but it is important to get the general picture. The basic problem with Barth's account, as I see it, is that he takes Kant's philosophy of religion as having a "closed and rounded quality" that leaves out God and that is then "disturbed" by Kant's view of radical evil.[62] It is better to see Kant's philosophy of religion as containing from the beginning his view of evil. If we do this, we will see that his philosophical theology is not in fact "closed to God from the inside," as Barth describes it.

Here are the seven ways in which Barth ends up exaggerating his difference from Kant. (1) Barth accepts that God is a regulative idea for Kant, and therefore "to speak of existence or non-existence is *per se* not to speak of God."[63] This was also the view of Van Til and Henry, as we saw previously. Barth does not acknowledge that within practical reason Kant thinks of the idea of God as *constitutive*. (2) Barth says that for Kant historical faith is "dead in itself"; it is not a living, not a salutary, faith.[64] Here, too, Van Til and

---

60. Karl Barth, *Protestant Theology in the Nineteenth Century: Its Background and History* (Grand Rapids: Eerdmans, 2002).

61. Ibid., 290.

62. Ibid., 283.

63. Ibid., 261.

64. Ibid., 270.

Henry agree with this reading of Kant.[65] But in this passage to which Barth refers,[66] Kant is quoting from James 2:17, "faith by itself, if it is not accompanied by action, is dead," and he is criticizing historical faith *without corresponding moral action.* He is not saying that historical faith if lived together with the moral disposition is dead or inert. (3) Barth takes it that Kant is saying, "Historical knowledge, which bears no inner relationship valid for all to the betterment of mankind," may be believed or not as we like.[67] But Kant's passage here is about "historical cognition that has no intrinsic relation, valid for everyone, to [moral improvement]."[68] Kant's point is that in some cases, and in fact in the present one he is discussing, there *is* an intrinsic connection between Scripture and its moral meaning that is valid for everyone. (4) Barth says, "The critical philosophy of religion cannot therefore speak of revelation."[69] Here again he repeats Van Til and Henry. But the two concentric circles in *Religion* are *both* described as revelation-historical revelation and the revelation to reason. Moreover, "pure rationalism," which Barth is right to attribute to Kant, *allows* special revelation, though it may not use it in either theoretical or practical maxims. I tried to explain this in the second section of this essay. (5) Barth treats *Conflict of the Faculties*[70] as teaching the same doctrine as *Religion,* and many of the passages he likes the least are from the former. But there are in fact important differences between these two texts. *Conflict* is already moving in the direction of the unpublished *Opus Postumum,*[71] which is problematic in various ways I will not now go into. (6) Barth has Kant saying that no historical example of the good disposition is necessary.[72] But Kant's passage actually says that while no example is necessary for us to take the idea of a human being morally pleasing to God as a model, the *practical validity* of this idea is assured by seeing an example, that is, Christ.[73] Finally (7) Barth (yet again like Van Til) quotes what I called (from Wolterstorff) "the Stoic maxim" and gives it the same interpretation.[74]

---

65. Cf. Van Til, *New Modernism,* 81; Henry, *God, Revelation and Authority,* 3:432.

66. *Religion* 6:111; ET, 143.

67. Barth, *Protestant Theology,* 271.

68. *Religion* 6:44; ET, 89.

69. Barth, *Protestant Theology,* 270.

70. Published in English in Kant, *Religion and Rational Theology,* 233-327.

71. Immanuel Kant, *Opus Postumum,* ed. Paul Guyer and Allen W. Wood (Cambridge: Cambridge University Press, 1993).

72. Barth, *Protestant Theology,* 274.

73. *Religion* 6:62-63; ET, 104-6.

74. Barth, *Protestant Theology,* 284. See *Religion* 6:44.

As I argued earlier, this interpretation makes Kant contradict himself within three sentences, and there is another interpretation that does not do so, which is to be preferred.

So Barth exaggerates the distance between his own theology and Kant's philosophy of religion. My main point, however, is a bit different from this. It is that Barth, after describing this "closed and rounded quality" in Kant's philosophy of religion, then wants to say that Kant himself "disturbs" this philosophy with his views on radical evil and on the church's need for an authoritative Scripture. The result is a "clash."[75] It is interesting to compare Barth's treatment of other figures, such as Novalis, where we find the same interpretive strategy. It is indeed a typical deconstructive strategy in the reading of a text, that we might find in many of Hegel's heirs, for example in Derrida's reading of Plato.[76] Barth is here closer to Henry than to Van Til. The picture is odd, however, because Kant's account in *Religion starts* with radical evil. Barth's YES to Kant at this point, and at the point where Kant insists on the need of the visible church for Scripture, should make us look at the rest of his philosophy of religion, or, as Kant himself prefers to call it, his philosophical theology, and try to make it consistent. To a remarkable extent we can do this by being careful to distinguish at every point *where* Kant is, so to speak, on the diagram of the two concentric circles. Barth himself acknowledges that Kant's account is not reductive, that he does not mean to eliminate the outer circle in favor of the inner one. Indeed Barth claims for himself the space Kant leaves for the biblical theologian. This is a great merit of Barth's account, because the texts where Kant leaves this space are often overlooked. But then we can say that when Kant talks about grace, or the need for God's assistance in various ways given our limitations, he is in the area either of the outer part of the larger circle in general, or in that part of the outer area that lies immediately adjacent to the inner circle, though it is not part of it.[77] In either case, he will only contradict himself if he means to eliminate the outer circle, and Barth denies that Kant means this. I myself think there are texts where Kant suggests he *does* look forward to its elimination, and then, as I said earlier, the key question will be *what* would be elimi-

75. Barth, *Protestant Theology,* 290.

76. See Jacques Derrida, *Dissemination,* trans. Barbara Johnson (Chicago: University of Chicago Press, 1981).

77. There are thus, strictly speaking, three concentric circles in the diagram, or at least three areas (since Kant does not say that the middle one is circular). The middle area is what Kant calls the "*parerga* to religion within the boundaries of pure reason; they do not belong within it yet border on it." *Religion* 6:52; ET, 96.

nated. But on Barth's reading there is no reduction, and so there is no need to accuse Kant of contradiction.

Finally, I want to say something briefly about the implications of Barth's treatment of Kant for our evaluation of the American evangelical critique of Barth with which I started. The dialectical nature of Barth's treatment makes this evaluation complex. My first claim is that there is nothing in Kant's basic epistemology that is itself unfaithful to the gospel. I tried to give an account in the second section of this paper of a Kantian philosophical theology that strikes me, with the one qualification I mentioned, as being faithful to the gospel, and that is constructed on the basis of this epistemology. Barth's NO to Kant's philosophical theology is in many respects very similar to the critiques by Van Til and Henry. This means that their attempt to criticize Barth as being too close to Kant in these ways misfires. They are actually allies of Barth in the criticism of Kant. Since I am defending Kant against many of these criticisms, I am in effect disagreeing with all three of them. On the other hand, and here I will end, Barth's YES to Kant's philosophical theology is a YES which Van Til and Henry might well have shared, I speculate, if they had been able to see these features of Kant as clearly as Barth did.[78]

78. I am grateful to Neil Arner, Paul Kim, and Scott Cleveland who gave me many helpful comments on earlier drafts, and to David Kelsey with help on some points of Barth exegesis.

A Theology of Experience?
Karl Barth and the Transcendental Argument

Clifford B. Anderson

What is the proper relation between personal religious experience and theological knowledge? Karl Barth's early theology (1905-32) can be read as a
struggle to answer this question. It is, of course, a question that engages
many evangelicals as well. Providing a full exposition of Barth on religious
experience and knowledge would require a monograph-length study, so I
will engage with the problematic only from the perspective of the influence
of Immanuel Kant's critical philosophy on Barth's concept of experience.
How did Kant — or more accurately, a certain contemporary school of neo-
Kantians — shape Barth's controversial ideas about the nature and function
of religious experience in theology?

I.

The influence of neo-Kantian thought-forms on the early theology of Karl
Barth has long been recognized. Barth himself noted the "remarkable crust of
Kantian-Platonic concepts" encompassing the second edition of his commentary on Romans[1] and Dietrich Bonhoeffer famously remarked that Barth had
achieved a great deal in that work "despite all the neo-Kantian eggshells."[2]

---

1. Karl Barth, *Credo* (Zollikon-Zürich, 1948 [1935]), 159. Johann Friedrich Lohmann
notes additional self-attestations of neo-Kantian influences on Karl Barth. See Lohmann,
Karl Barth und der Neukantianismus (Berlin: Walter de Gruyer, 1995), 376f.
2. Dietrich Bonhoeffer, *Widerstand und Ergebung: Briefe und Aufzeichnungen aus der*

The persistence of neo-Kantian thought-forms in Barth's mature theology is a subject of greater controversy among scholars. Cornelius Van Til argued in *The New Modernism* that not only did Barth not abandon his youthful Kantianism after his turn-from-liberalism, but that he went on in the *Church Dogmatics* to articulate an even more thoroughgoing form of the Critical Philosophy than had been defended by the "old" Modernist theologians against whom he was rebelling.[3] While claiming that a host of modern philosophers from Søren Kierkegaard to Ludwig Feuerbach had contributed to shaping Barth's (and Emil Brunner's) dialectical theology, Van Til attributed the most formative role to Kant. "All the doctrines of the Theology of Crisis . . . must be seen through the spectacles of the *Critique of Pure Reason*."[4] Neo-Orthodox defenders of Barth tended to play down the influence of Kant. Thomas F. Torrance, for example, complained that both "scholastic Romanism and scholastic Protestantism" interpreted Barth's theology of the Word of God as "Kantian subjectivism, when, in point of fact, it is the exact antithesis of that."[5] Chief among the breakthroughs in the second *Romans* commentary was, according to Torrance, Barth's resolve "to renounce the use of all idealistic and neo-Kantian conceptions in exegesis."[6]

A series of recent scholars, most prominently Bruce McCormack[7] and Johann Friedrich Lohmann,[8] have argued *pace* Torrance that some thought-forms from neo-Kantianism remained after Barth's turn-from-liberalism. They do not fully agree about which thought-forms persisted, however.[9] Barth's increasing expurgation of explicit references to neo-Kantian concepts in the decade between the second edition of the *Romans* commentary (1922) and the first volume of the *Kirchliche Dogmatik* (1932) no doubt obscured the continuing influence of such thought-forms. According to

---

Haft, ed. Christian Gremmels et al., Dietrich Bonhoeffer Werke, Band 8 (Gütersloh: Chr. Kaiser/Gütersloher Verlagshaus, 1998), 480.

3. Cornelius Van Til, *The New Modernism: An Appraisal of the Theology of Barth and Brunner* (Philadelphia: Presbyterian and Reformed Publishing Co., 1947), 371f.

4. Ibid., 366.

5. Thomas F. Torrance, *Karl Barth: An Introduction to His Early Theology, 1910-1931* (Edinburgh: T. & T. Clark, 1962), 99.

6. Ibid., 50.

7. See Bruce McCormack, *Karl Barth's Critically-Realistic Dialectical Theology: Its Genesis and Development, 1909-1936* (Oxford: Clarendon Press, 1995).

8. See Lohmann, *Karl Barth und der Neukantianismus*.

9. See Bruce McCormack, "Review of Johann Friedrich Lohmann's *Karl Barth und der Neukantianismus*," in *Orthodox and Modern: Studies in the Theology of Karl Barth* (Grand Rapids, MI: Baker Academic, 2008), 305-7.

George Hendry, what makes their continuing presence even more difficult to gauge is the fact that Barth typically removed such thought-forms from their philosophical context and reintroduced them in transformed guise in an explicitly theological setting.[10]

The question of whether an argumentative form analogous to Immanuel Kant's so-called "transcendental argument" was operative in Barth's early theology and persisted into his mature theology offers a good opportunity to examine this process of de-contextualization and re-contextualization. D. Tromp contended relatively early on that a distinctive form of the "transcendental method" was at work in the second edition of *Romans*[11] and George Hendry remarked relatively more recently that Barth carried through the transcendental method into the *Kirchliche Dogmatik*.[12] Both recognized, however, that Barth's use of the transcendental argument was not identical to Kant's.

What seems most peculiar about Barth's use of the transcendental argument, if he can be said to make use of that argumentative form, is his eschewal of experience. If Barth did use a transcendental argument somewhat similar to Kant's, he most certainly did not ground it in ordinary human experience. In *Karl Barth and the Strange New World within the Bible*, Neil MacDonald repeatedly emphasizes this point. "Though Barth's position on epistemology in the *Church Dogmatics* owes something to Kant's transcendental argument," MacDonald writes, "the form it took in Barth was not found in Kant."[13] That Barth refused to base his transcendental argument on any form of experience, including religious experience, fundamentally sets Barth apart from Kant.[14] MacDonald labels the argumentative form in the

---

10. George Hendry writes, "It became Barth's practice to conceal his philosophical obligations by translating them into general and less technical terms." See George Hendry, "The Transcendental Method in the Theology of Karl Barth," *Scottish Journal of Theology* 37 (1984): 213.

11. D. Tromp remarked in 1926 that Karl Barth applied "the transcendental method in theology." See D. Tromp, "Kritische Theologie: Over den Römerbrief van Karl Barth," in *Nieuwe Theologie (De School van Karl Barth)*, Geschriften Uitgegeven van Wege de Studie-Commissie der Ethische Vereeniging (Eerste Serie No. 6/8) (Barth: Hollandia-Drukkerij, 1926), 17. I am indebted to Johann Friedrich Lohmann for this reference (see Lohmann, *Karl Barth und der Neukantianismus*, 7).

12. See Hendry, "Transcendental Method," 219.

13. Neil B. MacDonald, *Karl Barth and the Strange New World within the Bible: Barth, Wittgenstein, and the Metadilemmas of the Enlightenment* (Carlisle, Cumbria: Paternoster Press, 2000), 210.

14. Ibid., 213.

Church Dogmatics "Barth's non-Kantian transcendental argument"[15] and endeavors to show by way of a comparison with Ludwig Wittgenstein that "though Kant defined a transcendental argument in terms of the conditions of the possibility of experience . . . it does not follow that all transcendental arguments necessarily ask of the conditions of the possibility of *experience*."[16] As a philosophical point, MacDonald is undoubtedly correct — there are forms of argument inspired by Kant's transcendental argument which do not refer to experience per se.[17] But I'd like to suggest that Barth learned this argument from a school of contemporary (neo-) Kantians who retained its connection with experience.

In what follows, I explore the connection between transcendental arguments and experience from an historical perspective by examining how Barth most likely appropriated the "transcendental method" from its philosophical context and how he reintroduced that method in his theology. I hope to show that Barth's transcendental argument was more neo-Kantian than straightforwardly Kantian and was more directly connected with his concept of experience than some interpreters have noticed.

II.

To speak about Karl Barth's appropriation of the "transcendental method" it is necessary, although not decisive, to briefly describe the function of that method in the critical philosophy of Immanuel Kant. In his *Critique of Pure Reason,* Kant employed a form of argumentation that reasons from a given actuality to its conditions of possibility. In his "Transcendental Aesthetic," for example, Kant contended that experience of the external world is possible if and only if space and time are not themselves empirical objects in the world, but rather forms of pure sensibility. In his "Transcendental Analytic," he argued that cognition of objects is not possible without presupposing fundamental logical categories such as causality and subsistence.

The form of argumentation that Kant employed has come to be known

15. Ibid., Chapter 10.

16. Ibid., 280.

17. Consider, for example, the use of "indispensability" arguments in W. v. O. Quine and Hilary Putnam. Such arguments bear some resemblance, as I have argued elsewhere (see Clifford Anderson, "A Pragmatic Reading of Karl Barth's Theological Epistemology," *American Journal of Theology and Philosophy* 22 [2001]: 251ff.), to transcendental arguments without making any direct connection to "experience."

as a "transcendental argument," although Kant himself did not employ that phrase in that sense.[18] Thomas Grundmann summarizes Kant's form of transcendental argument:

> Kant starts from human experience (empricial representation) as an undisputed fact and then seeks to show that the questionable presuppositions of *a priori* knowledge (certain *a priori* concepts) are necessary conditions of this experience.[19]

A key point is that Kant's transcendental argument moved from shared and generally accepted experience to the necessary (not just empirical, but ontological) conditions for its possibility. The validity of this form of argumentation has been the subject of philosophical discussion for more than two centuries. Did Kant mean to ward off Humean skepticism about knowledge based on experience with this argument? If so, is it really effective? As Ralph C. S. Walker points out, transcendental arguments are convincing only to those who do not doubt the veracity of their premises.

> The premises of a transcendental argument should be premises anyone must be prepared to accept if we are to be able to have a serious debate with them, the sort of debate that can convince them provided that they think rationally. Those who are mad, or inaccessible to reason, are not our concern.[20]

A key question that contemporary philosophers have addressed is whether and to what extent transcendental arguments are meant to ward off skepticism. Or do they serve broader purposes? If so, what are those purposes?

18. See Sami Pihlström, "Pragmatic and Transcendental Arguments for Theism," *International Journal for Philosophy of Religion* 51 (2002): 202. Pihlström notes that Kant does use the phrase in a different sense.

19. Thomas Grundmann, "Transzendentalphilosophie: Was ist eigentlich ein transzendentales Argument?" in *Warum Kant Heute: Systematische Bedeutung und Rezeption seiner Philosophie in der Gegenwart* (Berlin: Walter de Gruyter, 2003), 50. My translation.

20. Ralph C. S. Walker, "Kant and Transcendental Arguments," in *The Cambridge Companion to Kant and Modern Philosophy*, ed. Paul Guyer (Cambridge: Cambridge University Press, 2006), 256.

III.

The neo-Kantian revival in the mid-nineteenth century sought to answer such questions. Hermann Cohen and Paul Natorp, the innovators of the so-called "Marburg School" of neo-Kantianism, saw the transcendental argument as chief among Immanuel Kant's contributions to philosophy not because it defeated skepticism, but because it provided the starting point for critical epistemological reflection on human knowledge in all its dimensions. Helmut Holzhey remarks that the Marburg Neo-Kantians considered the transcendental method as "Kant's core idea."[21] "The new school found the spirit of Kantian philosophy, to which they considered themselves bound, in the concept of the transcendental method."[22] In fact, Cohen and Natorp valued Kant's transcendental argument so highly that they found it necessary to correct the master in places.

Cohen introduced a first correction of Kant quite early on in his career. In *Kants Theorie der Erfahrung,* a commentary on the *Kritik der reinen Vernunft,* Cohen asserted that Kant's philosophical critique of pure reason was actually a critique of *experience.*[23] "Kant discovered a new concept of experience," claimed Cohen near the opening of his commentary.[24] What was this new concept of experience? Cohen argued that Kant had transformed the concept of experience from what we naively take "experience" to refer to, namely, the psychological stream of experience of everyday life, and had given it a critical sense by aligning it with the concept of *scientific* experience. As Alan W. Richardson summarizes the significance of Cohen's reading, Kant had shown that "experience" was not really about perceptual psychology, but concepts codified in scientific theory.

> The object of Cohen's epistemology is Newtonian exact scientific knowledge. Experience is empirical knowledge of the world of Newtonian science; experience already expresses objective knowledge of the world, not

21. Helmut Holzhey, *Ursprung und Einheit: Die Geschichte der "Marburger Schule" als Auseinandersetzung um die Logik des Denkens,* Band I (Basel/Stuttgart: Schwabe & Co. AG Verlag), 51. Paul Natorp wrote, for example, "Als den Kerngedanken nun, zu dem alles Andere in Kant in Beziehung zu setzen, von wo aus es zu verstehen und zu bewerten sei, begriff Cohen den Gedanken der *transcendentalen* Methode." See Paul Natorp, "Kant und die Marburger Schule," *Kant-Studien* 17 (1912): 194.

22. Holzhey, *Ursprung und Einheit,* 50.

23. Hermann Cohen, *Kants Theorie der Erfahrung* (1871), Hermann Cohen Werke Band 1.3 (Hildesheim: Georg Olms Verlag, 1978), 3.

24. Ibid. My translation.

the "raw feels" of perception. Epistemology investigates how such knowledge is possible by understanding it to be not a given but an achievement that is possible only on the basis of certain necessary presuppositions. Those presuppositions are the *a priori* conditions of the possibility of experience.[25]

Extrapolating on Cohen's identification of experience with scientific knowledge, Paul Natorp introduced the idea of the "Monism of experience." As he put it in his *Einleitung in die Psychologie nach kritischer Methode* [Introduction to Psychology according to the Critical Method], there is fundamentally only one experience — the experience codified by natural science.[26] What we naively consider experience, namely, our individual perceptual encounters with the objects around us, represents merely a "symptom" of this single experience.[27] This is somewhat less paradoxical than it sounds. The point is that science presupposes that we all perceive the same objects from different perspectives.[28] Natorp and Cohen simply started with the shared objects of experience rather than the peculiar acts of perception by which we apprehend those objects.

A primary motivation for the Marburg School's alignment of the concept of experience with scientific knowledge was to overcome psychologizing interpretations of the critical philosophy. As Klaus Köhnke notes in his acclaimed history of the early neo-Kantian movement, Cohen sought to overcome the naturalistic interpretation of Kant put forward by Friedrich Albert Lange, among others.[29] Lange's naturalistic line of interpretation rendered Kant's categories of the understanding as psychological categories of the empirical mind. By connecting experience with the sciences, Cohen sought to separate the critical philosophy from psychological reductionism. The act of knowing really has nothing to do with epistemology; what counts is only the object of knowledge. Cohen's *Kants Theorie der Erfahrung* constituted a decisive step toward the transformation of Kant's critical philosophy

---

25. Alan W. Richardson, "Conceiving, Experiencing, and Conceiving Experiencing: Neo-Kantianism and the History of the Concept of Experience," *Topoi* 22 (2003): 60.

26. Paul Natorp, *Einleitung in die Psychologie nach kritischer Methode* (Freiburg: J. C. B. Mohr, 1888), §11.

27. Ibid., 73.

28. Ibid., 75.

29. See Klaus Köhnke, *The Rise of Neo-Kantianism: German Academic Philosophy between Idealism and Positivism*, tran. R. J. Hollingdale (Cambridge: Cambridge University Press, 1991), 151.

into a philosophy of science.[30] The transcendental method was conceived according to the Marburg School as critical reflection on the presuppositions not of human experience in general but on "scientific experience" in particular. As Cohen subsequently put the point, "All philosophy is dependent on the fact of science. This reliance on the fact of science counts as the eternal thing in Kant's system."[31]

A second alteration that Cohen made to Kant's critical philosophy arose from the combination of his estimation of the centrality of the transcendental method and his critical concept of experience. In his mature philosophical system, Cohen sought to apply the transcendental method more consistently than Kant had. Cohen contended in his *Ethik des reinen Willens* that Kant had failed to remain true to the transcendental method in his *Critique of Practical Reason* because he had not produced any transcendental deduction of the moral law. "There can be no question, however, that by this means an incurable error entered necessarily into the concept of the transcendental method. For if that method applies to logic, why should it not necessarily also apply for ethics?"[32] Cohen contended that the systematicity of reason required the natural sciences and the moral sciences to be treated equivalently. The transcendental method could not be applied in the logical part of the system but be neglected in the ethical part without injury to the unity of reason. This prompted Cohen to seek out a fundamental science in the moral sciences that could serve as an analog to physics in the natural sciences. Perhaps in dialogue with Rudolf Stammler, a legal scholar who had come under the influence of the Marburg School, Cohen settled on jurisprudence as the paradigmatic science in the ethical sphere.[33]

The transcendental method cannot be taken up in logic only to be rejected in ethics. As logic is contained in physics, physics must mediate [our knowledge of] logic. And just as physics consequently is rooted in

30. See Claudius Müller, *Die Rechtsphilosophie des Marburger Neukantianismus: Naturrecht und Rechtspositivismus in der Auseinandersetzung zwischen Hermann Cohen, Rudolf Stammler und Paul Natorp* (Tübingen: J. C. B. Mohr [Paul Siebeck], 1994), 20ff.

31. Hermann Cohen, *Ethik des Reinen Willens*, 6. Auflage, Hermann Cohen Werke 7.2 (Hildesheim: Georg Olms Verlag, 2002), 65. My translation.

32. Ibid., 227. My translation.

33. On the relationship between Cohen, Natorp, and Stammler, see Müller, *Die Rechtsphilosophie des Marburger Neukantianismus*. I am grateful to Johann Friedrich Lohmann for suggesting that I look into how Stammler adapted Marburg neo-Kantianism.

logic, law must also be rooted in ethics. So that is why jurisprudence mediates [our knowledge of] ethics and is founded in it.[34]

The application of the transcendental argument in ethics confirmed its centrality to Cohen's interpretation of the critical philosophy as a whole. And it opened the door to the application of transcendental arguments in domains beyond the natural sciences and jurisprudence. "Hermann Cohen came up with a remarkably fecund answer to the question of how to respond to skeptics about the possibility of knowledge in special domains: the fact that there is a science which presupposes given principles shows their legitimacy," remark Stephen Turner and Regis A. Factor. "Similar 'transcendental deductions' reasoning from the *'Faktum der Wissenschaft'* proliferated."[35] Paul Natorp was following the path blazed by Cohen when he argued that transcendental arguments should be applied in every part of the system, including religion.[36]

IV.

A tricky question in contemporary scholarship on Karl Barth is the way in which he appropriated thought-forms from both classical Kantianism and neo-Kantianism. On the one hand, some scholars have pointed to the influence of neo-Kantian thought-forms on the early theology of Barth.[37] On the other hand, other scholars contend that through his independent reading of Kant, Barth came to adhere to a more classical form of Kantian-

34. Cohen, *Ethik des Reinen Willens,* 227. My translation.
35. Stephen Turner and Regis A. Factor, *Max Weber: The Lawyer as Social Thinker* (London: Routledge, 1994), 16.
36. In "Kant und die Marburger Schule," Natorp asked, "Was also meinen wir . . . mit Kant und nur strenger noch als er, für jeder philosophische Aufstellung eine 'transcendentale' Begründung oder Rechtfertigung, eine *deductio juris* (wie Kant sagt) verlangen?" (196). He held that this demand consisted of two elements. "Das Erste ist die sichere Zurückbeziehung auf die vorliegenden, historisch aufweisbaren Fakta der Wissenschaft, der Sittlichkeit, der Kunst, der Religion" (196). "Und das nun is die Zweite, die entscheidende Forderung der transzendenten Methode: zum Faktum den Grund der 'Möglichkeit' und damit den 'Rechtsgrund' nachzuweisen, das heisst: eben den Gesetzgrund, die Einheit des Logos, der Ratio in all solcher schaffenden Tat der Kultur aufzuzeigen und zur Reinheit herauszuarbeiten" (197).
37. See Simon Fisher, *Revelatory Positivism? Barth's Earliest Theology and the Marburg School* (Oxford: Oxford University Press, 1988). See also Lohmann, *Karl Barth und der Neukantianismus.*

ism.[38] (To complicate the picture further, Barth also imbibed a distinct form of neo-Kantianism through his primary theological teacher, Wilhelm Herrmann.)[39] While there is no question that Barth studied Kant directly and reintroduced thought-forms from classical Kantianism into his theological epistemology which the Marburg School had eliminated from their philosophical theology, Barth was more indebted to the Marburg neo-Kantians than to Kant himself. In particular, Barth followed Cohen and Natorp both by regarding the point of departure for transcendental arguments as reflection on the presuppositions of the "fact of science" rather than of subjective human experience in general and by applying the transcendental argument in a context other than the natural sciences. A brief look at one of Barth's earliest texts helps to warrant this claim.

"*Ideen und Einfälle zur Religionsphilosophie*" [Ideas and Notions in the Philosophy of Religion] is an unfinished draft for a philosophy of religion which Barth sketched out in Geneva in 1910.[40] The draft is difficult to interpret because of its fragmentary character. In his sketch, Barth intended to reconcile Hermann Cohen, his principal philosophical influence, and Wilhelm Herrmann, his most beloved professor of theology.[41] The proposal was doomed from the start because it failed to deal adequately with the fundamental difference between Cohen's and Herrmann's concepts of experience. Whereas Cohen identified experience with objective knowledge, Herrmann identified religious knowledge with subjective experience.[42]

In the first section of the draft, Barth stipulated the relation between re-

38. For this point of view, see McCormack, *Karl Barth's Critically Realistic Dialectical Theology*, 226. See Paul La Montagne, "Barth and Rationality: Critical Realism in Theology" (PhD diss., Princeton Theological Seminary, 2001).

39. See Rainer Mogk, *Die Allgemeingültigkeitsbegründung des christlichen Glaubens: Wilhelm Herrmans Kant-Rezeption in Auseinandersetzung mit den Marburger Neukantianern* (Berlin: De Gruyter, 2000).

40. Karl Barth, "Ideen und Einfälle zur Religionsphilosophie," in *Vorträge und Kleinere Arbeiten, 1909-1914*, ed. Hans-Anton Drewes and Hinrich Stoevesandt, *Karl Barth Gesamtausabe* (Zürich: Theologischer Verlag, 1993), 126-38. For an extensive analysis of this draft, see Fisher, *Revelatory Positivism?* 240ff.

41. See editor's introduction to Barth, "Ideen und Einfälle zur Religionsphilosophie," 127.

42. As Christophe Chalamet nicely puts it, according to Herrmann, "Our experience of God is our knowledge of God." See Christophe Chalamet, *Dialectical Theologians: Wilhelm Herrmann, Karl Barth and Rudolf Bultmann* (Zürich: Theologischer Verlag, 2005), 39. The key to understanding Herrmann on religious experience is that he denied that our experience of God could ever become an object of scientific knowledge. See Chalamet, *Dialectical Theologians*, 54ff.

ligion, theology, and the philosophy of religion. His articulation of their tripartite relations parallels the relations in the Marburg School between the facts of science, scientific theory, and the philosophy of science. The methodological point of departure for the philosophy of religion is not a religious a priori (à la Troeltsch) but the fact of religious consciousness. "As Phil[osophy] about Rel[igion] the Philosophy of Rel[igion] is scient[ific], that is, methodological reflection on the fact of *Religion* which is somehow present to the scienti[fic] consciousness."[43] This way of conceiving its task provides the philosophy of religion with an empirically incontrovertible basis since the existence of human religiosity can hardly be denied even if the existence of its object can be disputed. The purpose of the philosophy of religion according to this draft is to articulate the conceptual scaffolding — that is, the basic philosophical categories — which make possible the scientific study of religion, otherwise known as theology. Whereas theology spells out the doctrinal concepts which structure religious experience, the philosophy of religion reflects on the fundamental categories of theology, that is, it reflects on the conditions of the possibility of religious experience. Barth sounds strikingly similar to Cohen when he asserted that "The determinate rel[igion], which constitutes the presupposition o[f] the phil[osophy] of Relig[ion], forms the method[ological] point of departure."[44] While Barth did not refer to the transcendental method when making his argument, his insistence that philosophy of religion must begin with the fact of religion (and not the postulation of any speculative a priori) indicates the telltale influence of the Marburg School's style of transcendental argument.

Barth's disagreement with the Marburg philosophers was not about methodology, but ultimately about how to relate subjective religious experience to the objective domains of culture. He agreed with Wilhelm Herrmann that both Natorp and Cohen had failed to relate religious experience adequately to culture. But Barth thought that each had failed in quite different ways. On the one hand, Natorp followed Schleiermacher by identifying religion with pre-conceptual sentiment or "feeling." For Natorp, religion is properly speaking not an objective domain of culture like science, ethics, or aesthetics, but rather the subjective side of these cultural domains. Religion is the psychological sub-current to all cultural activities. While appreciative of the comprehensiveness of this conception, which relates religion to every domain of culture, Barth rejected it because it failed to credit religion with any

---

43. Barth, "Ideen und Einfälle zur Religionsphilosophie," 129f.
44. Ibid., 131.

direct relation to objective reality. Religion as pure subjective experience has no objective existence. Hermann Cohen, on the other hand, rejected a subjective interpretation of religion, preferring to speak instead of the idea of God. To Cohen, the various world religious had brought to light in mythical form the philosophical unity of science and ethics. So Cohen provided an objective function for the idea of God. In his outline, Barth improvised on Cohen's interpretation of the idea of God. Religion is not a dimension of culture, but its goal. "In this fundamental function rel[igion] does not in any way get expressed as an individual constitutive factor, a proposal which must always lead to . . . complications," argued Barth, "but as its eternal feeling of direction, through which culture first becomes culture for living humanity."[45] While Barth resembled Cohen by arguing that the idea of God stands at the summit of the system of critical philosophy, his improvisation also incorporated his critique. By linking the concepts of "feeling" and "life" to the Idea of God, Barth was tacitly indicating his agreement with Wilhelm Herrmann's critique of Cohen, namely, that Cohen's critical philosophy had neglected to anchor itself in lived experience. If Natorp's philosophy of religion failed because it had neglected the objective side of religion, Cohen's philosophy of God proved inadequate because it lacked a subjective side.

Barth never completed the project he contemplated in this outline. The challenges of his pastoral ministry compounded by the outbreak of the Great War certainly contributed to his decision to shelve this academic undertaking. However, his awareness that he had failed adequately to synthesize Wilhelm Herrmann and the Marburg neo-Kantians was likely the main reason that he did not carry out his project. Barth tried to combine the Marburg School's reformulated transcendental argument with Herrmann's radically subjective concept of religious experience. But reflecting on the presuppositions of individual religious experience could hardly produce objective theological knowledge.

Something had to give. In the first and second editions of his *Romans* commentary, Barth pinpointed the liberal concept of experience he had inherited from Herrmann as a source of his theological frustration. In the first edition, he inveighed against lived religious experience as a source of theological knowledge: "An objective knowledge [*Erkenntnis*], not experiences and feelings [*nicht Erlebnisse, Erfahrungen und Empfindungen*]."[46] He agreed

---

45. Ibid., 134.

46. Karl Barth, *Der Römerbrief (erste Fassung), 1919*, ed. Hermann Schmidt (Zürich: Theologischer Verlag, 1985), 12. My translation.

with Marburg neo-Kantians that seeking to reach knowledge from subjective experience fell into the trap of psychologism. However, Barth thought Christians could at least corroborate their objective knowledge of God in the subjective prism of personal experience. "We do not *build* on our own experience if we know ourselves to be dead people with respect to sin. For experience brings us . . . to shame," he wrote. "But we are also not *without* experience; for God's Word cannot return empty."[47] In the second edition of the *Romans* commentary, Barth hardened his judgment significantly. There is no experience of sanctification. There is only experience of death. "The final experience, which we may gain from this world, and the *a priori* of all experience, meets us in the sentence: 'But I have died,'" Barth wrote in reference to Romans 7:9. "And it is the religious human being as such in which the final experience and the *a priori* of all experience meet."[48]

Barth did not uphold a constructive notion of religious experience in either edition of the *Romans* commentary. In the first edition, individual experience is ruled out as a building block of theological knowledge; in the second edition, the a priori of all experience is judgment in the face of divine revelation. While he had freed himself from Wilhelm Herrmann's notion of lived religious experience as the fundamental well of genuine theological knowledge, he did not resort to Hermann Cohen's concept of experience. What remained of religious experience was only a vacuum left by the gospel's destruction of any experiential awareness of God.

Barth's repudiation of religious experience in the *Romans* commentary was primarily directed against liberal theologians. However, his criticisms provoked an unanticipated response among the German evangelical (or "pietistic") communities. As Eberhard Busch has pointed out in *Karl Barth and the Pietists*, Barth dropped his explicit critique of the pietists — namely, that they fostered religious individualism — between the first and second editions of the commentary. But his criticism of religious experience struck a nerve among the pietists, who took themselves as its implicit target. "By viewing every critical comment about Christian 'experience' as a direct vote against Pietism," Busch remarks, "its supporters gain the impression that they are the main victims of Barth's theology."[49] The pietists emphasized, by con-

---

47. Ibid., 217.

48. Karl Barth, *Der Römerbrief* (Zollikon-Zürich: Theologischer Verlag, 1940), 233. My translation.

49. Eberhard Busch, *Karl Barth and the Pietists: The Young Karl Barth's Critique of Pietism and Its Response*, trans. Daniel W. Bloesh (Downers Grove, IL: InterVarsity Press, 2004), 164.

trast, that "it is not enough to say that God is God and that he is holy but that his reality must also be 'experienced.'"[50] Some pietists darkly suggested that Barth's failure to grasp the significance of personal religious experience in his theology could be chalked up to his being numbered among the unconverted.[51] Busch argues that the pietists by and large failed to interpret correctly Barth's interpretation of religious experience in the second *Romans* commentary, leading them to attribute false motives to Barth. However, he also remarks that "by insisting on the phenomenon of experience, the Pietists pointed out an open question, even an unsolved problem in the *Epistle to the Romans*."[52] Barth also came in time to see his interpretation of experience in the *Romans* commentary as flawed. His reinterpretation of religious experience in the *Church Dogmatics* can be linked, I think, to his rediscovery of the neo-Kantian reformulation of the transcendental argument.

V.

In the *Church Dogmatics*, Barth resorted once again to a characteristically neo-Kantian form of transcendental argument in his theological epistemology. His analysis of the Word of God moves from acknowledgment of its actuality to its conditions of possibility. Or, as he put it programmatically, "Where the actuality exists there is also the corresponding possibility."[53] The point is to respect the actuality of the given, not to begin with an abstraction. "The question [of the knowability of the Word of God] cannot then be posed *in abstracto* but only *in concreto;* not *a priori* but only *a posteriori*."[54] Theology begins with the acknowledgment of the actuality of the proclamation of the Word of God in the church. The proclamation of the Word of God is the "material" (*Stoff*) of dogmatic theology, as the title of §3 of the *Church Dogmatics* has it. The task of dogmatics then becomes the analysis of the presuppositions of the church's witnesses to the Word of God. Note the familiar use of the terms *analysis* and *fact* in Barth's description of the task of theology.

> But how can we perform this investigation? Clearly only by first considering and analysing the fact [*Faktum*] of this revelation — obviously the

---

50. Ibid., 200.
51. See ibid., 161.
52. Ibid., 199.
53. *CD* II/1, 5.
54. Ibid.

revelation which is attested to have taken place in Scripture and is promised as coming in proclamation; clearly only by analysing how the fact [*Faktum*] "God reveals Himself" is itself brought before us in the Bible and revelation; clearly only by analysing it as required by the fact [*Faktum*] itself and by the way it makes itself known to us.[55]

The point of theology is not simply to analyze the fact of the proclamation — theology does not leave "everything as it is" as Ludwig Wittgenstein famously circumscribed the task of philosophy in the *Philosophical Investigations*[56] — but also to return from the analysis of the presuppositions of proclamation to criticism of the church's practice of proclamation. In other words, clarifying the presuppositions of the proclamation enables theologians to discriminate, at least to some degree, between genuine and spurious — or faithful and unfaithful — forms of proclamation. Theology thus not only rises from proclamation to its presuppositions but also returns from those presuppositions to criticize proclamation.[57]

Could we summarize Barth's approach to theological knowledge in the *Church Dogmatics* by saying, "All theological knowledge begins with proclamation, but not all theological knowledge arises from proclamation"? Barth himself does not go as far as paraphrasing Kant, perhaps because he had already begun attributing the argumentative method of reasoning from actuality to the grounds of possibility to Anselm. Consider his interesting admixture of Kantian and Anselmian terms in the *Christliche Dogmatik im*

---

55. *CD* I/1, 291.

56. Ludwig Wittgenstein, *Philosophical Investigations*, trans. G. E. M. Anscombe (Oxford: Blackwell, 1997), I, §124.

57. Or, as Barth put it, "Wir stellen die Untersuchung des Offenbarungsbegriffs aber an, um die Voraussetzungen der Lehre von der Heiligen Schrift und der Lehre von der kirchlichen Verkündigung, auf die es uns ja praktisch ankommt, klarzulegen. Aus dem Offenbarungsbegriff muß es sich ergeben, inwiefern Bibel und Verkündigung als Wort Gottes zu verstehen sind, welche Korrespondenz zwischen beiden besteht und wie die zweite an der ersten zu messen ist. Die Untersuchung des Offenbarungsbegriffs gehört darum an den Anfang des Ganzen. Wir werden also im weiteren Verlauf unserer Prolegomena in drei Kapiteln von der Offenbarung, von der Heiligen Schrift, und von der Verkündigung der Kirche zu reden haben, so daß man das Ganze verstehen kann als eine Ausführung der in § 4 angekündigten Lehre von den drei Gestalten des Wortes Gottes, nur daß es nun nicht mehr auf den bloßen Aufweis dieser Gestalten abgesehen ist, sondern auf ihre innere Struktur und auf ihre Beziehungen untereinander, so daß der Weg — wir haben damals bei der Verkündigung als der problematischen Größe des ganzen Zusammenhangs eingesetzt - nun der umgekehrte werden, die Offenbarung also den Ausgangspunkt, die Verkündigung das Ziel bilden muß" (Barth, *KD* I/1, 309-10).

Entwurf when responding to the hypothetical objection that he was adducing dogma from the phenomenon of proclamation itself. "Was this not perhaps an attempt to construct *a priori* . . . the objective possibility of revelation . . . simply from the requirements of the dialectic of the concept of revelation, to deduce the God-man and to posit it as a necessary quantity?" Barth asked.[58] Barth provided several reasons why this charge did not apply. First, he was simply following the methodology of Anselm and Q. 12-17 of the Heidelberg Catechism. Second, he was not postulating about the possible reality of the Word of God, but about the condition of the possibility of that reality. "What we have constructed . . . was not the possibility, but the *conceptual* possibility of revelation, the condition under which the possibility of revelation must rightly be thought and spoken about."[59] Again, he compared this method to Anselm's *credo ut intelligere*. Finally, he also noted that his argument was not philosophical, but strictly theological. That is, he was not investigating the presuppositions of generally held philosophical truths, but of the fact of revelation. The method strictly tied the theologian to the domain of theology. Again, Anselm is cited for justification. Kant is not mentioned, despite the obvious parallels to Cohen's and Natorp's reformulation of the transcendental argument. My suspicion is that Barth's rediscovery of Anselm at this decisive stage in his theological career partially represented a rediscovery of the neo-Kantians' transcendental argument.

Barth took up the question of the relation between experience and faith in a systematic way in §6 of the *Church Dogmatics*. In that section, titled "The Knowability of the Word of God," Barth made some "un-Barthian"-sounding statements, which seem like concessions to the point of view he had rejected since his turn-from-liberalism. He says, for example, that "men can have a religious consciousness," that encounter between the Word of God and human beings might be described as "religious experience" (*Erlebnis*), and that even the concept of the religious a priori might be acceptable under a certain interpretation.[60] What makes this section particularly interesting for our purposes is the way Barth resorts to a form of the transcendental argument to determine the possibility of Christian religious experience.

Barth maintained his long-standing embargo against using subjective

---

58. Karl Barth, *Die christliche Dogmatik im Entwurf*, ed. Gerhard Sauter, *Karl Barth Gesamtausgabe* (Zürich: Theologischer Verlag, 1982), 304. My translation.

59. Ibid., 305. My translation.

60. *CD* I/1, 198 and 193.

religious experience as a building-block for faith. One of Barth's primary sparing partners in §6 is Georg Wobbermin. Wobbermin was, among other things, the German translator of William James's *The Varieties of Religious Experience*. Wobbermin was a sophisticated and philosophically inclined Lutheran theologian. He followed trends in contemporary philosophy closely and was among the first to engage with the nascent school of logical empiricism. In *Richtlinien evangelischer Theologie zur Überwindung der gegenwärtigen Krisis* [Guidelines of an Evangelical Theology for Overcoming the Contemporary Crisis], Wobbermin criticized Barth's understanding of the relationship between faith and experience.[61] He agreed with Barth that faith has a subjective pole and an objective pole and that the objective pole must take precedence over the subjective. However, he asserted that Barth did not merely give precedence to the objective side of faith — that is, the object (*Gegenstand*) of faith — but that he also effectively eliminated any reference to the subjective side — that is, the act (*Akt*) of faith. Wobbermin was particularly concerned that Barth simply excluded any reference to the personal experience of faith from his theology. "The personal experience of faith [*eigenpersönliche Glaubenserfahrung*] has to be completely excluded," writes Wobbermin about Barth's view.[62] This exclusion of the personal experience of faith led Barth to defend a kind of theological dogmatism which was more Roman Catholic than evangelical Protestant. Wobbermin held that though the subjective side of faith was always bound to its object, theologians cannot neglect the way that the experience of faith becomes part of our human experience in general. This "synthesis" of faith experience and ordinary experience produces the distinctive struggle between judgment and grace in our own lives that leads us to understand the significance of the gospel. Wobbermin argued that this "synthesis" of faith experience and ordinary experience represented our best witness to the indwelling presence of the Holy Spirit. "Experience of faith in the full meaning of the concept becomes a witness for the believer to the judgment and the grace of God; it becomes thus a witness to the working of the Holy Spirit."[63] According to Wobbermin, the experience of wrestling with the conflict of sin and grace is indispensable to understanding the object of faith.

Barth made unmistakable his rejection of Wobbermin's handling of the

61. Georg Wobbermin, *Richtlinien evangelischer Theologie zur Überwindung der gegenwärtigen Krisis* (Göttingen: Vandenhoeck & Ruprecht, 1929).

62. Ibid., 22. My translation.

63. Ibid., 127. My translation.

relation between subjective experience and the object of faith. "The difference between the view of Wobbermin . . . and the view presented here is as deep as it can possibly be within the Evangelical church," he wrote.[64] Why did Barth reject Wobbermin's proposal so definitively? After all, it seems roughly to have captured Barth's major concern of giving precedence to the object of faith when analyzing the experience of faith. Here is where I think returning to our theme, namely, the relation between the transcendental argument and the concept of experience, can clarify matters.

For Barth, experience of the Word of God is not something that Christians simply have. A significant amount of §6 is devoted to rejecting "Christian Cartesianism," or the claim that the reality of the Word of God can be established on the basis of some general human capacity, including the capacity for religious experience. Wobbermin's proposal, despite its emphasis on the objective pole of religious experience, amounts to "indirect Christian Cartesianism."[65] The difference between direct and indirect Christian Cartesianism is merely a matter of degree. The direct Cartesian uses the subjective pole of religious experience to establish the reality of its object. The indirect Cartesian simply uses the subjective pole as, in Wobbermin's language, a "methodical aid" to understanding the objective. Barth insinuated that indirect Christian Cartesianism may be more dangerous than direct Cartesianism because of its apparent acknowledgment of the priority of God's revelation to subjective human experience. Still, this way of relating personal religious experience to its object constantly threatens to turn inward and become self-focused. Christian Cartesianism makes the possibility of experiencing the object of faith, namely, the Word of God, into "man's own, a predicate of his existence, a content of his consciousness, his possession."[66] "When we try to find the content of divine Spirit in the (pardoned) consciousness of man," Barth wrote, "are we not like the man who wanted to scoop out in a sieve the reflection of the beautiful silvery moon from a pond?"[67] Barth was aiming at something qualitatively different than Wobbermin's quantitative and weighted distinction between the subjective and objective poles of religious experience.

How then did Barth establish the possibility of religious experience if he rejects any inference from the subjective pole to the objective? This move

---

64. *CD* I/1, 209.
65. Ibid., 213f.
66. Ibid., 214.
67. Ibid., 216.

seems to exclude any possibility of reasoning from experience at all. My contention is that he returned to the neo-Kantian adaptation of the transcendental argument, which he rooted in the actuality of proclamation. The *fact* of proclamation formed his starting point for reflection about the possibility of religious experience. Analysis of this *fact* shows that it presupposes not only that human beings can hear, understand, and know God's Word, but also that they can *experience* God's Word. "If knowledge of God becomes possible for men, this must mean that they can have experience of God's Word."[68] In other words, it must be possible for human beings not only to know, but also to experience the Word of God. "If this were not so," Barth contended, "the whole concept of the Word of God would have to be called a figment of the imagination, and Church proclamation, including dogmatics, would have to be called a pointless and meaningless activity, and therefore the Church would have to be called a place of self-deceptions without parallel."[69] Barth's recognition that experience of the Word of God is a presupposition of the *Faktum* that God's Word is spoken and heard in the church first provided solid footing from which to speak about Christian religious experience. Suddenly we find Karl Barth, the great opponent of religious experience, defending the possibility of religious experience with statements like "the possibility of human experience of the Word of God understood as the possibility of this Word itself, is one that we can and must affirm with certainty, with final human seriousness."[70]

Let's step back a bit. Barth declared himself willing to put his "hand in the fire" to defend the possibility of "the human experience of the Word of God" not because he trusted directly or indirectly in his own personal experience of God's Word, but because human religious experience counts among the conditions for the possibility of proclamation of the Word of God. If human beings cannot experience the Word of God, they cannot know the Word of God and cannot preach or hear the Word of God. But there is proclamation of the Word of God. So human beings must be able to experience God's Word. This is a transcendental argument in form, but it ultimately rests on faith — faith that the church's proclamation is actually proclamation of the Word of God.

This connection between faith and experience makes it quite appropriate that Barth concluded §6 with a section titled "The Word of God and

68. Ibid., 198; translation altered.
69. Ibid., 187f.
70. Ibid., 223f.

Faith." This section reinforces that subjective religious experience is not the ground of faith, but that faith in the Word of God is the condition for the possibility of religious experience. Or, as Barth asserted, "in faith men have real experience of the Word of God."[71] The key phrase is *in faith*. The experience of faith is not a possession, it is a confession which cancels out any notion of possession — hence, Barth's wonderfully paradoxical assertion in §6.3 that "by taking place as an experience this experience ceases to be an experience."[72] Or, to put the point in more neo-Kantian terms, religious experience is not a given, but only known as the presupposition of the fact of proclamation.

VI.

By way of conclusion, let me clarify what I perceive as the lingering influence of the neo-Kantian understanding of experience and the transcendental argument in Karl Barth. To what extent did Barth remain indebted to the Marburg neo-Kantians despite his efforts to distance himself from his philosophical "eggshells"? Our study of Barth's concept of experience allows us to answer this question with varying degrees of certainty.

First and quite evidently, Barth shared the Marburg School's repudiation of the empiricist standpoint in epistemology and their concomitant rejection of psychologism. Barth was consistent on this point from the first commentary on Romans to the *Church Dogmatics*. He wanted no truck with theories which either built up theology from the patchwork of religious experience or boiled down doctrines to the psychological experiences of sin and grace.

Second and more cautiously put, Barth significantly appropriated the Marburg neo-Kantians' transcendental argument. He argued that theology must not start from a priori principles or empirical experiences, but with reflection on the conditions of the possibility of proclamation. His readiness to deploy a transcendental argument outside the domain of the natural sciences, reference to the *Faktum* of theological proclamation as its starting point, and use of that argument not to ward off skepticism but to delineate the fundamental categories of theological science all speak to his indebtedness to the Marburg School.

71. Ibid., 238.
72. Ibid., 208.

Finally, and more speculatively, Barth incorporated elements of the Marburg neo-Kantians' concept of experience. Here the record is mixed. On the one hand, Barth moved progressively away from interpreting religious experience as a sort of admixture between the subjective act of experience and the object of experience. By the *Church Dogmatics*, he had turned religious experience itself into an object of faith. On the other hand, Barth never fully embraced Hermann Cohen's identification of experience with science. If he had, he might simply and easily have asserted that Christian religious experience is identical with the proclamation of the church and thus have written off the question of its subjective appropriation as a non-theological, psychological matter.

That Barth did not make this move may have resulted partially from the influence of Paul Natorp's more balanced consideration of the role of the subjective perspective in epistemology. His hesitation may also be due in part to the lingering effects of the liberal tradition's emphasis on lived experience. But the primary reason that Barth did not make this move was likely the chorus of evangelicals and pietists who protested against his neglect of the role that the experience of conversion played not only in the New Testament but also in their own lives.

Covenant, Election, and Incarnation: Evaluating Barth's Actualist Christology

Michael S. Horton

With the benefit of a little greater distance, evangelical and Reformed evaluations of Barth's theological legacy seem to have matured beyond lionizing and demonizing. For a host of reasons that are beyond the scope of this essay, I am indebted to Barth and Barthians for helping me to read God's Word more faithfully. In fact, to the extent that contemporary evangelicalism is threatened by the anthropocentric religious outlook that plagued Neo-Protestantism, Barth and his theological descendants can be recognized as indispensable conversation partners for confessional Protestants in a way that was far less likely only a generation ago. I am grateful for the opportunity to enter into this conversation and to have my interpretation and criticisms of Barth evaluated by his worthy heirs. In this essay I interact with Barth's Christology. Obviously, anything I say on this topic will be like trying to empty the Atlantic with a spoon. Yet throwing caution to the wind, I will pursue the massively broad topic of election and incarnation, comparing and contrasting Barth's actualistic Christology with the covenant theology of Reformed orthodoxy.

I. Covenant and Christology in Reformed Orthodoxy

The idea that predestination is the central dogma in Reformed theology from which every other belief is logically deduced originated with Alexander

Schweizer.[1] However, it reflects the distinctive tendency of nineteenth-century German historiography, and with respect to Reformed theology it has been effectively laid to rest by historical scholars.[2] Cautioning readers against abstract speculation concerning "God in himself" or simply "deity," the older systems typically defined the object of theology as God as he has revealed himself in scripture and pledged himself to us in Jesus Christ according to the covenant of grace.[3] Obviously, election played an important part in extrapolating that message. However, it does not function centrally, much less as a control-doctrine, in any of the Reformed confessions or catechisms. Even in the era of high orthodoxy, different nuances were tolerated, as evidenced in the relative friendliness of the supra-/infralapsarian squab-

---

1. Alexander Schweizer, *Die protestantischen Centraldogmen in ihrer Entwicklung innerhalb der reformierten Kirche,* 2 vols. (Zurich: Orell, Fuessli und Comp., 1854, 1856).

2. Rooted in the methodological approach of Heiko Oberman, David Steinmetz, and others, Richard Muller is joined by a growing number of historical theologians who have decisively refuted the Torrance school on the relation between Calvin and Calvinism. See, for example, Richard Muller, *After Calvin* (New York: Oxford University Press, 2004), which summarizes a lot of his research on this relationship; see Carl Trueman and R. S. Clark, eds., *Protestant Scholasticism: Essays in Reassessment* (Carlisle: Paternoster, 1998); Paul Helm, *Calvin and the Calvinists* (Edinburgh: Banner of Truth Trust, 1982); W. J. Van Asselt and E. Dekker, eds., *Reformation and Scholasticism: An Ecumenical Enterprise* (Grand Rapids, MI: Baker Academic, 2001); J. Beeke, *Assurance of Faith: Calvin, English Puritanism and the Dutch Second Reformation* (New York: Peter Lang, 1991); L. D. Bierma, "Federal Theology in the Sixteenth Century: Two Traditions?" *Westminster Theological Journal* 45 (1983): 304-21; idem, "The Role of Covenant Theology in Early Reformed Orthodoxy," *The Sixteenth Century Journal* 21 (1990): 453-62.

3. The seventeenth-century Reformed theologian Francis Turretin pointed out that even when treating the same topics, theology considers them in a different mode than metaphysics:

> But when God is set forth as the object of theology, he is not to be regarded simply as God in himself (for thus he is incomprehensible to us), but as he has been pleased to manifest himself to us in his word. . . . Nor is he to be considered exclusively under the relation of deity (according to the opinion of Thomas Aquinas and many Scholastics after him, for in this manner the knowledge of him could not be saving but deadly to sinners), but as he is our God (covenanted in Christ . . .). (*Institutes of Elenctic Theology,* vol. 1, trans. G. M. Giger, ed. James T. Dennison, Jr. [Phillipsburg, NJ: P & R Publishing, 1992], 16)

Calvin's attitude toward speculation is well known, as is his emphasis on God's condescension and accommodation to us, revealing God not as he is in himself but as he is toward us — not in his being but in his works. "Better to limp along this path," Calvin cautioned, "than to dash with all speed outside it" (*Institutes of the Christian Religion,* trans. Ford Lewis Battles, ed. John T. McNeill [Westminster: Philadelphia, 1960], 1.6.3).

bles (though, happily in my view, the infras seem to have won). Rather than adopt a central dogma from which all else could be deduced, Reformed systems came to be organized by the diverse yet integrated architecture of covenant theology.

The Westminster Confession speaks of the metaphysical distance between Creator and creature being so great that there could have been no relationship had God not condescended to us by way of a covenant.[4] Toward the end of the sixteenth century, there was an emerging consensus among the Reformed that scripture revealed three overarching covenants: a covenant of redemption *(pactum salutis)* made in eternity between the persons of the Trinity, the covenant of creation (also called the covenant of law/nature/works/life) with humanity in Adam, and the covenant of grace, which was God's unilateral promise after the fall to redeem, reconcile, and restore a great remnant of the fallen race and to bring them into the glory of the Sabbath rest through the triumph of the Last Adam.[5] I do not have the space here to elaborate this consensus, much less to explore its arguments and exegesis.[6] It will suffice to say that the Trinitarian structure and concentration on Christ the Mediator are key features of this federal theology.

Of course, the most controversial aspect of the confessional Reformed doctrine of predestination was (and remains) its view concerning the subjects of election and reprobation. Adopting an infralapsarian view without condemning supralapsarianism, the Reformed confessions typically speak of election as an active decree while reprobation is a permissive one. In fact, the Canons of the Synod of Dort conclude by confessing that the "Reformed Churches . . . detest with their whole soul" the view "that in the same manner in which the election is the fountain and cause of faith and good works, reprobation is the cause of unbelief and piety."[7] Although this doctrine was related more integrally to Christology, it is in

---

4. The Westminster Confession of Faith, Chapter 7.

5. These overarching covenants are also summarized in Chapter 7 of the Westminster Confession.

6. I have dealt with these developments in various places. For a more general treatment, see my book, *God of Promise: Introducing Covenant Theology* (Grand Rapids: Baker, 2006); for a more technical treatment, specifically directed to recent debates in Pauline studies over justification, see my *Covenant and Salvation: Union with Christ* (Louisville: Westminster John Knox, 2007).

7. Canons of the Synod of Dort, Chapter V, Conclusion, in *The Psalter Hymnal: Doctrinal Standards and Liturgy of the Christian Reformed Church* (Grand Rapids: Board of Publications of the CRC, 1976), 115.

this respect simply consistent Augustinianism and hardly unique to John Calvin or his heirs.[8]

Covenant theology placed the emphasis on the execution of the decree in history rather than on the decree itself. Consequently, human agency, genuine reversals and counter-reversals, and other elements critical to a dynamic narrative plot, kept Reformed theology from being reduced to a story that is already completed on the first page. In the place of static and often dualistic schemes such as nature and grace, the covenantal paradigm substituted the dynamism of a plot line of creation, fall, redemption, and consummation — in terms of both the *historia salutis* (redemption accomplished) and *ordo salutis* (redemption applied). Nevertheless, all of these diverse paths converge on the person of Jesus Christ, who is the mediator of creation and redemption.

In terms of Christology, Reformed scholasticism simply saw itself as a faithful interpretation of Chalcedon. Although attempts to pigeonhole Reformed Christology as Antiochene as opposed to Alexandrian are usually driven by polemics more than by real formulations, there is a discernable stress placed on the distinction and significance both of Christ's two natures in one person as well as the divine persons of the Trinity. As we will see, this encouraged Reformed orthodoxy to give equal attention to the personal properties of each member of the Godhead and to the one divine essence.

II. Defining Barth's Actualist Christology

By his own testimony, Barth's new Christological positions and emphases from Göttingen on were inspired by his readings in Reformed orthodoxy.[9] In fact, he believed that he was simply working out the implications of traditional Reformed Christology within an actualistic ontology that understands Christology in terms of "a single event." In this way, he said he had "'actualised' the doctrine of the incarnation."[10] From the beginning (II/1),

---

8. Dort's formula, "sufficient for the world, efficient for the elect alone," can be found in Peter Lombard and Thomas Aquinas, among others.

9. I am thinking especially of the anhypostatic/enhypostatic Christology.

10. *CD* IV/2, 105: "In a basic attachment to the Reformed tradition, but without following it in detail, and transcending it at some points, we have given this a sense and position which it did not have in all earlier Christology. We have 'actualised' the doctrine of the incarnation, i.e., we have used the main traditional concepts, *unio, communio* and *communicatio,* as concentrically related terms to describe one and the same ongoing process . . . a single event."

his axiom that God's being is in act generated new formulations across various loci, and by the remarkable fourth volume this actualist ontology reached its climax.[11] His stated motive is to eliminate any ontic as well as epistemological cleavage between God's actual being and God's self-revelation in Jesus Christ.[12] Unlike Reformed orthodoxy, Barth does seem to have made predestination (at least his own revised formulation of that doctrine) the central dogma of his system. In fact, we will see that in Bruce McCormack's elaboration and extension of Barth's doctrine of election, this point becomes especially obvious.

Let me offer a summary of what I take to be Barth's main line of argument concerning the relationship of election and Christology and then attempt the finer brush strokes as we go along.

First, although the tradition recognized the Son as well as the Father and the Spirit as the electing God, it failed (in Barth's view) to see the Son as the subject as well as the object of this act.[13] Instead, Barth advocates a "purified supralapsarianism." Election is God's choice, "preceding all His other choices," which is "fulfilled in His eternal willing of the existence of the man Jesus and of the people represented in Him."[14] Christ's election and the election of humanity are one and the same event. "In the beginning with God was this One, Jesus Christ. And that is predestination."[15]

Consequently, there is no room any longer for a distinction between elect and reprobate individuals with different ultimate destinies: one under the law and wrath, another under the gospel and grace, or a notion of a covenant or nature that is logically distinct from the covenant of grace. In the

---

11. See also George Hunsinger, *How To Read Karl Barth: The Shape of His Theology* (New York: Oxford University Press, 1991), 4-5. Hunsinger reminds us that Barth's theology cannot be reduced to actualism. Rather, it must be seen in connection with other motifs, particularly *particularism* (where Jesus Christ is the specific act or event that governs God's self-revelation), *objectivism* (God's self-giving in revelation/reconciliation regardless of human response), *personalism* (God, rather than something about God, as the object and subject of revelation), and *realism* (the possibility of true revelation by grace alone). "'Rationalism,' finally, again as used in this essay, is the motif which pertains to the construction and assessment of doctrine." It is the conceptual elaboration that "constitutes the theological task," as it employs exegesis and makes legitimate inferences from it (ibid., 5; emphasis added).

12. *CD* II/1, 262.

13. *CD* II/2, 43: "In the strict sense only He [Jesus Christ] can be understood and described as 'elected' (and 'rejected'). All others are so in Him, and not as individuals."

14. Ibid., 25.

15. Ibid., 145.

light of this history of the elect humanity in Jesus Christ, human resistance, rebellion, and unbelief are not ontologically real; it is the history of Jesus Christ (and therefore of God) that is decisive. Sin is the "impossible possibility," the shadow of the light cast by Christ. In truth, Jesus Christ is not the *last Adam,* but *precedes* Adam and in fact reduces "Adam" to non-being.[16] One may continue to object, to refuse to be defined by one's election and reconciliation in Christ, but that rejection is not finally decisive. "God does not permit [the human person] to execute this No of his, this contradiction and opposition."[17] Even God's No is overtaken by God's Yes; hence, Law must always be finally subsumed under gospel.[18] "*This* No is really Yes. *This* judgment is grace. *This* condemnation is forgiveness. *This* death is life. *This* hell is heaven."[19] Some might suggest that for Barth human existence under the reign of sin, death, unbelief, and condemnation is finally like the existence of the prisoners in Plato's cave. It is not the truth of their reality, but a terrible dream from which they need to be awakened.

Second, although the tradition insisted that Christ alone is the "mirror of election," Barth thinks that this had a merely noetic and pastoral rather than ontic and real force, since the fact remained that God's hidden and mysterious decree might not coincide with one's own election.[20] Barth sees his thesis, "Je-

16. See especially Karl Barth, *Christ and Adam: Man and Humanity in Romans 5,* trans. T. A. Smail (London and New York: Collier, 1962).

17. *CD* IV/3.1, 3.

18. *CD* II/2, 13: "The Yes cannot be heard unless the No is also heard. But the No is said for the sake of the Yes and not for its own sake. In substance, therefore, the first and last word is Yes and not No."

19. Karl Barth, *The Word of God and the Word of Man,* trans. Douglas Horton (New York: Harper & Bros., 1957), 120.

20. More consistently even than the Lutherans, who caricatured the Calvinist position, Reformed theology, says Barth, consistently maintained that election was grounded solely in Christ and it was there alone that we could find our own election (*CD* II/2, 62). Unlike the Thomistic interpretation, the Reformed view was thoroughly Christocentric and evangelical (62-63). Nevertheless, did Luther, Calvin, and the Reformed go far enough? Is there behind this a "higher truth" that we ought not to probe but is nonetheless part of the reality of the electing God? (63-64). As with his doctrine of revelation, the subject and object are always exclusively Jesus Christ. Just as revelation has to do with Truth (Jesus Christ) rather than truths (revealed propositions), election *is* Jesus Christ, not "a decision which precedes the being and will and word of Christ, a hidden God" who decreed the salvation of certain individuals and then subsequently decreed to call, justify, sanctify, and glorify them (64). Luther himself (*De servo arbitrio,* 1525) was the first to add the Christological reference only after a secret decree. The majestic will stood behind the *Deus incarnatus,* even if we were to content ourselves with the latter (66). Calvin simply followed in this train (66-67). I am not aware of

sus Christ as both the electing God and elected man," as a critical correction: yet "not really an innovation" but rather the clarification of the general trajectory of Reformation teaching.[21]

Third, this revised doctrine of election functions as a central dogma, deepening his actualist ontology and spreading it out across all of the various loci. "The election of grace is the sum of the Gospel — we must put it as pointedly as that," Barth insists. "But more, the election of grace is the whole of the Gospel, the Gospel *in nuce.*"[22] Barth recognizes that "Calvin and the Calvinists" emphasized the good news of election as a comforting doctrine.[23] Even Dort defined election in this evangelical manner, despite its affirmation of reprobation.[24]

Given the allegation among many of Barth's students that Calvin's successors made election a central dogma, it is interesting that Barth complains that predestination was not central enough for the Reformed scholastics.[25] These systems presupposed the classic "attributes" of God that tended to suggest that there was one God "for us" (living and active) who is quite different from God-in-himself. However, Barth argues, election is a constituent element in our doctrine of God not simply as a divine work *ad extra,* but as part of God's self-constituting identity.[26] So the orthodox were right to place election under the doctrine of God, "but we must do so far more radically than was the case in this very important Reformed tradition."[27] The upshot

---

any place where Barth's students have interacted with the impressive arguments against this reading of Calvin and Reformed orthodoxy, for example, by Richard Muller, *Unaccommodated Calvin* (New York: Oxford University Press, 2000), 46-48. See also the recent essay by Paul Helm, "John Calvin and the Hiddenness of God," in *Engaging the Doctrine of God: Contemporary Protestant Perspectives,* ed. Bruce McCormack (Grand Rapids, MI: Baker Academic, 2008), 67-82, which focuses most specifically on this issue.

21. *CD* II/2, 76.

22. Ibid., 13-14.

23. Ibid., 15.

24. Ibid., 17-18.

25. Barth rejected the notion that predestination was a "central dogma" in Reformed orthodoxy, much less that it functioned as "a kind of speculative key — a basic tenet from which they could deduce all other dogmas." "Not even the famous schema of T. Beza was intended in such a sense," Barth notes (ibid., 77-78). In fact, "If we read their expositions connectedly we are more likely to get the impression that from the standpoint of its systematic range and importance they gave to the doctrine too little consideration rather than too much" (ibid., 78). These comments stand in opposition to the school of Calvin interpretation associated with some of Barth's heirs, especially T. F. Torrance and J. B. Torrance.

26. Ibid., 79.

27. Ibid., 80.

of Barth's revised supralapsarianism is that "the work of God (the work of all works!) is not creation, but that which precedes creation both eternally and in effect temporally, the incarnate Word of God, Christ."[28] "It is for this reason that we understand the election as ordination, as God's self-ordaining of Himself."[29] Election, says Barth, is the primal decision on the basis of which the triune God *moves toward humanity*.[30] Nevertheless, there is no point in eternity or time where we encounter God apart from the redeeming grace of Jesus Christ.[31]

Barth does say that Reformed orthodoxy is to be commended for underscoring the freedom, mystery, and righteousness of the triune God without wandering off into speech about a "'supreme being' posited by human invention."[32] That Barth could still say this even in II/2 should remind us not to overstate his critique of the tradition. Nevertheless, it is first of all in God's election of grace, not in God's decision to create, that one discerns *all* the ways of God in relation to humanity.

Placing the decree to create and to permit the fall prior to the decree of election, Barth complains, infralapsarianism opened up space between creation and redemption, and the distinction between a covenant of creation and a covenant of grace made matters worse — opening the door to natural theology, historicism, and other ills of modern theology. Representing "an advance on medieval scholasticism," federal theology "tried to understand the work and Word of God attested in Holy Scripture dynamically and not statically, as an event and not as a system of objective and self-contained truths. . . . This theology is concerned with the bold review of a history of God and man which unfolds itself from creation to the day of judgment." It follows Calvin's emphasis on the dynamic history of the covenant in the history of redemption. However, he asks, did it not concern itself "with a whole series of events which are purposefully strung out but which belong together? . . . Can we historicize the activity and revelation of God? The Federal theologians were the first really to try to do this in principle."[33] "They say excellently that the Bible tells us about an event," says Barth, but fail to see that it is "only a *single event*" dependent on "the *single and complete decision* on the part of God. . . . Because of the difference of the attestation it

---

28. Ibid.
29. Ibid., 89.
30. Ibid., 90-92.
31. Ibid., 92-94.
32. Ibid., 24.
33. *CD* IV/1, 55.

cannot be broken up into a series of different covenant acts, or acts of re-demption, which follow one another step by step, and then reassembled into a single whole."[34]

After summarizing his translation of the older concepts of Reformed Christology in a more actualist direction, he anticipates the natural questions:

> How can a being be interpreted as an act, or an act as a being? How can God, or man, or both in their unity in Jesus Christ, be understood as history? How can humiliation also and at the same time be exaltation? How can it be said of a history which took place once that it takes place to-day, and that, having taken place once and taking place to-day, it will take place again?[35]

With this series of questions, Barth himself sets the terms for my interaction.

A. *Logos asarkos: Essentialism vs. Actualism?*

The Reformers sought to close the *door to speculation* by pointing to Christ, but Barth wanted to close the *ontological gap* between God's hidden and re-vealed will, so that, without speculating, we could know (perhaps univocally?) God's inner being. This principle is already laid down in I/1: "God, the Revealer, is identical with His act in revelation and also identical with its effect."[36] Understandably, this raises the question of the *Logos asarkos*. If there is no divine being standing behind God's self-revelation in Jesus Christ, can there be an eternal Son standing behind Jesus of Nazareth?

Barth takes up the subject of the *Logos asarkos* on the heels of his survey of the covenantal scheme of classical Reformed theology that I have already summarized. "In this free act of the election of grace the Son of the Father is no longer just the eternal Logos," says Barth, "but as such, as very God from all eternity He is also the very God and very man He will become in time. In the divine act of predestination there pre-exists the Jesus Christ who as the Son of the eternal Father and the child of the Virgin Mary will become and be the Mediator of the covenant between God and man, the One who ac-complishes the act of atonement." He adds,

---

34. Ibid., 56; emphasis added.
35. *CD* IV/2, 108.
36. *CD* I/1, 296.

This is the point which Coccejus and the Federal theology before and after Coccejus missed. Their doctrine of a purely intertrinitarian pact did not enable them to give an unequivocal or binding answer to the question of the form of the eternal divine decree as the beginning of all things. The result was that for all their loyalty to Scripture they inherited the notion that the covenant of grace fulfilled and revealed in history in Jesus Christ was perhaps only a secondary and subsequent divine arrangement (the foundation and history of a religion?) and not the beginning of all the ways of God. Their view of the covenant became dualistic.[37]

If these theologians of Reformed orthodoxy would only have attended to "the eternal divine Logos in His incarnation," says Barth, "they might well have overcome the other weaknesses in their doctrine: the abandonment of an original universalism in the conception of the covenant [which he attributes to Zwingli]; and finally the radical historicism of their understanding of Scripture."[38]

The question remaining is how far Barth's actualistic ontology should be extended. Although Barth himself was not thoroughly consistent, Bruce McCormack suggests, it should lead to the conclusion that the Trinity itself is constituted by God's electing decree.[39] It seems clear enough that Barth does not argue, at least explicitly, that the divine act of election constitutes the Trinity as such. In fact, McCormack is careful to concede as much. Yet it also seems clear enough to me at least that the trajectory of Barth's actualist Christology points in that direction. In fact, Emil Brunner already criticized Barth on this point.[40] I am glad that Barth is not as consistent as McCormack would

---

37. *CD* IV/1, 66. Barth is not quite fair in his definition, since these writers believed that there were two historical covenants, not one covenant conceived in a dualistic fashion.

38. Ibid.

39. Bruce McCormack, "Grace and Being: The Role of God's Gracious Election in Karl Barth's Theological Ontology," in *The Cambridge Companion to Karl Barth*, ed. John Webster (Cambridge: Cambridge University Press, 2000), 92-110; idem, "Seek God where he may be found: a response to Edwin Chr. van Driel," *Scottish Journal of Theology* 60, no. 1 (2007): 62-79; idem, "The Ontological Presuppositions of Barth's Doctrine of the Atonement," in *The Glory of the Atonement: Biblical, Historical & Practical Perspectives*, ed. Charles E. Hill and Frank A. James III (Downers Grove: InterVarsity Press, 2004), 346-66. As tantalizing and germane as those issues are to my paper, I will simply summarize my own reaction briefly, assuming familiarity with McCormack's thesis — especially the decisive significance of Barth's "breakthrough" via Pierre Maury's interpretation of election, which generates a more thoroughgoing actualism from II/2 on.

40. Emil Brunner, *The Christian Doctrine of God, Dogmatics: Vol. 1*, trans. Olive Wyon (Philadelphia: Westminster Press, 1946), 315.

like him to be on this point. However, it does point up for me the limits of an actualist interpretation of Chalcedonian Christology.[41] If an actualist ontol-

41. Edwin van Driel suggests, "For Barth, the incarnation does not constitute the divine being, but the divine being constitutes the incarnation. Incarnation is possible because of the kind of being God is." See Edwin Chr. van Driel, "Karl Barth on the Existence of Jesus Christ," *Scottish Journal of Theology* 60, no. 1 (2007): 45-61, here 52. Van Driel points to Barth's explicit statements concerning the natural and necessary character of the divine processions (*CD* II/1, 305-6). In response, McCormack argues that this is prior to II/2 and Barth's new concept of election ("Seek God," 64-65).

Setting this important point aside for the moment, van Driel poses some important material questions concerning McCormack's reading. If election is constitutive of God's being, van Driel wonders how we can fail to avoid the implication that "creation is likewise essential to God and constitutive of the divine being"? After all, incarnation implies humanity. "I therefore do not see how McCormack would end up at a different place than Hegel, even if his starting point — will rather than nature — is different." Who is it that is electing and willing in the first place? Surely there must be a divine being prior to election (van Driel, "Karl Barth," 54). On McCormack's thesis, Jesus Christ is basically electing himself. "This means that Jesus Christ existed before he elected to be Jesus Christ, because only thus can he be the subject of the election of Christ. . . . To think of a divine decision as involving a subject that precedes the decision is to think too anthropomorphically, McCormack suggests" (ibid., 55). Van Driel continues:

> [McCormack] appeals to the doctrine of the Trinity itself: God, in God's second mode of being, is the same divine subject as God in God's first mode of being, and therefore "if he makes a decision in his first form, he (the One subject) is necessarily making it in his second and third form as well. . . ." It seems to me this argument rather underscores than solves the problem. . . . The implication of the content of this decision is that God also exists in a second and third mode of being. . . . But what starts the argument is that God makes this first decision in God's first mode — that is, not in the mode of Jesus Christ, but in the mode of a God which precedes Jesus Christ. A mode not even being the *Logos asarkos* but more unknown than that. (Ibid., 56, citing McCormack, "Grace and Being," 104)

I might add that even if "the mode of a God which precedes Jesus Christ" is the first mode of being (the Father), the deeper problem — and, as I see it anyway, this is Barth's problem as well — is the modalistic tendency that motivated Barth's rejection of the covenant of redemption. There is a monistic undercurrent to Barth's doctrine of election that McCormack's interpretation strengthens. Mistaking distinctions (such as God's hidden and revealed will) for antitheses, the *Logos ensarkos* displaces the *Logos asarkos*, the unity of Christ's person displaces the two natures, the persons become lost in the essence of a "single subject," and election swallows reprobation.

At the end of the day, van Driel thinks that Barth is ambiguous. He is simply trying to say that the Logos with whom we have to do is the one whom the Logos determined to be in Jesus Christ (van Driel, "Karl Barth," 58). "If I am right, Barth's doctrine of election has no ontological consequences for the notions of immanent Trinity, *logos asarkos*, or God-

ogy will not suffice for Christology, then one wonders how successfully it can claim to have "'actualised' the doctrine of the incarnation." However, if it can only achieve this victory at the expense of understanding the Trinity as constituted by election, the price of consistency is high indeed.

Although Barth defends Calvin's formulation of the so-called *extra calvinisticum*,[42] he does express concern that the doctrine of the *Logos asarkos* allows for the possibility of a "hidden God" behind Jesus of Nazareth.[43] So once again we see that for Barth the specter of a hidden God abstracted from Christ is always entailed by a traditional Augustinian interpretation of double predestination.[44]

As McCormack reminds us, in identifying the *Logos asarkos* entirely with Jesus of Nazareth, Barth's resolution is to affirm simultaneously God's immutability and passibility. So there is no change to the deity itself. Other-

---

in-and-for-Godself. Instead of 'upstream' of election, the consequences will be 'downstream,' in Christology and anthropology" (ibid., 58-59). Barth did not want to replace divine and human natures with history — or if he did, he shouldn't have. "Now, if it is essential to Christ's identity, as Chalcedon held, that Christ is fully God and fully human, this means that, if this eternal act is indeed identical with Jesus Christ, then for one to be fully human it is enough if one is an intentional object. And could that be true?" (ibid., 61).

In response to van Driel, McCormack suggests that Barth did not eliminate the *asarkos/incarnandus* distinction, but identified them ("Seek God," 63). However, if that is the case, then I am not sure how innovative Barth really is at this point, as I concluded above. Second, McCormack reiterates his point that Barth only became "the post-metaphysical theologian" with II/2. Until then, Barth held the "belief of the ancient church that God's triunity was 'natural and necessary'" — independent of election. McCormack does not dispute van Driel's claim that the ancient church held that the Son "added" a human nature to the first. But this assigns suffering only to the human nature, a tactic that always leads in a Nestorian direction.

42. For example, Barth exonerates Calvin from caricatures of the so-called "extra," pointing out that it was held by Athanasius, Cyril, Hilary, and many others before him: "it was the abstract Lutheran denial of a being of the Logos *extra carnem* which was the real innovation" (IV/1, 181). At least qualifying McCormack's interpretation of Barth's critique of the tradition, Barth explicitly denies that Calvin, "any more than his predecessors," defended "an abstract Extra" that could imply a Nestorian separation of "the Son of God and the man Jesus." "On the contrary, it was his aim in that theory to hold to the fact that the Son of God who is wholly this man (*totus intra carnem* as it was formulated by a later Calvinist) is also wholly God and therefore omnipotent and omnipresent (and to that extent *extra carnem*), not bound or altered by its limitations" (ibid.).

43. *CD* IV/1, 181.

44. Yet Lutheran Christology had its own problems, as Barth points out (ibid., 181). If, in the union, the Son's deity could interpenetrate the humanity, why not the reverse? This was precisely the move that kenotic Christologies made in the nineteenth century.

wise, we are once again left wondering whether our talk about God's reconciliation of the world is actual in Jesus Christ.[45] There is no antithesis in
God, no cleavage between God "in Himself" and God "for us."[46] The God
who comes to us in Jesus Christ has always been majestic even in abasement
and abased even in majesty, entering time without ceasing to be eternal.[47]

*So the first point by way of analysis is that Barth tends to assimilate the
persons (or modes of being) to the one essence.* It is not only Jesus Christ whose
humiliation is seen as proper to his office, but in Jesus Christ we discern the
humiliation that is proper to God.[48] Here it seems that the divine essence
generally, not just the personal attribute of the Son, is to suffer as such. It is
not kenosis per se, but the assumption that kenosis involves *change,* that
Barth rejects.[49] "We cannot conceal the fact that it is a difficult and even an
elusive thing to speak of obedience which takes place in God Himself. Obedience implies an above and a below, a *prius* and a *posterius,* a superior and a
junior and subordinate."[50] However, such subordination should not be a
problem once we recognize that it does not entail any diminution of being.[51]

On this point at least, the answer to subordinationism from the perspective of Reformed orthodoxy is the distinction between ontological and
economic subordination, while the answer to modalism is the distinction
between the essence and the persons. It is clear enough what Barth is up to
here, though. His greatest concern is to identify the hidden and revealed God
in Jesus Christ — in other words, to know that Jesus Christ is God, and not
simply an "as-if." If the economy is not the same as God's immanent being,
then the atonement is not real.[52] Therefore, Barth insists that the superiority
and subordination is "in God Himself," in fact it is "essential to the being of
God." Not simply in the intratrinitarian relations but in the divine essence
"there is a below, a posterius, a subordination" — the personal attributes appear to be collapsed into the one essence.[53] I have searched in vain for a for-

---

45. Ibid., 183.

46. Ibid., 184.

47. Ibid., 188. See 192: "The mystery reveals to us that for God it is just as natural to be
lowly as it is to be high, to be near as it is to be far, to be little as it is to be great, to be abroad
as to be at home."

48. Ibid., 193.

49. Ibid.

50. Ibid., 195.

51. Ibid.

52. Ibid., 196-98.

53. Ibid., 200-201.

mulation something like: "There is an economic subordination of the Son to the Father in the life of the Trinity."[54] Although the incarnation involves God's unity with creaturely reality, this event is simply "the strangely logical final continuation of the history in which He is God."[55] Once more the distinction between essence and persons is missing.

It is not because of any wariness of using the language of essence as such, since this is his dominant term. Rather, it would seem that his reticence to employ such distinctions is motivated by the Trinitarian formulations that he has already made in previous volumes. Barth suggests as much when he repeats in IV/1, "By Father, Son and Spirit we do not mean what is commonly suggested to us by the word 'persons.'"[56] It is "one Subject, not three . . . the one God in self-repetition."[57] In some passages, Barth says that the subject of this humility or suffering is the divine essence as such.[58] In other passages, he attempts a typical Reformed (indeed, Chalcedonian) appeal to the two natures (IV/2, 203, 617). To complicate matters, he can say also that the subjects are the first and second modes of being (II/1, 357). So is it God's essence as such or the personal existence of the Son that is "obedient in humility"? It is hard to say, since "He is as man, as the man who is obedient in humility, Jesus of Nazareth, what He is *as God*," rather than what he is as the incarnate Son.[59] The weight falls on the side of the divine essence as the subject of immutable passibility.

A corollary of this monistic tilt in his concept of the Trinity is the tendency to collapse time into eternity. Barth challenges historicism (evident especially in Lessing's "ditch") by arguing that in *Urgeschichte* eternity has become time and the *Logos asarkos* has become the *Logos ensarkos*. Yet the time that eternity has now assumed is very much unlike the time identified with *Historie*. The former is the *real* history, eliminating the problem of relating the noumenal and the phenomenal, reason and history, the eternal Logos and Je-

---

54. It is worth reminding ourselves that the strength of Arius's position was his philosophical argument against division within a single essence and the breakthrough achieved by the Cappadocians was to distinguish at this point between a simple essence and a plurality of persons. Barth does not seem troubled by the Arian argument nor entirely comfortable with the Cappadocian response. I may be misunderstanding Barth on this point, but he seems to be saying that to whatever extent there is plurality in the Godhead, it is within the unified essence and therefore secondary to it.

55. *CD* IV/1, 204.

56. Ibid., 129.

57. Ibid., 205.

58. See *CD* IV/1, 44, 184, 192-93, 195, 199-201, 204; IV/2, 44, 86, 100, 203.

59. Ibid.

sus of Nazareth, God's inner being and revelation.[60] This "disperses the last appearance of contingency, externality, incidentality and dispensability which can so easily seem to surround the historical aspect of the Christ-event in its narrower sense." In God's eternal election, heaven is "worldly" and eternity is "this human history."[61]

> Therefore the sovereignty of God dwells in his creaturely dependence as the Son of Man, the eternity of God in His temporal uniqueness, the omnipresence of God in His spatial limitation, the omnipotence of God in His weakness, the glory of God in His passibility and mortality, the holiness and righteousness of God in His adamic bondage and fleshliness — in short, the unity and totality of the divine which is His own original essence in His humanity.[62]

None of this sounds, to me at least, quite as dialectical as advertised. Rather, there is a synthesizing tendency — fueled, of course, by antitheses — in which one attribute is finally swallowed up in another. With this synthesis, however, Barth's claim that in entering time God does not surrender God's eternity seems somewhat vacuous. After all, is there really an eternity that is *not* eternalized time or a time that is not temporalized eternity according to his argument?

Neither the incarnation nor the decree to become incarnate (i.e., election) seems to be the logical basis for the existence of the Son (and thus, the Trinity). However, because the incarnation is *for God* an event in eternity (i.e., God's history), the Son "ceased to all eternity to be God only, receiving and having and maintaining to all eternity human essence as well."[63] This

---

60. *CD* IV/2, 31: "We have to do with the eternal beginning of all the ways and works of God when we have to do with Jesus Christ — even in His true humanity. This is not a 'contingent fact of history.' It is the historical event in which there took place in time that which was the purpose and resolve and will of God from all eternity and therefore before the being of all creation, before all time and history, that which is, therefore, above all time and history, and will be after them, so that the being of all creatures and their whole history in time follow this one resolve and will, and were and are and will be referred and related to them. The true humanity of Jesus Christ, as the humanity of the Son, was and is and will be the primary content of God's eternal election of grace, i.e., of the divine decision and action which are not preceded by any higher apart from the trinitarian happening of the life of God, but which all other divine decisions and actions follow, and to which they are subordinated. . . . For God's eternal election of grace is concretely the election of Jesus Christ." See ibid., 33-34.

61. Ibid., 35.

62. Ibid., 86.

63. Ibid., 100.

cannot fail to appear to us as a retroactive causality, but we must remember that for Barth (following a traditional Boethian concept of eternity), even that which takes place in time is, for God, an event in an eternal moment.[64]

In this context, Barth mentions the changes this involves from states to a twofold history, although he says nothing about the Trinity as constituted by election.[65] He says he has followed the Reformed in broad outline. "But there can be no doubt that in our departure from this whole conception [viz., from the two states to the twofold history of Jesus Christ] we have left even Reformed Christology far behind. We cannot expect to be praised for our 'orthodoxy' from any quarter."[66]

Barth has no problem affirming an "essentialist" ontology. God's essence "does not, of course, need any actualisation," but is rather "the creative ground of all other, i.e., all creaturely actualizations." In fact, he adds, "Even as the divine essence of the Son it did not need His incarnation, His existence as man and His action in unity with the man Jesus of Nazareth, to become actual."[67] And this is the fourth volume! Independent not only of the incarnation but of election, the Son would have been who he is. What did require actualization was the hypostatic union. "It is the divine essence determined and characterised by His act, by His existence not only in itself but also in human essence. And as such it has to *become* actual."[68]

With these general lines of argument, we can see more clearly what Barth intended by the programmatic series of questions with which I began my summary:

> How can a being be interpreted as an act, or an act as a being? How can God, or man, or both in their unity in Jesus Christ, be understood as history? How can humiliation also and at the same time be exaltation? How can it be said of a history which took place once that it takes place to-day, and that, having taken place once and taking place to-day, it will take place again?[69]

If Barth is simply stipulating that when we speak of the eternal Son, even before his actual birth in Bethlehem, we should not think of someone other

---

64. Ibid., 101; cf. II/1, 608f.
65. Ibid., 106ff.
66. Ibid., 106.
67. Ibid., 113-14.
68. Ibid., 114.
69. Ibid., 108.

than the one we meet at this manger, then it is a salutary reminder but hardly an innovation. As McCormack points out, Reformed orthodoxy also spoke of the *Logos asarkos* as the *Logos incarnandus*.[70]

It may be that Barth did not really think that these theologians could really mean it or it may be, if McCormack's interpretation is correct, that Barth intends something more radical. On the material point, McCormack argues that the priority of God's being over decision does not make sense of the incarnation.[71] However, I remain unconvinced by the argument for that claim. McCormack stipulates, "There is no state, no mode of being or existence above and prior to this eternal act of self-determination as substantialistic thinking would lead us to believe."[72] It does not seem to me that Barth is

70. McCormack, "Grace and Being," 94. Furthermore, the *pactum* in federal theology is always the primordial, eternal, original purpose, basis, and goal for God's works, both in the covenant of creation and in the covenant of grace. Christ fulfills the terms of the covenant of creation (works) in order to dispense the gifts of his victory in a covenant of grace. Thus, there is no dualism, unless by dualism he is referring to a duality of election and reprobation.

71. McCormack, "The Ontological Presuppositions of Barth's Doctrine of the Atonement," 357.

72. Ibid., 359. Whatever we make of Barth's view of election and Trinity, I suggest that the terms "substantialist" and "essentialist" should be more concretely defined. I do not deny that there are problems associated with these categories, as there are with any conceptual toolbox we may prefer to formulate in our witness to the unique event of God-with-us. However, these terms do not carry the freight often associated with them in modern theology and which even McCormack seems to assume in the contrast of "essentialism" and "actualism." He does provide a footnote in the direction of specifying what he means by this term: "It should be noted that the definitions offered here are intended to be broad enough to encompass a variety of ancient Greek philosophies and not be limited in its reference to any particular one of them. It is the tendency, the direction, of 'substantialist' thinking that I am interested in here" (McCormack, "The Ontological Presuppositions of Barth's Doctrine of the Atonement," 356n15). However, "the tendency, the direction, of 'substantialist' thinking" is precisely what is at issue. McCormack has not eliminated the category from his own formulation; therefore greater precision concerning the particular variety of substantialism he has in mind should be offered. "Substance," he says, "is a timeless idea" that is abstracted "from an individual's lived history" (ibid., 357). However, this reads too much into the term. "Substance" does not say anything about the lived history of its bearer, one way or the other. McCormack states, "The Greek category of 'substance' (in all of its various forms) makes the self-identical element in 'persons' (which is our interest here) to be complete in itself apart from, and prior to, the decisions, acts and relations by means of which the *life* of the person in question is constituted" (ibid). But once more, this assumes that "substance" carries more freight than it actually does. A further elaboration is required for that conclusion and, I suggest, must be elaborated from a Christian perspective. As I understand it, "essence" or "substance" (*ousia* and *substantia/esse*) simply refer to something or someone about whom cer-

willing to go that far. He still retains some distinction between God's being for-himself and his being for-us, which contradicts the claim that election is prior to Trinity, even as it also qualifies Barth's own claim to have closed any ontic gap between God's being and God's self-determination in relation to humanity. However, given his emphasis on their exact (univocal?) identity, it is not surprising that many of his students have eliminated such distinctions altogether.[73]

---

tain qualities can be predicated. Building on this heavily freighted definition of substance, McCormack adds concerning the tradition's use of it: "And divine 'essence,' on this view, is something hidden to human perception and, finally, unknowable" (McCormack, "Grace and Being," 98). However, this is Kantian rather than orthodox (in either the Catholic or Protestant sense). Reformed orthodoxy affirmed God's knowability, but through analogical rather than univocal predication. If Barth was trying to get beyond the "metaphysical" thinking of classical Christology, he was in this respect simply, as he himself said, "a child of the nineteenth century."

McCormack says, "Barth, too, knows of an 'essence' (a self-identical element) in God, but for him 'essence' is given in the act of electing and is, in fact, constituted by that eternal act" (98-99). Does this not require some qualification of the claim that Barth has transcended essentialism, much less metaphysics in general? In fact, according to John Webster,

> Barth's point is rather different [than Ritschl's]: what he rejects is not the legitimacy of theological talk of God's being, but the assertion that theological talk of God's being is to be governed by general ontological principles rather than by attention to the acts of God in which he presents himself to the world: "What God is as God, the divine individuality and characteristics, the *essentia* or 'essence' of God, is something which we shall encounter either at the place where God deals with us as Lord and Saviour or not at all" (II/1, p. 261). (John Webster, *Barth* [London and New York: Continuum, 2000], 84)

It is this that motivated Barth's appeal to the category of "event." However, it is not at all clear to me that Barth is replacing the concept of essence with that of event, as a sharp "essentialist" versus "actualist" typology might suggest.

73. Barth preserves the "essentialist" distinction (and priority) between being and election while affirming their identity as to content. Jesus Christ "is the free grace of God as not content simply to remain identical with the inward and eternal being of God, but operating *ad extra* in the ways and works of God. *And for this reason,* before Him and above Him and beside Him and apart from Him there is no election, no beginning, no decree, no Word of God" (*CD* II/2, 95; emphasis added). Election determines God in his relation to creation, not in relation to his own existence as such. Election is consistent with, not constitutive of, that being. For example, on page 100, he adds, "In respect of the whole attitude and being of God *ad extra,* in His relationship with the order created by Him, can there be anything higher or more distinctive and essential in God than His electing?" The Son "was not at the beginning of God, for God has indeed no beginning. But He was at the beginning of all things, *at the beginning of God's dealings with the reality which is distinct from Himself.* Jesus Christ was the

Michael S. Horton

In my view, the tradition upheld the "union without confusion or separation" more consistently than Barth. Although Barth's dazzling vistas reveal illuminating comparisons that are easily obscured by less dialectical thinking, he so identifies history and eternity, the immanent and economic Trinity, God's being and revelation, revelation and redemption, that the only question left is in which direction the assimilation occurs. As a result, critics like Emil Brunner and G. C. Berkouwer could accuse Barth of eliminating history, while McCormack describes Barth's mature ontology as a kind of "historicizing." Is it therefore surprising that Barth's students would be somewhat divided between a more "Kierkegaardian" and a more "Hegelian" Barth? This leads to the further question.

B. *"Before" and "After" in God's External Works*

Barth's revised supralapsarianism generates an innovative ontology that reaches its climax in the doctrine of reconciliation. It affects his understanding both of what traditionally is called the accomplishment and application of redemption, but which is for him the same event. I will flesh out my own

---

choice or election of God in respect of *this* reality. He was the election of God's grace *as directed towards man*" (ibid., 102; emphasis added). If McCormack's interpretation of Barth (or the logical consequence of Barth's ontology) is correct, then God's being-for-us (the economic Trinity) grounds his inner essence (the immanent Trinity), collapsing God's being into history. In this case, Barth is not only deepening an earlier emphasis but contradicting his clear distinction between freedom-from and freedom-for that undergirds his understanding of divine aseity. On page 103 Barth adds, in fact, precisely "because as the Son of the Father He has no need of any special election, we must add at once that He is the Son of God elected in His oneness with man, and in fulfilment of God's covenant with man. Primarily, then, electing is the divine determination of the existence of Jesus Christ, and election (being elected) the human." Election is not the movement of one mode of being towards another, but God's "movement towards man" (ibid., 104). "Jesus Christ is Himself God as the Son of God the Father and with God the Father the source of the Holy Spirit, united in one essence with the Father by the Holy Spirit. That is how He is God. He is God as He takes part in the event which constitutes the divine being" (IV/1, 129).

It would seem that even if Barth intends to make election constitutive of God's Trinity, he does not refer this original unity of decision/essence to the Father alone. Further, "the event which constitutes the divine being" here involves the begetting of the Son and the procession of the Spirit, not election, and there is no mention of differences with I/1. On the contrary, he follows this by referring us back to I/1, sections 8-12 (ibid., 204). "When we are dealing with Jesus Christ there is no question of a temporal event in which He began to be the Son of God" (ibid., 206). The question remaining, on McCormack's reading, is whether there is an eternal event that is logically prior to his being.

account of this development first in terms of its implications for the *historia salutis* and then the *ordo salutis.*

First, in terms of the historia salutis, *Barth replaces the traditional categories of two successive states (humiliation and exaltation) with a single event: a twofold history of Jesus of Nazareth.*

The world "below" (history as such) may be but a shadow of the world "above" (real history), but for Barth what happens in the shadows affects reality at its heart. Or does it? That is the question that I have not been able to resolve in my own thinking about Barth. Is the historical life of Jesus really a temporal event, contingent although decreed? Or is it merely the phenomenal image cast by the noumenal revolutions in eternity? Is the move from the two states to the twofold history, and the more general resistance to the notion that redemption involves successive historical events, driven by particularism (viz., Jesus Christ) or is the particular already defined on the basis of a universal metaphysical scheme after all?

Barth insists that he is not departing from the content of classical Reformed Christology, much less of Chalcedon, but only from its form.[74] Even the older Christology used terms like *unio, communio,* and *communicatio,* implying movement. "How, then, does it come about that in spite of these concepts there is that static conception, that calm, at the centre of the older doctrine of the person of Christ? . . . Can we say 'Jesus Christ,' and therefore 'God and man,' 'Creator and creature,' without making it clear that we are speaking of the One who exists in this way only in the act of God, and therefore the occurrence of this history?"[75] Am I correct in concluding that for Barth the history defined by God's act *(Urgeschichte)* is the sublation of ordinary time *(Historie)* in an eternal moment that knows only the simultaneity of a single event of humiliation and exaltation rather than a succession of events (or "states")?[76]

Again, I am inclined to think that part of the motivation behind the move from the two states to a twofold history is Barth's attempt to answer the problem of Lessing's ditch. My concern, however, is that his notion of contemporaneity is too facile a response; instead of *mediating* the real "dis-

74. *CD* IV/2, 107-9.

75. Ibid., 109. He adds on the same page, "When we say 'Jesus Christ,' and therefore 'God and man,' with reference to the One who is both we say the 'humiliation of the Son of God and the exaltation of the Son of Man.' This is what the older Christology was trying to state in its doctrine of the 'states' of Jesus Christ. But in relation to the One who is both can we really speak of two different and successive 'states,' or even of 'states' at all?"

76. See, for example, ibid., 109-10.

tance" between the "then and there" and "here and now" of the Christ-event, Barth tacks again toward *synthesis*. For example, I suspect that one of the reasons for the charge of a weak pneumatology is that instead of giving appropriate weight to Pentecost and the Spirit's work of making us sharers in the history of Jesus Christ, all of the stress falls on the incarnation and atonement.

That Christ's work is often detached from his person can hardly be dismissed, although Calvin and Reformed orthodoxy underscored this inseparability especially in their Eucharistic teaching (viz., that the benefits of Christ could not be received without also receiving the person of Christ himself). However, Barth's strategy is to return to his pattern of an eternal moment that penetrates history in punctiliar moments of revelation. In this way, everyone is Christ's contemporary — not because the *Spirit* has united them to Christ, but because the Christ-event itself is always past, present, and future.[77] The unity of this event blurs the distinct achievements of Christ in the succession of redemptive-historical events. Consequently, I fail to see how the traditional view is too static while Barth's is more dynamic. Not only are election, incarnation, and the atonement different ways of saying the same thing; the subsequent events in the economy of grace are merely revelatory rather than constituent elements of God's redemptive work.

If there is a monistic drift to Barth's system, it cannot simply be written off as a debt to certain philosophical presuppositions.[78] Rather, it appears to be driven by two converging undercurrents that are doctrinal in character: namely, supralapsarianism and universal election (which is to say the election of Jesus Christ). These undercurrents converge in the thesis that "Nothing can precede his grace, whether in eternity or time."[79] Hence, the substi-

---

77. Ibid., 111. Barth says that every Christian has lived at least implicitly on the premise that Christ's death and resurrection "as it took place then takes place to-day and will again take place to-morrow" (ibid., 112).

78. There is a place for analyzing philosophical presuppositions in any attempt to contextualize the thought of a given figure. Too often, however, critiques of Barth's system have concentrated on his philosophical presuppositions (viz., whether he is a Platonist, nominalist, Kantian/neo-Kantian, Hegelian, Kierkegaardian, etc.), insufficiently appreciating the theological presuppositions that guide his thinking. In reading Barth's *Romans*, one need not strain to pick up the heavy Danish accent, with Plato also lurking in the shadows. However, as his dogmatics progresses, we hear Barth's own voice and it is the voice of a theologian. Here and there (especially in volume 4, if I remember correctly) he is even at pains to point out that his formulation is not a paradox or a synthesis.

79. *CD* II/2, 79.

tution of a two-fold history of a single event in the place of the traditional "states" of humiliation and exaltation.

The question that such a thesis provokes, of course, is how the persons of the Trinity — prior to creation, much less the fall — can properly be said to exist in a relationship of fault to which grace and mercy would be an appropriate response. It would be one thing if Barth's definition of grace were something like a general goodness, kindness, and self-giving benevolence. In this case, my criticism would be that his definition of grace is too expansive to account for its radical character. However, Barth has exactly the right concept of grace. It is more than generosity: "Grace means redemption. . . . Grace, in fact, presupposes the existence of this opposition [i.e., sin]."[80] Barth is rigorously consistent: if grace is defined as mercy shown to those at fault — in opposition to God's freedom and love — and there is no historical creation in integrity or fall into sin that precede this redemptive grace in time, then there cannot have been any moment when the creation was not inherently opposed to God. However, for Barth it means that the very notion of "prior to the fall" has to be adjusted. "*In himself and as such* man will always do as Adam did in Gen. 3."[81]

Where Reformed theology opposed the medieval dualism of nature and grace with the antithesis of sin and grace, ironically it is Barth who seems to retrieve the notion that grace is necessary before the fall. However, his formulation is more radical precisely because he recognizes grace not only as supernatural elevation of nature (as in the medieval ontology), but as mercy shown to those at fault. In this view, history — in fact, creation itself — cannot be the theater in which a genuine drama unfolds, because creation, fall, and redemption are not successive events but different aspects of the same event. The genuine narrative structure of the Bible is threatened and with it the very dynamism that Barth recognized in federal theology even amid his criticisms.

Berkouwer justifiably concludes that with no real transition from wrath to grace, "Barth's revised supralapsarianism blocks the way to ascribing decisive significance to history."[82] But it also blocks the way to ascribing decisive significance to the human partner in the covenant, since, as Barth says, "the temporal, observable, psychologically visible individual" is incapable of "eternal election or rejection." "The individual is not more than the stage

---

80. *CD* II/1, 355.

81. *CD* II/2, 122; emphasis added.

82. G. C. Berkouwer, *The Triumph of Grace in the Theology of Karl Barth*, trans. H. R. Boer (Grand Rapids: Eerdmans, 1956), 256-58.

upon which election and rejection takes place in the freedom of men, that is to say, in the freedom of the individual who rests in God and is moved by Him — the stage can surely bear no further weight!"[83]

Barth complained that the emphasis in Reformed orthodoxy (federalism) on the outworking of eternal election in temporal stages and covenants in history was "a fatal historical moment," paving the way for the assimilation of Revelation (Christ) to historicism.[84] Cocceius "earned the dubious credit for having introduced the idea of a temporal history of salvation into history."[85] With creation folded into redemption and nature into grace, Barth cannot accept a covenantal relationship that is not upheld by redemptive grace. The question, then, is whether humanity has ever existed in a condition that did not presuppose guilt and transgression of the covenant. "To say man," Barth writes, "is to say creature and sin, and this means limitation and suffering."[86] Berkouwer points out (via H. van Oyen) that Platonism and mythical conceptions of an uncreated darkness and light creep in. "There is no room in Barth's thinking for preservation as a sustaining and keeping work of God apart from the idea of *redemption*. For this reason the distinction between pre-fall and post-fall plays no role in his theology."[87] For Barth, judges Berkouwer, "Creation did not take place through the Logos asarkos (the pre-incarnate Word), but through *Jesus of Nazareth*."[88]

The real issue is not whether we think of creation Christologically, Berkouwer observes, but whether we reject or accept "the 'step-wise' character of God's works."[89] Attempts to "construct a *synthesis* of these two elements [decree and history or creation and redemption] which will be perspicuous to our understanding" inevitably cause us to "fall into the abyss of

---

83. *CD* II/2, 347.

84. Karl Barth, *Göttingen Dogmatics* (27.III), cited by Daniel L. Migliore, "Karl Barth's First Lectures in Dogmatics," an introduction to Karl Barth's *Göttingen Dogmatics: Instruction in the Christian Religion*, vol. 1, ed. Hannelotte Reiffen, trans. Geoffrey W. Bromiley (Grand Rapids: Eerdmans, 1991), xxxviii.

85. Karl Barth, *The Theology of the Reformed Confessions (1923)*, trans. Darrell L. Guder and Judith J. Guder (Louisville, KY: Westminster John Knox, 2002), 134. Interestingly, both Moltmann and Pannenberg refer to Cocceius and the federal theologians as precursors of their more historically oriented program. Once again this causes me to wonder whether some of Barth's students adopt his synthesis of eternity and time but reverse the direction: assimilating eternity to time, the immanent to the economic Trinity, etc.

86. *CD* IV/1, 131.

87. Berkouwer, *The Triumph of Grace*, 247.

88. Ibid., 250.

89. Ibid., 252.

either eternalizing God's works or historicizing them" — either monism or dualism.[90] A *"transition* from wrath to grace *in history* has already been excluded" and "wrath is no more than 'the form of grace.'"[91] Hence, the "ontological impossibility" of sin.[92] His supralapsarianism is motivated by this reaction against the "step-wise" character of God's works.[93]

For his own part, Barth was convinced that federal theology sowed the seeds of historicism.[94] "A theology of biblical history was now replaced by a theology of biblical histories."[95] Then we get (especially with Zacharias Ursinus) the twofold covenants: works and grace.[96]

From these criticisms we can discern at least some of the motives for Barth's stress on unity. One God, one covenant in which law is subsumed under gospel, one subject of electing grace, one eternal history of God actualized in one event: unity obtains a controlling status in Barth's dogmatics, which is perhaps one reason why it has been characterized as "Christian monism" and Barth himself had so little trouble identifying with the "biblical-theocentric monism" of seventeenth-century supralapsarianism.[97] God's movement toward the world is constituted by the election of grace, not creation. If election is the beginning of all God's works and ways with respect to humanity, however, there can be no other covenants or history prior to God's gracious redemption.

With its affirmation of a covenant of redemption *(pactum salutis),* federal theology even drew Christology and election into an inextricable connection. So why would Barth reject this move? Again, it is his attraction toward the one over the many:

> Can we really think of the first and second persons of the triune Godhead as two divine subjects and therefore as two legal subjects who can have dealings and enter into obligations one with another? This is mythology, for which there is no place in a right understanding of the doctrine of the Trinity as the doctrine of the three modes of being of the one God, which

90. Ibid., 253.
91. Ibid.
92. Ibid.
93. Ibid., 255.
94. Ibid.
95. Ibid., 58.
96. Ibid., 59. Strictly speaking, however, this two-covenant pattern can be found in Irenaeus and Augustine among others, as well as in Calvin — but that is for another day.
97. *CD* II/2, 135.

is how it was understood and presented in Reformed orthodoxy itself. God is one God, . . . the only subject, . . . the one subject.[98]

He adds, somewhat cryptically, "The thought of a purely inter-trinitarian decision as the eternal basis of the covenant of grace may be found both sublime and uplifting. But it is definitely much too uplifting and sublime to be a Christian thought. What we have to do with is not a relationship of God with Himself" — once again indicating his own reticence to speak of a relationship *between* the persons — "but the basis of a relationship between God and man."[99] It is not clear what Barth means by this criticism, since he was aware that federal theology articulated not only an intratrinitarian covenant but the divine-human covenants of creation and grace in which that primordial pact was executed. Not one stone is left upon another: all three covenants that form the architecture of Reformed theology are assimilated to a single covenant of grace — and one in which there is really no real progression in history from promise to fulfillment.

In an earlier phase, when he still seems to have been thinking in fairly "Kierkegaardian" terms about the relation of eternity *(Urgeschichte)* and time *(Historie)*, Barth would say that it is "not history but truth" that is at issue in revelation.[100] "Biblical history in the Old and New Testament is not really history at all, but seen from above is a series of free divine acts and seen from below a series of fruitless attempts to undertake something in itself impossible."[101] "The resurrection of Christ, or his second coming, *which is the same*

98. *CD* IV/1, 65.

99. Ibid., 66.

100. Barth, *The Word of God and the Word of Man*, 66. This is especially true when Barth himself in 1935, reflecting on the *Römerbrief*, conceded, "I had at that time no other desire than simply to set forth the meaning of Paul's letter to the Romans. This I did partly in a remarkable wrapping of Kantian and Platonic conceptions" (quoted in Berkouwer, *The Triumph of Grace*, 21n29). "This corresponds to the fact that in the foreword of the second edition of the *Römerbrief* Barth speaks about 'the better understanding of the real orientation of the ideas of Plato and Kant for which I am indebted to the writings of my brother, Heinrich Barth,' p. vii. Cf. also the self-criticism in the later volumes of the KD" (ibid., 21). Early on, there were charges of nominalism — even, for Brunner, "unheard of theological nominalism." Regardless of whether Barth fully answered these charges, it is sometimes difficult to overlook the similarities between his actualism and the occasionalism of Nicholas Malebranche, which Jonathan Edwards elaborated within a Platonic scheme. How is it that so many of Barth's interpreters, particularly critics, could only see *Historie* vanishing before *Geschichte*, while McCormack sees it as "Barthian historicizing" ("Grace and Being," 93) — different, of course, from nineteenth-century historicizing, but historicizing nonetheless?

101. Barth, *The Word of God and the Word of Man*, 72.

thing, is not a historical event."[102] Revelation occurs in an "eternal Moment" with no extension in time, which "God gives simultaneously to his Biblical witnesses and to those who accept their witness."[103] "Adam" represents a movement from an original relation of divine grace and human obedience to rebellion, whereas Jesus Christ brings about, as McCormack puts it, "a return to the 'Origin' (reconciliation). These two movements are not to be conceived of as sequential, but rather as parallel and simultaneous."[104]

In the *Church Dogmatics*, the only difference (although it is significant) is that Barth now speaks of truth and history, eternity and time, as more of a unity. Yet this unity is still defined by *Urgeschichte* — history as *this* history, that is, a completed history from the beginning. Or, as Eberhard Jüngel expresses it, "From the very beginning it is true that Jesus is victor."[105]

George Hunsinger reminds us that Berkouwer criticized Barth for "eternalizing" time (a separation finally leading to monism), while Robert Jenson extrapolates from Barth in the direction of a "historicizing" of eternity.[106] However, I wonder if both moves are entirely possible readings of Barth's own intentions: the Platonic and Hegelian moves together. Jenson insists that "the event of Jesus Christ's life, because it is the central event in the life of the eternal God, is the eternal presupposition of all else that happens."[107] If God's being is in act, and election is "the eternal presupposition of all else that happens," then again it would seem a small step to affirm with McCormack that the Trinity itself is constituted by election.

As we have seen, Brunner and Berkouwer recognized early on that Barth's all-encompassing re-formulation of election entailed a radical revision of theology. Barth speaks of "Jesus the eternally Elect Man," "the pre-existing God-Man, who, as such, is the eternal ground of all election," but Brunner pointedly asserts, "No special proof is required to show that the Bible contains no such doctrine, nor that no theory of this kind has ever been formulated by any theologian." If the eternal "existence of the God-Man were a fact, then the Incarnation would no longer be an *Event* at all; no longer would it be the great miracle of Christmas."[108] In fact, Brunner anticipates McCormack's thesis, though fearful of its implications:

102. Ibid., 90; emphasis added.
103. Ibid., 244.
104. McCormack, *Karl Barth's Critically Realistic Dialectical Theology*, 147.
105. Eberhard Jüngel, *God's Being Is in Becoming* (Edinburgh: T. & T. Clark, 2001), 94.
106. Hunsinger, *How To Read Karl Barth*, 15-16.
107. Ibid., 69, citing Jenson.
108. Brunner, *The Christian Doctrine of God, Vol. 1*, 347.

In the New Testament the new element is the fact that the eternal Son of God became Man, and that henceforth through His Resurrection and Ascension, in Him humanity has received a share in the heavenly glory; yet in this view of Barth's, all this is now anticipated, as it were, torn out of the sphere of history, and set within the pre-temporal sphere, in the pre-existence of the Logos. The results of this new truth would be extraordinary; fortunately Barth does not attempt to deduce them. The idea of the pre-existent Divine Human is an *ad hoc* artificial theory of the theological thinker, who can only carry through his argument that the Man Jesus is the Only Elect Human being by means of this theory.[109]

His "objectivism," Brunner judges, is an a priori construct that evades clear exegesis.[110]

Hence the transition from unbelief to faith is not the transition from "being-lost" to "being-saved." This turning-point does not exist, since it is no longer possible to be lost. But if we look at this view more closely, we see also that the turning-point in the historical Event is no real turning-point at all; for Election means that everything has already taken place in the sphere of pre-existence.[111]

Throughout II/1, the event of revelation (i.e., Jesus Christ) is past, present, and future. But this does not seem to require further revelation or revelatory (much less saving) events. God not only enters time; in Jesus Christ eternity becomes time, "permitting created time to become and be the form of His eternity. . . . He raises time to a form of His eternal being."[112] While this thesis at first appears to valorize history, it is only at the cost of history becoming something else.

I am unable to see how Barth's substitution of a single event for a series of events drawn together into a unity yields a more genuinely historical or dynamic Christological paradigm. Especially in volume 4, the incarnation and the cross form the real event of reconciliation while the resurrection, ascension, and parousia merely disclose and confirm for us that objective reality. Jesus Christ's resurrection and ascension are merely the first, and his return in glory the second, "universal, definitive revelation of that which He

---

109. Ibid.
110. Ibid., 349-50.
111. Ibid., 351.
112. *CD* II/1, 616.

has already done, and never ceased to do, in His existence as the Son of God and Son of Man."[113]

Where is Jesus-history to go after Golgotha? Surely it is not to be dissolved into the history of the church, as dominant Roman Catholic and neo-Protestant theologies had argued. Barth's incisive criticism of this assimilation of Christology to ecclesiology may even be more relevant to contemporary trends than it was in his own day. Nevertheless, for Barth, Jesus-history is finished at the cross.[114] The resurrection, Pentecost, and parousia do not represent new events arising out of Christ's life and death, but revelation, confirmation, and testimony. They fall on the "witness" side of Barth's revelation-attestation divide. He routinely speaks of God's electing grace receiving its "historical fulfilment in the incarnation" and "its revelation in the resurrection and ascension of Jesus Christ."[115]

It is not what these events accomplish in the further unfolding of redemptive history, but what they reveal about the single event that has happened, is happening, and will always happen. There is nothing left to be fulfilled beyond this history of Christ's incarnation and atonement.

> It does not need to be transcended or augmented by new qualities or further developments. The humiliation of God and the exaltation of man as they took place in Him are the completed fulfilment of the covenant, the completed reconciliation of the world with God. His being as such (if we may be permitted this abstraction for a moment) was and is the end of the old and the beginning of the new form of this world *even without His resurrection and ascension.* He did not and does not lack anything in Himself. What was lacking was only the men to see and hear it as the work and Word of God — the praise and thanksgiving and obedience of their thoughts and words and works. . . . It is here that His resurrection and ascension came in, and still come in.[116]

Thus, everything that happens on this side of Golgotha is necessary for human response, but not for human salvation per se. "His resurrection and ascension were simply the authentic communication and proclamation of the

---

113. *CD* IV/2, 100.

114. On this point and its implications, see Douglas Farrow, *Ascension and Ecclesia: On the Significance of the Doctrine of the Ascension for Ecclesiology and Christian Cosmology* (Edinburgh: T. & T. Clark, 1999), esp. 229-54.

115. *CD* IV/2, 107-9. See ibid., 118, 133, 140-41.

116. Ibid., 133; emphasis added.

perfect act of redemption once for all accomplished in His previous existence and history, of the Word of salvation once for all spoken in Him."[117] The resurrection simply reveals "God's decision concerning the *cross*."[118] It ensures that this event of Golgotha becomes "eternal history . . . and [is] therefore taking place here and now as it did then."[119] Even his return in glory "will still be the same revelation."[120]

Barth's doctrine of reconciliation offers tremendous insight into Christ as the redeemer, the vicarious substitute, the elder brother who is exalted and the Son of God who is humiliated for our sakes, but is he the first-fruits of those who sleep? Do the ascension, Pentecost, and Christ's return constitute anything *new* in redemptive history? Hans Urs von Balthasar spoke of Barth evidencing "a dynamic and actualist theopanism, which we define as a monism of beginning and end (protology and eschatology)," drawing on Idealist categories.[121] "Too much in Barth gives the impression that nothing much really *happens* in his theology of event and history, because everything has already happened in eternity."[122] My own analysis leads me to the same conclusions. The "step-wise" character of the divine economy gives to the biblical narrative a genuine movement with genuine twists and turns along the way. Jesus scolds his followers not for failing to recognize the simultaneity of his humiliation and exaltation, but for failing to realize that he first had to suffer and then enter into his glory (Lk. 9:28-45; 24:26; Phil. 2; 1 Pet. 1:11; Heb. 1:3ff., 2:9-10). The transition is historical, not noetic.

Second, in terms of the ordo salutis, *the application of redemption in our temporal history is assimilated to the accomplishment of redemption in the eternal time of the cross.* Just as Christ's humiliation and exaltation are two aspects of a single event rather than distinct "states" in temporal succession, the very notion of an *ordo salutis* becomes untenable. In fact, the application of redemption itself is absorbed into the atonement. Barth says, "As we now turn [from reconciliation and justification] to consider sanctification in and for itself, we are not dealing with a second divine action which either takes place simultaneously with it, or precedes or follows it in time. The action of God in His reconciliation of the world with Himself in Jesus Christ is uni-

---

117. Ibid.

118. *CD* IV/1, 309; emphasis added.

119. Ibid., 313.

120. Ibid., 142.

121. Hans Urs von Balthasar, *The Theology of Karl Barth: Exposition and Interpretation*, trans. Edward T. Oakes, S.J. (San Francisco: Ignatius Press, 1992), 94.

122. Ibid., 371.

tary."[123] In the humiliation and exaltation of Christ, humanity is both justified and sanctified.[124] "A psychologistic pragmatics in soteriology corresponded to the historicist pragmatics of Christology."[125] According to Barth (and I do not think he is wide of the mark on this point), pietism, as the beginning of the Enlightenment, turned this into an elaborate and untheological psychologism.[126] At the same time, Barth is also reacting against the historicism illustrated by Lessing's "ditch." The breach between "then and now" arose because of this forgetfulness of the unity of reconciliation in Christ's twofold history, he says. "He is the same there and then as He is here and now. He is the one living Lord in whom all things have occurred, and do and will occur, for all."[127]

However, it is not only pietism that is threatened by Barth's marginalization of the Spirit's application of redemption, but any notion of creaturely "means of grace."[128] This makes sense, however, in the light of his wider argument. Barth does have a duality; instead of redemption *accomplished* and *applied,* however, his duality is between *redemption* and *attestation* or *event* and *recognition.* So if the resurrection, the ascension, Pentecost,

---

123. *CD* IV/2, 501.

124. Ibid., 502.

125. Ibid. See also ibid., 507: "We presuppose that there is no such order in the temporal sense. The *simul* of the one redemptive act of God in Jesus Christ cannot be split up into a temporal sequence, and in this way psychologised. . . . No, they both take place simultaneously and together, just as the living Jesus Christ, in whom they both take place and are effective, is simultaneously and together true God and true man, the Humiliated and the Exalted."

126. Ibid., 502. Eberhard Busch points us to Barth's sharp reaction to a revivalist whose sermons delineated the various stages of conversion. See Busch, *Karl Barth and the Pietists,* trans. Daniel W. Bloesch (Downers Grove: InterVarsity Press, 2004), esp. 36-39.

127. *CD* IV/2, 503.

128. There is no such thing as "means of grace" (*CD* IV/4, 106, 129-30, etc.; see IV/3.2, 756, 783, 790, 843-901). The sacraments (oddly, unlike preaching) stand on the side of the church's work and witness and not on the divine side of saving events. "The confession of Christians, their suffering, their repentance, their prayer, their humility, their works, baptism, too, and the Lord's Supper can and should attest this event but only attest it." Jesus Christ is the one sacrament (IV/1, 296). "He is He, and His work is His work, standing over against all Christian action, including Christian faith and Christian baptism" (IV/4, 88). Not even the humanity of Christ is a direct revelation of God, despite its union with the Logos. Nevertheless, insofar as his deity is unveiled through the veil of his humanity, this alone attains the status of a sacrament (II/1, 53). The whole of the final fragment of the *Church Dogmatics* follows a contrast between the Spirit's work and the purely human response of water baptism.

and the parousia lie on the attestation/recognition rather than redemption/ event side of the line, it only follows that pneumatology, preaching, and sacraments can only fall on the "witness" side as well. Water baptism, Barth argues, is merely a human act of obedient answering; it is a response to the act of God, but it is not itself a divine action or means of grace.[129] No wonder there is a weak concept of mediation; in the eternal moment, there is no longer any "distance" to be traversed. We are contemporaries of Jesus of Nazareth. Conversion, justification, sanctification, and calling have already occurred for every person, even if one is not subjectively aware of it.[130] This is not to suggest, as is commonly done, that Barth does not take history seriously. The atonement is history. "To try to grasp it as supra-historical or non-historical truth is not to grasp it at all." Yet it is "the very special history of God with man." Indeed, "The atonement takes precedence over all other history."[131]

Third, as a logical corollary of the moves that Barth has made thus far, law is assimilated to gospel. At least at the theological level, it seems to me that the main reason that Barth resists talk of "before" and "after" in such matters is that this would open up a space for the God-world relationship that is logically prior to grace. As we have seen, it is a basic presupposition of Barth's revised supralapsarianism that law cannot come before gospel. This follows from the correlative assimilations of creation to redemption, and nature to grace. Even at the expense of calling into question a state of original integrity, law *cannot* precede gospel. Rather, the law is in the gospel, God's holiness is in his grace, his wrath is in his love, Barth says, adding, "God is holy because His grace judges and His judgment is gracious."[132] Every divine No always turns out to be a Yes after all. One meets one synthesis after another. So while the tendency of Rome and neo-Protestantism is to assimilate gospel to law, Barth assimilates law to gospel. Yet the result is the same: faith not only leads to obedience but *is* obedience. In fact, he adds, "We have already pointed out more than once the unity of the Gospel with the Law, and the character of faith as penitence."[133]

Berkouwer pointed to Hendrikus Berkhof's concern that the law in its accusing function had been eclipsed in contemporary preaching largely because of Barth's "conception of the relationship between gospel and law."

129. See the references in the previous footnote.
130. *CD* IV/1, 148.
131. Ibid., 157.
132. *CD* II/1, 363.
133. Ibid., 391.

This is not entirely fair, since for Barth the just sentence of the law and divine wrath are fully acknowledged. "This is no answer to Berkhof's criticism, however, because, according to Barth, this accusing function belongs exclusively to the law *as form of* the gospel. This is really the point at issue in Barth's inversion of the traditional order."[134] There can be no law prior to or apart from gospel because there is nothing prior to or apart from gospel. There is no "law of nature" alongside God's "word of grace." "Ethics is the 'ethics of grace' or it is no theological ethics."[135] "This priority of the law to the gospel which comes to such clear expression in Question 9 of the Heidelberg Catechism," says Berkouwer, "is wholly wanting in Barth's view of the law. . . . There is therefore also no room in Barth's conception for the view that man was placed under the law of the good Creator before the fall into sin and unrighteousness." There simply is no place for different epochs in redemptive history. His revised supralapsarianism will not allow him to say anything other than this: that whatever is between God and creatures, it always has been.[136] Consequently, punitive suffering is eliminated from Christ's work, since wrath is a form of grace.[137] Thus all of the syntheses that we have met along the way meet finally in the gracious election of Jesus Christ and in him all of humanity.

As with his changes with respect to the historical economy (the achievement of redemption), I fail to see how Barth's rejection of "before" and "after" in the *ordo salutis* (the application of redemption) represents the triumph of a dynamic over an ostensibly static soteriology. With Berkouwer and Brunner, I wonder how Barth can dismiss the emphasis that we find especially in the epistles on the transition from death to life, condemnation "under the law" to justification "under grace," wrath to grace, the dominion of the flesh to the dominion of the Spirit. The apostle explicitly says that we are no longer under law and wrath (though we once were), but under grace through faith in Christ. Granted, God's eternity is different from our temporal existence, but the relation appears to be equivocal rather than analogical in Barth's thinking. Eternally, the Son has been incarnate and has won our redemption. Just as the exaltation does not follow the humiliation of Christ,

---

134. Berkouwer, *The Triumph of Grace*, 321.

135. Ibid., 323.

136. Ibid., 324. "'God is humble and man is still proud!' Augustine exclaimed. One might be inclined to describe Barth's conception of the relationship between gospel and law, and of the proclamation of election, as the consciously theopaschitic systematization of this word of Augustine" (ibid., 326).

137. Berkouwer, *The Triumph of Grace*, 257.

sanctification does not follow justification. At the end of the day, our life and history seem to be merely a parable or an allegorical shadow of the real life and history of Jesus Christ.[138]

Therefore, Barth would not dispute the charge that in his dogmatics there is no real historical transition from wrath to grace. It is only in their pride that human beings want and therefore have a wrathful God (IV/1, 539), but it is subjective — an "as if," not reality but, like Adam, a shadow, the impossible possibility: "on the left hand" (541), the No that is finally overwhelmed by the Yes (543), the Whence that is overruled by the Whither (545), "a twofold but one" history of God with humanity (545). The self refusing this electing and reconciling grace is, like Adam, "a shadow, a ghost" in contrast to the self defined by Christ — "a real existence" (568). And this self is the same person: the *simul iustus et peccator* (576).

One reason I believe why Barth has often been accused of "Christomonism" is that everything is not only related to Christology but nearly merges into it. In fact, Christomonism subverts Christocentrism. In traditional Reformed theology, "Christ the Mediator" occupied a critical — even central — role in the system. However, when Christology swallows the horizon, Christ is no longer central; he is the whole picture. He is not the mediator through whom, in whom, by whom, and for whom all things were created, are redeemed, and will be renewed, but the Creator *simpliciter,* the only electing God and the only elected human. Brunner complains rather sharply, "It is the same erroneous Christ-Monism which we have met already in the doctrine of the Trinity."[139] Wrath is not a form of grace. According to the NT, only the elect are "in Christ" and they are "those who believe." The result of Barth's view is that "the possibility of being finally lost is eliminated."[140] It mistakes human responsibility for synergism.[141]

Besides ignoring the conditions in scripture, Brunner suggests that Barth eliminates "the vital tension, based on the dialectic of God's Holiness and Love, by means of a monistic *schema.*"[142] We do indeed need to start

---

138. The key "twofold history" versus "two states" passage may be found in *CD* IV/1, 132-38.

139. Brunner, *The Christian Doctrine of God,* 315.

140. Ibid., 315.

141. Ibid., 316.

142. Ibid., 334, 336. Brunner includes the doctrine of the double decree in this charge, although he fails to distinguish infralapsarian from supralapsarian interpretations. The former, I suggest, is not liable to this charge. In rejecting the "ruthless" doctrine of double predestination, Brunner simply identifies the conditional covenant with Israel with the uncon-

with the Trinity, but a view that realizes that "the Father and the Son are One, and yet not one." Similarly, God's holiness and love, "what God is in Himself" and "that which He is for us," election and revelation, converge "in Jesus Christ, in faith." "But outside of Jesus Christ, outside of faith, God's Holiness is not the same as His Love, but *there* it is His wrath; *there* what God is 'in Himself' is not the same as that which He is 'for us,' *there* it is the unfathomable, impenetrable mystery of the *'nuda majestas'; there* is no election, but rejection, judgment, condemnation. . . ."[143] Apostolic preaching in the New Testament announces forgiveness for all who believe, but it also warns that apart from faith there is the fearful expectation of wrath, not merely a lack of awareness of being saved.

Finally, it is significant that just as Barth backed away from eliminating all vestiges of "essentialism" in favor of actualism, he stopped short of embracing the doctrine of universal salvation (apokatastasis). Although all of humanity is elect in Christ, it would be an affront to God's sovereign freedom to assert that each and every person will finally be saved.[144] But does this not subvert Barth's intentions to close the ontic gap between God's being-in-himself and his being-for-us, just as he stopped short of making the incarnation necessary to God's being? Berkouwer judges that "Barth's preference for the supralapsarian view is nothing else than the reverse side of the ontological impossibility of sin."[145]

So there is still the possibility that either (a) not all are in Christ or (b) election and reconciliation fail to achieve what Barth has assured us they did achieve. The shadow remains. In fact, Barth remained agnostic concerning the future destiny of Judas Iscariot. Objectivism does not have the last word after all. Not only is there the anxiety over whether one is elect, which Barth attributes to Reformed orthodoxy, but now there is the possibility that despite being chosen, redeemed, called, justified, and sanctified, one may not at last be glorified but will be reprobate after all. If it is even possible for

---

ditional election in Christ. It is difficult to resist the impression that for Brunner election is self-selection by faith (ibid., 319). Although grace is always prevenient, human decision determines who is elect and who is not: the elect are those who believe and the non-elect are those who reject the gospel (319-20). At the end of the day, Brunner's doctrine of predestination seems basically Arminian (viz., election determined by faith), so I am not suggesting that we replace Barth's formulation with Brunner's. Nevertheless, I share the concerns he raises in these citations.

143. Ibid., 337. Brunner adds (in my concluded ellipsis), ". . . but no eternal decree."
144. *CD* II/2, 295, 417-18, 475-76.
145. Berkouwer, *The Triumph of Grace*, 256; cf. 117n45.

God's electing purpose to fail in one instance, then the specter of subjectivity, not to mention the ontological gap between God's being and will, rushes in with a vengeance.

For Calvin and Reformed orthodoxy, there is no ultimate gap between the immanent and economic Trinity (or *deus in se* and *deus pro nobis*). Calvin sharply rejected the nominalist idea of a God of arbitrary will and power behind or above the God revealed in Jesus Christ.[146] The hidden God is not different from the revealed God: all of the elect will be saved, without the possibility of one being lost. At the same time, the well-meant summons of the external Word to repent and believe the gospel is universal. That many do in fact embrace Christ is a miracle of God's electing grace, realized in history. Thus, there is no place for the ontological or epistemological cleavage that worries Barth, although his own reticence to eliminate any question of whether God's electing grace perfectly coincides with the outcome of salvation for everyone elected leaves a question mark over that question.

Conclusion

According to Hunsinger, Barth engages in "a dialectical strategy of juxtaposition."[147] John Webster refers to "Barth's lifelong tendency to think in terms of contrasts rather than correlations."[148] "As Barth strove to recover God's entire originality over against human nostrification of the divine, the threat of dualism certainly loomed over him," although sometimes simply pointing out differences is mistaken for dualism.[149] Yet whatever the real dangers of dualism, I have argued that it is frequently in the service of what von Balthasar calls his "actualistic monism."[150] In many cases — crucial to Barth's entire thought — we have seen that Barth's contrasts finally yield syntheses.

Like classical Reformed theology, Barth's system is logically coherent. However, unlike the former, the latter's consistency seems more to me like something deduced from a central dogma than like a series of sub-plots that display an over-arching plot centering on Christ. Barth *presupposes* that the

---

146. Calvin, *Institutes*, 3.23.2.

147. George Hunsinger, "Karl Barth's Christology," in *The Cambridge Companion to Karl Barth*, ed. John Webster (Cambridge: Cambridge University Press, 2000), 132.

148. Webster, *Karl Barth*, 28.

149. Ibid., 44.

150. Von Balthasar, *The Theology of Karl Barth*, 74, 79, 81, 99, 105, 108, 109, 140.

electing will of the single Subject, revealed in the single event of one covenant, executed in the one history that is eternal, encompasses every person. But what if God's revelation in Christ, known in scripture, contradicts even one of these theses?

Too one-sidedly focused on critique, my remarks have not adequately reflected my immense appreciation for the insights I have gleaned from Barth, especially his fourth volume. I have concentrated on areas of divergence mainly in the interest of having them tested — even refuted — by the likes of my esteemed interlocutors in this volume and in the hope that has already been expressed to me that this is only the beginning of a fruitful conversation. The Reformed tradition is unfinished, but that very fact demonstrates that it is still very much alive. Preparing his Göttingen lectures each day, Barth discovered that vitality. To some, his revisions represent improvement, to others declension. Regardless of where we are on that spectrum, we can still follow his own recommendation to draw more deeply from these older wells as together we seek to recover from what John Webster has called the "nostrification" of the gospel, in this land that Bonhoeffer finely referred to as "Protestantism without the Reformation."[151]

---

151. Dietrich Bonhoeffer, "Protestantism without the Reformation," in *No Rusty Swords: Letters, Lectures and Notes, 1928-1936*, ed. Edwin H. Robertson, trans. Edwin H. Robertson and John Bowden (London: Collins, 1965), 92-118.

History in Harmony: Karl Barth on the Hypostatic Union

Adam Neder

Given the central importance of Christology in Barth's theology as a whole, one would expect his most detailed description of the hypostatic union (*Church Dogmatics* IV/2, 36-116) to have been thoroughly examined and commented upon. Oddly enough, it hasn't.[1] And this despite the fact that it constitutes "the decisive center" of the Christology that opens *Church Dogmatics* IV/2, and from which his treatments in that volume of sin, sanctification, ecclesiology, and Christian love all proceed.[2] Barth himself could not have been clearer about the significance of this material.

> . . . I had to give particularly careful expression to the christological section which stands at the head and contains the whole *in nuce,* speaking as it does of the humanity of Jesus Christ. I cannot advise anyone to skip it either as a whole or in part in order to rush on as quickly as possible to what is said about sanctification, etc. For it is there — and this is true of

---

1. The lone exception in English is Bruce McCormack's essay "Karl Barth's Historicized Christology: Just How 'Chalcedonian' Is It?" (*Orthodox and Modern: Studies in the Theology of Karl Barth* [Grand Rapids: Baker Academic, 2008], 201-34) which addresses some of the themes that I will treat in this essay. For treatments of Barth's Christology in general, see George Hunsinger, "Karl Barth's Christology: Its Basic Chalcedonian Character," in *Disruptive Grace: Studies in the Theology of Karl Barth* (Grand Rapids: Eerdmans, 2000), 131-47; John Thompson, *Christ in Perspective: Christological Perspectives in the Theology of Karl Barth* (Grand Rapids: Eerdmans, 1978).

2. *CD* IV/2, 36.

every aspect — that the decisions are made. There is no legitimate way to an understanding of the Christian life than that which we enter there. As I see it, it is by the extent to which I have correctly described this that the book is to be judged.[3]

But arriving at such judgment is far from straightforward. Relatively clear on the surface, the material becomes elusive as one presses for greater precision regarding the details of Barth's view. Barth narrates the subject matter with such freedom of expression, from so many different angles, and with such a variety of accents and emphases, that one could easily draw the conclusion that he is attempting to solve the perennially thorny issues surrounding two natures Christology by arguing for all the basic positions at once. And in fact, there is some truth in the charge. But the root cause of the argument's elusiveness is actually located elsewhere — in Barth's audacious attempt, as he puts it, "to re-translate that whole phenomenology [of the two natures doctrine] into the sphere of a history."[4] The slipperiness of the prose is merely symptomatic of this massive translation project.

This essay elucidates the distinctive elements and emphases of Barth's doctrine of the hypostatic union through a close examination of his view of the *communio naturarum* — the mutual participation of the divine and human natures in God the Son. In order to do this, however, it will first be necessary to present the key Christological moves that he makes in *CD* IV/1, especially his claim that Jesus Christ is his history. For apart from an awareness of this material, the Christology of *CD* IV/2 cannot be understood or appreciated. Thus the essay is divided into two primary parts: first, a discussion of the Christology of *CD* IV/1, then a treatment of the doctrine of the hypostatic union in *CD* IV/2. I will conclude with a few questions about some of the more perplexing aspects of Barth's Christology.

Before moving through this material, however, for the purposes of this collection, I would like to briefly anticipate and address a well-worn criticism of Barth's project that has been especially influential in evangelical circles. According to critics such as Cornelius van Til, Barth's theology in general, and his Christology in particular, constitute an elaborate and nefarious ruse. By camouflaging his Christology in traditional language, Barth is pretending to be orthodox when in fact he is anything but.[5] In response to this

3. Ibid., x.
4. Ibid., 106.
5. Thus, the "danger is . . . that orthodox Christians, in spite of much experience with camouflage, will once more permit the wolf to enter their home and that to their own de-

accusation, allow me to mention just a few things. First, rather than conceal-
ing his differences with traditional dogmas, Barth went out of his way to
highlight and clarify precisely where he agreed and disagreed with them. As
we shall see, one of the more conspicuous features of his Christology is the
way he repeatedly (and often in detail) situates his position vis-à-vis Lutheran and Reformed formulations. In fact, not only did Barth draw attention to his innovations, he also made it perfectly clear that he did not expect
to be praised for his orthodoxy "from any quarter."[6] Thus, the charge of du-
plicity is unfair. Second, and more important, while fully conversant with
and significantly indebted to the vast resources of the church's reflection on
the person and work of Christ, Barth regarded himself to be *primarily* accountable to Holy Scripture, not church dogma, and thus asked that his
Christology be judged, above all, by its faithfulness to the New Testament
presentation of the living Lord Jesus Christ. Thus, one regularly finds Barth
justifying a Christological innovation with the argument that the New Testament depiction of Christ requires it (or something like it) and that the older
categories are inadequate to bear witness to this or that aspect of his existence. In other words, and quite simply, Barth understood himself to be free
to do *evangelical* theology — free, as he put it, to begin again at the beginning. And this approach, it seems to me, is one that evangelicals have every
reason to regard with sympathy rather than suspicion.

Part One

In *CD* IV/1, Barth approaches Jesus Christ's fulfillment of the covenant of
grace, the reconciliation of God and humanity in him, from the standpoint
of the self-humiliation of the Son of God. His most basic point throughout
this material, one that will emerge centrally in his treatment of the
hypostatic union in *CD* IV/2, is that Jesus Christ *is* his history. Jesus Christ,
Barth writes,

> is a being, but a being in a history. The gracious God is in this history, so is
> reconciled man, so are both in their unity. And what takes place in this
> history, and therefore in the being of Jesus Christ as such, is atonement.

---

struction" (Cornelius Van Til, *The New Modernism* [Philadelphia: Presbyterian and Reformed Publishing Co., 1946], 378).

    6. *CD* IV/2, 106.

Jesus Christ is not what he is — very God, very man, very God-man — in order as such to mean and do and accomplish something else which is atonement. But his being as God and man and God-man consists in the completed act of reconciliation with God.[7]

Thus, Jesus Christ is what he accomplishes. He is himself the atonement — the fulfillment of the covenant of grace — which God elects from all eternity. Barth employs the category of history *(Geschichte)* to indicate this inseparability of being and act.[8] To speak of Jesus Christ's history is to speak of the single twofold movement of divine humiliation and human exaltation that fulfills election, accomplishes reconciliation, and constitutes Jesus Christ's very being. The one person Jesus Christ — the *unio personalis* itself — is the one differentiated movement from Creator to creature and back again. Jesus Christ is one *within* this single, simultaneously divine and human, movement.

Without a firm grasp on this point, Barth's Christology is impossible to understand. Jesus Christ "exists as the Mediator between God and man in the sense that in Him God's reconciling of man and man's reconciliation with God are event."[9] The rest of the key Christological decisions that Barth makes in *CD* IV/1 unfold from this basic insight.

First, and most obviously, if Jesus Christ is his history, then the doctrine of reconciliation must be developed from a starting point in Christology. If Jesus Christ is the atonement, then "the christological propositions as such are constitutive, essential, necessary, and central in the Christian doctrine of reconciliation."[10] Barth's description of the whole sweep of reconciliation is an elaboration, as he puts it, of the name of Jesus Christ. Both its objective accomplishment and subjective reception occur in him, and thus Barth's doctrine of reconciliation is "completely dominated and determined by Christology."[11]

---

7. *CD* IV/1, 126.

8. The category of *covenant* functions similarly in his thought, emphasizing as it does the orderly, dynamic, and two-sided nature of the fellowship in which God and human beings exist. In fact, Barth often uses the phrases "Jesus Christ's history" and "the history of the covenant" synonymously.

9. *CD* IV/1, 123.

10. Ibid., 125.

11. Ibid., 128. Barth is often criticized for emphasizing the objective accomplishment of reconciliation to the exclusion of any meaningful subjective reception. In *Participation in Christ in Karl Barth's* Church Dogmatics (Louisville: Westminster John Knox Press, 2009), I show that the opposite is the case. Barth's teleological conception of the objective accom-

Second, if Jesus Christ is his history, then there can be no independent doctrine of the person of Christ abstracted from his work. The only legitimate two natures doctrine is one in which Jesus Christ's history exclusively provides the content and determines the relationships of the terms *divine nature, human nature, person,* and so on. For how would we know what these terms mean apart from him? As Barth puts it, "there can be no question of a doctrine of the two natures which is autonomous, a doctrine of Jesus Christ as God and man which is no longer or not yet related to the divine action which takes place in him."[12] While Barth regards the Chalcedonian definition as *in some sense* normative for all subsequent Christian thought, he is clearly dissatisfied with the history of the church's teaching on the person of Christ. In his judgment, Eastern Christology tends to abstract Christ's person from his work by adopting a "static" view of the *unio* of the person of the Logos with his human nature, rather than seeing it as "an act or a work."[13] Western Christology, on the other hand, tends to abstract Christ's work from his person by failing to show how Christ *is* his work.

> In himself and as such the Christ of Nicaea and Chalcedon naturally was and is a being which even if we could consistently and helpfully explain His unique structure conceptually could not possibly be proclaimed and believed as One who acts historically because of the timelessness and historical remoteness of the concepts (person, nature, Godhead, manhood, etc.). He could not possibly be proclaimed and believed as the One whom in actual fact the Christian Church has always and everywhere proclaimed and believed under the name of Jesus Christ. An abstract doctrine of the person of Christ may have its own apparent importance, but it is always an empty form, in which what we have to say concerning Jesus Christ can never be said.[14]

Barth's decision to identify Jesus Christ with his history is, among other things, an attempt to correct this fundamental weakness.

Third, if Jesus Christ is his history, then for the same reason that there can be no division between his person and work, there can be no division between the doctrine of the two natures and the doctrine of the "two states."

---

plishment of reconciliation in Christ actually elicits and guarantees the reality and significance of its subjective reception and realization.

12. *CD* IV/1, 133.
13. Ibid., 127.
14. Ibid.

Barth interprets the two states doctrine as an aspect of the two natures doctrine simply because Jesus Christ's exaltation and humiliation are not "incidental to his being."[15] Jesus Christ does not first exist in two natures, only then to exist in two states. Rather, the one history of exaltation and humiliation in which he lives "is the actuality of the being of Jesus Christ as very God and very man."[16] Thus, instead of two states, Barth prefers to speak of "the twofold action of Jesus Christ" — a twofold action that "constitutes his existence."[17] Jesus Christ is always at once (rather than sequentially) the Lord who became servant and the servant who became Lord, the humiliated Son of God and the exalted Son of Man. "Our question is whether this does not better correspond to the witness of the New Testament concerning Jesus Christ. Where and when is He not both humiliated and exalted, already exalted in His humiliation, and humiliated in His exaltation?"[18]

Fourth, if Jesus Christ is his history, then the eternal Son is the man Jesus. "Jesus Christ, very God and very man, born and living and acting and suffering and conquering in time is, as such, the eternal Word of God at the beginning of all things."[19]

> According to the free and gracious will of God the eternal Son of God is Jesus Christ as He lived and died and rose again in time, *and none other.* He is the decision of God in time, and yet according to what took place in time the decision which was made from all eternity. This decision was made freely and graciously and undeservedly in an overflowing of the divine goodness. Yet — for us to whom it refers and for whose sake it was taken — it was also made bindingly, inescapably and irrevocably. We cannot, therefore, go back on it. We must not ignore it and imagine a "Logos in itself" which does not have this content and form, which is the eternal Word of God without this form and content. We could only imagine such a Logos. Like Godhead abstracted from its revelation and acts, it would necessarily be an empty concept which we would, then, of course, feel obliged to fill with all kinds of contents of our own arbitrary invention. Under the title of a *logos asarkos* we pay homage to a *Deus absconditus* and therefore to some image of god which we have made for ourselves. . . . Is it real faith and obedience which concerns itself with this regress to a pre-

15. Ibid., 133.
16. Ibid.
17. Ibid.
18. Ibid.
19. Ibid., 49.

temporal being of the Word of God which is not His incarnate being, the being of the *Deus pro nobis?*[20]

In Jesus Christ, we encounter nothing less than "the most proper and direct and immediate presence and action of the one true God in the sphere of human and world history."[21] Barth goes as far as to say that the eternal relation of the Father and Son is *identical* with Jesus Christ's obedience to the Father in time. "In the work of the reconciliation of the world with God the inward divine relationship between the One who rules and commands in majesty and the One who obeys in humility is identical *[identisch]* with the very different relationship between God and one of His creatures, a man."[22] Barth never explicitly reduces the divine Son to the man Jesus. He prefers to say that the divine Son both *is* and *is also* the man Jesus. On the one hand, he is clear that the Son's self-humiliation in time (the *kenosis* of Phil. 2) occurs by way of addition — as the divine Son *becomes* the man Jesus whom he eternally elected to be. "In addition to His form in the likeness of God He could also — and this involves at once a making poor, a humiliation, a condescension, and to that extent a *kenosis* — take the form of a servant."[23] But Barth is equally clear that the eternal Son is *essentially* the man Jesus. The incarnation is an economy, but not "the kind of economy in which His true and proper being remains behind an improper being, a being 'as if.'"[24] There is only one eternal Son, and he is the man Jesus. "It is as this man that He is the Messiah, the *Kyrios,* or — in a final approximation to the mystery of His existence — the Son, or as the prologue to the Gospel of St. John has it, the Word of God."[25]

Fifth, if Jesus Christ is his history, and Jesus Christ is very God, then God is his history. God's being as Father, Son, and Holy Spirit is "his being in his own history," and the gospel of reconciliation announces that God has elected to include us in this history.[26]

> To put it in the simplest way, what unites God and us men is that He does not will to be God without us, that He creates us rather to share with us

---

20. Ibid., 52, emphasis added.
21. Ibid., 198.
22. Ibid., 203; *KD* IV/1, 222.
23. Ibid., 180.
24. Ibid., 198.
25. Ibid., 163.
26. Ibid., 205.

and therefore with our being and life and act His own incomparable being and life and act, that He does not allow His history to be His and ours ours, but causes them to take place as a common history. That is the special truth which the Christian message has to proclaim at its very heart.[27]

Reconciliation is not merely "an act of God," but is, more precisely, "God Himself in this act of His," since God "is who He is, and lives as what He is, in that He does what He does."[28] God's gracious election is his eternal decision to "activate" his Godhead in time, to exist as the man Jesus.[29] The decision is, of course, entirely free and unconstrained. But given its content, Barth can even claim that God's eternity "commands Him to be in time and Himself to be temporal."[30] This line of thought also explains Barth's otherwise baffling statement that Jesus Christ "is altogether man in virtue of His true Godhead whose glory consists in His humiliation."[31]

Yet alongside all of this, Barth repeatedly and emphatically declares that the incarnation does not involve a change in God's being. For such a change would immediately cast doubt upon and indeed nullify the atonement accomplished in him. The Son's descent into the far country of the flesh does not involve any subtraction or alteration of his deity. It occurs rather as the temporal realization of his eternal decision to "give to the world created by Him, to man, a part in the history in which He is God."[32] The incarnation is the enactment of a possibility internal to the being of God which he elects from all eternity. "This possibility," Barth writes, "is included in His unalterable being."[33] Thus in becoming the man Jesus, the Son "becomes what he had not previously been."[34] But he does so in full unity with the divine nature since this divine becoming occurs as the fulfillment of his eternal election to be the man Jesus. In fact this event occurs as "the strangely logical final continuation of the history in which He is God."[35]

This final assertion leads naturally to the last — and most startling — point in this section. If Jesus Christ is his history, then his obedience to his

27. Ibid., 7.
28. Ibid., 6.
29. Ibid., 134.
30. Ibid., 129.
31. Ibid., 130.
32. Ibid., 203.
33. Ibid., 187.
34. Ibid., 203.
35. Ibid.

Father in time is grounded in his obedience to his Father in eternity. In other words, Jesus Christ's obedience in time expresses *ad extra* "the mystery of the inner being of God as the being of the Son in relation to the Father."[36] For unless the self-humiliation of the Son of God in time is grounded in the Son's eternal relation to his Father, the incarnation would be an arbitrary decision that violates the divine unity and immutability and places God in contradiction with himself. God's being and act would be at odds with one another. If the Son is obedient to the Father in time, but not in eternity, then the incarnation could only mean that God enters into contradiction with himself. But how could God contradict and overcome human sin by entering into contradiction with himself? Moreover, Barth asks, where in Jesus Christ's history do we learn that God cannot be obedient? Is it not rather the case that if the one God is obedient, then he can be obedient? To suggest that obedience is incompatible with deity assumes a knowledge of the divine nature (and particularly of the divine unity and equality) acquired from some source other than Jesus Christ's history. But what source would that be? And why would it have priority over what Jesus Christ himself reveals to us?

> As we look at Jesus Christ we cannot avoid the astounding conclusion of a divine obedience. Therefore we have to draw the no less astounding deduction that in equal Godhead the one God is, in fact, the One and also Another, that He is indeed a First and a Second, One who rules and commands in majesty and One who obeys in humility.[37]

When we encounter Jesus Christ, we encounter God — not God in an improper sense, but God himself. And Jesus Christ shows us that "for God it is just as natural to be lowly as it is to be high, to be near as it is to be far, to be little as it is to be great, to be abroad as to be at home."[38] On the basis of Jesus Christ's history, Barth concludes that there is "in God Himself . . . a *prius* and a *posterius,* a superior and a junior and subordinate."[39] Thus, what superficially appears to be a subordinationist line of argument, a denial of the full deity of Jesus Christ, turns out to be the exact opposite. Barth argues for an eternal relation of dependence of the Son upon the Father precisely in order to affirm, safeguard, and purify the Church's confession that Jesus Christ is

---

36. Ibid., 177.
37. Ibid., 202.
38. Ibid., 192.
39. Ibid., 195.

homoousios with the Father. In fact, he does not think that the deity of Christ can be consistently affirmed in any other way.

Part Two

As I mentioned at the outset, even by Barth's standards, the discussion of the hypostatic union, which opens *CD* IV/2, is an especially dense and complex piece of theological writing. In this second section I will present the main lines of his argument as concisely as possible, and in the conclusion I will discuss a few of its more perplexing aspects.

Whereas in *CD* IV/1 Barth treats Jesus Christ's fulfillment of the covenant of grace from the standpoint of the humiliation of the Son of God, in *CD* IV/2 he treats the same history from the standpoint of the exaltation of the Son of Man. Humanity is the object of God's reconciling work, and thus the statement "I will be your God" (*CD* IV/1) necessarily precedes the statement "You will be my people" (*CD* IV/2). Yet the *telos* of the divine humiliation is the creation of a new human subject — one exalted into freely obedient covenant fellowship with God. In Jesus Christ, this subject becomes a reality. "For as an object of the truly and effectively reconciling grace of God, in his own particular, subordinate and secondary place and manner and function he is also a subject of this whole occurrence."[40] Since the exaltation of humanity to fellowship with God occurs in him, "the problem of the reconciled man, like that of the reconciling God, has to be based in Christology."[41] With these assumptions in place, Barth's treatment of the Christian life in *CD* IV/2 *had* to begin with a discussion of the hypostatic union.

Barth opens with a familiar observation. When the Word became flesh, he did not cease to be God, but as the unfolding of election, and in accordance with the will of the Father, he became *also* a man. In an act of pure mercy and grace, God in his mode of being as the Son became flesh. But what, Barth asks, does it mean to say that the Word became flesh? It certainly cannot mean that he adopted into unity with himself one man among other human beings, nor can it mean that he exists "in a duality" alongside an individual man.[42] For were that the case, the Son would not really have *become* flesh at all, and atonement would have been impossible, since that which oc-

40. *CD* IV/2, 4.
41. Ibid., 19.
42. Ibid., 48.

curs in the humanity of Jesus Christ is relevant for the rest of humanity only because Jesus Christ's humanity is the humanity of *God*. Thus, Barth rejects adoptionism and Nestorianism because neither can support Jesus Christ's work of reconciliation. In Barth's parlance, the Nestorian Christ would simply be *a* man, not *the* man.

To underscore this point, he affirms the *anhypostasis* or *impersonalitas* of the human nature of Christ. Jesus Christ exists as a man only as and because the Son of God exists as a man. The man Jesus "exists directly in and with the one God in the mode of existence of His eternal Son and Logos — not otherwise or apart from this mode."[43] Rather than uniting himself with a *homo* — an autonomously existing human being — "What God the Son assumed into unity with Himself and His divine being was and is — in a specific individual form elected and prepared for this purpose — not merely 'a man' but the *humanum,* the being and essence, the nature and kind, which is that of all men, which characterizes them as men, and distinguishes them from other creatures."[44] Barth defines this *humanum* (elsewhere he refers to it as *humanitas*)[45] as "the concrete possibility of the existence of one man in a specific form."[46] Thus Jesus Christ is "a man" — a truly human being — who does not exist independently *(anhypostasis),* but exists only in the Word *(enhypostasis).*

Furthermore, that God in his mode of being as the Son is the agent of this assumption means that he — not the man Jesus — grounds and sustains the hypostatic union. "The divine act of humility fulfilled in the Son is the only ground of this happening and being. On this ground the unity achieved in this history has to be described, not as two-sided, but as founded and consisting absolutely and exclusively in him."[47] Thus, the hypostatic union is not a relationship of cooperation, but is wholly a movement of divine grace and corresponding human gratitude. Among other things, on the soil of this Christology, Jesus Christ himself becomes the definitive rejection of Pelagian or semi-Pelagian conceptions of the relationship between divine and human action, since the man Jesus exists wholly by the grace of God.

Before moving into his discussion of the *communio naturarum* — the "mutual participation" of the divine and human natures in one another — Barth offers a helpful ten-page small-print excursus on the possibility of

43. Ibid., 49.
44. Ibid., 48.
45. Ibid., 27.
46. Ibid., 48.
47. Ibid., 46.

analogies for the hypostatic union.[48] "What does *unio* mean in this context?"[49] Could we perhaps look to other phenomena as instructive analogies for this event? Not surprisingly, Barth concludes that the *unio hypostatica* is sui generis, and therefore no such analogies exist. Or, more precisely, he concludes that the only possible analogy to the hypostatic union is that between Jesus Christ's heavenly existence and his earthly-historical existence (i.e., his existence prior to the incarnation and his existence as the head of his body — the *totus Christus*). But that, of course, is not so much an analogy as an indirect identity, since it is the same Jesus Christ who exists in these two forms. Nevertheless, readers will likely find this passage both helpful and interesting, since it offers a working example of the way that Barth's Christological innovations illuminate and critique a number of common misconceptions regarding the character of the hypostatic union.

Barth begins his treatment of "the doctrine of the two natures in the strict sense" with an observation that frames the whole discussion.[50] Were the two natures doctrine merely a speculative attempt to establish a general truth about the metaphysical union of divine and human natures in one person, it would be nothing more than "rationalistic enthusiasm bordering on lunacy."[51] Barth's own treatment proceeds from exactly the opposite direction. The possibility and legitimacy of the doctrine of the hypostatic union derive exclusively from the reality of Jesus Christ himself. Barth intends his Christology to be strictly a posteriori reflection. "This Subject, the one Jesus Christ, demands this statement, not as a statement about the possibility of uniting that which cannot be united, but as a statement about the uniting of that which is otherwise quite distinct and antithetical as it has actually taken place and been achieved in him."[52] Thus, the doctrine of the hypostatic union, including all of its embarrassing conceptual difficulties, is undertaken as a matter of obedience, and is exclusively accountable to its object, rather than to "Church dogma or general logic and metaphysics."[53] The inevitable offense which the latter will take in the face of this approach is simply acknowledged and ignored.

Barth organizes his treatment into two main sections — some broad observations about the mutual participation of divine and human natures,

48. Ibid., 51-60.
49. Ibid., 52.
50. Ibid., 61.
51. Ibid.
52. Ibid.
53. Ibid., 62.

followed by a "more precise explanation" of these observations under three headings *(communicatio idiomatum, communicatio gratiae, communicatio operationum)*. The opening passage contains the whole *in nuce:*

> From the unity with His own existence into which the Son of God as-
> sumes human essence while maintaining His own divine essence, there
> follows, as we have said, the union of divine and human essence as it has
> taken place and been actualized in Him. Jesus Christ, then, does not exist
> as the Son of God without also participating as such in human essence.
> And He does not exist as the Son of Man without participating as such in
> the essence of the Son of God and therefore in divine essence. On both
> sides there is a true and genuine participation. It is true and genuine in
> virtue of the act of God the Son . . . This two-sided participation, and
> therefore the union of the two natures in Him, arises and consists, there-
> fore, from Him. Hence it is "from above to below" . . . It is two-sided, but
> in this sequence, and in the differentiated two-sidedness which this and
> the difference of the two natures involves. . . . The unification of divine
> and human essence in Him, the One, and therefore His being as very God
> and very man, rests absolutely on the unity achieved by the Son of God in
> the act of God. But as it rests on this unity, and is its direct consequence, it
> is clear that it is not itself a unity, but a union in that two-sided participa-
> tion, the *communio naturarum*.[54]

The divine and human natures participate wholly and indivisibly in one another even as they remain "indissolubly distinct" as divine and human.[55] No
aspect of either nature is left unaffected by or excluded from this union, nor
is either nature changed into the other. Instead, the two natures are con-
joined in a dynamic and living union — not as a static *unitas,* but as a genuine *unio* — a genuine *history.* "They are a single event and being. . . . The
mystery of the incarnation consists in the fact that the simultaneity of divine
and human essence in Jesus Christ is real, and therefore their mutual participation is also real."[56]

Furthermore — and this point is crucial to notice — the hypostatic
union is grounded in the action of God the Son, not the action of the man
Jesus. God in his mode of being as the Son is the "acting Subject" in this event,
the one who unites the two natures in himself by giving to each one a differ-

---

54. Ibid., 62-63.
55. Ibid., 64.
56. Ibid., 65.

ent "determination" (*Bestimmung*).[57] Barth will describe the content of these determinations below. His primary concern here is to specify their ground and ordering. Neither the divine nature (which as such "has no existence" and therefore cannot act) nor the human nature (since it exists only in the Son) can be the acting subject of the union.[58] "The indispensable closer definition of this mutual participation must be this. The Son of God is the acting Subject who takes the initiative in this event . . . He Himself grasps and has and maintains the leadership in what His divine essence is and means for His human, and His human for His divine, in their mutual participation."[59] And since God the Son is the acting subject, the two determinations can only be ordered in one way: "The determination of His divine essence is *to* His human, and the determination of His human essence *from* His divine."[60] Therefore, the word "mutual" — in the phrase "mutual participation" — is completely misunderstood if taken to mean "reversible" or "interchangeable." Instead, since each nature has a different relationship to the divine Subject, each nature "has its own role" within their mutual participation.[61] "For all their reciprocity the two elements in this happening have a different character. The one, as the essence of the Son of God, is wholly that which gives. The other, exalted to existence and actuality only in and by Him, is wholly that which receives."[62] This ordering implies that while the determination of the divine nature means that the Son of God became the man Jesus, the determination of the human nature does not mean that the man Jesus became God. For if God the Son is the subject of the union, the Son of Man obviously cannot have assumed the divine nature into unity with himself so as to become the Son of God. Furthermore, since the man Jesus only exists as the Son of God *(anhypostasis)*, what sense would it make to say that the Son of God became what he always eternally was?

This is an admittedly difficult argument, which Barth could have made much clearer by drawing attention to the fact that his rejection of deification rests wholly on the doctrine of the *anhypostasis*. Nevertheless, the argument is also an ingenious way of ensuring that the exaltation of humanity to fellowship with God will not consist in the deification of human essence, but rather in the determination of human essence to be "filled and directed by

57. Ibid., 70.
58. Ibid., 65.
59. Ibid., 70.
60. Ibid.
61. Ibid., 71.
62. Ibid., 72.

the Holy Spirit, and in full harmony with the divine essence common to Father, Son, and Holy Spirit."[63] For if the man Jesus always *receives* his existence from God the Son, then his being is wholly a being in *response* to God. And since, as we have already seen, deity means giving rather than receiving, it follows that the idea of a deified humanity is a contradiction in terms.

Barth further clarifies his position by situating it vis-à-vis the Christologies of seventeenth-century Reformed and Lutheran Orthodoxy — something which he will continue to do in the material that follows. According to Barth, the Reformed and Lutherans agreed that the *communio naturarum* (the mutual participation of the two natures) is grounded in the *unio hypostatica*. But whereas the Reformed focused their attention on the "primary mystery" of the hypostatic union, the Lutherans were far more interested in the "secondary mystery" of the *communio naturarum*, and in particular in the communication of divine properties to the human nature of Christ such that the antithesis between God and humanity takes place "directly" in the human nature.[64] The Lutherans were primarily concerned, in other words, with the *effects* of the hypostatic union on the human nature — with the deification of the human nature. Thus, they criticized the Reformed for insisting that the union of the two natures is indirect (in the person of the union) rather than direct. The Reformed, on the other hand, "represented the diametrically opposite concern."[65] While they did not deny the *communio naturarum,* their emphasis was not on the effects of the union, but on the Subject of the union himself — "upon the Son of God as the Subject of the incarnation who creates and bears and maintains the *communio naturarum;* upon His act of equating divine and human essence, and not so much upon the consequent equation."[66] Their emphasis on the *unio hypostatica,* and thus on the abiding distinction between the divine and human natures even within the union, led them to reject the Lutheran procedure of directly attributing to the humanity of Christ predicates that belong to "the Logos existing in divine essence, and not to the human essence assumed by Him into unity with His existence."[67] Thus — and this is especially the case in the earliest Reformed Christologies — the Reformed rejection of the Lutheran position had nothing to do with a "barren intellectual zeal for the axiom: *finitum non capax infiniti,*" but rather with "a zeal for the sover-

63. Ibid.
64. Ibid., 66.
65. Ibid., 68.
66. Ibid.
67. Ibid.

eignty of the Subject acting in free grace in the incarnation, of the living God in the person and existence of His Son."[68] It is on this point, above all, that Barth sides with the Reformed. For his emphasis, like theirs, is always on the sovereignty of the divine subject and thus on the *event* of the union itself, rather than on the results of this union on either of the two natures.

That having been said, Barth does not dismiss the basic concern that underlies the Lutheran attraction to the *communio naturarum* — the exaltation which comes to human nature in the humanity of Christ. He opposes, rather, the particular description that the Lutherans gave to it. This is crucial to notice because it means that rather than merely rejecting deification, Barth's own doctrine of the *communio naturarum* attempts to address the legitimate concern which animates the Lutheran position — the exaltation of humanity — but to do so within the context of a basically Reformed Christology. In fact, Barth criticizes the older Reformed theologians for failing to give adequate attention to this question. Instead of recoiling in horror at the Lutheran view and dropping the problem altogether — a response which Barth describes as "much too negative" — they should have offered a compelling alternative.[69] "It is seldom a good thing to reject a problem which has once been seriously raised," and thus Barth offers his description of the *communio naturarum* as an attempt to "rescue the question from the impasse into which it was led by the Christological discussion of the older Protestants."[70] With these introductory remarks in place, Barth moves into his more focused examination of the *communio naturarum*.

Communicatio Idiomatum

The *communicatio idiomatum* is the most general of the three headings under which Barth elaborates the *communio naturarum*. We have already seen that the mutual participation of the divine and human natures occurs as an orderly event of divine giving and human receiving, and we have also seen that Jesus Christ is himself this event. "To see and think and say Jesus Christ is to see and think and say this impartation — divine and human essence in this relationship of real giving and receiving, God and man in the fellowship of this history."[71] But rather than directing their attention wholly toward

68. Ibid.
69. Ibid., 80.
70. Ibid., 83.
71. Ibid., 74.

this *happening* — toward this history — Lutheran theologians became preoccupied with what *happened* in the human nature itself. Their attention shifted, in other words, from the event of the communion of the two natures to a consideration of the human nature itself now supposedly decked out with divine attributes. But to conceive of Jesus Christ's humanity in this way, Barth argues, is to entertain "one long abstraction," since it involves considering the human nature in isolation from the history itself.[72] And according to Barth, this seemingly benign glance away from Jesus Christ himself to one of his natures is the fatal error of Lutheran Christology. For it results in both the confusion of the two natures (since the human nature is deified) and the unwitting separation of the two natures (to the extent that the supposedly deified human nature is isolated and considered in abstraction from event of the mutual participation). The latter error is especially ironic, since the separation of the two natures is precisely what the Lutherans were trying to avoid. Moreover, Barth argues that by regarding the deified humanity of Jesus Christ as the supreme purpose of the incarnation, and by treating it in isolation from the hypostatic union itself, the Lutherans unwittingly laid the groundwork for the *apotheosis* of humanity as such which occurred in the anthropology of later German thought.[73]

> For after all, is not the humanity of Jesus Christ, by definition, that of all men? And even if it is said only of Him, does this not mean that the essence of all men, human essence as such, is capable of divinization? If it can be said in relation to Him, why not to all men? But this means that in Christology a door is left wide open, not this time by a secular philosophy which has entered in with subtlety, but in fulfillment of the strictest theological discussion and ostensibly from the very heart of Christian faith. And through this door it is basically free for anyone to wander right away from Christology. . . . Surely it was not an accident that on the same soil of profound German thinking on which this Christology had once grown and been defended for two hundred years against the Calvinistic correction . . . there could and did arise, in the fullness of time, the wonderful flower of German Idealism.[74]

Thus, among other things, Barth's determination to conceive of the *communio naturarum* as a history, and his refusal to consider either nature

72. Ibid., 80.
73. Ibid., 81.
74. Ibid., 82.

apart from this event, should be regarded as a central component of his larger strategy of eliminating any trace of the idea that Jesus Christ is an instrument of salvation rather than salvation itself.

Communicatio Gratiarum

Recall again the three headings under which Barth develops his doctrine of the *communio naturarum* — the *communicatio idiomatum* (the mutual participation of the two natures), the *communicatio gratiarum* (the participation of the human in the divine), and the *communicatio operationum* (the common actualization of the two natures). Careful readers will wonder why the presentation is missing a heading. Why does Barth not offer a discrete treatment of the participation of the divine in the human — the so-called *genus tapeinoticum?*

The answer emerges in his discussion of the *communicatio gratiarum* — for it begins not, as one would expect, with a treatment of the participation of the human in the divine, but of the divine in the human. This way of ordering the material reveals a point of the highest importance. According to Barth, the discussion of the *communicatio gratiarum* must begin with an affirmation of the *genus tapeinoticum* because the determination of human essence for fellowship with God is first and primarily a determination of divine essence for fellowship with humanity. In fact, the former is exclusively grounded in the latter. If God does not really and genuinely participate in humanity, then humanity does not really and genuinely participate in God. If God is not really *affected* by the human life that he lives *(genus tapeinoticum)*, then humanity is not really exalted into fellowship with him *(communicatio gratiarum)*. Any attempt to describe the exaltation of humanity to participation in God that is not wholly grounded in and built upon the foundation of divine humiliation is doomed to failure.

Thus, Barth's doctrine of the *communicatio gratiarum* opens with a direct challenge to virtually the whole of the church's reflection on the meaning of human participation in God. For throughout its history the church's attachment to "the profoundly unchristian conception of a God whose Godhead is supposed not to be affected at all by its union with humanity" has kept it from fully acknowledging and embracing the divine humiliation.[75] By adhering to an abstract, and therefore inadequate, conception of the *immutabilitas Dei*, the church undermined the very foundation of its claim

---

75. Ibid., 85.

that human beings participate in God. In response to this colossal error, Barth counters that God's gracious election of humiliation for himself in the incarnation, rather than contradicting his deity, is the "supreme exercise and affirmation of His divine essence."[76] God is not prisoner to his Godhead, nor does he become a stranger to himself when he becomes human. Rather it belongs to the immutable divine essence "to be free for this decree and its execution, to be able to elect and determine itself in this form. No diminution comes to it by the fact that it is wholly directed and addressed to human essence in Jesus Christ, sharing its limitation and weakness and even its lostness in the most radical and consistent way."[77] Quite simply, if God freely and eternally elects to be God as this man, then his very deity is determined and affected by his decision to live this human life. "This does not take place at the expense but in the power of his divine nature. It is, however, a determination that He gives it. [His divine nature] acquires in man its *telos*. Directed and addressed to human nature, it acquires a form, *this* form."[78] To the extent that the church is unwilling to affirm this fact, it undermines the basis of its exaltation to fellowship with God, for human exaltation "has its ultimate depth and unshakeable solidity" only in the divine humiliation.[79]

Having insisted on this point, Barth is now ready to describe the content of the *communicatio gratiarum*. What does it mean to say that in Jesus Christ humanity participates in God? Barth's first instinct is to reiterate that the *communicatio gratiarum* does not entail the deification of Jesus Christ's human nature, for that would imply either a "direct or indirect identification" of the two natures, and such an identification would necessarily mean the transformation of both natures into something other than divine and human.[80] Against such a view, Barth conceives of the mutual participation of the two natures as an event of "confrontation."[81] Within the divine-human communion, the human nature is "determined wholly and utterly, from the very outset and in every part, by the electing grace of God."[82] Thus, the specific content of the exaltation of human essence is its determination for the freedom of obedience. Against the Lutheran suggestion that in addition to this the human nature also receives "the distinctive

76. Ibid.
77. Ibid., 85-86.
78. Ibid., 87.
79. Ibid.
80. Ibid.
81. Ibid.
82. Ibid., 88.

qualities of the divine nature" and is thereby deified, Barth offers a simple and yet penetrating response.

> It is hard to see where this necessity arises. It is hard to see why its total and exclusive determination by the grace of God is not enough. . . . Is temple or dwelling — a dwelling which is certainly filled with Godhead and totally and exclusively claimed and sanctified, but still a dwelling — not really enough to describe what we have to say of human essence in relation to this temple, this dwelling as such, in order that the dwelling of the Godhead in it may be a real one? If it is deified, does it not cease to be His temple? Or, to abandon the metaphor, does not a deified human essence cease to be our human essence, usable as such for the work of the Son of God for us and to us, and accessible and recognizable to us as such? If the human essence of Jesus Christ is deified, can He really be the Mediator between God and us? He is totally unlike even the most saintly among us in the fact that His human essence alone is fully, because from the very outset, determined by the grace of God. This is the qualitatively different determination of his human essence . . . It is genuinely human in the deepest sense to live by the electing grace of God addressed to man. This is how Jesus Christ lives as the Son of Man.[83]

Thus, human participation in the divine nature is exaltation to obedience — to human life in "harmony with the divine will," in "correspondence to divine grace," and in free dependence upon the Holy Spirit.[84] At this point, a number of obvious questions arise, two of which seem especially pressing.

First, why would Barth depict the communion of the two natures as a confrontation? Is this not an odd way to conceive of communion? Barth does not address this question here, but his response is not difficult to imagine. If God is and always remains the Lord, and if the Son of God is the subject of the union of the two natures, then the participation of the human nature in the divine nature must be an event of obedience. Since God is the Lord, he shares himself with the human creature by making himself the creature's Lord. He gives himself to the creature — extends his grace to the creature — by allowing the creature to live in the freedom of grateful obedience. Thus, if this communion takes place as an event of lordship and obedience, it has to take place as a confrontation. How could it be otherwise? To eliminate the confrontation would be to forfeit the communion and exchange it for some

83. Ibid., 89.
84. Ibid., 92.

kind of mystical merging of the creature into God. And while such a merging is perhaps possible with a generically conceived ground of being or primal One, it is impossible with the true God of the covenant who is and ever remains the Lord of his creatures. Thus, while counter-intuitive, Barth insists that divine-human communion takes place as an event of lordship and obedience, and therefore confrontation, precisely in order to affirm, rather than deny, real human participation in the real God. For without this distinction and distance between God and the creature, there could be no genuine union and communion between them.

This leads to the second question. Does Barth really mean that there is nothing more to human participation in God than obedience? Surely participation in God involves obedience, but is there not more to it than that? The answer to this question is anticipated in the answer to the previous question. If communion between God and the human creature is an event of divine giving and human receiving — if indeed it is genuinely human in the deepest sense to live according to the electing grace of God — then the whole of human life in fellowship with God has the character of grateful response. In obedience *(Gehorsam)*, those whom Jesus Christ has reconciled to God become (in themselves) who they already are (in him). Thus, rather than being restrictive, *Gehorsam* is Barth's comprehensive designation of every aspect of human life lived in proper response to divine grace. Moreover, since this fellowship of obedience occurs always and entirely by grace, Barth strenuously rejects the almost universal Christian affirmation that some sort of *gratia habitualis* is imparted to human nature in the course of the Christian life. Even the Reformed, who ought to have known better, were unable to resist the lure of this idea. But if the man Jesus "derives entirely from his divine origin" in election *(anhypostasis)*,[85] if he receives his humanity wholly in obedient response to divine grace, then to posit "a kind of status" infused into "the human essence of Jesus Christ as such" would be to look away from the history in which his being is received and enacted, and thus to entertain an abstraction.[86]

> *Habitus* comes from *habere*, and therefore denotes possession. But grace is divine giving and human receiving. It can be "had" only in the course of this history. . . . [W]e cannot look away from the event in which this receiving takes place. We can only look to the event in which it does also

85. Ibid., 91.
86. Ibid., 89.

take place. There can be no question, then, of a *habitus* proper to the human essence of Jesus Christ.[87]

Exaltation to fellowship with God is exaltation to total and perpetual dependence upon God. It is human life "filled and directed by the Holy Spirit, and in full harmony with the divine essence common to Father, Son, and Holy Spirit."[88] This is how God the Son lives as a man, and in union with him, this is how he frees us to live as well.

Communicatio Operationum

We have already seen that if Jesus Christ is his history, then the "person" of Christ is identical to the history in which the Son of God lives as the Son of Man. But that is just another way of saying that the *unio hypostatica* is identical to "the common actualization of divine and human essence as it takes place in Jesus Christ" — the *communicatio operationum*.[89] This means, therefore, that upon arriving at this heading, Barth has very little left to say. Not, of course, because the *communicatio operationum* is unimportant, but rather because *everything* he has said thus far about Jesus Christ is in fact a statement about the *communicatio operationum* — the concrete history in which Jesus Christ enacts and actualizes his being as both God and man.

> From the very first we have understood and interpreted the doctrine of the incarnation, which we have considered from all angles, in historical terms, as an actuality, as an *operatio* between God and man, fulfilled in Jesus Christ as a union of God with him. We have represented the existence of Jesus Christ as His being in His act. Relatively, therefore, this is not a great deal more to say . . . It may be said, indeed, that all the time we have been thinking and speaking within this concept of the *communicatio operationum*. Our only remaining task is to make one or two things more clear and precise. . . . We have "actualized" the doctrine of the incarnation, i.e., we have used the main traditional concepts, *unio, communio,* and *communicatio,* as concentrically related terms to describe one and the same ongoing process. We have stated it all (including the Chalcedonian definition, which is so important in dogmatic history, and rightly became normative) in the form of a denotation and description of a single event. We have taken it that the re-

87. Ibid., 90.
88. Ibid., 72.
89. Ibid., 104.

ality of Jesus Christ, which is the theme of Christology, is identical with this event, and this event with the reality of Jesus Christ.[90]

Barth's Christology is an extended attempt to eradicate every hint of "anything static at the broad center of the traditional doctrine of the person of Christ."[91] The "person" of the union is not a *unitas* (unity) but a *unitio* (uniting). Jesus Christ is not merely "the fusion of two elements," but is himself a movement, an act.[92] "He is in this *operatio*, this event. This is the new form which we have given to Christology."[93] To the criticism that a being cannot intelligibly be interpreted as an act, or a person as a history, Barth coolly responds that Christ alone is the "categorical law" governing all of our speech and thought, and if "historical" thinking is the most fitting form of witness to the *mysterium* of his being, then the question of its possibility is answered in its necessity.[94]

Barth extends this line of thought into the exceedingly difficult issue of the relationship between Jesus Christ's past, present, and future being. Crucially, he acknowledges that general modes of thought will always resist the claim that the history which took place "once and for all in the birth and life and death of Jesus Christ and was revealed for a first time in his resurrection," can also, in addition to belonging to a definite time in the past, take place in the present and future.[95] That this is even possible — much less actual — is revealed exclusively in the particular reality of the sacrament of the being of Jesus Christ himself.

> "Jesus Christ lives" means that this history takes place today in the same way as did that yesterday — indeed, as the same history. Jesus Christ speaks and acts and rules — it all means that this history is present. . . . It took place then, at its own time, before we were, when our present was still future. And it has also a forward reference. It is still future and will still happen — "even unto the end of the world." In other words, when we say that Jesus Christ is in every age, we say that His history takes place in every age. He is in this *operatio*, this event.[96]

90. Ibid., 105.
91. Ibid., 106.
92. Ibid., 109.
93. Ibid., 107.
94. Ibid., 108.
95. Ibid.
96. Ibid., 107.

Rather than attempting to justify the possibility of the co-inherence of these three temporal modes of Jesus Christ's one history according to external criteria, Barth claims that if the present and future Jesus Christ is the same as the one who lived, died, and was raised from the dead in a definite time in the past, then his history cannot be conceived in any other way. If Jesus Christ is the same yesterday, today, and forever, then his history has to be conceived along the lines that Barth is suggesting. "How can that which God did in Jesus Christ yesterday not be His act today and tomorrow? How can it be present and future only as the significance or influence of His then? For all its 'then-ness,' is it not once-for-all, and therefore His act today, which cannot and need not be continued or augmented or superseded? And will it not be the same tomorrow?"[97] Having emphasized this point, Barth concludes his discussion of the *communicatio operationum* with an observation that will serve as a natural transition to our concluding section.

Conclusion

Jesus Christ's existence is "the common actualization of divine and human essence."[98] In fulfillment of God's eternal decision for fellowship with humanity, the Son of God "activates" his divine essence by living as the Son of Man. In the first section of this paper, we encountered the same claim. The incarnation is not "the kind of economy in which His true and proper being remains behind an improper being, a being 'as if.'"[99] The eternal Logos is the man Jesus, not some abstract or unknown deity. As Barth puts it, "It is as this man that He is the Messiah, the *Kyrios*, or — in a final approximation to the mystery of His existence — the Son, or as the prologue to the Gospel of St. John has it, the Word of God."[100] Yet alongside this basic trajectory of thought, Barth adds another argument which, at the very least, complicates it.

> In the inner life of God, as the eternal essence of Father, Son and Holy Ghost, the divine essence does not, of course, need any actualization. On the contrary, it is the creative ground of all other, i.e., all creaturely actualizations. Even as the divine essence of the Son it did not need His incarnation, His existence as man and His action in unity with the man

97. Ibid., 111.
98. Ibid., 113.
99. Ibid., 198.
100. Ibid., 163.

Jesus of Nazareth to become actual. As the divine essence of the Son it is the predicate of the one God. And as the predicate of this Subject is not in any sense merely potential but in every sense actual. But His divine essence — and this is the new thing in Jesus Christ from the divine standpoint — needed a special actualization in the identity of the Son of God with the Son of Man, and therefore in its union with human essence. In this union it is not immediately actual. In this union it is addressed to what is of itself totally different human essence. It is directed to a specific goal *(apotelesmata)*, the reconciliation of the world with God. It is made parallel to divine essence, as it were, although with no inherent change. It is the divine essence of the Son in the act of condescension. It is the divine essence determined and characterized by His act, by His existence not only in itself but also in human essence. And as such it has to become actual. It needs an actualization which is new even from above, from the divine standpoint. It needs the *novum* of the execution of the eternal will and decree in which God elected man for Himself and Himself for man, giving this concrete determination to His own divine being.[101]

One could force this passage to cohere with the rest of Barth's argument by interpreting it to mean nothing more than that Jesus Christ's life history is the temporal actualization of God's eternal election of himself for humanity and humanity for himself. Perhaps when Barth says that the divine essence (a) is "in every sense actual" and (b) "becomes" actual in the incarnation, he just means that the Son of God actualizes divine essence by living as the man Jesus in fulfillment of the eternal election of grace. If so, then this passage would not move in the opposite direction of the argument set forth in the first two sections of this paper. The problem, however, is that Barth claims that the divine essence of the Son is in every sense actual *even apart from the incarnation*. But if the incarnation is God's "true and proper being" — rather than his being "as if" — how can the divine essence of the Son be *in every sense* actual prior to (and considered apart from) the incarnation? One way to answer the question is to say that prior to the incarnation the divine essence of the Son is actual only proleptically — in anticipation of the temporal fulfillment of election. And there are indeed passages where Barth expresses that thought. In addition to such passages, however, he also says, as he does here, that in the incarnation the divine essence becomes actual in a new *(novum)* and non-necessary way — i.e., in a new actualization of the di-

101. Ibid., 113-14.

vine essence of the Son who would have been the same God even if he had not become incarnate. But if God the Son is the man Jesus and the divine *essence* is really enacted in Jesus Christ's temporal history, then prior to the incarnation the divine essence cannot be actual "in every sense" — for the incarnation is at least one sense in which it is not already actual. As one begins to perceive this difficulty more clearly, it becomes harder and harder not to draw the conclusion that Barth has created a problem for himself that he does not quite know how to solve. One senses that he is at least partly aware of this when, as in the quotation above, he resorts to dubious claims such as that the divine essence "is made parallel to divine essence."

There is, however, a way of modifying Barth's argument that would not only clarify the confusion, but would also provide a more solid foundation for his central contention that in Jesus Christ we encounter deity in the full and proper sense. Recall Barth's claim that the incarnation is neither a paradox nor a violation of divine immutability since the Son's obedience in time is grounded in his eternal relation of obedience to his Father. If Barth had made clear that this eternal obedience, rather than being abstract, is identical with the Son's eternal decision to freely obey his Father's command to become incarnate in time for us and for our salvation, then there would be no room to doubt that Jesus Christ is *essentially* God. The incarnation would be the temporal fulfillment of this eternal *telos* of the divine essence. But to the extent that Barth distinguishes between an eternal relation of divine obedience, on the one hand, and the Son's temporal enactment of this eternal relation, on the other, he leaves room for the reader to draw the conclusion that the latter does not in fact belong to God essentially, but is merely one among many possible forms that the divine nature could have taken. The closest Barth comes, as far as I am aware, to closing this gap is in a passage quoted above: "In the work of reconciliation of the world with God the inward divine relationship between the One who rules and commands in majesty and the One who obeys in humility is identical [*identisch*] with the very different relationship between God and one of His creatures, a man."[102] But even here he says that the inward divine relationship is "very different" from the Son's life as a man, the implication being that while the incarnation is grounded in and coherent with the divine nature — the eternal relation of the Father and Son — it is not *identisch* with it. Had Barth sealed this opening once and for all, he would likewise have slammed the door on the possibility that the incarnation is inessential to the Son's identity as God. It should, of course, be

102. *CD* IV/1, 203; *KD* IV/1, 222.

pointed out that in addition to his basic claim that in Jesus Christ we encounter God in the full and proper sense, he makes other statements that lean in the direction of closing this gap, such as, for example, when he says that God's eternity "commands Him to be in time and Himself to be temporal."[103] Nevertheless, his failure to follow through on this and similar suggestions marks his Christology with a profound internal inconsistency.

Let us move now to a second problem. Like everyone else who affirms — in one way or another — the Chalcedonian claim that Jesus Christ is two natures in one person, Barth faces the exceptionally difficult challenge of sorting through what the church means when it confesses (a) that the Son of God is *also* the man Jesus and (b) that Jesus Christ is one person rather than two. Much of this paper has been devoted to showing how Barth "actualizes" the incarnation. Yet despite all of his innovations, he cannot avoid the perplexing question of what it means to say that the one God the Son lives *at once* as God and also as a man. Put in this way, a non-Nestorian Christ becomes extremely difficult to conceptualize. What exactly are we affirming when we say that one subject — one person — is at once one and another? How can God the Son become the human being who exists only in God the Son without somehow doubling himself? As we have seen, Barth's answer is to identify the "person" of the union with the one concrete history of giving and receiving in which Jesus Christ has his being. Even more specifically, he attempts to avoid Nestorianism by insisting that the mutual participation of the two natures is *total* on both sides. Jesus Christ is one person rather than two because there is no aspect of deity in which the Son of Man does not participate, and no aspect of humanity in which the Son of God does not participate. Jesus Christ is God the Son as the human Jesus, and the human Jesus as the Son of God, and he is both within the *one* concrete event of his history. "When we see Him, we cannot look here and there as though there were two side by side — a Son of God who is not Son of Man, and a Son of Man who is not Son of God. When we think of him, we cannot imagine two — a divinity which does not yet impart itself to the humanity, and a humanity which still looks forward to the impartation of the divinity, and therefore still lacks it."[104] Yet claims such as this, while helpful and perhaps true, do not sufficiently address the underlying question. Indeed, when one recalls that according to Barth the *unio hypostatica* is itself a union of lordship and obedience — a union of two distinct wills (divine and human) — the difficulty becomes even more acute.

103. *CD* IV/1, 129.
104. *CD* IV/2, 74.

While a host of other questions could be put to Barth's Christology, I would like to conclude with a crucial one that, to my knowledge, has never been raised. We have seen that Barth identifies Jesus Christ with his history. Jesus Christ is one person, and his work is one work, because the "person" of the union is identical to the history of the communion of divine lordship and human obedience in him. That is why the *communicatio operationum* turned out to be the key concept within which Barth interprets the *communio naturarum*. In addition to this thought, Barth emphasizes, especially in *CD* IV/1, that in Jesus Christ we encounter nothing less than *divine* obedience, the obedience of the eternal Son to his eternal Father. Notice that this is not merely indirect divine obedience — the *human* obedience of the Son of Man who is also the Son of God — but the direct and active obedience of God the Son. Yet when viewed alongside one another, these two lines of argument coalesce to create a conundrum.

If the *unio hypostatica* is an event of divine lordship and human obedience — if the man Jesus lives in harmony with the divine essence through perfect human obedience — then when the Son of Man obeys God, does he, in addition to obeying God the Father, also obey God the Son? In other words, is the Son of God, as God, somehow operative in the command that he obeys as the Son of Man? It is a difficult question for any Christology that affirms that Jesus Christ is divine and human in one person. But it becomes especially acute for Barth who (a) identifies the *unio hypostatica* with this dynamic of divine lordship and human obedience (implying that the man Jesus obeys God the Son) and (b) claims that in addition to this human obedience, God the Son is also *divinely* obedient.[105] But what could it mean to say that one and the same Son both issues and obeys the command? Barth never *directly* says that God the Son obeys himself. But he does say that God the Son founds and sustains his union with the man Jesus, and that this union has the character of divine lordship (i.e., command) and human obe-

---

105. Bruce McCormack's Barthian-inspired kenotic Christology is capable of responding to this difficulty inasmuch as McCormack identifies divine obedience with human obedience; see "Divine Impassibility or Simply Divine Constancy? Implications of Karl Barth's Later Christology for Debates over Impassibility" (unpublished lecture, Providence College, March 30-31, 2007); "Karl Barth's Christology as a Resource for a Reformed Version of Kenoticism," *International Journal of Systematic Theology* 8 (2006): 243-51. For reasons I hope to set forth in a subsequent essay, I think that McCormack's solution is an ingenious and promising dogmatic proposal in its own right. It is also, however, incompatible with Barth's doctrine of the *communicatio operationum,* and thus constitutes a major revision of Barth's view of the *unio hypostatica.*

dience, and that, of course, implies that the Son of God issues — along with the Father and Holy Spirit *(opera trinitatis ad extra sunt indivisa)* — the command that the man Jesus obeys.

Perhaps the problem will become clearer if we look at it from one final angle. If in any given moment of Jesus Christ's life, the divine Son obeys, how is this divine action related to his human action of obedience? Barth is adamant that divine action and human action, while united, are nevertheless distinct. Thus, the question cannot be resolved by identifying Jesus Christ's divine obedience and his human obedience. For in that case, there could be no two natures doctrine at all, especially since Barth conceptualizes the *unio hypostatica* as a history of divine lordship and human obedience, a communion of distinctly divine and human action. But if the two forms of obedience cannot be identified, then what is the best way to conceptualize their relationship to the command of God?

Having noted these difficulties, and acknowledged others, I would like to conclude by pointing out that the grand scale of Barth's Christological translation project — his innovative transposition of the whole of traditional two natures doctrine into the sphere of a history — almost guarantees that it will contain both major and minor conceptual problems. Yet is that not the case with all genuinely ground-breaking intellectual work? Is pioneering reflection in any field of discourse immune from such problems? At the very least, Barth's Christology deserves to be evaluated with the kind of sympathy that strains to listen to what he is trying to say rather than quibbling with the flaws in how he says it. Obviously, like everyone else, Barth's thought should be rigorously examined and criticized. But to do so without a keen awareness of the greatness of his achievement would be both petty and wasteful. For in addition to its obviously successful features, even the inchoate, under-developed, and inconsistent aspects of Barth's Christology are capable of disclosing previously unseen possibilities for Christological reflection — but only to those who read with charity. The more time one spends with Barth's Christology, and the more closely one attends to it, the clearer one perceives its sheer fecundity and suggestiveness. Yet in order to make genuine use of this great resource, Christian theology will have to struggle to understand the new Christological language that Barth is attempting to speak, and that process, it has to be said, is still in its early stages.

The Church in Karl Barth and Evangelicalism: Conversations across the Aisle

Kimlyn J. Bender

To ask whether Karl Barth and American evangelicals are friends is an interesting question to pose regarding two contentious partners. Certainly the actual relationship between them did not begin well, and the first challenge to answering such a question in any affirmative way entails that this history be overcome.

Barth's own interaction with American evangelicalism during his lifetime cannot be described as auspicious by any stretch of the imagination, with one particular episode especially significant and telling. At the request of the editor of the evangelical magazine *Christianity Today,* Geoffrey Bromiley wrote to Barth in the summer of 1961 asking whether he would be willing to answer questions from three prominent American evangelical theologians, questions that Bromiley forwarded with his letter.[1] Having surveyed the questions sent, some of them from Cornelius Van Til — who had already chastised Barth severely in print — Barth's reply to Bromiley was genial but also terse.[2] He must be forgiven, he said, if he could not and would not answer the questions, for he was busy with his teaching and writing re-

---

1. Barth's response to Bromiley's letter, as well as the questions posed, are included in Karl Barth, *Letters 1961-1968,* ed. Jürgen Fangmeier and Hinrich Stoevesandt, trans. and ed. Geoffrey W. Bromiley (Grand Rapids: Eerdmans, 1981), 7-8, 342-43.

2. Cornelius Van Til's criticisms of Barth appear in his book *The New Modernism* (Philadelphia: Presbyterian and Reformed Publishing, 1947). He would continue these criticisms in his later book *Christianity and Barthianism* (Philadelphia: Presbyterian and Reformed Publishing, 1962).

sponsibilities during his last semester as a professor before retirement. Yet even if he had the strength and time, Barth related, he would not enter a discussion based on such questions. A discussion presupposes a serious attempt to understand what he himself had written in the *Church Dogmatics* about related matters. But in his estimation, this prerequisite was conspicuously missing, readily apparent from the questions themselves, which Barth found superficial and trivial.[3]

But there was an even more important reason from abstaining from dialogue, as he writes:

> The decisive point, however, is this. The second presupposition of a fruitful discussion between them and me would have to be that we are able to talk on a common plane. But these people have already had their so-called orthodoxy for a long time. They are closed to anything else, they will cling to it at all costs, and they can adopt toward me only the role of prosecuting attorneys, trying to establish whether what I represent agrees or disagrees with their orthodoxy, in which I for my part have no interest! None of their questions leaves me with the impression that they want to seek with me the truth that is greater than us all. They take the stance of those who happily possess it already and who hope to enhance their happiness by succeeding in proving to themselves and the world that I do not share this happiness. Indeed they have long since decided and publicly proclaimed that I am a heretic, possibly (van Til) the worst heretic of all time. So be it! But they should not expect me to take the trouble to give them the satisfaction of offering explanations which they will simply use to confirm the judgement they have already passed on me. . . . These fundamentalists want to eat me up. They have not yet come to a "better mind and attitude" as I once hoped. I can thus give them neither an angry nor a gentle answer but instead no answer at all.[4]

While such a letter provides little hope for a fruitful dialogue between Barth and evangelicals, things are quite different today. Since the time of this letter, much has changed on the evangelical side of the aisle (and Barth himself is no longer with us to answer from his own side, of course). Just as

---

3. Barth, *Letters 1961-1968*, 7. Barth writes: "I sincerely respect the seriousness with which a man like Berkouwer studies me and then makes his criticisms. I can then answer him in detail. But I cannot respect the questions of these people from *Christianity Today*, for they do not focus on the reasons for my statements but on certain foolishly drawn deductions from them. Their questions are thus superficial."

4. Ibid., 7-8.

Barth could mellow in his old age, so evangelicalism seems to have mellowed (at least in some circles) with regard to Barth.[5] Within the past few decades especially, evangelicals have come to appreciate Barth as a fruitful dialogue partner, even if there remains an implicit and sometimes explicitly expressed wariness regarding his theology.[6] Yet the challenge pertaining to the question of the relation of evangelicals and Barth is no longer one of a problematic history, but is one of identity. To be specific: what is evangelicalism? To place Barth into a dialogue with American evangelicalism requires that we know what evangelicalism itself is.

This question itself may seem trite, but it is important to recognize that evangelicalism is a contested concept. The multifarious and complex nature of evangelicalism as a subculture has been much discussed and readily documented.[7] Indeed, evangelicalism is such a slippery term and so contentious a concept that some from both the Wesleyan and the Reformed wings of the movement have in effect called it meaningless and requested a moratorium on the use of the term.[8] Nevertheless, despite such minority voices, the majority of American historians and theologians continue to preserve it as a useful if imperfect designation for a broad consensus among a variegated grouping of American Christians.[9]

---

5. It is also important to remember that Bromiley himself, the great translator and devotee of Barth and one of the most important persons for Barth's early reception in North America, may be described as an evangelical and taught at an evangelical institution, Fuller Theological Seminary.

6. See especially Bernard Ramm, *After Fundamentalism: The Future of Evangelical Theology* (San Francisco: Harper and Row, 1983); Gregory G. Bolich, *Karl Barth and Evangelicalism* (Downers Grove: InterVarsity Press, 1980); Phillip R. Thorne, *Evangelicalism and Karl Barth: His Reception and Influence in North American Evangelical Theology* (Pittsburgh, PA: Pickwick Publications, 1995); and more recently, Sung Wook Chung, ed., *Karl Barth and Evangelical Theology* (Grand Rapids: Baker, 2006).

7. Randall Balmer, *Mine Eyes Have Seen the Glory: A Journey into the Evangelical Subculture in America*, 4th ed. (New York/Oxford: Oxford University Press, 2006); also Joel A. Carpenter, "The Fellowship of Kindred Minds: Evangelical Identity and the Quest for Christian Unity," in *Pilgrims on the Sawdust Trail: Evangelical Ecumenism and the Quest for Christian Identity*, ed. Timothy George (Grand Rapids: Baker, 2004), 27-42; and Mark Noll, *American Evangelical Christianity* (Malden, MA: Blackwell, 2001), 14.

8. Donald W. Dayton, "Some Doubts about the Usefulness of the Category 'Evangelical,'" in *The Variety of American Evangelicalism,* ed. Donald W. Dayton and Robert K. Johnston (Downers Grove: InterVarsity Press, 1991), 245-51; and D. G. Hart, *Deconstructing Evangelicalism: Conservative Protestantism in the Age of Billy Graham* (Grand Rapids, MI: Baker Academic, 2004).

9. While the usefulness and meaningfulness of the term has been called into question,

Evangelicalism is then usually defined in one of two ways: according to a narrative history that traces its genetic development, or by means of a list of key convictions that seeks to capture its essential nature. The first is a historical and sociological approach, while the latter strives for a theological definition. With regard to the first, it must be noted that while the narrative history is itself disputed, there is a broad consensus among historians that American evangelicalism arose as a movement with roots in the Protestant Reformation, the confluence of Puritanism and Pietism in the Great Awakenings and revivalism of eighteenth- and nineteenth-century America, and the Fundamentalist and Modernist controversy of the early twentieth century. These are, in fact, the periods in which the term "evangelical" came to prominence. This history is, of course, told a bit differently depending upon denominational perspective (for example, Wesleyan or Reformed, dispensational or Pentecostal, confessional or pietist).[10] Indeed, few concepts in American religious history are as disputed and amorphous as that of evangelicalism.[11] The history of evangelicalism is even traced by some all the way back to the first century and to those who embraced the *euangelion* of Christ, entailing that the first great divisive event in the church was not that between Protestant and Catholic, nor even Catholic and Orthodox, but between Christians and Jews.[12] Such a definition of evangelicalism is of course so broad as to render the term devoid of any meaning or usefulness. More common, however, is a historiography that begins in the Reformation and marks evangelicalism as

---

many historians and theologians defend the term while recognizing that it is nevertheless an "essentially contested concept." For example, see Robert K. Johnston, "American Evangelicalism: An Extended Family" in *The Variety of American Evangelicalism*, 253; 252-72. Johnston argues that while no uncontested definition for evangelicalism can be given, there are "family resemblances" between different denominational groups that allow them to be categorized under a common term, i.e., "evangelical." So also Richard Lints: "Evangelicals are like a collection of many siblings connected by some loose family resemblances. The differences between them are often as important as the similarities. The unifying strands will almost always admit of exceptions, and when the analysis becomes too fine-grained, it will lose some of its explanatory power" (*The Fabric of Theology: A Prolegomena to Evangelical Theology* [Grand Rapids: Eerdmans, 1993], 32). For a history of evangelicalism with special reference to its particular theology, see Roger Olson, *The Westminster Handbook of Evangelical Theology* (Louisville, KY: Westminster John Knox Press, 2004), 1-66.

10. Kenneth J. Collins, *The Evangelical Moment: The Promise of an American Religion* (Grand Rapids: Baker, 2005), 19-40.

11. As Collins notes, there is no definitive "evangelical metanarrative," but only smaller narratives that are combined through family resemblances and shared common themes (*The Evangelical Moment*, 22).

12. Collins, *The Evangelical Moment*, 22ff.

distinctly Protestant in nature. In its most strict form, evangelicalism refers to the neo-evangelicals (such as Harold John Ockenga and Carl F. H. Henry) of American post–World War II society who attempted to reform fundamentalism and overcome the deficiencies of its separatism and anti-intellectualism. Evangelical divisiveness and plurality are an inheritance of Protestant divisiveness and plurality and not unrelated to them. Evangelicalism is thus a reform movement within Christianity itself.

The other way of defining evangelicalism is by means of an essentialist, rather than historical, approach. The defining doctrines or convictions are most often stated as: (1) an authoritative and normative place for Scripture in determining all of faith and practice; (2) the necessity of conversion; (3) the centrality and definitive nature of Christ's atonement; and (4) the imperative of evangelism.[13] This evangelical quadrilateral has gained much acceptance as an accurate description of evangelical theological identity, and though other lists do exist, they usually amplify, rather than differ from, these four basic convictions.[14]

In brief, it is this prevalent definition of evangelicalism as a post–World War II phenomenon with roots in American Puritanism, Pietism, and revivalism — and as defined by these four convictions — that I will assume, rather than argue for, in this paper. Nevertheless, it should be noted that it here serves better as a descriptive rather than as a strictly normative term.

If we are then to answer the question of whether Barth and American evangelicals are friends or foes, we have to keep these challenges of history and identity in our purview. But this paper asks this question with regard to a specific theme, namely, that of ecclesiology as the topic of comparison between these dialogue partners, and here we reach a challenge that surpasses those of a troubled history and an elusive identity. This challenge can be illustrated by a bit of humor shared among some evangelicals involved in formal dialogue with Roman Catholics. As they put it: "The main difference between us and the Catholics is ecclesiology. They have one and we don't."[15] As Mark Noll comments, the joke is funny because it is at least partially true. In-

---

13. Collins, *The Evangelical Moment*, 21; also 41-61. This quadrilateral was definitively articulated by David W. Bebbington, *Evangelicalism in Modern Britain: A History from the 1730s to the 1980s* (London: Unwin Hyman, 1989), 1-19.

14. For example, see Lints, *The Fabric of Theology*, 49; also Olson, *Westminster Handbook to Evangelical Theology*, 6-7; and Johnson, "American Evangelicalism," 261.

15. Recounted in Mark Noll and Carolyn Nystrom, *Is The Reformation Over? An Evangelical Assessment of Contemporary Roman Catholicism* (Grand Rapids: Baker Academic, 2005), 145.

deed, one evangelical theologian has even floated the idea that "evangelical ecclesiology" may be an oxymoron.[16]

To see why this strange statement actually makes a bit of sense, we again must return to the question of identity. For unlike Lutheran, Reformed, Baptist, Congregationalist, and other communions, evangelicalism is not a confessional tradition, nor is it an institutional church or denomination (though George Marsden famously argued that it was).[17] It is a movement, and movements do not have ecclesiologies: churches do.[18] Remember that the list of four defining convictions for evangelicalism provided above did not include any specifically addressing ecclesiology. That absence is telling, for evangelicalism by its very nature is not a church (whether we understand a church in the sense of a local community of believers, a confessional or denominational body, or as an institutional structure) but rather is a movement that coalesced around a set of convictions and issues shared across various communions and denominations.[19] This is of course not to overlook the fact that evangelicals do belong to particular churches with particular ecclesiologies, so that we ought perhaps more accurately to speak of evangelical ecclesiologies in the plural rather than in the singular. Yet evangelicalism itself is both smaller than, and larger than, churches, while having its own unique ecclesial consciousness.[20]

First, evangelicalism is marked not so much by an ecclesiology as by *ecclesiolae in ecclesia,* a fellowship of persons within churches. At its most ex-

16. Bruce Hindmarsh, "Is Evangelical Ecclesiology an Oxymoron?" in *Evangelical Ecclesiology: Reality or Illusion?* ed. John G. Stackhouse, Jr. (Grand Rapids: Baker, 2003), 15-37. Hindmarsh himself believes that evangelicalism has its own "ecclesial consciousness," if not a developed specific ecclesiology per se.

17. George M. Marsden, "The Evangelical Denomination," in *Evangelicalism and Modern America, 1930-1980,* ed. George M. Marsden (Grand Rapids: Eerdmans, 1984).

18. This is of course not to deny that ecclesiologies differ even within traditions, and that not only evangelicalism, but confessional traditions themselves, are contested. For example, what does it mean to be Reformed? (And what is Reformed ecclesiology?) Van Til and Barth (both Reformed) would no doubt give quite different answers. Alasdair MacIntyre reminds us that *all* traditions are contested traditions, for a tradition is but "an historically extended, socially embodied argument." See MacIntyre, *After Virtue,* 2nd ed. (Notre Dame: University of Notre Dame Press, 1984), 222. For the diversity of Reformed thought since its inception, see Philip Benedict, *Christ's Churches Purely Reformed: A Social History of Calvinism* (New Haven and London: Yale University Press, 2002).

19. The word "church" itself is of course a multivalent term. See Erwin Fahlbusch, "Church," in *The Encyclopedia of Christianity: Volume 1 A-D,* ed. Erwin Fahlbusch, Jan M. Lochman, et al., trans. Geoffrey W. Bromiley (Grand Rapids, MI: Eerdmans, 1999), 477-78.

20. I borrow this term from Bruce Hindmarsh (see note 16 above).

treme, it trades the church for Philipp Jakob Spener's *collegia pietatis*, a college of piety, though it may also focus on doctrinal non-negotiables. Evangelicalism thus is smaller than churches insofar as it exists within them. It unites persons with shared convictions *within* traditional churches. Indeed, the ecclesiology of evangelicalism has often been an ecclesiology of division and separation as new denominations emerged from older ones in formal schism due to doctrinal differences or disagreements about the necessity of conversion. Separatism has been a recurrent feature of evangelical ecclesiologies.[21]

Evangelicalism is also larger than churches. It is marked by a penchant for producing large non-denominational and pan-denominational alliances and parachurch organizations that unite persons from various Protestant (and even Catholic!) confessions for common ministry, evangelism, and social action and service. Evangelicalism thus spans ecclesial borders. Indeed, its transdenominationalism is sometimes added as a fifth element to the four doctrinal marks above in order to identify what makes it most distinctive from other forms of Protestantism.[22]

If we do not understand evangelicalism as a movement both smaller than and larger than particular churches and confessional fellowships, we cannot make sense of both its sectarian proclivities and ecumenical achievements. These of course seem to be mutually exclusive, but they are not. Evangelicalism achieves the coalescing of a shared doctrinal and/or experiential identity within established churches. At times, the confessional and denominational identity of a particular church and its evangelical identity are functionally coextensive. At other times, however, an evangelical subconstituency forms its own identity that is more central and determinative than its confessional heritage (i.e., when one identifies oneself first as an evangelical, rather than as Reformed, Baptist, etc.). This new forged identity, when joined to disillusionment with and opposition to denominational directions and stances, may even lead to a separation from these confessional churches and the formation of new congregations and even denominations. Hence the sectarian element of evangelicalism.[23]

---

21. Carpenter, *The Evangelical Moment*, 33; for an insightful discussion of evangelicalism's peculiar ecclesial existence, see also Stanley Grenz, *Renewing the Center: Evangelical Theology in a Post-Theological Era* (Grand Rapids: Baker Academic, 2000), 287-324.

22. For example, John Stackhouse, *Evangelical Landscapes: Facing Critical Issues of the Day* (Grand Rapids: Baker, 2002), 48-50; see 163-65.

23. Leaving a confessional heritage or denomination can be done for less serious reasons as well. John Stackhouse can write: "Many evangelicals . . . feel free to leave one congregation, or even an entire denominational tradition, to find what to them is most important

But along with such sectarian proclivities, evangelicalism has also contributed to some of the most significant ecumenical achievements of the modern period, as Christians from numerous confessional and denominational traditions, from various churches, have joined with one another in both formal organizations and informal alliances to achieve shared evangelistic and activist goals in mission and relief. Such proclivities were already evident in the early British evangelicals, such as George Whitefield and John Wesley, who worked with those from various Christian traditions even while separated from them by confessions and other theological convictions. Such ecumenical endeavors led then, as now, to consternation among those less ecumenically inclined.[24] Evangelicalism is marked by sectarianism as well as ecumenism, by a demand for doctrinal purity that can lead to separation from mainline denominations, while at the same time downplaying confessional doctrines in favor of a shared conversional piety that transcends denominations themselves. Both of these must be recognized for us to consider evangelicalism honestly and accurately.[25]

The four-sided nature of evangelical ecclesial consciousness as sectarian and ecumenical, as well as pietistic and parachurch, lies at the root of evangelicalism's historical indifference to the institutional church and its general neglect of ecclesiology as a theological topic.[26] There can be no denying that evangelicalism has had significant effects upon American ecclesial life, not the least of which is a weakening of denominational and confessional identity. Whether one sees this as a positive or negative development depends on

---

in a church: usually some combination of the right basic doctrines, good preaching, good programs for the kids, and so on. Indeed, only among evangelicals does one encounter the revealing cliché, 'church shopping'" (*Evangelical Landscapes,* 28).

24. For an accounting of Whitefield's and Wesley's openness is this regard, see Mark Noll, *The Rise of Evangelicalism: The Age of Edwards, Whitefield, and the Wesleys* (Downers Grove: InterVarsity Press, 2003), 13-21; also Hindmarsh, "Is Evangelical Ecclesiology an Oxymoron?" 22-23; and Grenz, *Renewing the Center,* 292-93.

25. That Gary Dorrien only sees the sectarian, rather than the ecumenical, side of evangelicalism is thus a deficiency. See *The Remaking of Evangelical Theology* (Louisville, KY: Westminster John Knox, 1998), 3. I owe this insight to Stackhouse, *Evangelical Landscapes,* 183n35.

26. As George Marsden notes: "One of the striking features of much of evangelicalism is its general disregard for the institutional church." See Marsden, *Understanding Fundamentalism and Evangelicalism* (Grand Rapids: Eerdmans, 1991), 81; originally quoted in Grenz, *Renewing the Center,* 288, who then writes: "The lack of a full-orbed ecclesiological base is related to the 'parachurch' character of evangelicalism, which in turn has shaped the movement's particular ecumenicity. . . . The parachurch nature of evangelicalism has resulted in an unmistakable minimizing of ecclesiology" (288-89).

one's particular perspective and consideration of specific cases and aspects of this outcome.[27] Such a weakening can lead to a spiritualistic individualism that neglects the visible church and its sacraments, ordinances, and practices, as well as to a theological minimalism that dilutes rich and hearty confessional stews into a kind of thin theological gruel owing more to the market and to cultural trends than to the developed theological heritage of the churches. Such a weakening can also be due, however, to a recognition by Christians within one communion of a common confession of Christ and fellowship with others beyond the narrow confines of one's own denomination, accompanied by a new-found freedom from captivity to the confessional polemics of the past. Evangelical biblicism can foster both the bane of vacuous individualism, doctrinal indifference, and theological shallowness, as well as the benefit of freeing Christians to hear the voice of God anew and the freedom to circumvent, if not overcome, hard and fast confessional divisions of the past in common Christian witness for today.[28] Evangelicalism is unique, and it is uniquely puzzling.[29]

There can therefore be no simple answers when evaluating evangelical achievements and deficiencies with regard to ecclesiology. Even some of the significant elements of both Continental and British evangelicalism, as well

27. Stackhouse analyzes both the positive and negative effects of the increasing importance of parachurch organizations within evangelicalism in *Evangelical Landscapes*, 25-36. As he argues, "parachurch organizations cannot provide the full-fledged alternative cultures that Christian families, Christian small groups, and Christian churches can provide. . . . When Mr. and Mrs. Evangelical try to cope with a problem or succeed with an opportunity, InterVarsity and Focus on the Family and World Vision cannot talk with them in their living room, but local Christians bound to them in covenant *will* be there" (20).

28. See Stackhouse, *Evangelical Landscapes*, 174.

29. I would argue that evangelicalism at its best is a movement that may include doctrinal and conversionist themes, but that most positively serves as an ecumenical vision: it allows persons to transcend the feverish and narrow confines of their traditions, which must be nevertheless where all must live. Evangelicalism serves most significantly as a public space not for minimalist doctrinal commitments, but for ecumenical encounter and shared service and mission. In this, it serves as a hallway, to borrow an image from C. S. Lewis, or perhaps better as a parlor, where Christians dedicated to their individual churches, denominations, and traditions can meet for cordial (and sometimes heated) conversations as well as common mission. It is evangelicalism's institutions, such as its seminaries, and its publications, such as *Christianity Today*, and its publishing houses, such as Eerdmans, Baker, and InterVarsity, that serve as vehicles for theological discussions across denominational barriers and, I would argue, across evangelical and mainline divides (for example, Eerdmans crosses such barriers by publishing authors who unabashedly claim the evangelical label, and those who would reject that label entirely).

as that of America, that weakened traditional confessional identities cannot be simplistically judged and condemned. For example, the renewed missionary impulse of the eighteenth and nineteenth centuries led to the formation of ecumenical foreign missionary societies that up to that point had no parallel, and that then-current ecclesiological structures could not themselves provide. Such societies were the forerunners of modern parachurch organizations.[30] These societies provided for leadership opportunities outside hierarchical denominational structures and thus for greater lay involvement and leadership, thus lending them democratic and populist appeal. For no one was this more the case than for women. One of the often overlooked facts of the history of women in ministry is the place of these evangelical missionary societies, which were often organized, administered, and led by women, and this occurred long before the ordination of women in mainline denominations.[31]

All of this to say that evangelicalism has historically been loosely tied to traditional ecclesiological structures, most often existing *within* such structures (i.e., *ecclesiolae in ecclesia*), or in organizations spanning *alongside and across* them (i.e., parachurch organizations). This fact does not mean that evangelical organizations, both within and spanning across the churches, need be competitive with the churches; such organizations may work synergistically alongside of them.[32] Nevertheless, evangelicalism's unique character historically has led many evangelicals to downplay the church and certainly to neglect its centrality as a theological category (evangelicals have focused much more on the themes of Christ, atonement, and Scripture, and in doing so, are heirs of the Reformers in this regard). Stanley Grenz can thus state that ecclesiology is "the neglected stepchild of evangelical theology."[33] Only now, among second- and third-generation neo-evangelicals, and in

---

30. Carpenter, *The Evangelical Moment*, 34. "These new voluntary societies were to have profound implications for the churches. Like parishes or congregations, they were designed to bring people within hearing range of the gospel and to bring them into the church, but they did not fit into ecclesiastical systems of governance. So a new type of church organization grew up alongside old ones, and was parasitically related to them, but not under their authority. In the nineteenth century, there was an explosion of voluntary societies, as zealous evangelicals immediately saw opportunities to put these new organizational tools to work, for the reformation as well as the evangelization of their homelands" (34-35).

31. Ibid., 35. See also Justo L. González, *The Story of Christianity: The Early Church to the Present Day*, vol. 2 (Peabody, MA: Prince Press, 2001; 1985), 308.

32. Stackhouse, *Evangelical Landscapes*, 32.

33. Stanley Grenz, *Revisioning Evangelical Theology* (Downers Grove: InterVarsity Press, 1993), 165.

light of the increasing importance of ecclesiology in non-evangelical Protestant circles, have the ecclesiological deficiencies of evangelicalism been faced head on and ecclesiology taken up as a significant area of study.[34] More and more studies by evangelicals on ecclesiology are appearing, and this new wave of scholarship will have to address whether an evangelical ecclesiology is or is not an oxymoron.[35]

As I mentioned above, movements lend themselves to sociological description and perhaps even theological analysis. But movements themselves are not churches, and thus it takes some straining to argue that they possess ecclesiologies in their own right beyond those of the churches of their constitutive members. Nevertheless, setting aside this very large qualification, for the rest of this essay I want to focus on what Barth might criticize in, sympathize with, and contribute to contemporary evangelicalism and its understanding (or understandings) of the church. I will divide my comments into three broad headings: (1) areas where Barth would be quite critical of evangelicalism's understanding of the church and parachurch organizations, and how evangelicals might possibly respond to Barth; (2) areas where Barth can make a contribution to evangelicalism's understanding of the church today; and (3) areas where Barth might be quite sympathetic to evangelicalism and its understanding of the church and where they might share common ground. Let me also tip my hand at this point: I think that Barth provides evangelicalism with significant resources for a revitalized, rich, evangelical understanding of the church, and I want to encourage

---

34. Vanhoozer comments, "The doctrine of the church has, in the last decade or so, moved to the forefront of theological research and writing, primarily among non-evangelicals — so much so that ecclesiology has effectively displaced the doctrine of revelation as 'first theology.'" Vanhoozer, "Evangelicalism and the Church: The Company of the Gospel," in *The Futures of Evangelicalism: Issues and Prospects,* ed. Craig Bartholomew, Robin Perry, and Andrew West (Grand Rapids: Kregel, 2004), 63.

35. Some of the most important recent studies of evangelical ecclesiology are the papers collected in Stackhouse's *Evangelical Ecclesiology,* as well as those in *The Community of the Word: Toward an Evangelical Ecclesiology,* ed. Mark Husbands and Daniel J. Treier (Downers Grove: InterVarsity Press, 2005). See also Vanhoozer, "Evangelicalism and the Church," 40-99; as well as Grenz, *Renewing the Center,* 287-324. Howard A. Snyder has argued that evangelical ecclesiologies are patchwork amalgams of the Anglo-Catholic and Reformed/Lutheran-Catholic heritage, the Radical Reformation and Free Church tradition, the revivalist tradition, American democracy, and American entrepreneurship. Snyder, "The Marks of Evangelical Ecclesiology," in *Evangelical Ecclesiology,* 92-96. With such a mongrel pedigree, it is no wonder that it is so difficult to speak of a coherent notion of an evangelical ecclesiology.

evangelicals to take Barth's ecclesiology with utmost seriousness. So for the rest of this essay, I address three elements that Barth presents to evangelicalism: criticisms, contributions, and areas of consensus.

Let us begin with the problems. Insofar as evangelicals (not all, of course, but a significant number) neglect the visible institutional church, insofar as they align themselves more with parachurch movements and neglect or even denigrate the concrete assembly of believers in a church of word and sacrament or ordinance, Barth would spare no criticism. Such a judgment is not difficult to defend, and one piece from Barth's corpus is sufficient to ground it, namely, a short article addressing the Oxford Group Movement of the 1930s.[36] Barth's opposition to the Oxford Group Movement was not unrelated to the connections of some of its leadership to members of the Nazi Party, and I am not in any way implying that in this sense the Group Movement and evangelicalism can be compared or are at all similar. But as a renewal movement within the church, the Group Movement does provide an interesting test case for how Barth might respond to certain aspects of contemporary evangelicalism when Barth's specific charges against the Oxford Movement are examined.[37] In fact, a number of Barth's criticisms of this movement appear prescient for those who know American evangelicalism's weaknesses well.

First, Barth criticizes the Oxford Group for substituting a movement for the church. For those who were abandoning the church for the charisma and promise of the Oxford Group Movement, Barth indeed had stern rebuke. He writes: "Preaching, doctrine, teaching, pastoral work and the building up of the Christian congregation have nothing whatever to do with a 'movement.'"[38] Moreover, regardless of its shortcomings, the problems of the church could never entail its abandonment. When Barth himself in his early pastorate was enthralled with a movement, namely, the socialist movement,

---

36. For an introduction to Barth's background with the Oxford Group Movement, see Christoph Dahling-Sander, "Karl Barth-Emil Brunner. An uneasy correspondence from the very beginning." Available from: http://karlbarth.unibas.ch/fileadmin/downloads/letter2.pdf (accessed March 1, 2011). Once again, Barth's opposition to the movement was tied up with his fight against National Socialism. Though this is the case, I am not at all implying that Barth's criticisms of evangelicalism would have any correspondence to this aspect of the Group Movement.

37. For the following discussion, see Barth, "Church or Group Movement?" *The London Quarterly and Hoborn Review* (January 1937): 1-10. This article was originally published in *Evangelische Theologie* 6 (1936): 205ff.

38. Ibid., 4.

and was also quite critical of the church, he nonetheless did not abandon the church for socialism's call to action, to the chagrin of some of his socialist friends. Despite his harsh criticisms of the church in his commentary on *Romans,* leaving the church was never a serious question for him.[39] As he wrote to his friend Eduard Thurneysen in 1925, the protest against the church in those early years was a protest from within the church itself.[40] Barth's commitment to the church would never waver in this regard.

Second, Barth is very troubled by the anthropological starting point of the Oxford Group, in which the needs and contemporary situation of the modern person are determinative for the shape that the gospel message is to take and in fact, in his estimation, stand in judgment over it. He writes: "The Groups have put the 'world' in the position of a 'bank cashier' who tests the gold coin, i.e. the genuineness of the Christian proclamation."[41] For Barth, the gospel must be prior to such needs of the moment and cannot be captive to current blowing winds. To fail in this regard is to trade the Word of God for "a beautiful and moralistic programme" that can only be self-serving.[42] Barth wholly rejects such an apologetic of experience, whether moralistic or mystical, for Scripture's truth.[43]

In a related vein, Barth is also deeply distressed with both the triumphalism and the secular methods of the Groups in their attempt to

39. Barth writes: "The description of the Church which we have just given is often blamed as being typical of those who oppose the Church or who, at least, hold themselves aloof from it. But blame such as this does not affect us. When, however, our critics go on to propose that we ought to leave the Church if we think of it thus, we are bound to state that we could not contemplate such a proposal, and would do our best to dissuade others from even considering it. It would never enter our heads to think of leaving the Church. For in describing the Church we are describing ourselves." See Barth, *Der Römerbrief,* 2nd ed. (München: Chr. Kaiser Verlag, 1923), 355; English translation: *The Epistle to the Romans,* trans. Edwyn C. Hoskyns (Oxford: Oxford University Press, 1968), 371. For the development and content of Barth's ecclesiology, see Kimlyn J. Bender, *Karl Barth's Christological Ecclesiology* (Aldershot: Ashgate, 2005). Barth could later look back on his early reflections regarding the church during the *Romans* period as unduly harsh and one-sided: "It was a part of the exaggerations of which we were guilty in 1920 that we were able to see the theological relevance of the Church only as a negative counterpart to the Kingdom of God which we had then so happily rediscovered" (Barth, "The Humanity of God," in *The Humanity of God,* trans. John Newton Thomas [Louisville, KY: Westminster John Knox Press, 1960], 62).

40. *Revolutionary Theology in the Making: Barth-Thurneysen Correspondence, 1914-1925,* trans. James D. Smart (Richmond: John Knox Press, 1964), 216.

41. Barth, "Church or Group Movement?" 4.

42. Ibid., 8.

43. Ibid., 9.

Christianize the world. Barth, who opposed ecclesiastical and cultural triumphalism in any form, writes: "I do not know how long the world will submit to being conquered for Christ in such a secular way. But this I do know, that the creation of this magic land composed of secular values and standards has nothing to do with prayer, with hope and with the message of the Christian Church, and that the Church can only be compromised by the Groups." For Barth such triumphalism joined to worldly methods is a denial of the freedom and mystery of grace and the secularization of the church itself.[44]

Fourth, Barth also has a wariness of the cult of personality that the Groups seem to foster: "If a man with a title such as 'Secretary of State for the U.S.A.' utters only the very vaguest word in their favour, this becomes — I do not know why — a really magical testimonial."[45] Here again, the worldly position and standing of the testifier is seen to add credibility to the testimony, and this standing is being exploited by the Oxford Movement. For Barth, such could appear as little more than fawning for endorsements.

Finally, Barth is very disturbed by a movement that seems to lay more emphasis and weight upon the testimonial of a changed individual than the gospel of Christ. Here Barth's fear of an anthropological starting-point more commonly encountered in his interaction with Friedrich Schleiermacher, Emil Brunner, and Rudolf Bultmann (though also tellingly prefigured in his ambivalence to pietism) is readily evidenced in relation to a contemporary evangelical movement. As Barth accuses the Oxford Group: "Should one take the miraculous reports of the Group as an adequate and acceptable supplement to the Christian message? According to that very message Jesus Christ is the end and the way to the end. The way of the Group is not Jesus Christ, but the ostensibly changed man and what this man is pleased to report about himself. In this case can Christ be indeed the end of all things? I do not see a supplement here, I only see a contradiction."[46] Against such a

---

44. Ibid., 5; also 9-10.

45. Ibid., 4.

46. Ibid., 6. He also states: "The Groups' praise of God is too self-centered to be genuine praise; in the Bible it is *God's* help alone which is praised" (ibid., 8). Dahling-Sander summarizes Barth's criticisms of the movement this way: ". . . Barth placed the Oxford-Group-Movement together with its Swiss branch, the 'Middle-Party' in the church struggle in Germany as well as the Young Reformation Movement in the category of 'natural theology', which he fought against. Practically, it became for him the embodiment of the ambiguous nature of man, which seeks to justify and sanctify itself and, in so doing, take control of God. It deceives itself subjectively and 'acts' instead of allowing God to act."

movement, Barth poses the church, which "points away from the man who receives grace to the grace of God Himself."[47] For Barth, one had to choose between the church and the Group movement in an either/or decision. His own answer was to side with the church and exhort her to be and become the church which God would have her to be.[48]

Reading this short and little known piece from many years ago is illuminating for the present. Barth's opposition to any denigration and abandonment of the church for participation in a movement, to evangelistic triumphalism and the conflation of the church's mission with a cultural program, to secular methods driven by the needs of the time rather than from reflection upon the gospel itself, to the reduction of the gospel to a pragmatic moralism, to a cult of personality and to aggrandized testimonials often heavily salted with emotionalism as well as to a not-so-latent individualism: all are directly pertinent to a discussion of modern evangelicalism, at least in terms of its excesses often documented by many of its own adherents. In short, Barth's list from the past can only make many of us wince in the present. Certainly this is not to say that all of evangelicalism would fall under such criticisms, and, as noted above, many evangelicals themselves have made similar ones of the modern movement. But such criticisms are worth noting nonetheless.

Though Barth's criticisms were meant for a movement long ago, they do illustrate what Barth would no doubt oppose in much of current evangelical ecclesial life. Evangelicals themselves, however, might want to retort that Barth has overstated his case and offer their own questions to Barth. For instance, need the relation between Christian renewal movements or parachurch organizations and the church always be portrayed as one of conflict? Could there not be ones of genuine harmony and cooperation? Moreover, there is good biblical precedent, they might justifiably argue, for "becoming all things to all people" so that they might be saved (1 Cor. 9:22), as well as for recounting one's own encounter with God in order not to glorify the self but to turn others toward this God "who raises the dead" (2 Cor. 1:8-11). Did not the chief of sinners (as portrayed in Acts) often recount his inglorious past in order to point toward God's glorious future by speaking of a blinding light, a changed life, and a new destiny (Acts 22 and 26)?[49] Evangelicals would not have to start from scratch in forming their own questions and

---

47. Ibid., 8; also 10.
48. See ibid., 1, 2, 4.
49. One might also consider the final four chapters of 2 Corinthians in this regard.

counter-criticisms. Variations of the very ones I have just mentioned were raised by the distinguished Oxford New Testament professor B. H. Streeter, who defended the Oxford Movement in an April response in the same journal to Barth's January article.[50] I do not believe that Streeter provides anything that would make Barth retract his criticisms, although against Barth, Streeter made the astute point — and one that is to me irrefutable and too often forgotten — that the professor's lecture and the pastor's sermon can lend themselves to egoism as readily as an individual's testimonial.[51] Nevertheless, it is not hard to imagine that were Barth here today to converse with evangelicals, the discussion might sound something like the jousting between Barth and Streeter. I am not, however, going to try to stage such a debate or adjudicate it, a debate quite tied to how the objective and subjective poles of salvation are related. Instead, I want to move on to what Barth might uniquely contribute to evangelicalism's understanding of the church.

Most significantly, Barth provides a rich *theology* of the church that evangelicals may want to study and consider.[52] Barth's ecclesiology presents evangelicalism with an alternative to two mistaken approaches to which it has at times been prone, namely, a flight into visibility in which the theological nature of the church is sacrificed to sociological approaches, and a flight from the visible altogether by recourse to a doctrine of the invisible church. In other words, these are the problematic approaches of an ebionitic and a docetic ecclesiology, respectively. Let me address these in turn.

To say that evangelicals have neglected ecclesiology is not to say that they have neglected the church altogether. What they have neglected, rather, is a rich theological account of the church. An honest evaluation of evangelicalism must conclude that evangelicals have oftentimes conceded ecclesiology to sociology, history, and, in the worst instances, to entrepreneurship. Evangelicalism to a great degree does not have a richly Trinitarian, Christological, and pneumatological understanding of the church (though there are ever-increasing attempts to address this deficiency). There are at the very least two reasons for this lack of rich theological description. First, evangelicalism is most often understood as a sociological and historical

---

50. B. H. Streeter, "Professor Barth v. The Oxford Group," *London Quarterly and Hoborn Review* (April 1937): 145-49. Barth's and Streeter's short articles read together make for interesting reading.

51. Ibid., 148-49.

52. For a comprehensive discussion of Barth's theology of the church, see Bender, *Karl Barth's Christological Ecclesiology;* also, the essays by John Webster in *The Community of the Word,* 75-95 and 96-113.

movement (perhaps partly due to the prominent place that its historians play rather than its theologians). This view of evangelicalism in turn translates into a sociological view of the church rather than a theological one. Second, practitioners more interested in pragmatic and numerical success than theological reflection are often the ones who shape evangelical ecclesiology. In the words of Barth, they are often more impressed with extensive rather than intensive growth, numerical rather than spiritual increase (though, as Barth himself noted, these need not be mutually exclusive).[53] Nevertheless, to treat the church as a society among societies, as an organization among organizations, as a sociological entity marked by visible success accounted for by secular methods, is to take flight into the visible church and sacrifice its theological identity. What is required is a much more robust theological doctrine of the church.

Now it must be said that evangelical theologians are very aware of this. In his excellent essay, "Evangelicalism and the Church," Kevin Vanhoozer contends: "The church cannot be adequately understood unless one gives an appropriately 'thick description', one that goes beyond the human categories of sociology, even beyond the notion of 'community practices'. To describe all that the church is, one must have recourse to properly theological categories. For the church is, in the final analysis, a *theological* community."[54] In contrast, he states, "evangelicals by and large do not know what they believe about the church — neither about what it is, nor what it should be doing."[55]

Such an appeal to fundamental unawareness may overstate the case, confusing ignorance with an alternative view of the church, one that is sociological rather than theological in nature, an ecclesiology "from below" wherein the church is an aggregate of individuals self-chosen in a voluntary society.[56]

---

53. *CD* IV/2, 648.

54. Vanhoozer, "Evangelicalism and the Church," 71; see 70-71.

55. Ibid., 42.

56. As George R. Hunsberger writes, evangelical ecclesiology tends to see the church as "the modern social form of a *voluntary organization* grounded in the collective exercise of *rational choice* by its members rather than the form of a communion of saints that is made such by the will of the Spirit of God. There need be no dichotomy between the choices of God and the responses of those whom God calls, of course. But that dichotomy is precisely what emerges from a sense of Christian identity that is first and foremost individual rather than one that knows that human identity is both personal and relational, both individual and communal" ("Evangelical Conversion toward a Missional Ecclesiology," in *Evangelical Ecclesiology*, 118-19). For critiques of evangelicalism's individualism in relation to the church, see also C. Norman Kraus, "Evangelicalism: A Mennonite Critique," in *The Variety of American Evangelicalism*, 198; and Vanhoozer, "Evangelicalism and the Church," 58. Reformed thinkers in America

But evangelicalism is marked not only by a flight *into* the visible church, but also oftentimes by a flight *from* it.

In contrast to the former sociological understanding of the church, evangelicalism is often marked by a disregard for the visible church altogether and an embrace of a spiritual invisible church.[57] Such a view sees the visible church with its obvious difficulties as at best indifferent to and at worst deleterious for the spiritual life. It is the invisible church, the church as a "spiritual fellowship of the truly converted," that matters, such that involvement within the visible church becomes optional because it is in the end soteriologically irrelevant.[58] This viewpoint is evident when some evangelicals witness to others by contrasting the new life in Christ with the failures of the church. Such a viewpoint is of course not the case for many evangelicals. But it does seem to be the case for many American self-designated evangelicals answering George Barna's surveys.[59] One does not have to dig very hard to find within evangelicalism an indifference toward the visible church, if not a flight from the visible altogether.

Against both a flight into and that from the visible church, against both reductive sociological and pragmatic understandings of the church on the one hand and platonic and spiritualistic ones on the other, Barth presents a fully theological understanding of the church, a church that is divinely constituted, in which, as he says already in the *Göttingen Dogmatics,* the "invisible-becomes-visible [*sichtbarwerden*]."[60] The church is thus *more* than the visible, for it is divinely called, and not simply humanly constituted. But it is *never less* than visible, for its visibility is indeed part of its divinely

---

at times criticize evangelicalism for its low ecclesiology and penchant for using a parachurch definition of voluntary association united for practical purposes as an adequate ecclesiological description of the church. See Mark Noll and Cassandra Niemczyk, "Evangelicals and the Self-Consciously Reformed," in *The Variety of American Evangelicalism,* 216.

57. For evangelicalism's proclivity to abandon the visible church for the invisible one, see Vanhoozer, "Evangelicalism and the Church," 46-48; also Grenz, *Renewing the Center,* 297-99.

58. Vanhoozer, "Evangelicalism and the Church," 47.

59. See *The Barna Update,* "Americans Have Commitment Issues, New Survey Shows" (April 18, 2006). Available from: http://www.barna.org/barna-update/article/12-faithspirituality/267-americans-have-commitment-issues-new-survey-shows (accessed March 1, 2011).

60. Barth, *Unterricht in der christlichen Religion, III: Die Lehre von der Versöhnung/Die Lehre von der Erlösung,* ed. Hinrich Stoevesandt (Zürich: Theologisher Verlag Zürich, 2003), 364. This was Barth's first dogmatics and originated from his first professorship in the early to mid-1920s.

ordained existence. The doctrine of the church as both invisible and visible, with the first functioning as the basis of the second in an irreversible relation, thus exists in analogy to the doctrine of the person of Christ in Christology.[61] The church is the body of Christ, an image which Barth understands not as a weak metaphor but as an ontological reality in which the church truly exists as Christ's "earthly-historical form of existence" *(irdisch-geschichtliche Existenzform).*[62] Christ and the church are joined together in the *totus Christus,* Christ with his body, and Barth provides a place for the church in God's economy of salvation that is an important corrective to much of evangelicalism's reductive sociological description of the church in which the church is a collection of individuals, a solely voluntary society, and little else.[63]

Barth's ecclesiology is also a corrective, however, for ecclesiologies that trade concrete visibility for spiritual fellowship and personal piety and make the church peripheral or even irrelevant to God's saving activity. Against such a view, Barth presents a very different one, making the faith of the believer dependent upon the prior witness of the church, as when he states regarding the subjective reality of revelation in the first volume of the *Church Dogmatics:* "God himself and God alone turns man into a recipient of His revelation — but He does so in a definite area, and this area . . . is the area of the Church."[64] As he then continues:

> Put pointedly . . . there exist over against Jesus Christ, not in the first instance believers, and then, composed of them, the Church; but first of all the Church and then, through it and in it, believers. While God is as little bound to the Church as to the Synagogue, the recipients of His revelation are. They are what they are because the Church is what it is, and because they are in the Church, not apart from the Church and not outside the Church. And when we say "Church," we do not mean merely the inward and invisible coherence of those whom God in Christ calls His own, but also the outward and visible coherence of those who have heard in time, and have confessed to their hearing, that in Christ they are God's. The reception of revelation occurs within, not without, this twofold coherence.[65]

61. Ibid., 366.
62. *CD* IV/1, 661.
63. See *CD* IV/2, 59-60; see also *CD* IV/3.1, 216.
64. *CD* I/2, 210.
65. Ibid., 211.

Against the excesses of evangelical individualism, Barth posits the corporate reality of the church, a reality that is not peripheral to the economy of salvation but one grounded in God's sovereign election.[66] And against the evangelical penchant to downplay or even disregard the visible church and take flight to an invisible one, Barth posits that the church is necessarily visible and concrete as the "outward and visible coherence of those who have heard in time," ideas included in extensive sections of the *Church Dogmatics* where Barth speaks of such concrete issues as church law and church practices.[67] In short, Barth's ecclesiology is thoroughly grounded in God's free election of grace and integrated into the work of God's act of reconciliation rather than simply functional and peripheral to them. Barth provides a rich theological account of the church as a corporate and concrete people that can serve as a resource to protect against current deformities of ecclesiology resulting from an overemphasis upon pragmatism and the rising tides of a recently resurgent gnosticism.[68] Yet Barth's ecclesiology is more than a remedy for recent concerns.

What Barth provides is a richly developed ecclesiology that attempts to overcome a deficiency already latent to some degree in the Reformation bifurcation of soteriology and ecclesiology.[69] The bifurcation was perhaps unavoidable in its day, and the debate between Luther and the likes of Cajetan and Preieras was a necessary one, but it came with a price, namely, a division between soteriology and ecclesiology in which the former was used against the latter, evidenced in a minimalist Protestant ecclesiology that evangelicalism has attenuated still further. Luther and Calvin certainly labored to retain the centrality of the church in God's plan of redemption and cannot be pinned with today's individualistic excesses. But the times often dictated that the doctrine of salvation and that of the church were locked in a tragic zero-sum game, so that ecclesiology was even for the Reformers often defined in a negative and reactive rather than constructive manner. Their successors

---

66. *CD* II/2, 195ff.

67. *CD* IV/3.2, 865ff.; see also *CD* IV/2, 676ff.

68. Evangelicalism is always in danger of gnosticism, which seems, along with individualism, to be America's quintessential heresy. See Harold Bloom, *The American Religion: The Emergence of the Post-Christian Nation* (New York: Simon and Schuster, 1991). There is something perennially tempting about a gospel of simple knowledge, simply held, for an escape from a doomed world.

69. One way to state this is that the Reformers traded Augustine's ecclesiology for his soteriology. See Diarmaid MacCulloch, *The Reformation* (London/New York: Penguin, 2003), 111.

were much less successful than they. What Barth provides is a reuniting of soteriology and ecclesiology by getting at the heart of the matter, namely, the relation of Christ, and thus the gospel, to the church. His is an attempt to undo what was at the time a needed division but one that cannot last. Yet — and this cannot be stressed enough — this reunification is undertaken in a thoroughly Protestant manner, for Barth is after nothing less than articulating an ecclesiology equal in development and scope to that of Tridentine Catholicism, but one faithful to the Protestant vision, to join together again what in the Reformation was rent asunder, but to join them in a rightly ordered relation, to take Ephesians as seriously within the canon as Romans and Galatians.

Barth was keenly aware of the failure of the Reformation and post-Reformation to put forth an ecclesiology that was rich and developed, a failure in no small part due to its protest against the robust ecclesiology of Roman Catholicism. The answer to such a robust view of the church, Barth realized, could never be an ecclesiological minimalism, but a fully formed and compelling Protestant alternative to it. Just as the *Church Dogmatics* in some respects is on a par with Thomas's *Summa Theologica* in seriousness, weight, and scope (for Barth never repudiated the scholastic impulse of comprehensiveness in theology), so Barth's doctrine of the church provides an ecclesiology for Protestantism as high as that of Roman Catholicism. It is thus a serious resource to be considered for an ecumenical ecclesiology for Protestantism today that stands between the organic ecclesiology of Roman Catholicism, and the self-selected sociological ecclesiology of so much of evangelical Protestantism. What Barth gives us is a rich ecclesiology that aspires to be catholic even as it is thoroughly evangelical (in the widest sense of the term), Protestant in nature and congregational in form. To rip off Richard Dawkins in a way that he would no doubt despise, Barth may provide a significant resource for remaining an "intellectually fulfilled Protestant" by providing an ecclesiology that is sufficiently serious and compelling to be a viable alternative to those of the Catholic and Orthodox traditions.

Barth can provide this due to a theology of the church that fully incorporates the church into the economy of grace without making it the steward of grace. In other words, while Barth takes seriously the unity of the *totus Christus,* the unity of Christ and the church in a way that evangelicalism often has not, this unity always remains for him a unity in distinction, never a simple unity. Christ is united with his church, but he is never subsumed into her. In other words, Barth never ceases to be a Protestant in his ecclesiology even while correcting Protestant deficiencies. He provides a truly catholic evangelical (over against, for example, a Roman Catholic or evangelical catholic) doctrine of the church.

Certainly it must be said that the distinction between Christ and the church is carefully preserved in evangelicalism, but it is often preserved by making the church peripheral to God's act of reconciliation. What Barth provides is an ecclesiology in which there is a true union of Christ and the church, but where this union remains ever differentiated and irreversible in nature; where Christ is never subsumed into the being and agency of the church; where the church is a witness to, but not an extension of, the incarnation, and thus a proclaimer, rather than dispenser, of grace. One in which the church is both divine event and human institution, but with these also in an irreversible order, the first giving rise to the second, the second never the church without the first. In short, what Barth offers evangelicals to consider is a doctrine of the church that once again sees the church as a mystery and an article of faith. This in the end may be Barth's greatest contribution to evangelicalism regarding the question of the church, if evangelicals are willing to take him seriously on this score. Such a consideration need not of course mean that evangelicalism's unique and best contributions to ecclesiology cannot be preserved. Perhaps even evangelicalism's voluntarism and its emphasis upon the individual (though not its individualism) could thus be theologically transformed and reconstituted by being grounded in the freedom of God and the priesthood of all believers, respectively, though this is the topic for another paper.[70]

In closing, I want to add that I think that this conversation can get off the ground and that Barth and evangelicals can even be friends, in spite of significant differences that may continue to exist between them. I believe this can take place because Barth and evangelicals are very close on a number of central and important issues, of which I will mention three. The first is that both embrace the scandal of the gospel, namely, the centrality of Christ and his unique and supreme and irreplaceable identity standing at the heart of all of the ways and works of God. This sets them apart from so many others today, sadly. If the great divide in modern Christianity is between those who embrace and those who reject the scandal of the gospel, then Barth and evangelicals stand together on one side of the aisle.

Second, in correspondence to this Christological particularity, Barth

---

70. For a provisional attempt at such a reconfiguration, see Roger Olson, "Free Church Ecclesiology and Evangelical Spirituality: A Unique Compatibility," in *Evangelical Ecclesiology*, 161-78.

and evangelicals both give evidence of a shared commitment to a radical particularity in ecclesiology, in that the primary agent of God's work in the world is not the institutional structure of a church per se, but is the concrete congregation of believers in a particular place and time. If all politics is local, and the church as the concrete sign of the kingdom is a divinely actualized event that gives rise to a new form of politics in the world, then the church, too, is local. The universality of the church is therefore found in its radical particularity, and the fundamental nature of the church is related not first and foremost to an institutional or denominational structure but to the local body of believers. For the church is before all else an event that gives rise to a historical existence in a particular location, and thus the church is first and foremost a congregation rather than an institution (hence Barth's preference for the German *Gemeinde* rather than *Kirche*).[71] In a manner that could no doubt be embraced by most evangelicals, Barth articulates this conviction when he states: "When I say congregation, I am thinking primarily of the concrete form of the congregation in a particular place. . . . *Credo ecclesiam* means that I believe that here, at this place, in this visible assembly, the work of the Holy Spirit takes place."[72] Moreover, like Barth, many evangelicals are not likely to be swayed by an argument that the answer to today's secularism can effectively be held off with an appeal to a new creedalism or recovery of an episcopal ministry and return to strong clergy and laity distinctions.[73]

71. See Barth's address at the Amsterdam Assembly of the World Council of Churches in 1948 in *Man's Disorder and God's Design* (New York: Harper and Brothers, 1948), 67-76; see also Barth's discussion of the difference between these terms in *Evangelical Theology: An Introduction,* trans. Grover Foley (New York: Holt, Rinehart and Winston, 1963), 37. For a robust and compelling defense of an evangelical congregationalism, including a theological defense of a chastened emphasis upon the individual and of voluntarism, see Olson, "Free Church Ecclesiology and Evangelical Spirituality," 161-78.

72. Barth, *Dogmatics in Outline,* trans. G. T. Thomson (New York: Harper & Row, 1959), 142-43. Elsewhere he can say: "We assume that by the Christian community or Church is not meant an establishment or institution organized along specific lines, but the living people awakened and assembled by Jesus Christ as the Lord for the fulfillment of a specific task" (*CD* III/4, 488). Such a view of the church as local and concrete does not deny the reality of the universal church, but it does prioritize and respect the integrity of the local congregation and refuse to universalize forms and structures of community life that are best left to local and indigenous decision.

73. Barth's opposition to hierarchical vicariate offices can be seen at least as early as his dogmatic lectures in Göttingen. See Barth, *Unterricht in der christlichen Religion,* III, 372-77; see also *CD* III/4, 488-90; and *CD* IV/2, 690-95. For an early commentary on the limitations of creedalism, see Barth's "The Desirability and Possibility of a Universal Reformed Creed," in *Theology and Church,* trans. Louise Pettibone Smith (New York: Harper & Row, 1962), 118.

Creeds and bishops may have helped in the past and may have value in the present, but they are not enough and may even do more harm than good (may one assume that Bishop John Shelby Spong says the creed in the liturgy?). So Barth and evangelicals may find common cause in a commitment to a very different catholicity and a very different ecclesial concreteness than the high church and highly centralized and hierarchical ecclesiology espoused by the so-called "evangelical catholics" of today, one that focuses on concrete congregational existence rather than institutional offices and structures, as well as one that is eschatological, rather than romantic, regarding questions of ecumenism.[74]

The final similarity between Barth and evangelicals is that both define the church not only by its self-constitutive practices (as does the Augsburg Confession, for example) but make mission as evangelism and service central to the church's existence, though for evangelicals mission is often thought of as what the church *does,* whereas for Barth's actualistic ecclesiology mission is what the church *is.*[75] Nevertheless, evangelicals, who often are much better in their practice than their theory, would no doubt completely concur with Barth's statement that "the Church is either a missionary Church or it is no church at all."[76] Evangelicals indeed now seem to live this out more than their mainline counterparts.

Barth himself regretted that this missionary impulse was not to be found in the magisterial churches of his day, while readily evident in the sects, as he referred to them.[77] But the end of Christendom, which Barth saw as occurring around him, has now come to pass in the West, so it is perhaps best to retire Ernst Troeltsch's categories once and for all and recognize similarities among all like-minded missional Christians. And when we retire such categories, perhaps this too can remove one more barrier to making conversations between Barth and modern evangelicals possible and productive.

74. For such an example of an evangelical-catholic approach, see Carl Braaten, "The Special Ministry of the Ordained," in *Marks of the Body of Christ,* ed. Carl E. Braaten and Robert W. Jenson (Grand Rapids, MI: Eerdmans, 1999), 123-36. Braaten has little regard for evangelicalism, it seems (see 134). For a very different assessment of episcopal ministry than Braaten's by one within both the high church and evangelical traditions, see Paul F. M. Zahl, "Up the Creek: Paddling in the Maelstrom of the Mainline," in *Pilgrims on the Sawdust Trail,* 177-81; see also his response to the articles in *Evangelical Ecclesiology,* 213-16.

75. See *CD* IV/3.2, esp. 795-96.

76. *CD* III/3, 64. Barth claimed to have recovered this missionary impulse not from magisterial Protestantism, but from Anabaptism and Pietism (*CD* IV/3.1, 11-38, esp. 25 and 28).

77. *CD* III/4, 505.

The Being and Act of the Church:
Barth and the Future of Evangelical Ecclesiology

Keith L. Johnson

I. The Evangelical Problem

In *The Younger Evangelicals*, Robert Webber provides an often surprising account of the changing commitments of the most recent generation of evangelical scholars and church leaders. One shift that he notes among these younger evangelicals is their desire for "a more visible concept of the church."[1] This desire stems, in part, from their reaction against what they perceive as the overly individualistic tendencies of modern evangelicalism. They believe that these tendencies lead to the same kind of "ahistoricism and spiritual subjectivism" that Philip Schaff called "the great disease which has fastened itself upon the heart of Protestantism."[2] Younger evangelicals have dedicated themselves to fighting this disease. Right doctrine and a commitment to evangelism are no longer enough; they want, in Webber's words, "an embodied presence of God's reign in an earthed community."[3] To find it, they are turning to high forms of liturgy, ancient spiritual practices, sacra-

1. Robert Webber, *The Younger Evangelicals: Facing the Challenges of the New World* (Grand Rapids: Baker Books, 2002), 109.

2. Both citations are found in D. H. Williams, *Retrieving the Tradition and Renewing Evangelicalism: A Primer for Suspicious Protestants* (Grand Rapids: Eerdmans, 1999), 14. Also see Philip Schaff, *The Principle of Protestantism*, trans. John Nevin (Chambersburg, PA: Publication Office of the German Reformed Church, 1845), 107. Williams's book can be read as an example of the trend Webber describes.

3. Webber, *The Younger Evangelicals*, 109.

mental worship, and a renewed engagement with the historic faith through catechisms and confessions. They are, in other words, looking beyond the evangelical tradition for resources that supply new and more concrete forms for their faith and the ministry of their churches.

When seen in the context of this trend, the recent conversion of Evangelical Theological Society President Francis Beckwith to Roman Catholicism is not as surprising as it first appears. As he tells it, his journey toward Rome began with the sense that something wasn't right with his faith. He responded by turning to the Church Fathers, to books like Mark Noll's *Is the Reformation Over?*, and to the *Joint Declaration on the Doctrine of Justification*.[4] These sources led him to engage more deeply with Catholic theology, and eventually, with the Roman Catholic Church itself. In Catholicism he found the resources to overcome the deficiencies he perceived in evangelicalism. Here is how he describes the reasoning behind his conversion:

> The Catholic Church frames the Christian life as one in which you must exercise virtue — not because virtue saves you, but because that's the way God's grace gets manifested. As an evangelical, even when I talked about sanctification and wanted to practice it, it seemed as if I didn't have a good enough incentive to do so. Now there's a kind of theological framework, and it doesn't say my salvation depends on me, but it says my virtue counts for something. It's important to allow the grace of God to be exercised through your actions. The evangelical emphasis on the moral life forms my Catholic practice with an added incentive. That was liberating to me.[5]

Beckwith's problem of not having "a good enough incentive" to live a sanctified life is shared by many evangelicals. The problem is a theological one, and it stems from a failure to properly situate the church in the doctrine of God.[6] If we see our justification exclusively as a forensic event

---

4. See the Lutheran World Federation and the Roman Catholic Church, *Joint Declaration on the Doctrine of Justification* (Grand Rapids: Eerdmans, 1999); Mark Noll and Carolyn Nystrom, *Is the Reformation Over? An Evangelical Assessment of Contemporary Roman Catholicism* (Grand Rapids: Baker Academic, 2005).

5. This quotation is taken from an interview from May 9, 2007, on the *Christianity Today* website.

6. John Webster has often made this point. For example: "A properly evangelical ecclesiology has to take its place within the scope of doctrinal affirmations which spell out the Christian confession of God, Christ, the Spirit, election, reconciliation, sanctification and the rest." See John Webster, "The Visible Attests the Invisible," in *The Community of the*

whose effects are felt only beyond our concrete and historical existence, then we will fail to see that God's justifying work includes in itself a subjective correlate that touches our lives here and now.[7] In other words, if we fail to articulate a clear line of sight between our justification in Christ and what we are to *do* as the church, then we will fail to understand why what we do in the church really *matters*. All that we will have left to us is what Beckwith calls "the moral life" — and that, as evangelicals have learned, cannot sustain a church.

From one angle, then, Beckwith's conversion seems like the logical outworking of the younger evangelical desire to overcome their individualistic tendencies with a more "visible" church. This visible structure is a hallmark of the Roman Catholic Church; as participants in the very historical body of Christ, one's life in the Church *matters,* and one's actions in the church "count for something" in one's faith.[8] But is there a Protestant way to accomplish the same goal? Can we, in other words, overcome evangelical ecclesiological deficiencies without going the way of younger evangelicals like Beckwith? My paper argues that Karl Barth offers a possible solution to our dilemma, and that this solution is preferable to the one Beckwith chose. To establish this claim, however, I'm going to have to address a persistent criticism of Barth's ecclesiology — a criticism similar to the one younger evangelicals level against their own tradition. Only then will we be in a position to see what Barth has to offer.

II. Criticism of Barth's "Bifurcated" Ecclesiology

The criticism in its most common form is that Barth has a "bifurcated" ecclesiology. The roots of this critique can be found in some of Barth's earliest critics, but more recent manifestations are found in the work of Nicholas

---

Word: Toward an Evangelical Ecclesiology, ed. Mark Husbands and Daniel B. Treier (Downers Grove: InterVarsity Press, 2005), 112.

7. Karl Barth makes this point: "We cannot be content merely with that foreordination and predisposition of man for his vocation, as though it were not necessary for his own vocation also to take place as an event in his own life. To do this is tantamount to thinking that the star which guided the wise men to Bethlehem finally shone upon an empty manger." See *CD* IV/3.2, 497-500.

8. Barth himself recognized this point; see Karl Barth, "Roman Catholicism: A Question to the Protestant Church," in *Theology and Church,* ed. T. F. Torrance (London: SCM Press, 1928), 314.

Healy, Stanley Hauerwas, Joseph Mangina, and Reinhard Hütter.[9] Hütter's critique prompts the most interest, because his is the most incisive. He worries that Barth offers us "a theology without any tangible ecclesial roots."[10] It is an ecclesiology, he argues, which exists in "an endless dialectical play" between two rejected alternatives without ever offering an "ecclesially concrete" option of its own.[11]

We find this "dialectical play" in the opening pages of *Church Dogmatics* I/1. On one side of the ecclesial spectrum is Neo-Protestantism. In this view, Barth argues, the church exists as a specific actualization of "something generally human."[12] We find the prime example in Friedrich Schleiermacher's *Glaubenslehre*, where he describes the church as "nothing but a communion or association relating to religion or piety"[13] and as "a society which originates only through free human action and which can only through such continue to exist."[14] Barth rejects this ecclesiology because it understands the church in terms of "human possibility" and "the general historicity of human existence" rather than from "the acting of God himself."[15]

On the other side of the spectrum is Roman Catholicism. Catholic ecclesiology holds that the church is not a human possibility but a divinely established institution. However, Barth argues, the church has this status only because Jesus Christ is "absorbed into the existence of the Church, and is thus ultimately restricted and conditioned by certain concrete forms."[16] The result of this absorption is that the divine act is changed "into that

---

9. See Stanley Hauerwas, *With the Grain of the Universe: The Church's Witness and Natural Theology* (Grand Rapids: Brazos Press, 2001); Nicholas M. Healy, "The logic of Karl Barth's ecclesiology: analysis, assessment, and proposed modifications," *Modern Theology* 10, no. 3 (1994); Reinhard Hütter, "Karl Barth's 'Dialectical Catholicity': *Sic et Non*," *Modern Theology* 16, no. 2 (2000); idem, *Suffering Divine Things: Theology as Church Practice*, trans. D. Scott (Grand Rapids: Eerdmans, 2000).

10. Hütter, "Karl Barth's 'Dialectical Catholicity,'" 144.

11. Ibid., 143. For a similar analysis, see John G. Flett, "God is a Missionary God: *Missio Dei*, Karl Barth, and the Doctrine of the Trinity" (PhD diss., Princeton Theological Seminary, 2007), 68-78.

12. *CD* I/1, 38. This view, Barth says, "understands the being of the Church and itself decisively as a definition of the reality of man, of piety."

13. Friedrich D. E. Schleiermacher, *The Christian Faith*, ed. H. R. Macintosh and J. S. Stewart (Edinburgh: T. & T. Clark, 1928), 5.

14. Ibid., 3. Barth points out that these definitions "have their origins in English Congregationalism" and "they and they alone could authorize Schleiermacher to commence his basic work of introduction with statements borrowed from ethics." See *CD* I/1, 38.

15. *CD* I/1, 38-39.

16. Ibid., 40.

which is enclosed into the reality of the Church," meaning that what should be a "personal act of divine address" instead has become "a constantly available relationship."[17] For Barth, this means that grace has become nature, and "the action of God immediately disappears and is taken up into the action of the recipient of grace."[18]

Rejecting both alternatives, Barth offers a third option: the church as "*actus purus.*" The church as *actus purus* emphasizes that the church results from a divine act "comprehensible only from and through itself."[19] The church's existence, in other words, results from the free action of God rather than from historical and cultural factors.[20] The church as *actus purus* distinguishes the church's ministry from the divine act. The being of the church, Barth argues, results from "an event of personal address" rather than "a continuously available relationship" or "a transmitted material condition."[21] Thus, in contrast to the positions on both ends of the spectrum, Barth insists both that the church "depends on God's ongoing act" for its being (*contra* Neo-Protestantism), and that "God does not divest himself into the historical contingency of the church" in this act (*contra* Roman Catholicism).[22]

Hütter criticizes this third option for subsisting in a "ceaseless critical oscillation" between the two rejected alternatives, leaving Barth's church a theological and historical impossibility.[23] If the true identity of the church rests on God's free act — and if this act is something the church receives "moment by moment" in the event of God's personal address — then the true meaning of the church is "something which in no way and to no degree subsists" in the church itself.[24] By definition, therefore, Barth's church "cannot be embodied."[25] While Barth's church witnesses to Christ, it does not serve as "the means through which believers begin to participate in the new life [Christ] brings," and the result is a "hiatus between the church (in a full theological sense) and the ordinary, empirical practices of the Christian community across time."[26] Barth's church, in other words, is an abstraction.

---

17. Ibid., 41.
18. Ibid.
19. Ibid.
20. For this insight, see Flett, "God is a Missionary God," 70.
21. *CD* I/1, 41.
22. Flett, "God is a Missionary God," 69.
23. Hütter, "Karl Barth's 'Dialectical Catholicity,'" 143.
24. Ibid., 147.
25. Ibid.
26. Joseph L. Mangina, "Bearing the marks of Jesus: The church in the economy of sal-

The root of the problem, Hütter contends, lies in Barth's weak pneumatology. Barth's ecclesiology is predicated upon "a strict *diastasis* between Spirit and institution."[27] This is what is meant by the charge of a "bifurcated" ecclesiology. A breach exists between divine and human action in the church so that — to employ Beckwith's phrase — human action doesn't "count for something" in the church. An action "counts" in this view when it makes a real contribution to the church's true identity, meaning, or purpose, and for Hütter, this is precisely what Barth's ecclesiology does not allow. This problem results from Barth's depiction of the Holy Spirit as simply "Christ's mode of action," who is thus "accorded no work of its own in relation to church doctrine" or practices.[28] In other words, Barth offers us a disembodied and deficient pneumatology, and because he "never quite brings himself to explain how our human agency is involved in the Spirit's work," it is unclear how human participation in the church makes any difference, or "counts," at all.[29]

As an alternative, Hütter offers an ecclesiology in which the church exists as a "way of life, i.e., a distinct set of practices interwoven with normative beliefs, concretely and distinctly embodied."[30] He accomplishes this by means of a "*pneumatological enhypostasis* of the core church practices."[31] The heart of this proposal is the idea that God binds himself to the church by the Spirit in such a way that the Spirit "is identical with distinct practices or activities, institutions, offices, and doctrines" of the church.[32] "The Holy

---

vation in Barth and Hauerwas," *Scottish Journal of Theology* 52, no. 3 (1999): 270. Mangina draws similar conclusions about Barth as Hütter does in his work, but he does not follow Hütter's proposed alternative.

27. Hütter, *Suffering Divine Things*, 115.

28. Ibid., 113.

29. This quotation is from Stanley Hauerwas, who shares the same concern. See Hauerwas, *With the Grain of the Universe*, 145. Hütter articulates his concern this way: "Barth is unable to interpret or render ecclesiologically fruitful in any pneumatologically relevant fashion what he calls the 'mediate forms', and his development of the relational nexus of church, church doctrine, and theology ultimately remains ecclesiologically unstable because the pneumatology itself remains deficient." See Hütter, *Suffering Divine Things*, 113. For similar thoughts, see Mangina, "Bearing the marks of Jesus," 192.

30. Hütter, "Karl Barth's 'Dialectical Catholicity,'" 149.

31. Hütter, *Suffering Divine Things*, 133.

32. Ibid., 119. He says: "In the form of these core practices, the church subsists enhypostatically in the Holy Spirit, and through them the Holy Spirit performs its economic mission, namely, the eschatological re-creation of humanity, a re-creation whose beginning is faith and whose growth is growth in faith, transforming human beings precisely in and through ongoing affliction by drawing them into God's eschatological communion." See ibid., 133.

Spirit is thus realized not 'spiritualistically' in the immediacy of the in-spiration of the Spirit into individual religious consciousnesses, but in the form of concrete church practices which as such are to be understood as the gift of the Spirit in the service of God's economy of salvation."[33] No breach exists, therefore, between divine and human action in these church prac-tices. Rather, because these practices "inhere in the salvific-economic mis-sion of the Spirit,"[34] the church serves as the "organ of actualization" of this mission.[35] This makes the church both an embodied and indispensable real-ity, and thus its true identity is not located in something beyond itself, but precisely in those ecclesial practices "through which the Spirit does his sanc-tifying work."[36] In a very real sense, then, human action "counts for some-thing" in this view.

Hütter is not alone in proposing an ecclesiology of this sort. John Milbank, a central proponent of the Radical Orthodoxy that Robert Webber regards as so attractive to younger evangelicals, speaks similarly of a "hypostatic descent of the Spirit" in the church.[37] Beckwith may or may not hold this precise view, but his implicit critique of evangelical ecclesiology shares the same theological roots. His movement toward an embodied and sacramental ecclesiology, his shift to a Roman Catholic doctrine of justifica-tion in which his virtue plays a part in God's salvific purpose for his life, and his desire that his actions in the church "count for something" follow the same path taken by Hütter against Barth. And as we have seen, there are many other evangelicals on the same road.

---

33. Ibid., 127.

34. Ibid., 133.

35. Ibid., 126. He emphasizes that this view implies that cooperation takes place be-tween God and the human so that the human is "present fully as agent . . . *actively* present in praise, confession, prayer, obedience, and discipleship." See ibid., 125.

36. Hütter, "Karl Barth's 'Dialectical Catholicity,'" 150. Consequently, he argues, we must see the church existence as participating in the triune communion: "The church at once becomes transparent as both the body of Christ and as a creation of the Holy Spirit; bearing the eschatological earnest of the Holy Spirit itself, it already receives a portion in the life of the triune God." See Hütter, *Suffering Divine Things*, 119.

37. John Milbank, *Being Reconciled: Ontology and Pardon* (New York: Routledge, 2003), 105. He makes a similar claim earlier in the book: "It is for this reason that the gift of intrahuman forgiveness offered by the whole Trinity to Christ's humanity is passed on by Christ to us as the hypostatic presence amongst us in time of the Holy Spirit, the bond of ex-change and mutual giving within the Trinity. As participators through the Sacraments and membership of the body of Christ in the divine humanity, we now also begin to be capable of a forgiveness on sufficient authority and without taint of rancor" (ibid., 62). See also ibid., 41-42, 100, 105, 133, and 208. See Webber, *The Younger Evangelicals*, 72-75.

The reason for this trend may lie in the perception among younger evangelicals that the only solution to their problems rests in an ecclesiology of Hütter's sort. That is, if the choices are either (a) a direct connection between our ecclesial practices and divine action — such as we see in Hütter's proposal — or (b) no connection at all between our ecclesial practices and divine action — such as we see in the evangelical *status quo* — then the decision to move in Hütter's direction makes sense. But is there another option? Can we establish a connection between divine and human action in the church so we can say our actions in the church "count for something" in some sense? Or, to put it another way, can we connect the church as God's act to the church as an earthly-historical community in some other way than by moving in the direction in which Hütter and many evangelicals are traveling?

I believe that such an alternative is not only possible but that Barth provides it. Barth's construal of the connection between divine and human action, however, will not meet Hütter's criteria for the kind of connection that is necessary. That is, while human action "counts" in Barth's view, it does not "count" in the way Hütter wants it to. It does "count" enough, however, to complicate Hütter's critique. And as we will see, the implications of Hütter's — and by extension, Beckwith's — vision for the church make their option less attractive for evangelicals than it first appears; conversely, the strength of Barth's account corresponds to the best insights of the evangelical tradition. To understand why this is the case, we have to venture into the center of Barth's theology.

III. Barth and the *concursus Dei*

Barth, as we have seen, believes that the church is an *actus purus*, a divine action, and it exists "only in the power of the divine decision, act, and revelation accomplished and effective in Jesus Christ."[38] This means that the church must not be understood as a natural state of affairs but as a divinely established reality; and yet it is not a reality which takes divine properties upon itself, but rather, it is one that remains at all times "an earthly-historical event."[39] This distinction raises our question: how can this di-

---

38. *CD* IV/3.2, 727. Paul Nimmo puts this idea well: "For Barth, then, the Church simply *is* in the event of divine action in which God lets people live as servants of God, and in which they respond accordingly." See Paul T. Nimmo, *Being in Action: The Theological Shape of Barth's Ethical Vision* (London: T. & T. Clark, 2007), 68.

39. *CD* IV/2, 696.

vinely established reality be an "earthly-historical event" at the same time? In other words, how can the existence of the church be a divine action and not be divorced in some sense from the human beings who make it up? The answer to this question will go to the heart of addressing Hütter's critique. For that, we need to spell out Barth's understanding of the relationship between divine and human action found in his account of the *concursus Dei* in *CD* III/3. This section is important because Barth's ecclesiology can be understood rightly only in light of what he says here.

We will proceed first by outlining Barth's understanding of the *concursus Dei*, and then we will put this doctrine to the test in the context of the church. This test will show that, far from advocating a bifurcated ecclesiology, Barth seeks to articulate a particular kind of visibility, one that corresponds historically to the divine and human fellowship completed once and for all in the being and work of Jesus Christ. As such, Barth's ecclesiology provides a solution to the problems younger evangelicals find in evangelicalism that is both distinct from and preferable to the one offered by Beckwith or Hütter. It also raises questions about whether their kind of ecclesiological visibility is an attractive option for evangelicals at all.

The *concursus Dei* is the doctrine that attempts to describe the relation of two seemingly incompatible notions: "the lordship of God" and the "free and autonomous activity of the creature."[40] The relation between the two is not obvious, and for that reason Barth says that the doctrine's formulation is "not an assertion but a confession."[41] We must not "begin with empty concepts," he insists, "but with concepts which are already filled out with Christian meaning."[42] In other words, if we want to know what continuity between divine and human action looks like, then we must proceed from the right theological ground. This is an important point, given that many of Barth's critics presuppose what continuity between divine and human ac-

---

40. *CD* III/3, 90.

41. Ibid., 142. On this point, George Hunsinger says that this doctrine "presents not a quandary to be solved, but a miracle to be respected and a mystery to be revered." Hence, the "theologian's job, accordingly, is not to explain away the miracle or resolve the mystery, but rather to describe an event that ultimately defies explanation." It is thus an event "absolutely incomprehensible on any terms other than its own, and that can only be known from its actual occurrence. It cannot be deduced from any principle, normalized by any law, or divested of its incomprehensibility by any conceptual scheme." See George Hunsinger, *How to Read Karl Barth: The Shape of His Theology* (New York: Oxford University Press, 1991), 185-224.

42. *CD* III/3, 117.

tion must look like and then criticize Barth because his understanding of divine and human action does not fit their preconceptions. There is, however, more than one way to think about divine-human continuity, and one's starting point matters a great deal. For Barth, the only correct theological starting point is God's act in Jesus Christ by the power of the Spirit.[43] This question would be "insuperably difficult," he says, if we only had "the framework of a general philosophy" from which to derive our answer.[44] But we do not have a philosophy: we have God's act of revelation.

Barth's use of the phrase *actus purus et singularis* comes to mind here.[45] When we refer to God's act, we refer to the specific act of the election of Jesus Christ in the covenant of grace, and as such, our particular election in him. This is part of the reason why, for Barth, the *concursus Dei* can only be considered in light of the doctrine of election. When we start with Christ, we see that the lordship of God over the creature is the "execution of the election of grace resolved and fulfilled by God from all eternity."[46] This covenant of grace provides the specific framework from which the relationship of divine and human action must be considered. It cannot be regarded from any other basis.

Two implications follow from this connection between election and *concursus* for Barth. First, we must say that all human history, including the action of autonomous human beings, finds its meaning and purpose in God's electing act. We simply do not exist apart from God's determination to be God-for-us, and this determination shapes, orders, and forms every aspect of our lives. All creation, Barth says, "took place on the basis of this purposed covenant and with a view to its execution," and as a result, "the meaning of the continued existence of the creature, and therefore the purpose of its history, is that this covenant will and work of God begun in creation should have its course and reach its goal."[47] This means, for Barth, that "the history of the covenant of grace accompanies the act of the creature from first to last."[48] Every time a creature acts, Barth says, "God is there as the One

43. Ibid., 141.
44. Ibid., 139.
45. See *CD* II/1, 264ff.
46. *CD* III/3, 36.
47. Ibid.
48. Ibid., 92. Nimmo thus is right to argue that "*concursus Dei* is not only noetically revealed in Jesus Christ: it is also ontically constituted and teleologically directed in the eternal election of Jesus Christ." See Paul T. Nimmo, "Karl Barth and the *concursus Dei* — A Chalcedonianism Too Far?" *International Journal of Systematic Theology* 9, no. 1 (2007): 60.

who has already loved it, who has already undertaken to save and glorify it, who in this sense and to this end has already worked even before it itself began to work, even before the conditions, and the pre-conditions, and the pre-pre-conditions of its working were laid down."[49]

This first implication of the connection between election and *concursus* leads to the second: when we talk about the "execution of the election of grace," we are talking about the specific and particular will of God for the reconciliation of human beings.[50] Barth says that "when we say 'the will of God' we have to understand His fatherly good-will, His decree of grace in Jesus Christ, the mercy in which from all eternity He undertook to save the creature, and to give it eternal life in fellowship with Himself."[51] The doctrine of the *concursus Dei*, therefore, "seeks to explain how it is that God executes *this* [specific] will in time."[52] For Barth, this means that we cannot say that God positively wills everything that human creatures will. For example, God does not will the evil that creatures do, nor does God actively will every particular thing that takes place in nature or history. He wills "all things" only in the sense that he "wills this world and its history *as the context* in which the covenant of grace is played out."[53] Hence, Barth says, God's "*causare* consists, and consists *only*, in the fact that He bends [human beings'] activity to the execution of His own will which is His will of grace, subordinating their operations to the specific operation which constitutes the history of the covenant of grace."[54]

These two implications from the doctrine of election lay the groundwork for two seemingly contradictory assertions Barth makes in the

49. *CD* III/3, 119. See also ibid., 92, where Barth explains further: when a creature acts, "the gracious will of God is executed in that which borders upon it, in its environment, in the nexus of being in which it has its duration. Whatever that may or may not mean, the creature is not alone on the way, but as it goes it is accompanied by God, by the God who is this Lord." On this point, John Webster notes: "That history simply is, anterior to all human choosing; it is a condition in which we find ourselves, and not something which we bring about through an act of will." The reality of human existence, as Barth says, is that before the very first human acted "God had already acted, offering his grace, making his mercy in Jesus Christ operative and effective to the creature, revealing the majesty of his beloved Son." The same is true for every creature. See John Webster, *Barth's Moral Theology: Human Action in Barth's Thought* (Grand Rapids: Eerdmans, 1998), 123.

50. For this insight, see Bruce L. McCormack, "The Actuality of God: Karl Barth in Conversation with Open Theism," in *Engaging the Doctrine of God*, ed. Bruce L. McCormack (Grand Rapids: Baker Academic, 2008), 223-31.

51. *CD* III/3, 117; cited in McCormack, "The Actuality of God," 225.

52. McCormack, "The Actuality of God," 228.

53. Ibid., 225.

54. *CD* III/3, 105; cited in McCormack, "The Actuality of God," 228.

concursus Dei about the relationship between divine and human action. The first assertion is that while we cannot consider human action apart from its relation to divine action, this relation does not undermine the integrity of this action *as a human action*.[55] How are we to understand this idea? From Barth's doctrine of election, we know he understands the relationship between God and humanity in terms of "two distinct aspects": God's election to be Lord and Helper of humanity and, included in this election, the corresponding election of humanity to be "witnesses of God's glory."[56] This, Barth argues, means that "the being and essence and activity of God as the Lord of the covenant between Himself and man includes a relationship to the being and essence and activity of man" — the one demands the other.[57]

Note that there is a "relationship" between the two, not a blending of their "being and essence and activity." Barth believes that even though human actions "have no significance or value apart from God's covenant will," we must insist that they remain *human* actions which "constitute an occurrence distinct from the activity of God."[58] The covenant of grace gives these actions their form, but it does not violate the integrity of these actions as *creaturely* actions.[59] God, Barth says, "does not play the part of the tyrant" toward the creature.[60] "Man is not nothing. He is God's man. He is accepted by God. He is recognized as himself a free subject, a subject who has been made free once and for all by his restoration as the faithful covenant partner of God."[61] In some sense, then, Barth believes that God works *with* the creature by making the creature a partner in his covenant. He explains:

> If God had willed to act alone, or by means of non-autonomous agents or instruments, there would have been no need to institute a covenant, and

---

55. *CD* III/3, 122.

56. See Nimmo, *Being in Action*, 10.

57. *CD* II/2, 511; cited in Nimmo, *Being in Action*, 11.

58. *CD* III/3, 36; cited in Nimmo, "Karl Barth and the *concursus Dei*," 66.

59. See *CD* III/3, 122.

60. Ibid., 92.

61. *CD* IV/1, 89-90. Webster provides a helpful explanation of what Barth means by "freedom": "Freedom is not — as it has come to be in modernity — a free-standing, quasi-absolute reality which both characterizes and validates the unique dignity of the human person. Rather, freedom is consent to a given order or reality which encloses human history, an order which is at one and the same time a loving summons to joyful action in accordance with itself, and a judgment against our attempts to be ourselves by somehow escaping from or suspending its givenness. Freedom is the real possibility given to me by necessity." See Webster, *Barth's Moral Theology*, 112.

the fulfillment of his will in creation need not have taken the form of a covenant-history. Again, grace would no longer be grace if its exercise consisted only in the elimination or suppression as autonomous subject of the one to whom it was extended. The gracious God acts not only *towards* the creature but also — however we explain it in detail — *with* the creature.[62]

Hence, Barth believes that the covenant of grace — because it is a covenant of *grace* — "ensures that the creature in the *concursus* retains its own identity and integrity and full personhood."[63] The creature, Barth says, is "allowed to be, and live, and work, and occupy [its] own sphere, and exercise [its] own effect upon [its] environment, and fulfil the circle of [its] own destiny."[64]

Barth's second assertion — the one which seemingly contradicts the first — takes the form of a caution. He insists that something else must be said about the relationship between God and the human: "man is an active, not an inactive recipient," he says, "yet even in his activity he is still a *recipient*."[65] In this relation, "the creature does not have [just] any kind of companion. *God* is with it . . . [and God] is so as the sovereign and almighty Lord."[66] Barth's point is that God's actions are not conditioned by God's creatures: God "would not be God at all . . . if there were a single point where He was absent or inactive, or only partly active, or restricted in his action."[67] Hence, when we say that God accompanies and cooperates with us in the covenant of grace, we also must say that "His activity determines our activity even to its most intimate depths."[68] Barth says: "As He Himself enters the creaturely sphere — and He does not cease to do this, but does it in the slightest movement of a leaf in the wind — His will is accomplished directly and His decisions are made and fulfilled in all creaturely occurrence both great and small."[69] In other words, because divine action "conditions abso-

---

62. *CD* III/3, 93. This point builds upon an earlier affirmation: "The fact that the divine lordship extends beyond the creation of the creature means also and primarily that he maintains it in its own actuality, that he gives it space and opportunity for its own work, for its own being in action, for its own autonomous activity." See ibid., 91.

63. Nimmo, "Karl Barth and the *concursus Dei*," 66.

64. *CD* III/3, 148.

65. Karl Barth, *The Christian Life: Church Dogmatics IV, 4: Lecture Fragments* (Grand Rapids: Eerdmans, 1981), 29.

66. *CD* III/3, 132.

67. Ibid., 133.

68. Ibid., 132.

69. Ibid., 133.

lutely the activity of the creature,"[70] we must say that "the will of God is unconditionally and irresistibly fulfilled" in this activity.[71] Every human action stands under the sovereign will of God in his covenant of grace, and thus, every action serves the purposes of God's covenant because the divine will cannot be conditioned by anything other than God himself. As a result, Barth asserts that "we have to understand the activity of God and that of the creature as a single action."[72] What he means by this assertion is that, within the context of the covenant of grace, God "is so present in the activity of the creature, and present with such sovereignty and almighty power, that His own action takes place in and with and over the activity of the creature."[73]

How are we to make sense of these seemingly contradictory assertions? How are we to understand that, on the one hand, God's covenant of grace ensures the integrity of human beings as autonomous creatures, but on the other hand, God accompanies the creature as its *Lord* so that divine activity and creaturely activity are united as a single action? Barth's answer to this question brings us into the heart of the *concursus*, and it also brings us to the heart of his vision for how human action might "count for something" in the church. He argues that, in the relationship between divine and human action, "we have to do with the mystery of grace in the confrontation and encounter of two subjects who cannot be compared and [who] do not fall under any one master-concept."[74] We make a mistake if we think of God and creature as "two species of the same genus."[75] No — when God acts, Barth says, his work "is not merely done after a higher and superior fashion, but within a completely different order."[76]

What does this claim mean? Barth insists that it does not mean that God simply provides the hidden meaning or content of all human action, as if there were two parallel lines with the higher one determining the meaning of the lower one.[77] It also does not mean that in these actions the Creator be-

---

70. Ibid., 113.
71. Ibid., 117.
72. Ibid., 132.
73. Ibid.
74. Ibid., 135.
75. Ibid., 102.
76. Ibid., 135.
77. Ibid., 133. The problem is that this view posits God's action merely as a "higher or absolute force on beings whose force is less." This would mean that God and the human stand in ontological continuity with one another because their action, while differing in potency, occurs on the same plane. See *CD* III/3, 135-36.

comes a creature, or the reverse, that a creature becomes the Creator. The *concursus* is a miracle, but it is not a repetition of the miracle of the incarnation.[78] Rather, Barth says, it means that

> God, the only true God, so loved the world in His election of grace that in fulfillment of the covenant of grace instituted at the creation He willed to become a creature, and did in fact become a creature, in order to be its Saviour. And this same God accepts the creature even apart from the history of the covenant and its fulfillment. He takes it to Himself as such and in general in such sort that He co-operates with it, preceding, accompanying, and following all its being and activity, so that all the activity of the creature is primarily and simultaneously and subsequently His own activity, and therefore a part of the actualisation of His own will revealed and triumphant in Jesus Christ.[79]

We can summarize this claim by saying that there is a "genuine antithesis" between God and creature in the midst of a "genuine encounter" between them. They remain distinct subjects utterly unlike one another, each with its own integrity, and yet within the context of the covenant of grace, the divine action is fulfilled "in, with and over" the human action. This means for Barth that there is a true continuity between divine and human action, but it also means — and this is an important point — that this continuity is not a static or permanently available one. No, this continuity occurs in the *event* of divine act and human correspondence, in the specific and particular encounter of two utterly distinct subjects. These encounters, Barth says, are "not therefore so many 'cases' in the one rule, but *individual events* which have their own importance and have to be considered in and for themselves."[80]

Barth describes these encounters as events of Word and Spirit, and this pattern helps us grasp his explanation of how this divine-human encounter works. In these events, there is a genuine encounter between two distinct subjects, but they are subjects who relate to one another in a particular order — an order which implies a definite responsibility on the part of the human

---

78. As Barth says elsewhere: "It is one thing that God is present in and with everything that is and occurs, that in Him we live and move and have our being . . . but it is quite another that He Himself became and is man. Even this union and unity cannot therefore be compared or exchanged with the *unio personalis* in Jesus Christ." Hence, as Nimmo argues, "the encounter between two beings in actualization and two natures in actualization is qualitatively different." See *CD* IV/2, 53, and Nimmo, "Karl Barth and the *concursus Dei*," 66.

79. *CD* III/3, 105.

80. Ibid., 138.

subject. Barth says: "the free God elects and wills. The free man must elect and will what God elects and wills. God is the giver and man is the recipient."[81] "God is gracious to man," Barth says, "not man to God. And man is responsible and indebted to God, not God to man."[82] This means that "God directs, orders, and commands, while man can exercise his responsibility only by obeying God's command. That God might withhold his direction and man [withhold] his obedience is not foreseen in the covenant of grace."[83]

This pattern and order of the divine act on the one hand, and human correspondence to it on the other, reveals what Barth has in mind when he employs Word and Spirit to describe the *concursus*. On the basis of this pattern, he says that there is a continuity of action between God and the creature because God "is in both cases the one who acts, in the one case as Word and the other as Spirit."[84] At all moments, however, the genuine antithesis between God and creature remains intact, because even as their actions stand in continuity in this event, no "absorption or assimilation of creaturely activity into the divine" occurs.[85] God remains God and acts as God; the creature remains creature and acts as creature. They exist in a relation of command and obedience, but it remains at all times a relation between distinct subjects. Thus, Barth believes that because the creature's act occurs in correspondence to the Word and as a result of the Spirit's awakening, life-giving, and summoning power, we can say that her creaturely action is an action of the Spirit.[86] Defining human action in this way, Barth says, does not prejudice the autonomy, freedom, responsibility, or genuineness of the human's actions.[87] The Holy Spirit does not overpower the human in this event, because while she acts in the space cleared for her by the Spirit, she really *is* the one who acts, and she does so *as a creature* in free obedience

---

81. Barth, *The Christian Life*, 29.

82. Ibid., 27.

83. Ibid., 29. He elaborates further: "Also excluded is that in the dealings between God and man there might be something other than command and obedience, namely, negotiable arrangements and agreements reached on the same plane, a kind of contract or fellowship in which the definite order of first and second is either eliminated or even reversed."

84. *CD* III/3, 142.

85. Ibid., 149.

86. Barth clarifies this point in a later volume: "man's faith can no more dissolve into a divine act than God can dissolve into the human act of faith. Even in their unity in Jesus Christ himself, God does not cease to be God nor man to be man." See Barth, *The Christian Life*, 27-28.

87. *CD* III/3, 144.

to the demands of God's Word.[88] Likewise, Barth says, the Spirit does not impart "a quality or quantity of the divine essence or operation to the creature and its activity" in this event.[89] Making human action the *enhypostasis* of the Spirit, for example, would create a unity of action, but it would undermine both the distinction between God and creature, and the nature of this unity as an event with two distinct aspects. It would be a move, in other words, impossible on the soil of Barth's covenant of grace.

Thus, because it is viewed in terms of an event of encounter between two distinct subjects, Barth believes we can say that in Word and Spirit the activity of God and that of the creature stand in continuity with one another; but we cannot say either that God simply overpowers the creature or that there is a permanent or readily available union of divine and human action. To think in such terms, Barth says, would be "to forget that the activity of God is the activity of his continually free grace, an activity from above downwards, a condescension in which God is beyond comparison."[90] It would also be, he says, to forget that while "any identification, comparison, or interchange of God and man is ruled out, so is any separation between them. In the covenant of grace [God and the human] are distinct partners, but precisely in their distinction they are partners who are inseparably bound to one another."[91]

To summarize: in the *concursus*, every human action finds its meaning and purpose in the covenant of grace, which is God's particular will for the reconciliation of the world in Jesus Christ by the power of the Spirit. While God and the human stand in a genuine antithesis as two distinct subjects, their actions exist in continuity as God acts "in, with and over" the human in the event of Word and Spirit, an event which mobilizes the human, at the proper level, into corresponding action as an immediate consequence of, and as an active participant in, this event. This continuity of action is not by nature but by grace, an *event* of continuity in which the distinction between the two subjects remains intact. With these insights in hand, we have a natural avenue into the question of the acting being of the church. Do the insights of the *concursus Dei* inform the life of this community? Indeed, they do. The *concursus* shows that

---

88. This is why we can say with Nimmo that God's act of grace, love, and freedom in the covenant includes a corresponding expectation and demand for something from the covenant partner, and this something establishes a "clearly defined space . . . within which meaningful human action can take place, as the Being in action of God calls forth a particular being in action of the ethical agent." See Nimmo, *Being in Action*, 11.

89. *CD* III/3, 136.

90. *CD* III/3, 149.

91. Barth, *The Christian Life*, 28.

our actions in the church "count for something" in Barth's theology, although they "count" in a different sense than they do for Beckwith or Hütter. This difference will present Barth's unique answer to the evangelical problem, and I will argue that this answer offers a better alternative for evangelicals as they consider the shape of evangelical ecclesiology in the future. I will make this case by turning to Barth's construal of water baptism, because the distinctions made there tread directly upon both the critiques made against his ecclesiology and the issues central to the *concursus Dei*.[92] From there, we will be in a position to see the full scope of Barth's solution to the younger evangelicals' dilemma.

IV. Water Baptism and the *concursus Dei*

Barth's key move in the baptismal fragment of *CD* IV/4 is to draw a distinction between baptism with the Holy Spirit and baptism with water. By "baptism with the Holy Spirit," Barth means God's free work of grace which is the sole "origin of human faithfulness" and "the foundation of Christian life."[93] Our life in Christ, in other words, is an event in which God alone is the actor and the subject. Baptism with water, conversely, is a "truly human work,"[94] one in which the human commits a "wholly free, conscious and voluntary decision."[95] Water baptism thus is not a "superhuman or supernatural"[96] act but rather is a "human decision which follows the divine change effected for man."[97] Hence, for Barth, baptism with the Holy Spirit and baptism with water "are two very different things as man's free work on the one side and God's free work on the other."[98]

This construal prompts the charge that Barth creates a "disjunction" between divine and human action in baptism.[99] That is, by dividing baptism

92. For a more extensive treatment of the relationship between *concursus* and water baptism, see Nimmo, *Being in Action*, 126-30. I am deeply indebted to Nimmo's work here, as it helped me recognize the implication of this connection for Barth's theology.

93. *CD* IV/4, 4.

94. Ibid., 102.

95. Ibid., 163.

96. Ibid., 143.

97. Ibid., 162.

98. Ibid., 88.

99. John Macken, *The Autonomy Theme in the "Church Dogmatics": Karl Barth and His Critics* (Cambridge: Cambridge University Press, 1990), 80; cited in Nimmo, *Being in Action*, 128.

into two acts — the act of the Holy Spirit as the foundation of the Christian life, and the human act of obedience and correspondence to the divine act — Barth posits "the *wholly different action* of two inalienably distinct subjects."[100] This charge ties directly into the previously mentioned critique of Barth's ecclesiology. The criticism, in this instance, would be that Barth divides water baptism from any connection to divine action, meaning that, as an ecclesial practice, it is bifurcated from the divine act in which the Christian finds her true existence and in which baptism finds its true meaning. God does not act in water baptism, grace is not mediated through it, and thus this human act does not "count" with respect to the true basis of the Christian life or the true ministry of the church.[101]

What are we to make of this charge in light of what we've seen in the *concursus Dei?* One the one hand, we can agree with the critics that there are two "inalienably distinct subjects" in the act of water baptism. We know from the *concursus* that God and the creature are not "species of the same genus," and thus, we know that "divine action and human action, like their respective agents, are utterly incomparable."[102] On the other hand, we also know that in the context of the covenant of grace, an "intimate and direct connection" exists between divine and human action so that we must consider them "a single action." In other words — on Barth's terms — in the event of Word and Spirit, the divine action is fulfilled "in, with and over" the creaturely action so that the creaturely act *in its very creatureliness* fulfills God's covenant will. On the basis of this insight from the *concursus,* therefore, we can say that "precisely *as* a truly human action, the act of water baptism is accompanied by a divine action and is thus in no way independent of divine action."[103] If they were divided from one another — if, in other words, the human act of water baptism was wholly independent of divine

100. Macken, *The Autonomy Theme in the "Church Dogmatics,"* 86; see also Nimmo, *Being in Action,* 127.

101. Keep in mind that an action "counts" when it makes a contribution to one's true identity, meaning, or purpose. The charge that baptism does not fit that bill is commonly made among Barth scholars. T. F. Torrance articulates the charge well: the meaning of water "baptism is not found in a direct act of God but in an ethical act on the part of man made by way of a response to what God has already done on his behalf." The implication is that by relegating this ecclesial act to the human sphere alone, it is diminished in meaning, divided from the true basis of the church and Christian life. See T. F. Torrance, *Theology in Reconciliation: Essays toward Evangelical and Catholic Unity in East and West* (Grand Rapids: Eerdmans, 1976), 99.

102. Nimmo, *Being in Action,* 127.

103. Ibid.

action — then, as Paul Nimmo notes, "a rift would appear" between the doctrines of the *concursus* and baptism in Barth's theology.[104]

Although such a rift is often appealed to among Barth scholars, it is not evident in *CD* IV/4. In fact, Barth's construal of baptism in *CD* IV/4 is simply the working out of the *concursus Dei* in an ecclesial context. In the volume's opening pages, Barth says the "real question" under discussion is the "reality of the origin of [man's] free partnership with God in God's covenant of grace."[105] The answer to this question, he says, can be found in the divine "actualization of [man's] creaturely determination and consequently of his natural powers."[106] The emphasis on the actualization of the human agent by God emerges explicitly later in the volume, and the working out of the *concursus* is most evident here. Note the use of Word and Spirit in the following quotation: "God, who as such is the *auctor primarius* of all creaturely occurrence, is specifically in the work and word of Jesus Christ through the Holy Spirit the free Lord of the action of the community which bears witness to Him, and therewith of its baptism too."[107] The deployment of Word and Spirit is the same as in the *concursus:* God "is in both cases the one who acts, in the one case as Word and the other as Spirit."[108] Yet, just as in the *concursus,* Barth insists that God's action in Word and Spirit does not detract from the creatureliness of this action. The creature, he says, is "taken seriously as the creature which is different from God."[109] Barth thus argues that "[God's] action within and on [the community], His presence, work and revelation in their whole action, and therewith in their [water] baptism, does not supplant or suppress their action" or "rob it of its significance."[110] In other words, Barth is saying that human causality in water baptism cannot be excluded from its relationship to divine causality, because from the *concursus* we know that in Word and Spirit "*all* creaturely activity finds its locus within the context of the divine activity."[111] Thus, "precisely as a true

104. Ibid.

105. *CD* IV/4, 6.

106. Ibid.

107. Ibid., 105.

108. *CD* III/3, 142.

109. *CD* IV/4, 35.

110. Ibid., 105-6. This is what Barth has in mind when he argues that "the omnicausality of God must not be construed as his sole causality." In the context of the covenant of grace, the human being can exercise "a free and responsible choosing and rejecting, affirming and negating, a human decision." This is what we see in particular in the act of baptism. See *CD* IV/4, 22 and 163.

111. Nimmo, *Being in Action*, 127.

and real human response, water baptism is not without the activity of God."[112] As Barth says (and note the parallel to the language of *concursus* here): "How could [water] baptism . . . be a true answer if the action of God were not *present* and did not *precede* and *follow* in his work and Word?"[113] On such grounds, we can say that Barth's doctrine of baptism and his doctrine of the *concursus Dei* "stand in profound continuity" with one another.[114]

What can we conclude from this examination of water baptism? There are three things. First, we conclude that there is no sharp "disjunction" between divine and human action in water baptism. The human act of water baptism is preceded, accompanied, and followed by divine action and thus does not occur independent of it.[115]

Second, we conclude that water baptism as a human act stands in continuity with God's act, but that it does so only on the terms of the covenant of grace. This qualification, as we have seen, means that "continuity" must be understood in a very specific sense. It is a continuity that occurs in the event of Word and Spirit: thus there is no infusion or imparting of the divine essence or operation to the creature in this act. There is not, in other words, a permanent or readily available sacramental union between divine and human action in water baptism. One could argue for such sacramentalism, Barth says, only if "God were acting in the place of men and men in the place of God."[116] But that is *not* what happens in water baptism. Yes, God's action in the covenant of grace takes place "in, with and over" the human act of water baptism so that the act of God and the act of the creature become, in this event, a "single action." But this action occurs by way of "two [distinct sub-

---

112. Ibid.

113. *CD* IV/4, 106.

114. Nimmo, *Being in Action,* 129-30.

115. Nimmo draws this same conclusion; see *Being in Action,* 128.

116. *CD* IV/4, 106. Webster comments that Barth is launching a "protest against the ease with which the sacramental activity of the church can come to put itself on par with, or can even supplant, the being and activity of Jesus Christ himself." See John B. Webster, *Barth's Ethics of Reconciliation* (Cambridge: Cambridge University, 1995), 166. Healy offers a similar observation: "Thus although the church remains under the 'special care of [God's] free grace,' grace has not been committed 'into the hand of his community.' To be sure, the church is to teach us and direct our thought and action, and it is the task of special ethics to point out 'certain lines' and 'directives' that the church must instill in us. But neither the Word nor the Spirit is bound to the church; the church, and thus the Christian, are bound to them." See Nicholas M. Healy, "Karl Barth's Ecclesiology Reconsidered," *Scottish Journal of Theology* 57, no. 3 (2004): 293.

jects] who stand in clear encounter, God on the one side and man on the other."[117] In other words, this action occurs in the event of Word and Spirit as God clears the space for true and free *human* action which corresponds with his own action. *This* is what Barth means by continuity between divine and human action. Such continuity does not "disparage, weaken, or demean the true and proper dignity of [water] baptism," he argues, but rather enhances it by placing this creaturely act in its rightful place within the context of God's eternal covenant of grace.[118]

This leads us to the third conclusion we can draw from this account: the human act of water baptism "counts for something" as an ecclesial practice, but it "counts" in a particular sense. Whereas Hütter's ecclesial practices "count" in the sense that they make tangible contributions to the true identity, meaning, and purpose of the church, Barth's ecclesial practices "count" in the sense that human actions accomplish something internal to the relationship between God and the human in the context of the covenant of grace. This accomplishment is the response of witness, which is human participation in God's act of self-revelation. The picture Barth paints is this: Jesus Christ, the one who was crucified at Golgotha there and then, lives and reigns as the resurrected one here and now. As the living one, Christ is not idle in the world but active. By the power of the Holy Spirit, he is active in proclaiming here and now the work of reconciliation accomplished there and then. Jesus Christ alone is "authorized and competent" to proclaim this Word of God, but "he does not will to be alone" in this proclamation.[119] Through the power of the Spirit, he summons Christians to serve as heralds who proclaim this Word of God alongside him. Barth says: "[God] calls them — and it is in this sense that we may really speak of their cooperation in His prophetic work — to the *ministerium Verbi divini*, to the service of God and His Word. This then, the divine Word, the Word of Christ, is the *telos* and meaning of their service."[120] In short, for Barth, human action in the church "counts" when it is an act of witness to the Word of God, which is nothing other than God's act in Jesus Christ. This is precisely what we see in the act of water baptism. As a human act, it is the "first exemplary work of faith,"[121] a human witness to God's prior act, a response of obedience that proclaims the Word of God to the world. This vision of what "counts" is cer-

---

117. *CD* IV/4, 163.
118. Ibid., 107.
119. *CD* IV/3.2, 606.
120. Ibid., 607.
121. *CD* IV/4, 44.

tainly different from Hütter's and Beckwith's vision of what "counts," but it is not a vision which disqualifies human action altogether. Rather, Barth places human action in "its proper, limited but nevertheless real, human sphere."[122] It is a sphere defined by the covenant of grace.

V. Barth and the Future of Evangelical Ecclesiology

With Barth's account of divine and human action in the church in hand, we are in a position to address our central question: what are the implications of his ecclesiology for the younger evangelicals' desire to overcome evangelicalism's problems with a more visible church? I think Barth helps us see that the evangelicals who want their actions to "count" in Hütter's and Beckwith's sense are burdening themselves with the responsibility of what should be God's work, while distracting themselves from their own unique and truly evangelical task.[123] To put it another way: I think Barth's solution to the evangelical problem frees us to be truly *evangelical*, which the solution Beckwith chose does not. To illustrate why this is the case, I am going to outline one of the most important implications of their respective solutions: the effect their ecclesiology has on their understanding of the vocation of the church with respect to non-Christians. Given our missionary heritage, this issue carries special importance for evangelicals.

As they confront the problems at hand, those evangelicals who are turning to an authoritative tradition, a high liturgy, a robust sacramentalism, and a thick engagement with Roman Catholic ecclesiology have found a resource that provides an answer to their problem. In such a framework, ecclesial practices can be seen as vital to the Christian life and faith, and as we have seen, these practices can even serve as the indispensable means of God's grace in the world. This framework can thus legitimate an ecclesiology in which human action and virtue matter. Beckwith's comments about his move to the Roman Catholic Church illustrate this fact well. As he notes, Roman Catholicism provides a way for him to understand God's grace being

---

122. Webster, *Barth's Moral Theology*, 170.

123. This point comes from Webster: "Hütter underplays the fact that one of Barth's primary motives in rejecting a mediatory understanding of the church's action was a desire not to burden the church with responsibility for what is properly God's affair, and thus a desire to liberate the church for its own proper work. To deny that church action is mediatory is, for Barth, not to detract from its status but to establish the limits within which it can fulfill its real office with liberty." See ibid., 146.

exercised through his actions and in turn, this allows his virtue to "count for something" with respect to his faith. Indeed, as he sees it, the justification begun by Christ is preserved and increased by his own grace-filled cooperation with God's act. His life of virtue and obedience, formed by ecclesial practices, thus plays a vital role in the manifestation of Christ's justifying work in his life. His action makes a contribution to his identity in the church as well as to the meaning and purpose of his faith. For him, the evangelical ecclesiological problem has been overcome.

The ecclesiological cost of this type of solution, however, proves to be too high, and this is especially evident when we consider this solution's effect on the form of the church's vocation. To see the nature of this problem, we turn to Barth's worry that an ecclesiology which focuses upon the mediation of God's grace through church practices inevitably makes the reception and possession of this grace the primary end of human action in the church. In his view, when the *telos* of the church is the facilitation of the ongoing reception, preservation, and cultivation of Christ's benefits in our lives, then the distribution of these benefits through ecclesial practices becomes the church's primary vocation. This is the action that "counts" in the church. The task of witnessing and proclaiming God's Word to those outside the church becomes secondary to the task of cultivating God's grace in the lives of those inside the church. As a result, Barth argues, the "being and act of the church [becomes] a circle closed in on itself": the church's reason for existing resides in the reception of the gift of God's grace, and the church witnesses to God precisely in its reception of this gift.[124] This description sounds very much like Webber's account of the vision many younger evangelicals have for the church. For them, "The church does not 'have' a mission. It *is* mission, by its very existence in the world."[125] The inevitable result of this kind of ecclesiology, Barth contends, is that the "Church becomes an end in itself in its existence as the community and institution of salvation."[126] It never needs to look outside its own walls to realize its true vocation.

Barth's ecclesiology — seen in light of the *concursus Dei* — offers us a different vision for the *telos* of the church. His vision begins with the reality that our justification in Christ is a complete and finished work: we stand enclosed in the history of Jesus Christ. The reconciliation that objectively oc-

---

124. See *CD* IV/3.2, 766.
125. Webber, *The Younger Evangelicals*, 113.
126. *CD* IV/3.2, 767.

curred there and then needs no further subjective actualization in our lives here and now in order to be effective. John Webster describes this idea well:

> The perfection of Jesus Christ's work is such that it stands in need of no human or created mediation. Christ's work is characterized by what might be called "inclusive perfection": its completeness is not only its "being finished," but its effective power in renewing human life by bringing about human response to itself. Consequently, the relation of "objective" and "subjective" shifts. The objective is not a complete realm, separate from the subjective and, therefore, standing in need of "translation" into the subjective. Rather, the objective includes the subjective within itself, and is efficacious without reliance on a quasi-independent realm of mediating created agencies.[127]

Note again: the objective work of Christ includes within itself the subjective realization of that work. This means that the church does not continue the being of Christ in a changed form, distributing Christ's benefits in history by means of its practices. This distribution has already occurred, and every human stands under the banner of Christ's reconciling work. Subjective participation in this reconciliation, Barth says, simply has "the character of *revelation,* of the *Word* of God demanding expression" in the lives of the humans who hear it.[128] This expression, following the pattern we saw in the *concursus Dei,* takes place by the power of the Holy Spirit. Indeed, the mission of the Spirit is to form a community that exists in correspondence to the word of Christ's reconciling work. The Spirit works as the awakening and life-giving power of this community. It is, as Barth says, "the summoning power of the divine promise, which points the community beyond itself, which calls it to transcend itself and in that way to be in truth the community of God — in truth, i.e., as it bears witness to the truth known within it, as it knows itself to be charged with this witness and sent out to establish it."[129]

The being of the church thus is realized in its "service of witness and proclamation."[130] It finds its meaning and purpose, Barth says, beyond "the

---

127. Webster, *Barth's Ethics of Reconciliation,* 127-28.

128. *CD* IV/3.1, 38.

129. *CD* IV/1, 152.

130. *CD* IV/2, 133. On this point, Healy notes: "Accordingly, the witness of the church is truthful witness just to the extent that it points to the truth that is not itself, or not in the first place at least. Christians are to live 'ec-centrically,' looking beyond themselves. The church is ec-centric, too, in that it 'exists for the world' in visible form." See Healy, "Karl Barth's Ecclesiology Reconsidered," 293.

reception and experience of its members, [and] beyond all that is promised to them personally."[131] In short, the church's being is in its act — and its act is its proclamation of God's Word to the world. *This* is what it means to be the church, and human action in the church "counts" inasmuch as it participates in this activity of witness. For Barth, then, Christ's reconciling work does not reside *in* the church; it propels, charges, and enlists the church as a partner in the proclamation of this work to the world.[132] "The true community of Jesus Christ," Barth says, "is the community which God has sent out into the world in and with its foundation. As such, it exists for the world."[133] Our *telos* is not simply to *be* the church; our *telos* is to find our being in our action as we work as partners in God's covenant of grace by proclaiming his word to the world.

To conclude: this illustration of how each solution to the evangelical problem frames our understanding of the church's vocation provides an example of one way Barth can serve as a good conversation partner for the evangelical future. For all our problems, the strength of evangelicalism lies in the reality that the task of proclaiming the word of the gospel to the world is ingrained in our theological DNA. Mission is who we *are* — it is what "counts" for evangelicals. Ironically, as the younger evangelicals have discovered, our strong focus on mission has become the source of our weaknesses. Our overly flexible ecclesiology, our nearly exclusive focus on the individual aspects of salvation, our reliance on technique over doctrine, and our goal of being relevant to the culture all have their roots in our desire to be effective in sharing the gospel with those who have not heard it. The unintended consequence of these tendencies has been ahistoricism, subjectivism, and the lack of an incentive to make our actions in the church count. Barth supplies a way for us to overcome this problem. In his solution, human action in the church counts. It does not count for our own benefit, however; it counts for the benefit of those who have yet to hear. In this sense, Barth's ecclesiological commitments overlap with the best insights of the evangelical tradition, and he helps evangelicals see why these insights truly matter.

---

131. *CD* IV/3.2, 764.

132. Healy's insights are again helpful: "In sum, perhaps Barth's greatest legacy in the area of ecclesiology was his massive awareness of the providential rule of God, and thus of the fundamental joyfulness of the gospel. He understood Christianity to be adventurous, to be about letting God lead us, work in and with us, the church, so that we may enjoy partnership with God. We can trust God to act to preserve the body of Christ in its historical and Spirit-filled form until the eschaton." See Healy, "Karl Barth's Ecclesiology Reconsidered," 299.

133. *CD* IV/3.2, 768.

So That He May Be Merciful to All:
Karl Barth and the Problem of Universalism

Bruce L. McCormack

For most evangelicals today — even those most sympathetic with many of Karl Barth's concerns — the real sticking point with his theology lies in his universalistic tendencies. Differences with respect to his doctrine of Scripture can be negotiated — and have been, most recently by Kevin Vanhoozer.[1] His use of German idealistic philosophies (ranging from Immanuel Kant to G. W. F. Hegel) in his efforts to explicate theological subject-matters can be shown to be controlled by those subject-matters — and has been.[2] So that should not be an insuperable problem either. The problems that have proven to be most intractable all have to do in one way or another with the allegation of universalism.

Let me give two quick examples. First, Barth's actualistic ontology would probably be taken more seriously were it not for the fact that the ground of the "exaltation" of human "nature" in the history of Jesus of Nazareth is to be found in the election of all human beings in Him. It is because all are in Him

1. Kevin Vanhoozer, "A Person of the Book? Barth on Biblical Authority and Interpretation," in *Karl Barth and Evangelical Theology: Convergences and Divergences*, ed. Sung Wook Chung (Bletchley, England, and Grand Rapids: Paternoster Press and Baker Academic, 2006), 26-59.

2. See Bruce L. McCormack, *Karl Barth's Critically Realistic Dialectical Theology: Its Genesis and Development, 1909-1936* (Oxford: Clarendon Press, 1995), 43-49, 129-30, 216-40, 327-74; idem, "Der theologiegeschichtliche Ort Karl Barths," in *Karl Barth in Deutschland (1921-1935): Aufbruch-Klärung-Widerstand*, ed. Michael Beintker, Christian Link, and Michael Trowitzsch (Zürich: TVZ, 2005), 15-40.

by virtue of election that He can constitute, through His lived obedience, human being as such. Second example: Barth's treatment of the descent into "hell" ought, on the face of it, to make eminent sense to evangelicals long committed to penal substitution theories of the atoning work of Christ. If the death of Christ is thought to be equivalent to the eschatological punishment which the elect otherwise would have had to endure, then that death cannot be simply biological but must surely include the experience described in Rev. 20:14 as the "second death," the descent into hell. That is, after all, the punishment that all evangelicals believe awaits the unredeemed. What makes Barth's reflection on this theme unacceptable in spite of such a reasonable extension of the traditional Protestant understanding of the atonement, however, is his belief that Christ suffered "hell" on behalf of all; that all were "in Him" in His descent. It is one thing to believe in a universal atonement *if* one insists (in good Arminian fashion) that the human will to resist can triumph over God's will to save — for in that case, hell will still be populated. The Calvinist wing of the evangelical movement may not like the Arminian solution, but at least they will not move to have them expelled from the Evangelical Theological Society for it. But it is another thing altogether to couple belief in a universal atonement with a robust affirmation of irresistible grace. If Christ truly experienced *eschatological* punishment on behalf of all, then "hell" ought to be an empty set. Zero inhabitants. And that, of course, is the real problem that evangelicals have with Barth's teaching on the descent into hell.[3]

So it is universalism that is the worry in all other worries. And universalism is a deal-breaker for evangelicals because it is so clearly out of step with the biblical witness — or so the great majority of evangelicals would like to think. But is the possibility of a universal salvation really so unthinkable in the light of the NT witness?

In this paper, I am going to re-visit the problem of "universalism" in Barth's theology in an effort to help those evangelicals with serious doubts to take him a bit more seriously. Mind you, I am not going to try to convince anyone that Barth's view is the *only* possible view to hold in the light of the NT witness. But I do think that it is *one* possible view, and that it belongs to a range of possibilities left open by the NT. And that is a matter of great significance where evangelicals are concerned. Evangelicals, after all, are "people of the book." The only thing that finally counts for them — the only thing

---

3. For a thorough treatment of Barth's teaching on this theme by a very able evangelical theologian, see David Lauber, *Barth on the Descent into Hell: God, Atonement and the Christian Life* (Burlington, VT: Ashgate, 2004).

that *should* count! — is the biblical warrant for any putative truth claim. So I am going to begin with a treatment of Paul's eschatology in the context of the NT generally. Then I am going to turn to Barth's early engagement with Paul, an engagement which in many ways set his course for life — at least where his attitude to "double predestination" and the extent of the atonement are concerned. I will then turn to Barth's mature doctrine of election and seek to assess its significance for the problem of "universalism."

I. Atonement and Eschatology in the New Testament

A. Preliminary Comment

There is a tension, I want to suggest, that runs through the very heart of the New Testament witness, between those passages that bear witness to the saving intentions of God in setting forth a Mediator and the passages that bear witness to the Final Judgment at the end of time. The first are characterized by a universalism of divine intent; Christ died for all. The second are often (though not exclusively) characterized by particularism, a separation in the Final Judgment of the sheep from the goats (Matt. 25:31-46). Faced with this tension, evangelical exegetes have typically sought to remove it through one of two strategies. "Calvinist" exegesis has taken the eschatological passages as a clear and definite starting point for thought and treated the atonement passages as obscure and requiring careful explanation if they are to be harmonized with the eschatological passages. "Arminian" exegesis, too, has taken the eschatological passages as a clear and definite starting point but regarded the universality of God's saving intentions as witnessed to in the atonement passages as equally so. So their strategy for harmonizing rests in the introduction of a third factor between God's intentions and the final outcome — viz. a human will, which God allows to trump His will to save. God wants to save all but cannot because He places too high a priority on human freedom to be willing to impose faith irresistibly. Though these strategies differ, they share two things in common: (1) both presuppose that faith in Jesus Christ is an absolutely necessary condition which must be met if any individual is to be numbered among the eschatologically saved and (2) both presuppose that elimination of the tension is necessary if the New Testament is to retain its authoritative status in Christian theology.

In relation to these two presuppositions of traditional evangelical exegesis, I would like to say that I agree with the first but disagree with the second.

I think there are good and sufficient reasons *not* to eliminate the tension but to allow it to stand — reasons that I will elucidate in the first major section of this essay. And because I think that to be the case, I also think that both traditional Calvinist and traditional Arminian exegesis misfire — and misfire at precisely the same point. Both treat the propositions found in Scripture as standing in a strictly logical relationship to one another, so that any tension that might exist among them must finally be regarded as a contradiction — which would obviously threaten biblical authority. My own view is that the tension I have identified is not rightly understood as a contradiction. Rather, it is a function of the tension between history and eschatology, between time and eternity, between certitudes and mysteries, between what may be said with great definiteness and what must finally be left open-ended and unresolved. I can illustrate this best by setting forth an outline of Pauline eschatology.

B. Paul's Eschatology and the Problem of Universalism

Paul is nothing like us. That is not simply because he is an apostle. It is because his theology is shot through with eschatology. Paul expected the Lord's imminent return and most of us do not. We — and by that I mean all of us, evangelicals and non-evangelicals alike — have accommodated ourselves to life in this world. Survival, the extension of our own lives and the preservation of our churches in a world that has become increasingly post-Christian, has become our abiding preoccupation. Not so with Paul. He breathed an air that is too rarified for us. And most of us find that air stifling — suffocating even. And so we seek to domesticate him, to make him more like us. But he continually resists such efforts. He stands over against us as a prophet of the coming Kingdom and of the Day of the Lord in which that Kingdom will be inaugurated.

It may well be that the great mystics through the centuries have come closest to adopting a posture or attitude that corresponds to Paul's. Certainly they shared his "other-worldliness." They, too, longed to be with Christ. But there is little or no apophatic element in Paul. His expectation and longing are conditioned not by an unknowability of God which will be transcended in the eschaton but by three eschatological certainties: (1) that the cross and resurrection of Jesus constitute together the great incursion of the future of God into time, (2) that the Spirit poured out at Pentecost is the power that makes Paul's congregations to be eschatological communities whose faith and love are conditioned by hope, and (3) that the coming "Day of the Lord" will consist in a "Final Judgment" — a universal and public declaration of the truth of that which God accomplished in the death and resurrection of Jesus, combined with an assessment of the works of all who have professed faith in Christ (1 Cor. 3:11-15).[4] It is against the background of these commitments that the problem of universalism arises in Paul's writings.

The problem of universalism has been much debated in the last twenty years by Pauline researchers. That it exists at all is the consequence of the collision of two strands of his teaching: first, his belief that God sent His Son into this world to be the Savior of all, combined with the understanding that what Christ accomplished in His death and resurrection was not merely the *possibility* of redemption but its *reality;* and, second, his belief that only those would be saved who were granted the gift of faith in Jesus Christ, combined with the thought that since God has not deigned, within the limits of history, to give faith to all, the giving of faith to some and withholding it from others must necessarily result in a division of the human race into two groups (believers and unbelievers, those who have been made alive and those who are perishing).

First, on the side of the extent of the atonement, the death of Jesus Christ constitutes for Paul the turning point between two ages. The classic text in this regard is Rom. 5:18-19: "Therefore just as one man's trespass led to condemnation for all, so one man's act of righteousness leads to justification and life for all. For just as by the one man's disobedience the many were made sinners, so by the one man's obedience the many will be made righteous." The basic contrast here is between two acts, one of which resulted in the reign of sin and death over the whole human race and the other of which brought an end to that reign. The first act is the sin of Adam; the second is the death of Jesus Christ. The question which has always plagued exegetes in relation to this passage is whether the two occurrences of "all" in v. 18 have the same reference. No one questions that the condemnation resulting from Adam's sin pertains to every human being without exception. What is disputed is the reference of the second "all." It would seem odd if Paul were to have shifted the reference from one clause to the next within the bounds of a single sentence — but such a move might well have a precedent.

In 1 Cor. 15:21-22, we find a similar statement: "For since death came

---

4. See Udo Schnelle, *Apostle Paul: His Life and Theology,* trans. M. Eugene Boring (Grand Rapids: Baker Academic, 2005), 593-94. To my mind, the weakness in Schnelle's presentation lies in the fact that he thinks that what Christ accomplished is the "potentiality" of redemption, not its reality. See ibid., 579.

through a human being, the resurrection of the dead has also come through a human being; for as all die in Adam, so all will be made alive in Christ." Here, too, we have two occurrences of "all." But in this case, the second "all" has a different reference than the first — as is made clear by vv. 23-24: "But each in his own order: Christ the first fruits, then at his coming those who belong to Christ. Then comes the end, when he hands over the kingdom to the Father, after he has destroyed every ruler and every authority and power." The resurrection of the dead which immediately precedes the Final Judgment seems here to be restricted to "those who belong to Christ" — so that the second "all" of v. 22 refers not to every human being without exception but only to those who have faith in Christ. It is they who will be made alive. It is interesting to note that no mention is made here of a raising of those who do not belong to Christ or of an eschatological judgment which awaits them. Those who have not believed would seem to be left behind, lying in the grave.[5] And so it is at least possible that the final "all" spoken of in v. 28 includes only believers. "When all things are subjected to him, then the Son himself will also be subjected to the one who put all things in subjection to him, so that God may be all in all." It may be that God is "all" only in the "all" that remain — the others having passed into oblivion. That is, at least, one possibility. I will return to that point in a moment.

But let us return now to Rom. 5:18. Does 1 Cor. 15:22 provide a precedent for how the two "alls" in Rom. 5:18 should be construed? I would say that it does not — for the following reasons. First, what happened in Adam clearly "happened to and for all human beings, without their personal act of decision and participation."[6] Subsequent decisions and acts by each and every human being after Adam merely repeat his decision and act; they do not bring it or the condemnation resulting from it into being. For the parallel that Paul is developing in 5:18 to be complete, that must be true of what happens in Christ as well. Second — and following directly upon the previous point — what is envisioned in both clauses is envisioned as *real*. The turn of the ages which has taken place in the death of Christ has happened not merely potentially (and contingent upon a decision that human individuals might or might not make subsequently) but really and truly.[7] The eschatological wrath of God spoken of in 1:18 and alluded to in 3:19 has been poured

---

5. See on this point M. Eugene Boring, "The Language of Universal Salvation in Paul," *Journal of Biblical Theology* 105 (1986): 281.

6. Ibid., 286.

7. Here against the reading of 1 Cor. 15:23 by Udo Schnelle. See Schnelle, *Apostle Paul*, 579.

out according to 3:25. What Christ has accomplished, then, is the *reality* of redemption, not merely its possibility — a possibility that requires a further act to be made complete. Third and most important: the literary context requires that the second "all" be as universal in its scope as is the first. Verse 17 says, "If, because of the one man's trespass, death exercised dominion through that one, much more surely will those who receive the abundance of grace and the free gift of righteousness exercise dominion in life through the one man, Jesus Christ." The contrast here is between the effect of the act of the first man and the effect of the act of the second. The second act establishes the reign of God through the destruction of the dominion of sin and death. That is the significance of the "much more surely." "Paul repeatedly makes the point that Christ is not simply parallel to Adam but [that] his deed is *much more* significant than Adam's. Paul's main point would be wiped out if, in fact, the 'real' meaning of the passage as a whole is that sin and death ultimately prevail over most of humanity, for in that case the saving deed of Christ would be 'much less' than the condemning deed of Adam."[8] To be sure, the saving deed of Christ must be received according to v. 17. But *how* it is received and *when* are questions left unresolved at this stage of Paul's argument in Romans. What we must not conclude without further ado is that "receiving" is an act which can only take place within the limits of history. For in chapter 11, Paul will give us reason to think that reception (i.e., the act of faith) may, in some instances at the very least, takes place beyond the limits of history. Here, too, we touch upon a point that will have to be taken up again in a moment.[9]

The second strand of Paul's thinking suggests very strongly that eschatological salvation is limited to those who have believed in Christ in this world. The list of such passages would include the following. 1 Cor. 1:18, 9:22, 11:32, 15:18; 2 Cor. 2:16-16; Gal. 2:15-16, 5:19-21; and Phil. 1:28. First Cor. 1:18 is typical: "For the message of the cross is foolishness to those who are perishing, but to us who are being saved it is the power of God." There is clearly present here a division of the human race into two groups: one whose end is life and the other whose end is "destruction" (see Phil. 3:19).

Now several strategies have been proposed in an effort to "solve" the problem created by these two strands of Paul's thinking. All of them have

---

8. Boring, "The Language of Universal Salvation in Paul," 285.

9. Among the other passages belonging to the universalizing strand of Paul's thinking, the following would have to be considered in a larger study: 2 Cor. 5:14; Eph. 1:10; Phil. 2:10-11; Col. 1:20; 1 Tim. 2:4-6; and Titus 2:11.

been discussed at some length in an article written some twenty-five years ago by M. Eugene Boring. That article has attained "classic" status among researchers; virtually everyone refers to it — whether in agreement or disagreement.[10] According to Boring, the most basic decision to be made has to do with whether Paul has a coherent eschatology.[11] Some have said no; others have said that the ambiguities are only apparent and not real. Among those who hold that Paul has a fully coherent eschatology, three approaches may be distinguished: (1) those who hold that Paul's thinking on the subject underwent development, (2) those who have subordinated the particularist passages to the universalizing passages, and (3) those who have subordinated the universalizing passages to the particularist passages.[12] Boring himself tends to side with J. Christiaan Beker, who held that while Paul's eschatology is not finally coherent, it is possible to identify a "deep structure" to his thinking which tilts decidedly in the universalizing direction. Boring's contribution to this line of thought lies in the argument that Paul worked two "encompassing images" which took him in different directions. Use of *judicial* images takes Paul in the direction of a "two-group" eschatology; use of *kingly* images takes him in the direction a "one-group" eschatology. Boring's view, at the end of the day, is that the propositions generated while Paul worked with one of these "encompassing images" are irreconcilable with the propositions generated by the other "encompassing image."[13] But the good news is that both sets are needed if we, as readers of Paul, are not to harm ourselves on one side or the other. "The limited salvation statements proceed from, and conjure up, the image of God-the-judge and its corollary, human responsibility. Without these statements, the affirmation of universal salvation could only be heard as a fate; evangelism would lose something of its urgency, and Paul's hecklers would be justified in saying that we can and even should go on sinning because it magnifies God's grace (see Rom. 3:5-8, 6:1). The universal-salvation statements proceed from, and conjure up, the image of God-the-king, who finally extends His *de jure* gracious reign *de facto* to include all His creation. Without *these* statements, Paul's affirma-

10. See Charles Cousar, "Continuity and Discontinuity: Reflections on Romans 5-8," in *Pauline Theology, Volume III: Romans,* ed. David M. Hay and E. Elizabeth Johnson (Minneapolis: Fortress Press, 1995), 196-210; Richard H. Bell, "Rom. 5:18-19 and Universal Salvation," *New Testament Studies* 48 (2002): 417-32; Thomas Schreiner, *Paul: Apostle of God's Glory in Christ* (Downers Grove: InterVarsity Press, 2001), 182-88.

11. Boring, "The Language of Universal Salvation in Paul," 270.

12. Ibid., 270-74.

13. Ibid., 275.

tions of a salvation limited to Christian believers must be heard as affirming a frustrated God who brought all creation into being but despite his best efforts could only salvage some of it, and as claiming that it does not ultimately matter that Christ has come into the world if the apostle or evangelist does not get the message announced to every individual."[14]

I think myself that there is something to what Boring says, though I also think he has made three mistakes. First, he has failed to reckon sufficiently with the extent to which judicial images serve the kingly in Paul's thinking. God's reign over the world is established for Paul through the exercise of His justice. To say that much does not automatically guarantee that Paul's eschatology is coherent but it does serve to call into question the way in which Boring has sought to address the issue of coherence. Second, in his statement of the baleful consequences of holding only to Paul's affirmations of limited salvation, he speaks only of God's will being frustrated. That judgment would apply only to traditional Wesleyan-Arminian exegesis of Paul and not, obviously, to the traditional Calvinist who holds to a limited atonement. The latter has its problems too, but the fact that Boring's recitation of the benefits of holding the tension open does not really address Calvinist exegesis suggests that there is something wrong with his description of the tension. And that leads me to the third and most important point. Boring dismisses the possibility of development in Paul's thinking much too quickly. To be sure, Paul's development did not take him from a commitment to a limited eschatological salvation to universalism. It consisted rather in the growth in understanding that Paul experienced with respect to the fate of his kinsmen and women "according to the flesh" (Rom. 9:3) — a question of great existential import for Paul personally.[15]

In 1 Thessalonians (the first of Paul's letters), he makes it quite clear that he regards the wrath of God to have fallen upon "the Jews" — and he gives no indication that this wrath will ever be removed. It is simply an accomplished fact. "For you, brothers and sisters, became imitators of the churches of God in Christ Jesus that are in Judea, for you suffered the same things from your compatriots as they did from the Jews, who killed both the Lord Jesus and the prophets, and drove us out; they displease God and oppose everyone by hindering us from speaking to the Gentiles so that they might be saved. Thus they have constantly been filling up the measure of their sins;

14. Ibid., 291.

15. For the description of Paul's development that follows, see Schnelle, *Apostle Paul,* 588-92.

but God's wrath has overtaken them at last." And in Gal. 6:16, Paul uses the phrase "the Israel of God" as synonymous with the church composed of both Gentiles and Jews — an "Israel," therefore, which is not synonymous with ethnic Israel. But in Rom. 9-11, we catch sight of a significant advance in Paul's thinking.

Paul begins in Rom. 9:6-8 by distinguishing — as he had done before — between ethnic Israel and "spiritual" Israel. But what follows is not a two-stage understanding of God's dealings with Israel as we might have expected on the basis of 1 Thessalonians but a three-stage understanding of the history of salvation. The first stage was the election of Israel as a peculiar people of God in the Old Testament. The second stage was inaugurated by the coming of Israel's Messiah into this world. But God "hardened" all but a remnant of the Jews so that they stumbled over Christ. But stumbling, it turns out, is not God's final word. Rom. 11:11-12, 15: "So I ask, have they stumbled so as to fall? By no means! But through their stumbling salvation has come to the Gentiles, so as to make Israel jealous. Now if their stumbling means riches for the world, and if their defeat means riches for Gentiles, how much more will their full inclusion mean? . . . For if their rejection is the reconciliation of the world, what will their acceptance be but life from the dead?" The entire meditation culminates in vv. 25-26a, where Paul tells his readers of a "mystery" which has been disclosed to him — and disclosed, in all probability, only after the writing of 1 Thessalonians and Galatians. "So that you may not claim to be wiser than you are, brothers and sisters, I want you to understand this mystery: a hardening has come upon part of Israel, until the full number of the Gentiles has come in." "Until the full number of the Gentiles has come in": that surely refers to the end, the final act in history. What happens next is something that takes place beyond the limits of history and coincides with the parousia. Rom. 11:26-27: "And so all Israel will be saved; as it is written, 'Out of Zion will come the Deliverer; he will banish ungodliness from Jacob.' 'And this is my covenant with them, when I take away their sins.'" The saving of "all Israel," it would seem, is an event which will be triggered by the appearance of the Deliverer, at which point there will be a resurrection of the dead — a point already alluded to in v. 15: ". . . what will their acceptance be but life from the dead!" But it is the appearance of the Deliverer which brings about faith in Him.

Note that nothing has changed concerning the indispensable condition for sharing in eschatological salvation. Christ must be received; faith in Him is still necessary. The "mystery" of which Paul speaks does not mean a setting aside of that condition. The "mystery" has to do rather with how saving faith

will then be engendered. In His appearing, the word of God is no longer mediated by human preachers. He who is the Word confronts the chosen people directly and immediately.[16] When this happens, "all Israel" is saved —
and thus it will be shown definitively that "the gifts and calling of God are irrevocable" (v. 29).

That Paul has been thinking throughout of ethnic Israel in what he
writes is clear — and pretty much admitted on all sides today. The chief
exegetical question has to do with the word "all." What does Paul mean in
saying that "*all* Israel will be saved"? It's worth noting that even a traditionally minded exegete like Douglas Moo grants: (1) that the "acceptance" of Israel constitutes a "third step in the salvation-historical process," (2) that this
will occur when the eschatological resurrection of the dead takes place
(v. 15), and (3) that "the current partial hardening of Israel will be reversed
when all the elect Gentiles have been saved" — all of which adds up to the
thought that the "regathering of Jews that reverses the judgment of Israel's
exile and that ushers in the eschatological age"[17] will happen when Christ returns. But does "all Israel" mean every Jewish person, living or dead? Moo's
answer is no. He appeals to the fact that Paul has spoken throughout chapters 9-11 of two corporate entities (Jews and Gentiles) and concludes, "The
corporate significance of 'all Israel' makes it impossible to reckon the actual
percentage of Jews living at that time who will be saved. But the contrast between the remnant and 'all Israel' would suggest a significantly larger percentage than was the case in Paul's day."[18] Parenthetically, it is a bit strange
that Moo would restrict the question of the "actual percentage" to "Jews living at that time." For he acknowledges the importance of the resurrection of
the dead where the timing of the event is concerned. So why not Jews who
have died as well? But to say this much does not take us any closer to a resolution of the meaning of "all."

I have to say that Moo's reading is certainly a plausible one. It may even
be the most plausible reading. I do not think that it is the only plausible
reading, however. What it does not account for well is Paul's emphasis on the
fact that "the gifts and the calling of God are irrevocable" (v. 29). That claim
would be more obviously substantiated by the view that "all Israel" refers

16. I owe this insight into Paul's "mystery" to the outstanding article by the Reformed
exegete, Otfried Hofius. See "'All Israel Will be Saved': Divine Salvation and Israel's Deliverance in Romans 9-11," *Princeton Seminary Bulletin Supplementary Issue No. 1* (1990): 19-
39.

17. Douglas Moo, *The Epistle to the Romans* (Grand Rapids: Eerdmans, 1996), 723-24.

18. Ibid., 724.

simply to "ethnic Israel" and, therefore, to every Jewish individual, living or dead. That would, at least, help to explain why Paul then opens the aperture even wider in v. 32: "For God has imprisoned all in disobedience so that he may be merciful to all." Here again, we are confronted by one of those sentences in Paul's writings which makes reference to "all" in each of its two clauses. Clearly, the first "all" is universal; it would be very strange if the second were not universal as well.

So has Paul suddenly become a "universalist" in chapter 11? To say that would be to say way too much. No mention is made here of an eschatological conversion of the Gentiles, comparable to the acceptance of the Jews. Paul speaks with confidence only of a "full number" of the Gentiles whose conversion will take place prior to the resurrection of the dead — a phrase which gives every appearance of being a limited number within the whole. And so what Paul sets forth here is certainly not a *doctrine* of universal salvation. But the fact that he now knows — in light of the "mystery" disclosed to him — that God is able and willing to redeem Israel beyond the limits of history is worth pondering. My own view is that Paul is not certain. Rom. 11:32 allows us to *hope* that all may be saved; it does not confirm it as a fact.

Now as I say, this reading of Rom. 9–11 is not the only plausible one. The traditional interpretation cannot be excluded. It too is a plausible reading and one that has enjoyed the support of a great host of exegetes from Augustine to John Calvin and on down to the present day.[19] But I do want to insist that what I have offered you here is *also* a plausible reading.

In sum, what I have tried to show here is two things. First, Paul's thinking about eschatology underwent a conspicuous development. Such development as occurred, however, is best understood in terms of an expansion and clarification of what was said earlier, certainly not in terms of a "change of mind." The truth is that it is not entirely clear that Paul ever had a "two group *eschatology*," as Boring put it. The resurrection of the dead seems in some passages to be restricted to those who will share in eschatological salvation (see 1 Cor. 15:23). The rest are "destroyed" — a term which is left sufficiently ambiguous in some instances that one might be forgiven for thinking that what Paul has in mind is that such people are left in the grave (see Phil. 3:19). Moreover, Paul held that believers too would face judgment, a judgment of their works in which their dross would be consumed and the gold refined — a rather "fiery" judgment then (see 1 Cor. 3:11-15 with 2 Cor. 5:10

---

19. See Thomas Schreiner, *Paul: Apostle of God's Glory in Christ* (Downers Grove: InterVarsity Press, 2001), 182-88.

and Rom. 2:6-10). But if believers can be "refined" in this way, then undoubtedly the same is true of those Jews who, according to Rom. 11, are raised precisely for their final "acceptance" — and of any other that God might choose to raise from the dead for this purpose. If that is the case, then it would be proper to maintain that Paul has only a one-group *eschatology* — while leaving open the possibility that others are simply destroyed. But then, if all of this be true, then Paul's thinking has been deepened and clarified by what he had to say on these themes. But he does not simply contradict his earlier teaching.

Second, I have tried to show that the tensions in Paul's thinking are better understood as tensions between history and eschatology, between what is given to us to know in the here and now and that for which we are allowed to hope. What we know for certain is that faith in Christ remains the indispensable condition of salvation. What we know is that we are called here and now to share the good news with each and every man, woman, and child. What we know is that the bestowal of faith by God within time is not universal but particular — and this most certainly erects a division. All this we know. For the rest, we can only hope.

C. The Place of Paul's Eschatology in a Canonically Responsible New Testament Theology

Conspicuous by its absence from Paul's theology is any mention of "hell." One might well think that the talk of the wrath and fury, tribulation and distress which awaits those who do evil in Rom. 2:8-9 is equivalent to "hell" but Paul never uses that word. The concept of "hell" does play a sizable role in the teaching of Jesus and in the Book of Revelation, of course. Taken by itself, this difference between Jesus and Paul would not be a problem. The two views could easily be harmonized simply by regarding what Jesus has to say as a further expansion upon what Paul knows to say. The problem, however, is that Paul is committed to a universal atonement[20] — as well as the understanding that faith in Jesus Christ is effected in human beings by God's grace

---

20. In addition to Rom. 5:18 and 1 Cor. 15:22, which we have already considered, the following should also be taken into account: 2 Cor. 5:14, 15, 19. Paul also speaks of the possibility that one for whom Christ died might yet "perish" in Rom. 14:15 and 1 Cor. 8:11. Paul is not unique in holding this view, of course. Aside from John's Gospel, where exegetical grounds for a limited atonement can be found in 6:37, 39, 44 and 17:9, a universal atonement seems everywhere to be affirmed. See 1 Tim. 2:4, 6; 4:10; Titus 2:11; Heb. 2:9, 10:29; 2 Pet. 2:1; 1 John 2:2, 4:14.

alone. And the combination of these two elements creates a difficulty of no small proportions. For if grace is irresistible, if faith is God's to give as He wills and Christ died for all, then, logically, God's will ought to be to give the gift to all and universal salvation should be the result. Alternatively, we could take up our starting point in the "two-group" eschatologies of Jesus and the Seer and look back through the lens provided by the Pauline understanding of the relation of grace and faith and the only logical option would be to affirm a limited atonement. Universal salvation on the one side and limited atonement on the other; those are the only two logical possibilities which arise on the soil of the Pauline understanding of faith as a sovereign work of God. And because Jesus' teaching on hell, especially, was taken to be the fixed pole, Reformed theology in its orthodox expressions always concluded to a limited atonement. The net effect of that decision was, of course, that Paul's commitment to a universal atonement had to be negotiated out of existence.

I would suggest that there is a better way of dealing with this, the most profound and important of the tensions found in the New Testament. I am certainly conservative enough in my understanding of biblical inspiration to believe that if something appears in the New Testament, it is there because God wanted it there. So if a tension exists, there must be a reason for it. And if I had to guess, I would say that the reason has to do with the fact that those awakened to faith in Jesus Christ in this world are still sinners. If God told us the answer to the problem in advance of the eschaton, we would harm ourselves on one side or the other. If He were to tell us that a universal salvation will be the final outcome, we would very likely become lax, antinomian even. The sense of urgency that is pervasive in Paul's Christian existentialism would be lost. If, on the other hand, God told us that limited atonement is the true resolution of the tension, we would very likely despair of our salvation. How could anyone be certain that the atoning death of Christ was really intended for him or her? And so I would venture to guess that the tension I have described is divinely intended — in order to protect us from ourselves.

In short, I think it was a mistake for the Westminster Assembly to seek to resolve this question on the side of limited atonement in advance of the return of Christ in glory — just as I think that it would be a mistake for any church today to teach universalism. Again, these are simply the logical possibilities that arise on the soil of the Reformed understanding of the relation of grace and faith. As such, they constitute the walls within which we are to live in this world. All of us will tilt more to one side than the other. And if individual theologians wish to conclude to one or the other — for the sake of exploring implications and relationships among the various Christian doctrines, they should be allowed to do so. That belongs to their unique calling. But churches need to be responsible for all the faithful. And for that reason, I would say, neither limited atonement nor universalism should ever be made church dogma.

We are now in a position to appreciate Karl Barth's position on the problem of universalism.

II. What Barth Learned from Paul

It is of the utmost significance that Barth's doctrine of election first began to take shape as the result of an intensive engagement with Paul's epistle to the Romans. That doctrine would later undergo a fairly massive correction by being given a Christological grounding.[21] But even then, elements that Barth had first derived from Paul's writings would remain present in it that are important for understanding his "universalism." I will here focus my attention on two of these elements.

First, Barth has the grip of a bulldog on the Pauline understanding that a *real* turning of the ages took place in the death and resurrection of Jesus Christ; not an ideal or merely potential turning, but a fully realized turning of the ages. "The dualism of Adam and Christ, the old world and the new world, is not a metaphysical dualism, but a dialectical one. It exists only insofar as it sublates itself. It is throughout the dualism of a movement, of a recognition, of a way *from* here *to* there. The entire situation would be misunderstood if somehow the conception of a duality swinging to and fro in equilibrium or the two parts of an hour-glass reversing at will were to arise. . . . For the crisis of death and resurrection, the crisis of faith, is the turn from the divine No to the divine Yes and never, at the same time, the reverse as well."[22] The turn from the old world to the new, from the divine No to the divine Yes, has taken place in the death and resurrection of Jesus Christ.

---

21. On the development of Barth's doctrine of election, see McCormack, *Karl Barth's Critically Realistic Dialectical Theology*, 267-68, 371-74, 455-62; Matthias Gockel, *Barth and Schleiermacher on the Doctrine of Election: A Systematic-Theological Comparison* (Oxford: Oxford University Press, 2006); Suzanne McDonald, "Barth's 'Other' Doctrine of Election in the *Church Dogmatics*," *International Journal of Systematic Theology* 9 (2007): 134-47.

22. Karl Barth, *Der Römerbrief, 1922* (Zürich: TVZ, 1940), 155; ET, *The Epistle to the Romans*, trans. Edwyn C. Hoskyns (Oxford: Oxford University Press, 1968), 176-77.

The death of Jesus is the eschatological event par excellence, the inbreaking of the Final Judgment into time. In it, God has — through the actions of the human Jesus — put to death all human possibilities by which we might try to be something over against God. Jesus, he says, "places Himself completely under the judgment which rests upon this world. He places Himself there where God can only still be present as the question of God. He takes the form of a servant. He goes to the cross and dies there. At the high point, at the goal of His way, He is a purely negative magnitude; not a genius, not the bearer of manifest or hidden psychic powers, not a hero, a leader, a poet, or thinker. . . . *Therefore*, God exalted Him, *therein* is He recognized as the Christ, *thereby* He becomes the light of the last things which shines forth above everyone and everything. Truly we see in Him God's faithfulness in the depths of hell. The Messiah is the end of the human. There, too, precisely there, God is faithful. The new day of the righteousness of God wants to dawn with the day of the 'sublated' human."[23] In putting to death *all* human possibilities — even the greatest and most sublime of those possibilities which Barth identifies with "religion" — Jesus has made God known as the end of all things, as their boundary and limit. But not only that! The judgment of God, which is enacted through Jesus' obedient death, is itself mercy and grace. Judgment is mercy! For God does not leave Jesus in the grave. He raises Him from the dead. A full understanding of the revelation of God that takes place in the death of Jesus requires that the cross be seen in the light of the resurrection. In that this takes place, it is understood that God kills only in order to make alive. He puts all human possibilities to death so that all that remains is the divine possibility of a restored relationship with Him. The revelation of God in the death of Jesus is a revelation that is itself reconciliation. And for that reason, the death of Jesus is understood by Barth — even at this very early stage of his development — as "vicarious satisfaction."[24]

The second thing Barth took from Paul has already been adumbrated in the first point. The turning of the ages which has taken place in the cross and resurrection of Christ is not only real; its scope is *universal*. Precisely as the eschatological event in which sin and death are destroyed, the death and resurrection of Jesus is an event with cosmic implications. A new world has been inaugurated. For Barth, Rom. 11:32 is the "key to the whole of the epistle to the Romans."[25] "For God has imprisoned all in disobedience so that he may be

23. Ibid., 71-72; ET, 96-97.
24. Ibid., 137; ET, 160.
25. Ibid., 407; ET, 421.

merciful to all." With respect to this astounding claim, Barth says, "What Paul (and not only Paul!) means when he speaks of God, righteousness, humanity, sin, grace, death, resurrection, law, judgment, salvation, election, rejection, faith, love, hope . . . is decided by how one understands or does not understand this passage. It is the standard by which all is measured, the scale in which all is to be weighed. It is, in its way, for everyone who hears or reads the Epistle, itself the criterion of that *double predestination* whose final meaning it wants to make clear."[26] Had we time to consider the whole of Barth's exegesis of chapters 9 through 11, we would find that there is much in it that goes well beyond what Paul entitles us to say — as a matter of strict exegesis. But here, at least, he has most certainly laid hold of Paul's eschatological hope. And because he has, he finds it necessary to reconstruct the traditional Augustinian-Calvinist doctrine of predestination from the ground up.

This is not the place for a complete treatment of Barth's earliest doctrine of election. It will be sufficient to highlight those elements in it that would undergo change later, change that would strengthen Barth's drift toward universalism.

Barth's doctrine of election in this phase functioned on two distinct levels. We have already discussed the first of these, viz. the movement from a universal reprobation to a universal election, which took place in the death and resurrection of Jesus Christ. But in that the resurrection has happened only to Jesus and not yet to us, the turn has taken place (past tense) only in Him. It takes place (present tense) for us individually only insofar as faith in that event is awakened in us, moment by moment. Barth understands faith not as a gift given once and for all time, in the initiating moment of the Christian life, but as something that must be given ever and anew in each subsequent moment — or not given, as God wills. "Election," then, is something that takes place in the here and now of our lives in that God awakens faith in us.[27] But, then, that also means that where and when

---

26. Ibid.

27. Ibid., 308; ET, 324: "[B]efore every moment in time, God foreordains; and the very brokenness and indirectness of our relationship with Him sanctions and authenticates the calling of those who love Him. Men are therefore foreordained by God, because they are known of Him: *If any man love God, the same is known of him* (1 Cor. 8:3). Here it is that we encounter the secret of predestination to blessedness, which Augustine and the Reformers represented in mythological form as though it were a scheme of cause and effect, thereby robbing it of its significance. No doubt human love of God, the ordination of men to Sonship, and their calling to be witnesses of the Resurrection, are genuine occurrences, consequent upon God's knowledge of men and taking place in the knowledge of the true and only

God "passes over" anyone, that person lives in that moment as one who is "reprobate." "Reprobation" is, in fact, our natural condition in this world. It is only in those moments that we genuinely believe that we are "elect" — which is to say, it is only in those moments that we participate (actualistically) in the turn from reprobation to election that has already taken place in Christ. Election and reprobation so conceived is not a matter of a "protological determinism."[28] It is a matter rather of a singular, supra-temporal activity of God which is "repeated," in a sense, in those moments when an individual is awakened to faith. Moreover, it is precisely because of the supra-temporal character of election and reprobation that Barth knows of no doctrine of a final *apokatastasis* in this commentary. He knows only that in the cross and resurrection of Christ a turn of the ages took place that is universal in its scope. What this means for any particular individual is left for God to determine.

In sum: what Barth learned from Paul was: (1) to understand the death and resurrection of Christ as a complex eschatological event, and (2) to understand that eschatological event as having universal or cosmic consequences. How he then constructed his doctrine of election went beyond Paul's three-stage understanding in Rom. 9–11 by universalizing what Paul says of the history of God's dealings with Israel to make of it a story that concerns all men and women in principle. Two and a half years later, Barth would begin to elaborate the Christology that would one day require a massive correction in this account of election. And when that day came, the problem of "universalism" would take on new contours.

III. Barth's Later Doctrine of Election and the Problem of "Universalism"

The central thesis of Barth's doctrine of election is that Jesus Christ is both the electing God and the elect human. By means of that thesis, Barth effected

---

God. But this must not be taken to mean that His love has brought into being a particular temporal human being and having and doing, which is the result of a divine causation which took place concretely as the first of a series of temporal occurrences. Predestination means the recognition that love towards God is an occurrence, a being and having and doing of men, which takes place in no moment of time, which is beyond time, which has its origin at every moment in God Himself, and which must therefore be sought and found only in Him."

28. Gockel, *Barth and Schleiermacher on the Doctrine of Election*, 113.

a revolution in both the doctrine of God and theological anthropology. It is the second of these revolutions we are interested in here.[29]

That Jesus Christ is the object of election means two things: it means first that He is the One chosen to take the place of all men and women and on their behalf to suffer divine judgment, death in God-abandonment and the experience of hell. But in order to be able to take the place of sinners in this way, He had to be innocent of sin Himself. He had to be perfectly obedient to the will of His Father. His way to the cross is the expression of that obedience. Now aside from the emphasis on the experience of hell, there is nothing in this that need awaken worries on the part of evangelicals. And even the emphasis on the descent into hell is arguably, as I mentioned earlier, a variation on the evangelical understanding of penal substitution.

What creates the worries is the fact that Barth appears to make the election of Jesus Christ to judgment, death, and the experience of hell to be *exhaustive* of the meaning of reprobation. "He is *the* Rejected, as and because He is *the* Elect. In view of His election, there is no other rejected but Himself."[30] What remains for the rest of us — what we are elected to — is a share in His exalted humanity and the verdict of justification pronounced on Him in the resurrection. Even more significantly: all of this — both His rejection and our election — is wholly *actual* in Him. Our own calling in time, then, is not the realization of a possibility but the completion of a reality. The purpose of our calling — and of that awakening to faith and obedience that is an ongoing feature of the Christian life — is that we might be brought into conformity to our true being in Jesus Christ.

Note that predestination is still "double" in this view, but it has been reordered so that its object on both sides (reprobation and election) is Jesus Christ. No longer is Jesus Christ merely the means to one of the two ends established in a prior decree (as both traditional supralapsarianism and traditional infralapsarianism had it). There is no decree above and prior to the decree to provide a Mediator. Jesus Christ is Himself, in His Person, the content of the *one* decree of God. God's eternal will is to redeem a lost human

---

29. I have treated the significance of Barth's doctrine of election for his doctrine of God elsewhere. See Bruce L. McCormack, "Grace and Being: The Role of God's Gracious Election in Karl Barth's Theological Ontology," in *The Cambridge Companion to Karl Barth*, ed. John Webster (Cambridge: Cambridge University Press, 2000), 93-104; idem, "The Actuality of God: Karl Barth in Conversation with Open Theism," in *Engaging the Doctrine of God: Contemporary Protestant Perspectives*, ed. Bruce L. McCormack (Grand Rapids: Baker Academic, 2008), 185-242.

30. *CD* II/2, 353.

race in Him — that is the sole content of predestination. Thus, election is "a chiasmic movement in which the elected of God elects rejection in order that the rejected may be elected."[31]

That all of this constitutes a departure from Barth's earliest doctrine of election is obvious. Election and reprobation as a swinging pendulum descriptive of the believer's situation in the here and now has been "stabilized," so to speak, by being made descriptive of the being and existence of the one Word of God, Jesus Christ. That this move inclines Barth even more surely in the direction of "universalism" is also clear. Certainly, it is hard to imagine a more solid basis for a final reconciliation of all things than the one Barth has laid in his doctrine of election and reprobation. And if what is accomplished in Jesus Christ is the reality of redemption and not merely its possibility, then surely all *must* be saved!

Is Barth, then, a "universalist"? Many have said so, including not only notable opponents of Barth's theology but some he counted as friends.[32] In spite of the fact that he, too, understood Jesus Christ to have experienced "hell" and on that basis wanted to maintain hope for all, Hans Urs von Balthasar judged Barth's doctrine of reprobation to be overly "systematized" and thereby made much too definite.[33] On the face of it, it might well seem that von Balthasar is right. Certainly, it is hard to imagine a more solid basis for a final reconciliation of all things than the one Barth has laid in his doctrine of election and reprobation. And if what is accomplished in Jesus Christ is the reality of redemption and not merely its possibility, then surely all *must* be saved. And, therefore, all *will* be saved.

And yet, Barth himself drew back from such a conclusion. "If we are to respect the freedom of divine grace, we cannot venture the statement that it must and will finally be coincident with the world of man as such (as in the doctrine of the so-called *apokatastasis*). No such right or necessity can legiti-

---

31. Tom Greggs, "'Jesus is Victor': Passing the Impasse of Barth on Universalism," *Scottish Journal of Theology* 60 (2007): 201.

32. Emil Brunner, *The Christian Doctrine of God,* trans. Olive Wyon (Philadelphia: Westminster Press, 1950), 346-53; G. C. Berkouwer, *The Triumph of Grace in the Theology of Karl Barth,* trans. Harry R. Boer (Grand Rapids, MI: Wm. B. Eerdmans, 1956), 111-16, 287-96; Hans Urs von Balthasar, *Dare We Hope 'That All Men Be Saved'? With a Short Discourse on Hell* (San Francisco: Ignatius Press, 1988), 44-45, 94. For defenses against the charge, see Joseph D. Bettis, "Is Karl Barth a Universalist?" *Scottish Journal of Theology* 20 (1967): 423-36; George Hunsinger, "Hellfire and Damnation: Four Ancient and Modern Views," in *Disruptive Grace: Studies in the Theology of Karl Barth* (Grand Rapids, MI: Wm. B. Eerdmans, 2000), 242-48.

33. Von Balthasar, *Dare We Hope,* 44-45.

mately be deduced. Just as the gracious God does not need to elect or call any single man, so He does not need to elect or call all mankind. His election and calling do not give rise to any historical metaphysics, but only to the necessity of attesting them on the ground that they have taken place in Jesus Christ and His community. But, again, in grateful recognition of the grace of the divine freedom we cannot venture the opposite statement that there cannot and will not be this final opening up and enlargement of the circle of election and calling. . . . We would be developing an opposing historical metaphysics if we were to try to attribute any limits . . . to the loving-kindness of God."[34] What Barth is saying in this passage is that we have to leave room for the divine freedom. On the face of it, this has to seem perplexing — even vexing. What would freedom in God mean once so solid a foundation for universal salvation has been laid? Is it a freedom to change God's mind? Surely Barth does not think that! Presumably it was in view of such reflections that von Balthasar finally decided that Barth's protestations against the doctrine of an *apokatastasis panton* was merely "rhetorical."[35]

My own view, however, is that Barth's protest is not merely "rhetorical." Nor is it directed solely against those versions of "universalism" which would make of grace a *principle* from which the salvation of all would be logically derived.[36] To be sure, Barth is a steadfast opponent of all such principles.[37] But that is not the ultimate reason for his protest in the just-cited passage. The ultimate reason appears in his rejection of all "historical metaphysics." What is at stake in Barth's rejection of an *apokatastasis panton* is ultimately his understanding of the *reality* of Jesus Christ. Jesus Christ is not only the One who has come (in the incarnation); He is also the One who comes (in

---

34. *CD* II/2, 417-18.

35. Von Balthasar, *Dare We Hope*, 94. The word "rhetorical" is taken by von Balthasar from the fine work by Walter Kreck. However, Kreck did not himself believe Barth to be engaged in mere rhetorical flourish. The word "rhetorical" appears in Kreck's text in the midst of a rhetorical question — which Kreck answered in the negative. See Walter Kreck, *Die Zukunft des Gekommenen*, 2nd ed. (Munich: Chr. Kaiser Verlag, 1966), 144f.

36. In his recent article, Tom Greggs argues that those who, in the past, have sought to defend Barth from the charge of "universalism" have done him something of a disservice. It is crucial, Greggs says, to notice what Barth's rejection entails — as well as what it doesn't entail. What it doesn't entail is any retraction of what Barth said in his doctrine of election. What Barth is opposing is simply the attribution to him of a "triumph of grace" — as the title of Berkouwer's well known book had it. Greggs is certainly right about this — but that is not all that is at stake in Barth's protest against the doctrine of an *apokatastasis panton*. See Greggs, "Jesus is Victor," 196-212.

37. *CD* IV/3, 173-80.

the power of the eschatological Spirit) and the One who will come (in His visible return). He is all three in a unity that is secure in Him but which will only be fully received by us in the eschaton.[38] This is not at all to say that what has already taken place in the incarnate life of the Mediator is somehow insecure or that God might simply change His mind! "Jesus Christ as He is attested for us in Holy Scripture is the *one* Word of God which we are to hear, trust and obey in life and in death."[39] It is rather to say that until Christ comes in glory, even the very best Christology (and the doctrine of election which finds its root in it) can only be a witness to the reality that Christ is. It cannot provide an exhaustively true account of that reality.

And so Barth concludes, ". . . there is no good reason why we should forbid ourselves, or be forbidden, openness to the possibility that in the reality of God and man in Jesus Christ there is contained much more than we might expect and therefore the supremely unexpected withdrawal of that final threat, i.e. that in the truth of this reality there might not be contained the super-abundant promise of the final deliverance of all men. . . . If we are certainly forbidden to count on this as though we had a claim to it, as though it were not supremely the work of God to which man can have no possible claim, we are surely commanded the more definitely to hope and pray for it."[40] At the end of the day, Barth's position on "universalism" is the same as von Balthasar's. Universal salvation is something for which we ought to hope and pray but it is not something we can teach. That von Balthasar could regard Barth's teaching on reprobation as an exercise in illegitimate systematizing only shows that he has failed to grasp the full implications of Barth's claim that even the best theology can only be a witness to the truth, not the thing itself.

Conclusion

If we were to seek the biblical warrant for Barth's view, it would have to be found above all in Eph. 1:4: ". . . He chose us in Christ before the foundation of the world to be holy and blameless before Him in love." But the justification for Barth's view cannot finally be reduced to a single passage. For what

---

38. On this point, see Kreck, *Die Zukunft des Gekommenen*, 145.

39. Karl Barth, *Texte zur Barmer Theologischen Erklärung*, ed. Martin Rohkrämer (Zürich: TVZ, 1984), 2-3 (emphasis mine).

40. *CD* IV/3, 477-78.

Barth has done is what any systematic theologian who takes the *canon* of Holy Scripture seriously must do: he has read across documents found in the New Testament. He has had to think together the points of view of the various authors. And, as a consequence, he has attempted to synthesize Paul's universal tendency with Jesus' teaching on "hell." To be sure, the results are startling in their novelty. But they ought not to be dismissed for that reason.

The church's engagement with Holy Scripture is a *history* which is not yet finished. Evangelicals do not treat tradition as a second source of revelation; they do not place it on the same level as Scripture. And for that reason, they must always be ready and willing to submit their doctrines to close scrutiny in the light of Scripture in order to ask: have our doctrines been as effective a witness to the truth as it is in Jesus Christ as we have hoped? And in carrying out this task, they must be ready and willing to receive instruction from even the most unexpected quarters.

Evangelical Questioning of Election in Barth: A Pneumatological Perspective from the Reformed Heritage

Suzanne McDonald

As someone whose theology has been shaped in a British context, I have to confess that I am something of an outsider looking in on the debates sparked by the American evangelical response to the theology of Karl Barth.[1] These are not the debates that have shaped my personal engagement with Barth, and many of the questions raised by this particular history have not been the ones to dominate the reception of Barth in the United Kingdom.

Perhaps because of this, I find myself approaching the issue of the "problem" of universalism for the American evangelical response to Barth's doctrine of election from a somewhat quirky perspective. In the first instance, I am not convinced that the question of universalism is the primary problem that evangelicalism might encounter in Barth's doctrine. Second, and as a way of drawing out some of the wider issues his doctrine raises, I will be exploring Barth's account of election from a *pneumatological* perspective.

Since Christology is the focus of Barth's monumental re-working of the doctrine, it is hardly surprising that Christological issues have often dominated the response to it. Even so, it seems to me that the Reformed evangelical questioning of Barth has overlooked some of the strengths of its own heritage by not raising the role of the Spirit and the relationship be-

---

1. At the time I delivered this essay as a paper, I opened by expressing my deep appreciation for Bruce McCormack's presentation of the scriptural possibilities for a Reformed doctrine of election, and would like to reiterate that appreciation here.

tween Christology and pneumatology in election as pointedly as it might have done.[2]

First, however, to the question of whether universalism is the most significant problem that Barth's doctrine poses to evangelicals. This issue most certainly is and has been a major point of contention. From the outset, the Reformed and wider evangelical critique of Barth's doctrine of election has focused on what is at the very least a decided tilt toward universalism in Barth, and it sees this as the outcome of what it considers to be a falsely ordered Christological concentration. For Barth, the whole of election is encompassed in the person of Jesus Christ, the one reprobate who bears the rejection of all, that all might share in the Yes to humanity which is God's self-election in Christ. In so doing, says this form of evangelical critique, God's judgment and justice are absorbed into the trajectory of his grace and mercy, and reprobation is swallowed up in election, first in the person of Christ and then in relation to humanity as a whole, as the whole of humanity shares in Christ's election. The logical and *theo*logical outcome of such an election Christology appears to be universalism, and the suspicion is that the person of Jesus Christ has become an ideal universal in whom all antinomies are brought together and resolved.

Looking back to some of the earliest critiques from Reformed evangelicalism, this approach finds perhaps its strongest polemical expression in the work of Cornelius Van Til, who develops it in directions that not all Reformed evangelicals, conservative or otherwise, have been willing to follow.[3] Nevertheless, these basic contours form the crux of the wider evangelical critique of Barth's doctrine of election: the questioning of Barth's Christological method and the concomitant critique of an outcome which seems to lead to

---

2. The vocabulary for classifying various sub-categories of "evangelical" theology is increasingly complex: Reformed and Arminian, obviously, but add to that conservative, post-conservative, ecumenical, narrative, post-liberal, and so on. For reflections on the nature of contemporary evangelical theology, see Timothy Larsen and Daniel Treier, eds., *The Cambridge Companion to Evangelical Theology* (Cambridge: Cambridge University Press, 2007) and for contemporary evangelical responses to Barth, see Sung Wook Chung, ed., *Karl Barth and Evangelical Theology: Convergences and Divergences* (Grand Rapids: Baker, 2006), and, since this paper was delivered, David Gibson and Daniel Strange, eds., *Engaging With Barth: Contemporary Evangelical Critiques* (Nottingham: Apollos, 2008). My essay offers a response to Barth's doctrine of election from within a Reformed perspective, drawing on the historic theological roots of the Reformed evangelical heritage.

3. See his *The New Modernism: An Appraisal of the Theology of Barth and Brunner* (London: James Clarke & Co., 1946); *Barth's Christology* (Philadelphia: P&R Publishing, 1962); *Christianity and Barthianism* (Philadelphia: P&R Publishing, 1962).

the resolution-cum-dissolution of judgment into grace in our speaking about God and reprobation into election in our speaking about human beings. Evangelicalism has questioned Barth's scriptural warrant for the notion that the whole of election is concentrated in Christ, and that all humanity can be said to be included in Christ's own election. It finds it unsurprising that this leads to a position that evangelicalism has likewise found scripturally difficult to justify: apparent universalism, whether Barth admits to it or not.

Instead, the conservative Reformed evangelical response has followed historic Reformed orthodoxy by suggesting that in and through Christ, election is revealed as the demonstration of the mercy of God on the one hand and the justice of God on the other, in relation to two classes of people: the elect and the reprobate, those who by grace respond to Christ in faith and those who do not. In this account, the New Testament witness is seen to indicate that Christ is not so much the bearer of universal judgment as the universal criterion of judgment.[4] It is one's response to Christ — bearing in mind the Reformed insistence that God is wholly sovereign over our response to him — that is the touchstone for God's dealings with us *either* as Savior *or* as Judge. As we are given to respond to Christ, so we demonstrate our election or reprobation.

Clearly, then, universalism is *a* problem when it comes to Reformed evangelical responses to Barth and the irreconcilable differences between Barth's approach to election and that of historic Reformed orthodoxy. It is a problem too in the evangelical questioning of whether Barth's doctrine of election is internally coherent or not. In the debate over whether Barth should have declared himself to be a universalist, critics have consistently argued that given his understanding of God's self-election to be God-for-us in Christ, and the inclusion of all in Christ's election, it is somewhat difficult to see how Barth can refuse to maintain *apokatastasis*.[5]

I will turn to the pneumatological issues that this raises shortly. For the moment, we need to note that Barth appeals in this context most frequently to the freedom of God.[6] God cannot be confined to theological systems and

---

4. The comparison is neatly made in another early evangelical response, Clive Brown, *Karl Barth and the Christian Message* (London: Tyndale Press, 1967), 134.

5. The *locus classicus* of the debate on this question is to be found in Berkouwer and Bettis. See G. Berkouwer, *The Triumph of Grace in the Theology of Karl Barth*, trans. H. R. Boer (London: Paternoster, 1956); J. D. Bettis, "Is Karl Barth a Universalist?" *Scottish Journal of Theology* 20 (1967): 423-36. Oliver Crisp has recently revived the debate in "On Barth's Denial of Universalism," *Themelios* 29 (2003): 18-29.

6. So, for example, *CD* II/2, 422, where Barth insists upon God's "free will . . . in relation to the world" as the basis upon which some may be rejected. Salvation can only ever be an

the inexorability of human logic. George Hunsinger's summary captures the essence of Barth here: that universal salvation cannot be deduced or excluded as a possibility, since "[n]either the logical deduction nor the definite exclusion would properly respect the concrete freedom of God."[7] For Barth, the freedom of God is such that, in principle at least, he may indeed choose ultimately to exclude some from sharing in the fullness of Christ's election.

The persistent criticism remains that having described the way in which God freely determines himself to be one who elects to take humanity's rejection upon himself in the person of the incarnate Son, it is extremely unclear on what terms Barth can then maintain that God is free to choose *not* to save in Christ. This is the essence of G. C. Berkouwer's a posteriori argument against Barth's denial of universalism, as part of his account of Barth's theology as a whole in terms of "the triumph of grace."[8] The focus of Barth's direct reply to Berkouwer lies elsewhere than the universalist tendencies of the triumph of grace (or, in Barth's preferred designation, of the reality that Jesus is Victor).[9] So one of the substantive points of Berkouwer's critique of election in Barth remains whether, on Barth's own terms, God can indeed be free to exclude anyone from participating in Christ's election, given the way in which God has freely determined to be God in his self-election.[10]

Clearly, then, universalism is a serious problem on both these counts: both as Reformed evangelicalism makes its choice between historical orthodoxy on election and Barth's radically re-worked alternative, and as it probes the issue of whether Barth's position is internally coherent or not. Nevertheless, universalism in itself and as such does not seem to me to be *the* problem. Major issues at stake between the evangelical conception of election and Barth's lie elsewhere.

"unexpected grace," since "[e]ven though theological consistency might seem to lead [towards *apokatastasis*], we must not arrogate to ourselves that which can be given and received only as a free gift" (*CD* IV/3, 477).

7. George Hunsinger, *Disruptive Grace: Studies in the Theology of Karl Barth* (Grand Rapids: Eerdmans, 2000), 245.

8. Berkouwer's criticism is rightly described by Colwell as a "devastating" argument against Barth. John E. Colwell, *Actuality and Provisionality: Eternity and Election in the Theology of Karl Barth* (Edinburgh: Rutherford House Books, 1989), 271; see also his extended discussion of a priori/a posteriori necessity in Barth in ibid., 221ff.

9. For Barth's response to Berkouwer, see *CD* IV/3, 175-80.

10. Part of the problem here lies in the slippages in Barth's use of the term "freedom," particularly between freedom as self-determination and freedom as choice. See, for example, G. S. Hendry, "The Freedom of God in the Theology of Karl Barth," *Scottish Journal of Theology* 31 (1978): 229-44, for an account of the fluidity with which Barth uses the term.

This is in part because the universalism question — the issue of the extent of salvation — is in some respects a second-order question. There are more fundamental theological questions to pursue before we can ask that one, and which will determine our answer to it. One of the more fundamental questions that might be explored in this regard, and the one I will be raising here, is: how are we found to be "in Christ"? Barth recognizes, and Reformed evangelicalism recognizes, that, following the New Testament, this is effectively a basic definition of election in relation to us. Those who are in Christ are elect. The elect are those of whom we can say, "They are in Christ."

Some of the strongest wider questions that a Reformed evangelical perspective can put to Barth have to do not with universalism, nor even with Barth's Christological concentration as such, but with this question of how one is found to be in Christ and what this means for the relationship between Christology and pneumatology in election. In other words, there are questions here to do with how the Trinitarian shape of election is understood. While the relationship between election and Trinity in Barth raises many areas for discussion, the particular Trinitarian issue I shall be focusing upon is the way in which both the historic Reformed tradition and Barth interpret the notion that the works of God *ad extra* reflect the being of God *ad intra* in the context of the unfolding of God's election in time, and in particular, the way in which the Spirit's role is understood.[11]

In order to make this clear, I will draw upon the roots of the Reformed evangelical heritage by turning to John Owen, perhaps best known for his staunch defense of the Canons of Dordt against resurgent Arminianism.[12] While Owen will be my example, Owen and Reformed orthodoxy more widely speak with one voice in relation to the fundamental Trinitarian shape and pneumatological dynamic of election. I choose Owen in part because he is a theologian who shows us his workings, and so every step of his scriptural and theological reasoning is spelled out clearly for us. And what we find is that at the heart of his doctrine of election there is the rigorous application

---

11. For a fuller treatment of the argument to follow, see my *Re-Imaging Election: Divine Election as Representing God to Others and Others to God* (Grand Rapids: Eerdmans, 2010).

12. Here, I will be primarily calling upon his *Christologia* and *Pneumatologia,* which draw out the Trinitarian shape and pneumatological dynamic of election more broadly. See John Owen, *Pneumatologia, or A Discourse Concerning the Holy Spirit,* vols. 3 and 4, *The Works of John Owen,* ed. William H. Gould (London: Johnstone and Hunter, 1850-55); *Christologia, or A Declaration of the Glorious Mystery of the Person of Christ — God and Man,* vol. 1, *Works,* 1-272.

of the principle that the works of the Triune God *ad extra* are the expression of the Triune being of God *ad intra*.

It is axiomatic for the whole of Owen's theology that the economic acts of God express the being of God, or in his own terms, that "the order of the dispensation of the divine persons towards us ariseth from the order of their own subsistence."[13] Inner-Trinitarian relations are a touchstone for the right understanding of all doctrines, and election is no exception. Carl Trueman has been instrumental in the renewed appreciation of Owen's Trinitarian patterns of thought, and he rightly observes that for Owen, the shape of election "is a specifically functional and soteriological application of the *filioque*."[14]

In a clear reflection of the inner-Trinitarian order of being, we find that it is the Father and the Son who together determine the extent and nature of the redeeming work to be undertaken by the Son in our humanity.[15]

Owen speaks of "the counsels of the Father and the Son, as to the redemption and salvation of the church, wherein they delight and mutually rejoice in each other."[16]

13. Owen, *Pneumatologia*, 61.

14. Carl R. Trueman, *The Claims of Truth: John Owen's Trinitarian Theology* (Carlisle: Paternoster, 1998), 146.

15. Although a detailed discussion is outside the scope of this essay, note that because the Son is eternally *incarnandus*, Owen explicitly places Jesus Christ at the heart of the eternal determination of the decree, e.g., God the Father "delighteth in these his eternal counsels in Christ . . . [and] because they were all laid in him and with him, therefore [Christ] is said to be his 'delight continually before the world was'" (*Christologia*, 59). *Christologia*, Chapter IV, "The Person of Christ the Foundation of all the Counsels of God," 54-64 *passim*, provides an extended discussion of the Father and the Son in relation to the decree of election and, through his eternal determination as *incarnandus*, the eternally elected person of Christ. Evangelicals and others have accepted Barth's own interpretation of his innovation in this area, and so have maintained the assumption that the tradition has no notion of Christ as the co-author of the decree. See, e.g., Bruce McCormack, "Grace and Being: The Role of God's Gracious Election in Karl Barth's Theological Ontology," in *The Cambridge Companion to Karl Barth*, ed. John Webster (Cambridge: Cambridge University Press, 2000), 92-110; and, recently, Sung Wook Chung, "A Bold Innovator: Barth on God and Election," in *Karl Barth and Evangelical Theology*, 60-76, esp. 74ff. It seems to me that historical scholarship suggests a need to re-assess Barth's view of the matter; see especially Richard Muller, *Christ and the Decree: Christology and Predestination in Reformed Theology from Calvin to Perkins* (Durham, NC: The Labyrinth Press, 1986). The difference between Barth and the tradition in this regard is not that for the former Jesus Christ is co-author of the decree and for the latter he is merely instrumental to it, but the kind of decree of which Jesus Christ is co-author.

16. Owen, *Christologia*, 58. It is typical of Owen's pneumatological care and Trinitarian thoroughly to ensure that we do not consider the Spirit as a "stranger" to the counsels of the Father and the Son, as if he were simply the agent of a decree established without his in-

As it is particularly the Father and the Son who together determine the nature of the electing decree and its content, in turn, as the full expression of the *filioque* dynamic, it is the task of the Spirit to ensure the fulfillment in the economy of that which has been determined by the Father and the Son. As the logically sequential third in the being of God, so it is the Spirit's task to bring to completion and perfection the determinations of the Triune God in the economy.[17] Hence, as the Spirit owes his being to the Father and the Son, so Owen remarks that the Spirit's task in the unfolding of election "is not an original but a perfecting work." It is therefore

> the peculiar work of the Holy Spirit to make those things of the Father and the Son effectual unto . . . the elect . . . [so that] in the work of the new creation, God . . . intends the especial revelation of *each person of the whole Trinity* distinctly.[18]

As such, while the Spirit's work has its source in and depends upon that of Father and Son, we are constantly and carefully reminded of their dependence upon the Spirit. It is only through the Spirit's work that theirs is brought to its fulfillment. After the eternal counsel of the Father and the Son, and the mediation of the Son,

> [t]here yet remains *the actual application* . . . that [we] may be partakers in the mediation of the Son; and herein is the Holy Spirit to be manifested and glorified, that he also, together with the Father and the Son, may be known, adored, worshipped.[19]

---

volvement. Rather, since he proceeds from both the Father and the Son, "he is equally participant of their counsels," and has an infinite knowledge of them (*Pneumatologia*, 196).

17. As the logically sequential "third" in the Trinity, in every work of God, as Owen puts it, "the *concluding, completing, perfecting acts* are ascribed to the Holy Ghost" (*Pneumatologia*, 94; all italics original unless otherwise noted).

18. Owen, *Pneumatologia*, 189-90. Not surprisingly, the way in which the Spirit accomplishes this clearly corresponds to the notion of the Spirit as the *vinculum amoris* who both expresses and completes the mutual love of Father and Son in the Trinity. His person and work mean that he particularly is the one who conveys the love of God to humanity and enables the human response of love to God in return. So, for example, "As the descending of God towards us in love and grace issues or ends in the work of the Spirit in us and on us, so all our ascending towards him begins therein" (ibid., 200; see also ibid., 157, where Owen reminds us that no grace or mercy comes to us from God except by the Spirit, and neither is there any return of faith or love by us to God "but what is effectually wrought in us . . . by him alone").

19. Ibid., 190.

The work of each person of the Trinity is therefore co-determinative in the coming-to-fulfillment of the electing decree, with the dependence of each of the persons on the others.[20] Yet, because of the nature of inner-Trinitarian relations, it is in fact the Spirit's work upon which the fulfillment of the determination of the Father and the Son finally hinges.

We need to be careful to note, however, that this is not merely the rigorous application of an abstract Trinitarian principle. It is because of what Owen finds in the self-revelation of God in scripture that he is able to speak reflexively of the relationship between the eternal being of God and the economic acts of God. So it is that this understanding of the Spirit's role in the economy of election arises because the New Testament witness indicates to us that it is the Spirit who brings the completed work of Christ to bear upon us and in us, as the agent of union with Christ and new creation in Christ. Owen rightly discerns that in the New Testament, election is inseparable from the nexus of themes drawn together round the notion of being found to be "in Christ." In turn, everything about our being found to be "in Christ" presupposes and entails the work of the Spirit in us. The concept of being "in Christ" by the Spirit — of personal union with Christ effected by the Spirit — lies at the heart of Owen's understanding of election and the Christian life. In a characteristic summary, Owen states that "whatever is wrought in believers by the *Spirit of Christ*, it is in their *union* to the person of Christ, and by virtue thereof," such that the Spirit's task in election can be summed up straightforwardly as, "To unite us to Christ; and . . . to communicate all grace unto us from Christ, by virtue of that union."[21] There can be for Owen no concept of our being "in Christ," and so of being elect "in Christ," that does not also necessarily include the work of the Spirit. Our election might be summed up by the concept of being "in Christ by the Spirit."

In addition to the significance of the Spirit's role toward us in election, we need to be clear about another aspect of the Spirit's person and work in this regard. As the one through whom the terms of the covenant are accom-

20. My thanks go to George Hunsinger for sharpening my use of terms here (although I am sure he will continue to disagree as graciously as he did during the conference with the implications that I will go on to draw from them!). Originally, I had spoken throughout of the "co-decisive" role for the Spirit with the Son in election. As he pointed out, that might suggest that the Son's role was in some way "indecisive." I have chosen "co-determinative" here as a shorthand for the way in which the earlier Reformed tradition expresses the mutual interdependence of the three persons in the outworking of the decree in the economy, recognizing that it is still potentially misleading, but, I hope, less so.

21. Owen, *Pneumatologia*, 516.

plished in the economy, the Spirit is the guarantor of the unity of God's electing determination *ad intra* and its unfolding *ad extra*. Only if we grasp the centrality of this can we appreciate that what is at stake in the Spirit's role in election here is not simply logical consistency, nor even an attempt to ensure that full account is taken of the New Testament presentation of the Spirit's work, but also the integrity of the being and act of God.

At the fulcrum of the relationship between the unfolding of the decree in time and the integrity of the Godhead is the mutual binding of the Spirit's work and that of the ascended Christ. The Spirit's work in election depends upon Christ's act of bestowal in his ascended high-priestly mediation, and in turn, the fulfillment of Christ's work and so of the eternal decree depends upon the work of the Spirit.

It is as the Spirit brings about the efficacious application of the work of Christ that there is a basic unity in the Son's role in election, and as such, between the inner-Trinitarian relations that constitute the being of God, the electing decree of God, and the saving acts of God in human history. As co-author of the electing decree with the Father, the Son determines with the Father those who will be saved and the manner in which that salvation will be wrought. As the incarnate Son and primary object of the Father's electing will, the Son accomplishes through the Spirit all that is needful for that salvation. In his ascended mediation, on the basis of the decree, the eternally elect receive the gift of the Spirit and so are brought to participate in the salvation determined for them in Christ before the foundation of the world. The Spirit's role in bringing to bear upon the elect what has been accomplished in Christ is the lynchpin of the unity of the being and act of God in election, *ad intra* and *ad extra*. It is this which makes the decree a fully Trinitarian determination and action, and it is this which honors the New Testament witness to the co-determinative role for the Spirit in election, as the one who delineates those who are — and are not — "in Christ."

Here, then, are the theological contours that shape Owen's upholding of individual double predestination. Whatever we make of this understanding of the electing decree, what we have is not so much the Aristotelian as the *theological* logic of the Reformed orthodox view of election. Owen's position is the consequence of a total and rigorous commitment to the unity of the person and work of the Son in election, and also of the person and work of the Spirit. In the context of this paper, we need to note particularly the emphasis that is placed on the co-determinative work of the Spirit in relation to that of Christ. This is bound up both with Owen's understanding of the scriptural witness and with the theological principle that the works of God *ad extra* reflect the being of God *ad intra*. It is as the one who proceeds from the Father and the Son that the Spirit is the one whose work is both dependent upon that of Father and Son, and the one upon which Father and Son depend for bringing theirs to fulfillment. Owen describes an economy of election that reflects the Triune being of the God who elects, in which each person of the Godhead equally is glorified, worshipped, and adored.

Turning now to Barth, in his monumental re-working of the doctrine in *Church Dogmatics* II/2, we find that his radical Christological re-orientation of election means that the focus is no longer God's determination of the eternal destinies of every single individual. Instead, election is the primary ontological category for God himself, as the fundamental self-determination by which the Triune God is who he is, in his free decision to be God-for-us in Christ.[22] In the person of the incarnate Son, God is revealed as the one who chooses to enter into gracious relationship with humanity, and as such elects *himself*. Since this electing God is known only in Jesus Christ, election has a shape and a character of which we can be graciously assured. It is the sum of the gospel; it is light and not darkness.[23]

Predestination is indeed eternal, unconditional, and double, as the historic Reformed tradition affirms, but the whole of the decree is now concentrated in the person of Christ.[24] In the "Yes" of the Son — his willingness to take our humanity, and his obedience in that humanity as the true covenant partner of God — the Son takes upon and exhausts in himself the "No" of humanity's rejection of God. For Barth, Christ alone is therefore the locus of both election and rejection, and election has a clear teleology. The Son's election is to bear our reprobation, so that the "No" of God is solely for the sake of the "Yes," rejection for the sake of the consummation of the election of grace.

The basic Trinitarian structure that shapes his account of election in fact differs little from that of Owen. Following a *filioque*-shaped pattern, the inner-divine electing self-determination in Barth is between the Father and the Son. Election is described specifically as "the decision made between Father and Son from all eternity."[25] In fully Trinitarian terms, he describes the

22. Explored in "Jesus Christ, Electing and Elected," in particular (*CD* II/2, 94-144). See also ibid., 76-93: "The Place of the Doctrine in Dogmatics."

23. Ibid., 13.

24. Developed particularly in "The Eternal Will of God in the Election of Jesus Christ," ibid., 145-94.

25. Ibid., 90.

eternal choice of the Father to be gracious toward humanity in offering the Son; it is the Son's choice to offer himself up in obedience to the Father, and it is the Holy Spirit's resolve to preserve the unity of the Godhead in the incarnation.[26] The Holy Spirit is also the one who brings the accomplished work of election in Christ to bear upon us. Is that not precisely the same role for the Spirit, and precisely the same fundamental Trinitarian pattern in the unfolding of election as that which we find in Owen?

The answer to this question is both yes and no. In this regard we need to turn to the implications for us of God's self-election in Christ. What we find is that the concentration of the whole of election and reprobation in the person of Christ creates a twofold division in humanity that reflects the manner of the whole of humanity's participation in Christ's election. Humanity is not divided into the elect and the rejected. It is divided into the called and the uncalled, the believing and the unbelieving, and this is not at all the same thing. What we have is the elect and the apparently rejected, who as yet do not realize that in fact they too are included in Christ's election.[27]

For Barth, the whole of humanity represents one side or the other of Christ's election — either the reprobation that Christ has taken on in order to overcome it, or the prolepsis of the intended destiny of humanity with God which is the purpose of God's self-election for us. This sharing of all humanity in one side or the other of Christ's election is seen in the way that Barth presents the election of the community, in its twofold form of Israel-and-the-church, and we see it also in his discussion of the election of the individual, in which Barth speaks of the division of humanity as a whole into the "elect" believing community of the church, and the apparently rejected: the rest of humanity which is still elect in Christ but as yet unaware of or hostile to the reality of its election.

Barth is clear that the distinction between the elect and the apparently rejected consists in the presence or absence of the gift of the Spirit. By the Spirit the believing community is enabled to know, and to live more and more in accordance with, the foundational reality of its election and the knowledge that the only truly rejected one is the Son.[28] The function of the believing community is to witness to the reality that all share in Christ's election. It is because those outside the believing community, in Barth's words, "lack the gift of the Holy Spirit" that they remain deaf to the

---

26. Ibid., 101; see also ibid., 105-6.
27. Ibid., 351.
28. Ibid., 319; see also ibid., 349.

proclamation and continue to live *as if* rejected in spite of the reality of their election.[29]

We might summarize by saying that the elect believing community is to be distinguished *functionally but not ontologically,* and *pneumatologically but not Christologically,* from the rest of humanity. Crucially, while the Spirit's work is both noetic and ontic — in other words, it is by the Spirit that we are given to *know* the nature of God's self-election in Christ, and are enabled to *live* accordingly — to be "in Christ" is the Christologically achieved *ontological* reality for all, even if they never in fact receive the gift of the Spirit and so never come to recognize their election.[30] An objective change in the entire human situation before God has already occurred in Christ apart from the Spirit's work.[31]

Barth therefore speaks categorically of Christ as the one who takes from the apparently rejected "the right and possibility *of his own independent being and gives him His own being.*"[32] Hence he points out that "[i]t is *not for his being but for his life* as elect that [the apparently rejected] needs to hear and believe the promise."[33] The Spirit's noetic and ontic work has no bear-

---

29. Ibid., 345; see also ibid., 346: those outside the community of the visibly elect "do not possess the Holy Spirit," and so cannot witness to the truth of election, but continue in their ultimately "futile attempt to live the life of one rejected by God."

30. Ibid., 321. Barth makes similar points in his account of human being in his doctrine of creation, e.g., that as we are with Jesus and so with God, we are "elected in the divine election of grace, i.e. elected along with or into Jesus," such that humanity "must and may be described as elected along with the man Jesus" (*CD* III/2, 145). Colwell rightly states that for Barth, the ontological definition of humanity is "that of man *(sic)* as reconciled to God in Jesus Christ" (*Actuality,* 261).

31. For Christ's election as the eternal presupposition and basis of the reality of the whole human situation before God see, e.g., *CD* II/2, 321. For the "decisive alteration of the human situation" already brought about by God's self-election in Christ, see also, e.g., *CD* IV/1, 310ff.

32. *CD* II/2, 453; my italics. Barth precedes this statement with the definition of the divinely imposed limit to the threat of rejection, which is that "the rejected man exists in the person of Jesus Christ only in such a way that he is *assumed into His being* as the elect and beloved of God" (ibid.; my italics). As such, Barth continues by insisting that there can be no independent existence of the rejected *as* rejected, but that they exist only as those for whom Christ elected irreversibly to bear rejection.

33. This encapsulates the distinction between what we might call the "ontological" (the Christological determination of our being) and the "ontic" (whether or not we are brought into lived correspondence with this ontological reality) in Barth's doctrine of election, and the division of these aspects into the Christological and pneumatological respectively. This point must be borne in mind, for example, in relation to Barth's use of "ontological" language concerning the Spirit's role in sanctification. This does indeed make a real "alteration"

ing on the ontological reality of our actual election in Christ, but only on whether we live our lives in accordance with our election or not. Those who remain, in Barth's words, "without the Spirit" are nevertheless "in Christ." One can be — indeed most of humanity *is* — elect in Christ apart from and in the absence of the Spirit's work.

Here we see one of the major fault lines between Barth's position and that of the Reformed evangelical heritage. The earlier tradition maintains that there can ultimately be no "in Christ" apart from the Spirit's work, and that the Spirit's work ultimately delineates, not simply whether or not one recognizes that one is elect in Christ, but whether one is elect in Christ or not. Of course it is not that one only "becomes" elect through the work of the Spirit in the economy. The elect are eternally elect in Christ before the foundation of the world. The point is that the way in which the historic Reformed tradition understands the Trinitarian nature of the decree and its unfolding in time means there can finally be no participating in Christ's election that does not also include the work of the Spirit.

As Owen has illustrated, the historic Reformed tradition therefore maintains a delicate balance between Christology and pneumatology in election, in which Christ's work and the Spirit's are both mutually interdependent and equally determinative. There is no election in Christ that can in any way bypass the Spirit's work in uniting us to him by faith. As such, as we have seen, it is the Spirit's work upon which Christ's completed work depends for its fulfillment in the economic unfolding of election. This is a reflection both of the implications of the scriptural witness and the expression in the economy of inner-Trinitarian relations, such that while the work of the Spirit is wholly dependent upon that of the Father and the Son, that of the Father and the Son is also wholly dependent upon the Spirit.

By contrast, Barth's radical concentration of the whole of election in Christ means that the outworking of the *filioque* effectively issues in a subordination of pneumatology to Christology in election. The pattern of the dual procession still holds: the Spirit remains the one who brings the electing determination of Father and Son to bear in the economy. Nevertheless, the significance of the Spirit's role has been radically relativized. Election as it relates to humanity is less clearly a fully Triune act, in which the Spirit's work is co-determinative with that of the Father and the Son; rather it is a reality that has already been accomplished for all in God's self-election in Christ,

---

in our being (so, e.g., *CD* IV/2, 259) but it does not affect or alter the Christological ontology that defines the existence of each and every person.

which may or may not be made known to individuals by the Spirit. Barth is clear that the participation of all in Christ's election need not include the Spirit's work. The Spirit's work simply delineates one manner of that participation but not the other.

Barth follows his own theological logic by being equally clear that our response of faith or unbelief is not constitutive of either election or salvation. As Hunsinger describes it, Barth's position is one of "soteriological objectivism": that is to say, salvation is entirely constituted, complete, and effective for all apart from our response or lack of response. What Barth will not countenance is any form of "soteriological existentialism" — the notion that our subjective appropriation can be thought of as decisive for or constitutive of salvation.[34] For Barth, our response or lack of it is taken up and included within the election of Christ, and serves to illustrate one or the other aspect of Christ's election: either the rejection of our election which Christ has rendered void, or the recognition of our election in Christ, and with that the realization that Christ is the only rejected and all are elected in him.

Here is another flashpoint for the Reformed evangelical critique of Barth. More often than not, however, that critique contents itself with simply pointing out that Barth's election Christology is so all-embracing that it seems to downplay the significance of human response, and that this is of a piece with his trajectory toward universalism. By contrast, the evangelical reaction draws attention to the implications of the New Testament, which suggest that our response of faith in Christ becomes the criterion for salvation and judgment.

There are two problems with this kind of critique. The first is that if we are not careful, a Reformed evangelical response begins to sound like an Arminian one. So we must always make clear the point on which Barth and Reformed evangelicalism are agreed: that God is wholly sovereign over our response to him. The second related problem is that the critique that there is insufficient weight given to our response stops short of taking the critical theological step. The significance or otherwise accorded to our response is the significance or otherwise accorded *to the work of the Spirit,* and it is therefore also a statement about the relationship between Christ's work and the Spirit's in election and salvation. The Reformed evangelical heritage has the scriptural and Trinitarian resources to pose some sharp questions to Barth in this regard.

If taking a pneumatological perspective allows Reformed evangelicalism

---

34. George Hunsinger, *How To Read Karl Barth: The Shape of His Theology* (Oxford: Oxford University Press, 1991), Chapter 5, "Truth as Mediated: Salvation," *passim*, see esp. 113-14.

to put some old questions to Barth in slightly different ways, using a pneumatological lens also gives us a different focus for questions concerning the internal coherence of Barth's doctrine. While it is wholly consistent with the logic of his election Christology that the Spirit's work relates to the *functional* setting apart of the witnessing community, but not to the *ontological* inclusion of humanity as a whole in the election of Christ, we also need to note that this is not the only way that the Spirit's role is presented in *CD* II/2. There are pneumatological problems *within* Barth's mature doctrine of election which take us to the root of the wider questions concerning the coherence of Barth's account.[35]

With this we come once again to the vexed question of universalism in Barth's doctrine. As is frequently rehearsed, Barth is able to assert on the one hand that the godless still live under the threat of actual rejection, and of eternal condemnation, and on the other, that the godless cannot in fact annul their election, since that threat is "rendered powerless by Jesus Christ," who has borne the rejection of the apparently rejected.[36]

The overwhelming thrust of Barth's account of God's single act of election in the person of Jesus Christ is that, in Barth's words, "[w]ith Jesus Christ the rejected can only *have been* rejected. He cannot *be* rejected any more."[37] Indeed, "faith in the divine predestination . . . means faith in the non-rejection of man. . . . [I]t is God Himself who is rejected in His Son . . . that we might not be rejected. . . . [P]redestination is the non-rejection of man."[38]

Yet Barth steadfastly refuses to maintain *apokatastasis*. This refusal is consistently based upon two key themes: preserving God's freedom, as noted earlier, and what is effectively an appeal to the Spirit's role. Berkouwer asks with a rhetorical flourish what right Barth's rejection of *apokatastasis* can possibly have.[39] The answer is: a pneumatological one. If Barth's assertion

35. Hunsinger reminds us that the paradoxes in Barth's doctrine of election result from attempting to inhabit the "field of tension" between asserting the efficacy of the saving work of Christ for all, the impossibility of actively participating in this except through faith, and Barth's concern to affirm the non-constitutiveness of faith for salvation (*How To Read Karl Barth*, 106-7, 110-12). While this captures the essence of the "field of tension" in Barth, the extent to which this captures the NT's "field of tension" might be questioned, particularly with regard to the issue of how one is found to be "in Christ" and the role of faith in salvation (and so the implications of the New Testament witness for the relationship between Christology and pneumatology for election and salvation).

36. *CD* II/2, 321-22; see also ibid., 318-19, 346.

37. Ibid., 453.

38. Ibid., 167.

39. Berkouwer, *Triumph*, 116.

that the Son's assumption of our reprobation to himself may ultimately apply to some but not to others, and if this is not to be an exercise of arbitrary freedom on God's part, then it requires an election pneumatology in which, after all, it is the Spirit who delineates those who are "in Christ" and those who are not. This is precisely what is implied when we turn to aspects of Barth's account of our election of God.[40]

On the one hand, Barth insists that the choice of the godless is in fact "void," since "he belongs eternally to Jesus Christ." The rejection he deserves is borne and cancelled by Christ.[41] On this basis, as we have noted, the Spirit's work in enabling our response is significant for the way in which we live now — either in recognition of our election, or in ignorance and opposition to it — but is in no way determinative of the ultimate reality of our election. This is the overwhelming thrust of Barth's doctrine of election and is the predominant understanding of the relationship between Christology and pneumatology.

Nevertheless, there are occasions when Barth also appears to insist that the Spirit's work *is* necessary, not simply for the apprehension of our election in Christ, but for its reality. Positively, Barth remarks that "in faith in [Christ] it is decided . . . who belongs to the fulness" of God's people in Christ.[42] He acknowledges that the New Testament unequivocally identifies election with faith, and so with the work of the Spirit: "[e]lection means faith,"[43] he says, and the people of Jesus Christ are "all who believe in Him and are therefore the object of divine election."[44]

Negatively, the rejected is the one who "isolates himself from God by resisting his election as it has taken place in Jesus Christ."[45] The rejected are those from whom God has turned away *because they have turned their backs upon God.*[46] Later in his corpus, Barth goes so far as to state that "[t]o the man who persistently tries to change the truth into untruth, God does not

40. For our election of God as taking place within, and as the purpose of, God's self-election in Christ, see *CD* II/2, 177.

41. Ibid., 306. Barth again emphasizes, "In the negative act of this void choice of nothing, he [the godless] is vanquished and overtaken even before he begins by that which God has eternally decreed for him and done for him in the election of Jesus Christ" (316), and he cannot "reverse or change the eternal decision of God. . . . [H]e can accomplish nothing which abolishes the choice of God" (317).

42. Ibid., 300.

43. Ibid., 427; see ibid., 426-28.

44. Ibid., 430; see also ibid., 127.

45. Ibid., 449.

46. Ibid., 455.

owe eternal patience and . . . deliverance."[47] It would seem, then, that if there is to be ultimate rejection, this will be in part as a result of the perverse obstinacy of human choice against God in the face of God's choice for us.

If the significance of Barth's election Christology holds, then the ambiguity of Barth's stress upon our choice is not of ultimate significance.[48] If final reprobation is a genuine possibility as a result of our decision to reject our election in Christ, then this emphasis upon choice is deeply problematic, to say the least.[49] Berkouwer stresses Barth's desire to maintain the "open situation" of the gospel proclamation as the source of the contradiction in this aspect of his doctrine.[50] In fact, the crux of the issue is that in a very significant sense, the gospel proclamation is *not* open in this way.

Once again we need to be reminded that those who reject their election remain deaf to the proclamation and unable to live in accordance with the reality of their election in Christ *because they have not received the gift of the Spirit.* We may indeed continue to resist our participation in Christ's election, but our only possibility of freely choosing to share in it lies in God's own decision to bestow the Spirit to this purpose. If God chooses to grant this gift to some and not to others, and if a negative response contains the real threat of ultimate exclusion from participation in election in Christ, then there are aspects of Barth's doctrine of election that tacitly remain within the dynamic of individual double predestination. His desire to avoid the universalist implications of his election Christology leads to a lurch back

47. *CD* IV/3, 477. He goes on to remark that while we cannot count on the withdrawal of this final threat, because we have no claim on God, we may pray for it and hope for it (477-78). While we may have no claim on God, once again, we must ask whether Barth has taken sufficient account of the claim made upon the being and act of God by God's own free self-determination as he has described it.

48. So, for example, our assurance is to be located in the will of God for salvation, expressed in his self-election, which is "unconditional in its certainty, preceding all self-determination and outlasting any change in self-determination on the part of the creature" (*CD* II/2, 31).

49. Sung Wook Chung refers to this as a tension between "Calvinistic" and "Arminian" tendencies in Barth's doctrine, but rightly points out that Barth would resist any accusation of Arminianism ("A Bold Innovator," 74). In fact, as I shall go on to note, given Barth's understanding of the Spirit's role, the tension is not so much between Calvinistic and Arminian tendencies as between the only two "logical" possibilities for a fully Reformed understanding of God's sovereign election of grace — universalism or individual double predestination. For a clear presentation of these as the only two possibilities within an Augustinian-Reformed theological framework, see Oliver D. Crisp, "Augustinian Universalism," *International Journal for Philosophy of Religion* 53 (2003): 127-45.

50. Berkouwer, *Triumph*, 116, 122.

toward individual double predestination through what is effectively an appeal to the gift and work of the Spirit.

So, seen from a pneumatological perspective, the Reformed evangelical questioning of Barth can once again take a slightly different direction than the usual. The issue might be seen not so much in terms of Barth's inconsistency in not declaring himself a universalist on the basis of his election Christology, but in terms of whether there are aspects of Barth's pneumatology that are pulling in such a different direction to his Christology that his doctrine of election is at risk of imploding.

All of this takes us back to the point that while universalism is *a* problem for the Reformed evangelical response to Barth, it is not necessarily *the* problem. It serves to point us to some of the more fundamental issues at stake between Barth's re-orientation of the doctrine and Reformed orthodoxy. The differences between Reformed evangelicalism and Barth here are not simply a matter of Barth's radical Christological concentration. There are questions for Reformed evangelicalism to put to Barth concerning whether his election Christology allows room for a sufficiently robust election pneumatology alongside it. The problem is not simply that Barth's Christology seems to lead straight to universalism, but whether Barth's understanding of the "in Christ" of election can accommodate a rigorous enough account of the "by the Spirit" of election.

All of this is *not* to say, of course, that Reformed (or any other) evangelicals are to leap to the general conclusion that Barth's pneumatology is weaker than that of the earlier Reformed tradition. There has recently been a highly appreciative overview of Barth's pneumatology, demonstrating how it might assist various strands of evangelicalism to *recover* their Christological and pneumatological balance.[51] Nevertheless, it is to say that looking hard at the pneumatological dynamic as well as the Christological shape of the doctrine of election raises some pointed questions that bring focus to, and push further, the evangelical questioning of Barth's doctrine of election.

Looking through a pneumatological lens allows a Reformed evangelical perspective to bring a somewhat different angle to well-worn critiques, and it also points to some possibilities for taking the discussion in new directions. Continuing to probe the relationship between Barth and evangelicalism is at its most fruitful when it not only re-visits old debates but also opens up fresh areas of discussion. In doing so, it bears the additional fruit of be-

---

51. Frank Macchia, "The Spirit of God and the Spirit of Life: An Evangelical Response to Karl Barth's Pneumatology," in *Karl Barth and Evangelical Theology*, 149-71.

coming a catalyst for further constructive work. Neither Reformed evangelicalism nor Karl Barth has said the last word on the doctrine of election. So it seems to me that from an evangelical perspective Barth's stress on election as fundamentally for the sake of blessing, and his questioning of whether the primary focus of the decree is indeed the determination of the eternal destiny of individuals, ought to give us pause because there is much in the scriptural contours of election to challenge some default habits of thinking on these points. But it also seems to me that the historic Reformed tradition has somewhat the better of the scriptural and Trinitarian balance between Christ's work and the Spirit's in the unfolding of election. There is scope aplenty here in the ongoing engagement between evangelicalism and Barth for thinking afresh about how we might re-express the nature and purpose of election in Christ by the Spirit.

PART III

CONTEMPORARY TRAJECTORIES

But Did It *Really* Happen? Frei, Henry, and Barth on Historical Reference and Critical Realism

Jason A. Springs

"Postliberal theology" is a slippery term. Though it has become common in contemporary theological usage, the referent intended by the term frequently varies. It is used to refer to a select set of works produced by a diverse group of theologians who taught or studied at Yale during the 1960s and '70s; but it is also used to refer to any thinker whose theological approach is informed by "non-foundational" philosophical insights, who refuses systematic apologetics in theological discourse, and who situates these commitments within a framework oriented by the witness of Scripture in the life of the Christian church. In my judgment, in as far as the moniker "postliberal theology" stands in as a placeholder for the complex and impressionistic range of family resemblances shared by a variety of theological projects, it has outrun its usefulness. So used, the term must function at such a high level of generality in order to encompass so many important differences and unresolved debates that it borders on sheer inaccuracy. As such, its effect is to pigeonhole and caricature, much in line with Ralph Waldo Emerson's dictum "if you know my sect then you can anticipate my argument." If this is how the term "postliberal" has come to function in contemporary theological exchange, then we have all the reason we need to let it go by the boards.

At the same time, however, the term need not be inherently detrimental if used delicately and suggestively, in ways that invite careful inquiry and detailed analysis. In order to be helpful for purposes of understanding, comparison, and criticism, the family resemblances toward which it gestures must be identified and assessed on a case by case basis, with careful attention to detail and under the proviso that resemblance is not identity. An array of shared concerns need not imply agreement on the substance of those concerns, any one of which may be the basis of sustained disagreement. Any assessment of "postliberal theology" will do well to concretely engage particular thinkers in critical comparison and contrast, and cautiously move along at the level of detail.

Criticisms aimed at "postliberal theology" have been as wide-ranging as the resemblances that comprise it. Some evangelical critics have charged that postliberal theologians' tendency to be unapologetic about their basic theological commitments cedes the upper hand to philosophical skepticism. In refusing to work at historically verifying the events reported in Scripture, for instance, they forgo historical viability or "what really happened." As such, they devote their efforts to explicating the supposedly autonomous world inside the biblical text. On one hand, such critics claim, postliberal theologians lack faith in the historical reliability of the scriptural witness. On the other hand, and perhaps more important, they stand in dereliction of their apologetic duties by refusing to engage critical history. Certain exchanges on these points have proven especially fruitful precisely because they have moved past labels and caricature to sustained and mainly charitable debate at the level of detail. In Part I of this essay I examine one such encounter — perhaps the most famous encounter between a postliberal and an evangelical theologian on the question of reference — the exchange between Carl F. H. Henry and Hans Frei.[1] This encounter warrants careful consideration and analysis not only as a model for what a detailed encounter between postliberal and evangelical theologians might look like, but also because it affords an opportunity to clarify Frei's position on what may be the most nagging concerns about his theology — the question of historical reference.

The difficulty that reference poses for Frei does not stop with the question of history. If some evangelicals are especially concerned about historical reference, various Barth scholars are equally concerned about Frei's position on a closely related form of extra-textual reference. The latter ask how Frei can posit Scripture as the Word of God manifest linguistically in the way that he does without giving up the *realism* of Scripture's claims

---

1. Carl F. H. Henry, "Narrative Theology: An Evangelical Appraisal," and Hans Frei's response in *Trinity Journal* 8 (1987): 3-24. This particular debate has been mediated by George Hunsinger in an essay entitled, "What Can Evangelicals and Postliberals Learn from Each Other? The Carl Henry-Hans Frei Exchange Reconsidered," in *The Nature of Confession: Evangelicals and Postliberals in Conversation,* ed. Timothy R. Phillips and Dennis L. Okholm (Downers Grove, IL: InterVarsity, 1996).

about God. How, for instance, are we to make sense of Frei's claims that "[F]or the Christian interpretive tradition truth is what is written, not something separable and translinguistic that is written 'about'"?[2] Does such a claim give up God's revelation in Scripture actually corresponding to the reality of God outside of the text? If claims like this one compromise a realist account of theological reference then it becomes difficult to see how Frei can avoid slipping into a "linguistically idealist" account of revelation in which the text itself becomes the "linguistic presence" of God. On the basis of such anti-realist concerns some critics claim that Frei's work diverges from Karl Barth's at a fundamental level, and in a way that Frei appears not to have understood.

These charges concerning historical and theological reference are closely related. Both raise worries about construing the biblical text as a self-contained "world unto itself," reminiscent of Jacques Derrida's declaration that "there is nothing outside the text."[3] In the following paragraphs I work through both of the challenges that extra-textual reference poses to Frei's theology. Based upon close examination of the full range of resources available in his writings, I argue that Frei makes available means by which to successfully navigate both of these challenges, even if he himself never managed to articulate such means with sufficient clarity. I conclude that, while their differences are important, Frei's theology is far more consistent than it is inconsistent with what some scholars have come to refer to as Barth's "critical realism."[4]

I. Frei, Henry, and Historical Reference

In *The Eclipse of Biblical Narrative* Hans Frei demonstrated how scriptural reasoning and textual interpretation in eighteenth- and nineteenth-century Europe had come to be regulated by fairly recent, and highly theory-laden, conceptions of "meaning," "interpretation," and "understanding." When

---

2. Hans Frei, "Theology and the Interpretation of Narrative" (1982), in *Theology and Narrative: Selected Essays*, ed. George Hunsinger and William Placher (Oxford: Oxford University Press, 1993), 108; hereafter cited as *TN*.

3. Jacques Derrida, *Of Grammatology*, trans. Gayatri Chakravorty Spivak (Baltimore: Johns Hopkins, 1976), 156.

4. For a succinct account of this feature of Barth's theology, see Bruce McCormack, *Orthodox and Modern: Studies in the Theology of Karl Barth* (Grand Rapids, MI: Baker, 2008), 109-66.

Frei surveyed the terrain of modern biblical scholarship, he identified a problematical impasse between theological liberals and conservatives. Frei posed the dilemma:

> On the one hand, there are liberal affirmations to the effect that the logical and real subject of resurrection statements is the faith of the disciples, that statements about the resurrection do not describe events but the *significance* of other events, that the resurrection was spiritual, that it isn't crucial to Christianity, etc. On the other hand, conservatives not only claim that Jesus is the subject of the statements about the resurrection but that these statements describe the manner of his resurrected state. . . . [They propose to] adduce evidence about the credibility of the witnesses, the veracity of the authors, the possibility that God can perform miracles because he's in charge of the universe . . . and [then] make the transition from hermeneutics, or exegesis of the texts, not only to the affirmation of their veracity but also to a clear statement of the mode in which these events happened (e.g., the resurrected body of Jesus was or was not subject to the law of gravity).[5]

Now, in passages such as these, Frei may be as guilty of lumping together "liberals" and "conservatives" as those who lump him under the "post-liberal" rubric. To my mind, it is precisely for this reason that Frei's engagement with Carl Henry is so instructively concrete.

Henry began his critical analysis of Frei by gesturing toward the significant agreements they shared. They shared, for instance, the conviction that "Scripture is a harmonious unity, that historical criticism has not invalidated the relevance of Scripture, that the biblical world is the real world which illuminates all else and that Jesus is the indispensable Savior."[6] Even so, as Henry saw it, Frei's averse reaction to the modern uses of the Bible as a historical source, in effect, dismissed the reality "behind the text" as either theologically unnecessary or fortunately no longer available from the perspective of critical-historical methodology. In other words, Frei either bracketed or sidestepped altogether questions about the Bible's reference to historical reality. In fact, at times he appeared to reduce the biblical reports to literature. Henry countered, "The notion that the narrative simply as narra-

---

5. Hans Frei, "Historical Reference and the Gospels: A Response to a Critique of *The Identity of Jesus Christ*," in *Hans W. Frei: Unpublished Pieces: Transcripts from the Yale Divinity School Archive*, ed. Mike Higton, 65, 64.

6. Hunsinger, "What Can Evangelicals and Postliberals Learn from Each Other?" 137.

tive adequately nurtures faith independently of all objective historical concerns sponsors a split in the relationships of faith to reason and to history that would in principle encourage skepticism and cloud historical referents into obscurity."[7] Henry thought this entirely unacceptable. He wanted to know, quite simply, did Jesus come back to life or did he not? Was he resurrected and did he leave his tomb empty, or not?

Frei's immediate response to such questions sounded equivocal. "Well, yes," he replied. "If I am asked to use the language of factuality, then I would say, yes, in those terms, I have to speak of an empty tomb. In those terms I have to speak of the literal resurrection." Frei, however, quickly interposed a proviso. "But I think those terms are not privileged, theory-neutral, trans-cultural, an ingredient in the structure of the human mind and of reality always and everywhere."[8] With this proviso Frei sought to question the normative assumptions by which some event might be determined historically verified or verifiable. And, initially, it sounds like Frei is making a move customary of the so-called "postmodern" turn away from the very possibility of "objectivity." I want to suggest, however, that this is the wrong way to characterize Frei's reservation.

On the one hand, Frei derived his concern about the "theory-ladenness" of modern historical research from his recognition that such forms of investigation have been based upon several philosophically empiricist presuppositions. Such presuppositions include the idea that "the facts" stand independently of, and separable from, the reports that render them, and that accurate or inaccurate correspondence to those facts makes claims or beliefs about them true or false. These presuppositions include, further, that one ought to tailor the strength of one's assertion of factuality or belief in the truth of one's claim in proportion to the reliability of one's evidence and the public testability of one's claim. Frei's reservations about historical investigation of the Gospel accounts, by contrast, are grounded in his belief that the particular subject matter he has in view is unique in kind. This latter concern provides Frei's primary motivation for treating questions about Scripture's historical reference with cautious hesitation.

As Frei saw it, the uniqueness of the biblical subject matter resists the tendency of modern historical investigation to confine the biblical witness to the status of a factual report. This subject matter does not altogether *preclude* the concerns of modern historical investigation. However, it refuses to

7. Henry, "Narrative Theology," 11.

8. Frei, "Response to 'Narrative Theology: An Evangelical Appraisal,'" *Trinity Journal* 8 (1987): 24.

be circumscribed by the limits of modern historical understanding alone. Frei continued in response to Henry:

> Even if I say that history is first of all the facts — and I do have a healthy respect for evidence — I come across something else. Is Jesus Christ (and here I come across the problem of miracle) a "fact" like other historical facts? Should I really say that the eternal Word made flesh, that is, made fact indeed, is a fact like any other? I can talk about "Jesus" in that way, but can I talk about the eternal Word made flesh in him that way? I don't think so. . . .[9]

These are not words of one who brackets questions of history or suspends questions of reality reference, as is occasionally charged.[10] In fact, in sorting through these difficulties Frei identified two distinct senses of reference operative in the biblical witness. The first he referred to as old-fashioned "historical reference," and the second he called "textual reference."[11]

Historical reference is central to Frei's project under the proviso that there can be no "systematic correlation" between God's revelation in scripture and human procedures of historical investigation. George Hunsinger characterizes this way of relating historical investigation and the gospel narratives as "ad hoc minimalism." This position is "ad hoc" because, while it incorporates historical investigation, it refuses to reduce or finally constrain the integrity and efficacy of the biblical witness to the criterion of historical verifiability. It is "minimalist" because "Faith needs no more from modern historical criticism . . . than two very minimal assurances: first, that Christ's resurrection has not been historically disconfirmed, and second, 'that a man, Jesus of Nazareth, who proclaimed the Kingdom of God's nearness, did exist and was finally executed.'"[12]

Of course, while minimal, the role that historical reference plays in Frei's account is anything but negligible. In fact, in some circumstances, it could prove decisive. While Frei believed that the resurrection could not be historically proven, he held out the possibility that it could be historically

---

9. Ibid.

10. For criticisms along these lines, see Alister McGrath, "An Evangelical Evaluation of Postliberalism," in *The Nature of Confession*, 41-43; N. T. Wright, *The Resurrection of the Son of God* (Minneapolis: Fortress, 2003), 21-23.

11. Frei, "Response to 'Narrative Theology,'" 22.

12. Hunsinger, "What Can Evangelicals and Postliberals Learn from Each Other?" 143, citing pp. 151 and 51 of the 1975 Fortress Press edition of *The Identity of Jesus Christ*.

disconfirmed. Historical *dis*confirmation would indicate that the claim that Christ's resurrection had happened had been a fabrication all along. In this scenario, accordingly, the alleged resurrection would be just another piece of falsifiable *Historie* for which historical investigation would be both necessary and entirely sufficient. If, however, Jesus is who the Bible portrays him to be, then we are dealing with an event that happened in time, but for which probability or evidence is woefully insufficient. "[I]f the resurrection is true, it is unique, but if false, it is like any other fact that has been proved false: there is nothing unique about it in that case."[13]

What Frei called "textual reference" enters into the account at this point, first of all, because there can be no access to the events that happened "then and there" apart from some terms of description. In other words, the "facts of the matter" do not stand by neutrally, awaiting analysts to assume a view from nowhere in order to access them in unadulterated objectivity. Any account will be relative to some frame of reference, terms of depiction, and investigative interests and purposes. Moreover, taken purely on historical-critical terms, the Gospel accounts are troublingly fragmentary. Empirical evidence for or against "what really happened" is insufficient to generate sustained scholarly consensus. Working to sidestep intractably speculative debates about factuality — such as the nearly self-parodying sequence of quests for the historical Jesus — Frei began with a simple assumption about what happened then and there. He wrote:

> I plead guilty to a kind of fall-back on common sense, to which someone may say I have no right. I am assuming that somebody roughly fitting Jesus of Nazareth as described in the Gospels really did live. If and when it is shown that this assumption is unwarranted and the person invented, I will no longer want to be a Christian. Until then, I plan to go on being one and saying, "We know him only under a description. . . ."[14]

The Gospel accounts of Christ's life, death, and resurrection provide the indispensable description of the events depicted there for two reasons. First,

13. Frei, *The Identity of Jesus Christ* (Eugene, OR: Wipf and Stock, 1997), 183. Bruce Marshall explores the epistemic implication of one such scenario of disconfirmation and explains why such a possibility need not compromise believers' confidence in the certainty with which they hold those beliefs. See Marshall's *Trinity and Truth* (Cambridge: Cambridge University Press, 2000), 167-69.

14. Frei, "Historical Reference and the Gospels," 67. Hunsinger's treatment of Frei on this point is helpful; see his "The Daybreak of the New Creation: Christ's Resurrection in Recent Theology," *Scottish Journal of Theology* 7, no. 2 (2004): 14-16.

they concretely render the person and work of Christ. The events they render cannot be grasped in their full significance in abstraction from what the Gospels depict and how they depict it. As Frei put the point, "'The Word was made flesh and dwelt among us, full of grace and truth' — is something that we don't understand except as a sequence enacted in the life, death and resurrection of Jesus."[15] The full consequence of that to which these accounts attest eludes a "neutral and detached" perspective. This subject matter makes a claim upon the lives of its readers. This is not a claim about intelligibility; it does not mean, in other words, that the claim that Jesus is the crucified and risen Savior is *intelligible* only to those for whom this claim becomes self-involving. It means, rather, that when grasped by the full significance of these stories, Jesus is no longer recognized merely as "the one of whom it is said 'on the third day he rose again from the dead,'" he is recognized as the one who on the third day rose again from the dead. The latter case is uniquely self-involving because, in Frei's words, "unlike other cases of factual assertion, the resurrection of Christ shapes a new life."[16]

The second and decisive reason that the Gospel accounts of Jesus' death and resurrection are indispensable for Frei is the divine authority of Scripture. The events portrayed by the accounts of Jesus' death and resurrection claim to entail the entrance of Eternity into time, the Infinite into the finite. As such, readers should neither expect to comprehend them exhaustively, nor to maintain control over the terms by which they make themselves available. In fact, to presume that the finite terms in which we humans live and move and have our being could comprehensively contain this Infinite, and that we could have these at our disposal to know and do with as we see fit, would only speak against the credibility of such an account. A claim on behalf of the Infinite that could be submitted wholly and entirely to the finite would testify against itself. It would cease to be Infinite. Moreover, the pretense of human beings to do so would amount to a form of idolatry — an account of God's revelation fashioned after humanity's image. Hence, if the Gospel accounts indeed portray the uniquely unsubstitutable Savior as they claim to, then the only descriptions finally adequate to this subject matter are those that God used — and uses — to convey it. Ultimately, it is God's use of them that makes them adequate. As the means by which God reveals God's self these accounts are indispensable for that knowledge and encounter. Frei explained:

15. Frei, "Response to 'Narrative Theology,'" 21.
16. Frei, *Identity*, 59.

The truth to which we refer we cannot state apart from the biblical language which we employ to do so. And belief in the divine authority of Scripture is for me simply that we do not need more. The narrative description there is adequate. "God was in Christ reconciling the world to himself" is an adequate statement for what we refer to, though we cannot say univocally how we refer to it.[17]

Notice here that, for Frei, the adequacy of the Gospel accounts is not merely a matter of *how* they depict what they depict, nor merely the fact that they give their readers "enough to go on" regarding what happened then and there. Their adequacy is, most basically for Frei, a matter of the divine authority of Scripture.

Where does this leave historical reference? It means that the positive contribution historical reference makes to the *kerygmatic* efficacy of these accounts, while necessary, is secondary and dependent. The proper ordering of this relation led Frei to add that "the text is witness to the Word of God, whether it is historical or not."[18] Frei's point with this claim is that, whether or not each detail happened as described in the Gospel accounts, these accounts nonetheless convey the identity of Jesus Christ by portraying what he was like and what he has accomplished.[19]

Of course, when it came to discussing how such a conception of "reference" fit into this complex equation Frei frequently became sparing — if not squeamish — in his explanatory terminology. He exerted great caution to avoid either systematic or even overly cogent explanation (e.g., an attempt to cover every explanatory detail so completely as to drain all flexibil-

17. Frei, "Response to 'Narrative Theology,'" 22.

18. Ibid.

19. For an expansion upon this point, see William Placher, "Scripture as Realistic Narrative: Some Preliminary Questions," *Perspectives in Religious Studies* 5 (Spring 1987), 32-41; see Placher, *Narratives of a Vulnerable God,* chaps. 1 and 4 (esp. pp. 92-95). Placher's explanation of this point is helpful enough to quote at length. He writes: "Reading these stories, one learns who Jesus is — that is, one learns both the characteristics of his human life and the fact that that human life was somehow the self-revelation of God. Many of the individual episodes serve as biographical anecdotes, 'true' if they illustrate his character authentically even though the particular incident they narrate never happened, and the overall shape of the narrative portrays something of Jesus' identity. While such an identity description need not be correct in all its particulars in order to get someone's identity right, its general themes do have to capture a person's essential features, and *some* of its particulars may be crucial. . . . [I]f Jesus never taught about love, or if the disciples, as Reimarus argued two hundred years ago, conspired to invent the story of the resurrection so that they would not have to go back to fishing, then the Gospels are wrong about Jesus" (ibid., 92).

ity and mystery from the account), or speculation abstracted from the central claims and features of the biblical accounts. Hence, on one hand he asserted that "[B]elief in Jesus' resurrection is more nearly a belief in something like the inspired quality of the accounts than in the theory that they reflect what 'actually took place.'"[20] And yet, this claim can be abstracted from his further stipulations only upon pain of misunderstanding Frei's position. He added:

> [A]t one point a judgment of faith concerning the inspiration of the descriptive contents and a judgment of faith affirming their central factual claim would have to coincide for the believer. He would have to affirm that the New Testament authors were right in insisting that it is more nearly correct to think of Jesus as factually raised, bodily if you will, than not to think of him in this manner. (But the qualification "more nearly . . . than not" is important in order to guard against speculative explanations of the resurrection from theories of immortality, possibilities of visionary or auditory experience, possibilities of resuscitating dead bodies, miracle in general, etc.[21]

Much later in his writing Frei described this approach to the Gospel accounts of Jesus' death and resurrection as one in which readers

> . . . read the accounts as meaning what they say, so that their subject is indeed the bodily resurrected Jesus. They also believe that a miracle — the miracle of the resurrection in particular — is a real event; however, it is one to which human depiction and conception are inadequate, even though the literal description is the best that can be offered, not to be supplanted or replaced by any other and therefore itself not simply metaphorical in character. *In this view text and reality are adequate, indeed, indispensable to each other but not identical. Inadequate by itself, the literal account of the text is adequate to the reality of the events by divine grace.* The text is not a photographic depiction of reality, for not only are the accounts fragmentary and confusing, but they depict a series of miraculous events that are in the nature of the case unique, incomparable, and impenetrable — in short, the abiding mystery of the union of the divine with the historical, for our salvation from sin and death.[22]

20. Frei, *Identity,* 182.
21. Ibid.
22. Frei, "How It All Began: On the Resurrection of Christ," *Anglican and Episcopal History* 53, no. 2 (June 1989): 139-45 (here 141).

Read in tandem, the foregoing passages provide as close to a stereoscopic sense of Frei's understanding of the status of historical reference in Scripture as may be available. The first passage demonstrates how Frei thought that Scripture's witness to, and proclamation of, the person and work of Christ retains an element of *Historie* as a non-fungible ingredient.[23] It clarifies, moreover, that this ingredient (historical reference) is secondary to, and dependent upon, the Gospels' depictive rendering of their subject matter (their "sense"). The second passage makes clear that, ultimately, even the adequacy of the sense of the text depends upon God's self-revelatory activity. For, while the "literal description" is "the best that can be offered" in the way of human conception and depiction of what happened then and there, on its own it remains inadequate to the nature of the case. It becomes "adequate to the reality of the events by divine grace."[24] Frei amplified this point in his response to Carl Henry:

> Once again, yes, "Jesus" refers, as does any ordinary name, but "Jesus Christ" in scriptural witness does not refer ordinarily; or rather, it refers ordinarily only by the miracle of grace. And that means that I do not know the manner in which it refers, only that the ordinary language in which it is cast will miraculously suffice.[25]

Notice that in the above passages Scripture's witness to, and proclamation of, the person and work of Christ occurs both in virtue of what happened there and then *and* what God does here and now. It is thanks to the miracle that God wrought once for all (there and then) to which the Gospel witnesses attest, *and* the miracle God continues to enact again and again in and through

---

23. While Frei stands with Barth against abstraction and speculation, Frei's account of historical reference differs from Barth's in a crucial way. Hunsinger has identified the character and significance of this difference, writing: "In his treatment of the question of knowledge, Barth did not keep the same balance between historicity and transcendence. He focused almost entirely on the transcendent aspect while denying any significance to modern historical inquiry (IV/2, pp. 149-50). The possibility of disconfirmation, as explored by Frei, apparently did not interest him; consequently, Frei's thoughtful emendation of Barth's position was arguably more nuanced and satisfying. Nevertheless, Barth richly developed the transcendent aspect in a way that remains unsurpassed. He was untiring in his stress that if Christ was risen from the dead, so as to be present as the risen Lord, then his own self-witness as the One who lives was always necessarily decisive. Faith depended not on historical investigation but on an encounter with the living Christ." See Hunsinger, "The Daybreak of the New Creation," 17.

24. Frei, "How It All Began," 241.

25. Frei, "Response to 'Narrative Theology,'" 24.

that attestation that we have what we need in the way of access to the reality of God. This convergence of factors entails factual claims. But any factual claims are conditioned by the uniqueness of the subject matter. Because this subject matter is unique in kind, in the final analysis "[t]he witness of Scripture to God is sure, not of itself, but because the witness of God to Scripture is faithful and constant."[26]

Of course, Frei's account of "textual reference" assuaged Carl Henry's misgivings no more than did his position on "historical reference." Henry persisted in his claim that Frei had exchanged a notion of reference to something outside the text (what he called "text-transcendent reference") for the "literary presence" of the Word of God.[27] Clearly, Frei struggled to articulate his ideas about reference throughout his career. And indeed, in his latest work — fragments pieced together and published after his death — some passages occasionally sound as if Frei thinks that the presence of God is purely textual or linguistic. For instance, he wrote:

> [W]e don't have more than our concepts of God. We don't have a separate intuition, a preconceptual or prelinguistic apprehension or grasp of God in his reality. . . . But we don't need it either; for the reality of God is given in, with, and under the concept and not separably, and that is adequate for us.[28]

Here we have an awkwardly phrased point that will strike some as flatly anti-realist (that "we have the reality [of God] . . . only linguistically"). However, what at first may appear as a most egregious form of linguistic idealism in his understanding of revelation may appear differently when situated within the trajectory and development of Frei's body of work. If we situate this claim with sufficient care, I think we will find that what Frei means here is that the possibility of God's self-revelation in and through human concepts

---

26. Frei, *Identity*, 194. For all of the reasons above, I think that Nicholas Wolterstorff is mistaken when he claims that "the traditional view that proper reading of the scriptures is a mode of revelation in the present (and was a mode of revelation in the past) is as absent from Frei's line of thought as it was from Locke's. That this is 'the Word of God' does not function in his argument." Wolterstorff, "Is Narrativity the Linchpin? Reflections on the Hermeneutic of Hans Frei," in *Relativism and Religion*, ed. Charles M. Lewis (London: Palgrave Macmillan, 1995), 101.

27. Henry wrote, "Narrative hermeneutics removes from the interpretative process any text-transcendent referent and clouds the narrative's relationship to a divine reality not exhausted by literary presence" ("Narrative Theology," 13).

28. Hans Frei, *Types of Christian Theology*, ed. George Hunsinger and William C. Placher (New Haven and London: Yale University Press, 1992), 79.

and language is predicated on the actuality of God conscripting, breaking, and utilizing those concepts for the purposes of God's self-revelation. Hunsinger points out that this makes Frei's understanding of the mode of reference of these concepts doubly analogical. "They refer not only to Jesus in his earthly life (whether we can verify that factuality by modern methods or not) but also and at the same time to the risen Jesus Christ who lives to all eternity, and who attests to us through those narratives here and now."[29]

Frei's claims on this point reflect a contention that he reiterated at various points throughout his writings — the claim that the content of God's miracle of grace makes revelation *inseparable from,* yet *not identical to,* its form. Frei arrived at this position largely as a result of his extended engagement with Barth and the Protestant Reformers on the nature and character of the scriptural witness. He wrote:

> The odd, philosophically ambiguous status of "reference" in this tradition, for which literal and historical, word and thing were congruent in a semiotic rather than epistemological representational way meant that the text did not communicate — as though by way of a channel of absence — the presence of God. The text did not refer to, it was the linguistic presence of God, the fit embodiment of one who was himself "Word," and thus it was analogous to, though not identical with, Incarnation.[30]

If we read these claims as more or less consistent with Barth's account (which I believe we have grounds to, as I argue in what follows), then the miracle of grace that makes "textual reference" possible is God's taking up human conceptual practices — words, concepts, and the claims and assertions they constitute — and breaking and transforming them for God's self-revelatory purposes. And yet, at the same time, God's revealing activity leaves the human character of those concepts, claims, and assertions intact.

Charges arise that Frei's treatment of "textual reference," and his reliance upon an *analogical* mode of reality reference in particular, results in a non-dialectical account of revelation that overlooks God's continuing activity in revelation. If correct, such charges drive a deep wedge between Frei and Barth. Bruce McCormack, for instance, argues that Frei's claim that we have God's revelation "in, with, and under" our concepts works to "dangerously flatten out" the dialectical relation of God's being and the language

---

29. Hunsinger, "What Can Evangelicals and Postliberals Learn from Each Other?" 145-46.

30. Frei, "Theology and the Interpretation of Narrative," in *TN,* 108.

that witnesses to him. If this deficiency in Frei's thinking is not terminal in itself, it at least indicates a point at which Frei not only departed from Barth, but risked positively distorting Barth's theology.[31]

As McCormack sees it, Frei's account of Barth is indicative of a misunderstanding of the development of Barth's thought "that has dominated the Anglo-American reception of Barth's thought in fundamental ways."[32] It is rooted in the account of Barth's theology provided by Hans Urs von Balthasar in 1951, claiming that Barth's 1931 book on Anselm of Canterbury represents his turn to the use of analogical thought forms — "the point at which Barth abandons his dialectical method and adopts a more 'objective' and 'positivistic' approach to theology."[33] This account is fundamentally flawed, and by centering his treatment of Barth upon it, Frei's theology replicates those flaws. McCormack explains:

> What is missing in the Anselm book, from the point of view of the *Church Dogmatics,* is an adequate emphasis on the network of dogmatic assumptions which would prevent the theological "science" described in [the Anselm book] from becoming just one more complacent, bourgeois discipline, namely, (1) attention to the fact that theology can succeed in its task of speaking adequately of God only if God *does* something and (2) the comprehension of this realistic emphasis on divine action in terms of a *Realdialektik* of veiling and unveiling, which would locate the reality of God in a realm beyond that accessible by means of direct intuition and thereby make clear the fact that the reality of God cannot simply be grasped, controlled, manipulated. It is this set of dogmatic presuppositions which would forever make theology, for Barth, a *human* impossibility. It is possible as a divine possibility, or it is not possible at all. Not for Karl Barth a definition of theology in terms of the learning of a linguistic skill! Frei seems to have understood all this with regard to the early Barth of the second edition of *Romans.* . . . But Frei believed that the Anselm book constituted a methodological "revolution" in Barth's thought.[34]

31. McCormack, *Orthodox and Modern,* 123.

32. John Franke, "Karl Barth, the Postmodern Turn, and Evangelical Theology," in *Karl Barth and Evangelical Theology: Convergences and Divergences,* ed. Sung Wook Chung (Grand Rapids, MI: Baker, 2006), 273.

33. Ibid., 272-73. Hans Urs von Balthasar, *The Theology of Karl Barth: Exposition and Interpretation,* trans. Edward T. Oakes, S.J. (San Francisco: Ignatius, 1992); Karl Barth, *Anselm: Fides Quaerens Intellectum: Anselm's Proof of the Existence of God in the Context of his Theological Scheme* (London: SMC Press, 1960, 1985), hereafter *Anselm.*

34. McCormack, *Orthodox and Modern,* 124n45.

In as far as Frei split apart dialectic and analogy his reading of Barth resulted in a "positivistic biblicism" — so great an emphasis upon "the *givenness* of God in revelation (e.g., through collapsing revelation into the text of the biblical witness) that Barth is made into a revelational positivist."[35] McCormack explains that the dialectical dimension of Barth's account means, by contrast, that "God makes the language of the biblical witness conform to himself and, in that God does so, we do indeed grasp God in his reality."[36] McCormack positions Frei as having committed such a fallacy in his dissertation on Barth's doctrine of revelation, then transmitting that fallacy to many American neo-Barthians. In the pages that remain, I conduct a bit of textual excavation of Frei's earliest writings in order to demonstrate that positioning Frei's account of Barth in this way overlooks the nuance and complexity of his account of analogy and dialectic, and results in a fairly schizophrenic — and basically inaccurate — view of his treatment of Barth, and his theology more broadly.

II. Frei, Barth, and Analogy

In his doctoral dissertation of 1956 Frei described Barth's 1931 book on St. Anselm of Canterbury as "absolutely indispensable for a knowledge of the revolution in his thought between the two editions of the *The Doctrine of the Word of God*."[37] The "revolution" in question was Barth's movement from an earlier reliance upon a dialectical theological method to an analogical thought form. This term that Frei uses — "revolution" — is today portrayed

---

35. Ibid., 158, 113.

36. Ibid., 123n44.

37. Hans Frei, *The Doctrine of Revelation in the Thought of Karl Barth, 1909-1922: The Nature of Barth's Break with Liberalism* (New Haven, CT: Yale University Dissertation, 1956), 194; hereafter cited as *Barth's Break with Liberalism*. Frei further developed this suggestion in a dense discussion of Barth's work for an article adapted from his dissertation, and included in a 1957 *Festschrift* for H. Richard Niebuhr. See Frei, "Niebuhr's Theological Background," in *Faith and Ethics: The Theology of H. Richard Niebuhr*, ed. Paul Ramsey (New York: Harper & Brothers, 1957), 9-64. This essay includes pages 174-202 of Frei's dissertation. In both this essay and in his dissertation Frei bases this characterization of the shift primarily upon Barth's own retrospective admission that the Anselm book "characterize[s] the change in his thinking in the decade following 1928." Barth's remarks appear in "How My Mind Has Changed," *Christian Century* 56, nos. 37 and 38 (September 13 and 20, 1939). For an overview of von Balthasar's thesis, its problems, and the ensuing developments, see Bruce McCormack's *Karl Barth's Critically Realistic Dialectical Theology* (Oxford: Clarendon Press, 1995), 1-28.

as representative of his understanding of the development of Barth's thought. It conveys the "revolutionary" difference between Barth's adoption of an analogical mode of reference in the *Church Dogmatics* as opposed to his earlier, "dialectical" period.[38]

I admit from the start that, at various points, Frei did convey the distinct impression that his position on these points can be adequately summed up in terms of a "revolution" or "radical transformation" in Barth's thinking — elsewhere described as a "turn from dialectic to analogy, from critical to positive theology, from epistemology and trans-epistemology to the priority of ontology over epistemology."[39] On one hand, Frei wrote:

> It remains true for him that God is always *Subject-in-Act*. But now [after his turn to analogical thought form] Barth affirms that in grace, in Jesus Christ, this God, who is subject and nothing else, gives himself as object to us. God remains mysterious, but in this mystery it is he that is revealed. He that is hidden, reveals himself in hiddenness. He who becomes God for us is nothing and no less than God himself. The living God gives himself as object, thereby affirming and not denying his living freedom.[40]

Frei continued by expanding upon the significance of this development in Barth's thinking. He added:

> Hence, then, there is — not identity but correspondence and congruity, radical congruity between Creator and creature, grace and nature, but on the basis of grace and revelation alone. Barth has turned to a doctrine of analogy . . . the analogy between our words, concepts, intuitions and their

38. "Where von Balthasar was at least tempted to see the *Christliche Dogmatik* as initiating Barth's turn to analogy, for Hans Frei that volume belonged without question to the dialectical period and the shift which was thought to take place with the Anselm book was seen to be dramatic in character — in Frei's word, it represented a 'revolution' in Barth's thought" (McCormack, *Karl Barth's Critically Realistic Dialectical Theology*, 4); "Frei believed that the Anselm book constituted a methodological 'revolution' in Barth's thought" (McCormack, *Orthodox and Modern*, 124n45); "On the one hand, Frei could speak of the Anselm book in 1931 as having wrought a 'revolution' in Barth's thought and could find evidence for this in an alleged retreat from actualism in the doctrine of God (though what he meant by the latter point is not especially clear). . . . And yet, Frei is also well aware that the mature Barth of the *Dogmatics* continued to insist that God is revealed in hiddenness, in the givenness of an object with which God is not identical" (ibid., 160n159). See Franke, "Karl Barth, the Postmodern Turn, and Evangelical Theology," 272-73.

39. Frei, *Barth's Break with Liberalism*, 198.

40. Ibid., 197.

object, God, through the self-giving of God in is Word. This is the *analogia fidei*.[41]

In the context of Frei's dissertation one can detect in these particular passages almost celebratory tones. As Frei sees it, Barth's "turn" to the *analogia fidei* from dialectical thought form succeeded in breaking through barriers erected between humanity and God by Immanuel Kant and Friedrich Schleiermacher.[42] "Barth no longer has to insist that in his radical realism, the knowledge of God is simply *ac-knowledgement* of myself as being known: in knowledge, as in existence, Barth seems now to say, I am actually and meaningfully confronted by the One who is the lord of grace."[43] The result is that theology becomes a human possibility. This is because, and solely because, God confronts humans in the miraculous activity of self-revelation.

As Frei understood the unfolding of Barth's thinking, while "dialectic" came to be no longer "as necessary," neither was it merely dispensable. Even amidst his effusiveness about the breakthrough that Frei takes Barth to have achieved, Frei never jettisoned "dialectic" from his account of Barth's theology. Hence, after the "turn" to the *analogia fidei*, it remains the case that "all theological theses are inadequate to their object," and "there is no identity between the *Credo* and its *res*."[44] Frei characterized Barth's "turn from dialectic to analogy" as a *de-emphasis* rather than a rejection of dialectic.[45] Frei continued, "It is not so necessary now (since Barth thinks that he has drawn sufficient attention to the fact) to affirm that we cannot, of ourselves, predicate any qualities of God, that he is the unpredicable or unintuitable center between positive and negative attributions and judgments."[46] Frei reiterated that "similarity of predictability" occurs in virtue of God's own act of "making himself similar to the creature, and yet remaining identical with himself in this act." This is where Frei stood at roughly the two hundred-page mark of his nearly six hundred-page dissertation. Clearly, he has made fairly distinct claims about the movement in Barth's thinking from dialectical to analogical thought form. Indeed, were we to limit our grasp of Frei's account to

41. Ibid., 199.
42. Ibid., 200.
43. Ibid., 198.
44. Ibid., 196.
45. Ibid., 198.
46. Ibid., 197-200. Frei identifies the *analogia fidei* in *KD* I/1, 250ff.; II/1, 63-93, 252-67. In the following sentence he identifies the *analogia relationis* between God and man in *KD* III/2, 262ff.

these claims the terms "revolution" and "turn" might adequately character-ize his account. However, an understanding of Frei's account of dialectic and analogy in Barth's thinking that limits itself to dramatic and revolutionary terms turns out to be woefully inadequate, and basically inaccurate.

In the final hundred pages of Frei's dissertation a markedly different picture of the relationship between analogy and dialectic in the develop-ment of Barth's thought emerges. What he earlier characterized as Barth's *turn* from dialectic to analogy Frei now assesses under a different aspect. In the later chapters Frei characterizes this development in Barth's thinking as a gradual development that had occurred steadily over the course of the 1920s. Clearly, Frei still writes in terms of two "stages" in Barth's thinking. None-theless, his motivating concern in the later chapters is to highlight, clarify, and account for the *continuity* between these stages. In fact, his final disser-tation chapter traces Barth's use of an analogical thought form as far back in his thinking as the 1922 edition of *The Epistle to the Romans.*

Here Frei portrays dialectic as an indirect *giving* by which God reveals God's self without "erecting a corresponding magnitude of response on a creaturely level." As such, he writes, "faith must negate itself, point away from itself; yet not in such a way as to dissolve the reality of the creaturely ac-tion that it is, since it is human, not divine activity." Frei continues:

> But dialectic, if it succeeds in this negative, indirect task of pointing away from faith itself to the actuality of faith in revelation alone, fails thereby to indicate that this actuality in revelation which takes place in faith is never-theless an undissolved, untranscended human act, i.e., that a miracle takes place and not a sublation of the created spirit into the Holy Spirit. In or-der to indicate this miraculous fact Barth even at this early and thor-oughly dialectical stage of his thinking has to draw upon some sort of doctrine or [*sic*] analogy. It is pale and vague indeed; nevertheless it is there, precisely in conjunction with the understanding of faith. In some concrete way he must indicate the relation of this wholly divinely — actu-alized fact of faith, this sheer gift of revelation, to its natural setting. He does so within the context of dialectical negation and movement; never-theless he does so.[47]

47. Frei, *Barth's Break with Liberalism*, 520ff., 557, 568; Frei explicates long passages from the 1922 edition of *The Epistle to the Romans,* trans. Sir Edwyn Hoskyns (London: Oxford Uni-versity Press, 1933), 39ff., 78ff. Note that the word "or" in this passage is an error. Frei intends to write "of." Nearly forty pages later he provides a correct restatement of this point, writing, "The more [Barth] turns to *a doctrine of analogy* (which was, as we have seen, not quite absent

As these lines indicate, according to Frei's reading the dialectical character of the miracle of God's revelation does not eliminate human agency. This is because a faint but nonetheless emerging conception of analogy promises to mediate the radical otherness of God's agency and its relative likeness in human agency. In the miracle of faith (as the recipient mode of God's act of revelation) human agency becomes "a pointer to the absolute." However, while quite real, the human element remains "relative, the witness, the parable."[48] Frei read this "positive valuation of 'parable'" by Barth as the first evidence of analogy within a predominately dialectical framework. He took this use of "parable" to point toward an analogical thought form because of Barth's use of that concept to, at once, mediate an apparent contradiction and yet permit the full stringency of that contradiction to remain intact. Thus, while humanity could never speak directly of God, nonetheless, God's miracle of grace enabled human words and capacities to adequately witness to God.

Frei read this use of parable and witness as an important early development in what he characterized as "Barth's steady shift toward a doctrine of analogy."[49] Of course Frei pointed out that any such early uses of analogy at that point in Barth's work occurred "wholly within and on the basis of dialectic." At that earlier point in Barth's development, Frei wrote, "[analogy] has no independent position of its own." Nevertheless, Frei identified Barth's use of analogical thought form as present and effective even at the height of what he refers to as Barth's "dialectical period."[50]

What made "analogy" such a promising insight for Frei's concerns? In Barth's hands, analogy became a tool by which to conceptualize the "correspondence in predicable qualities between [God] and his creatures." At the same time, it kept in view the guiding insight that "it is of [God's] own grace that this is so, through the historical miracle that he has wrought."[51] Frei stressed the historical character of this miracle as a miracle that occurred in the concrete particularity of Christ's person and work (his *Geschichte*). Christ's incarnation makes possible the indirect, but nevertheless authentic,

---

even at the height of the dialectical period, in his understanding of faith), the more we see through revelation a freedom that is in God himself" (557, italics and underscore added). At the end of the parenthetical remark in the preceding sentence Frei refers his reader by way of a footnote to his previous demonstration of this point, citing the passage quoted above (520).

48. Barth, *Die Christliche Welt* (1923), cols. 249f.; Frei also cites pp. 193ff. Quoted by Frei in *Barth's Break with Liberalism*, 522.

49. Frei, *Barth's Break with Liberalism*, 520ff., 557, 568.

50. Ibid., 522-23.

51. Frei, "Niebuhr's Theological Background," 52.

correlation between "our [human] words, concepts, intuitions and their object" — God.[52] Thus, Frei wrote, God effects a "correspondence and congruity, radical congruity between Creator and creature, grace and nature, but on the basis of grace and revelation alone."[53] In no way does this congruity rely upon an ontologically inscribed point of intersection between creation and Creator. It occurs in God's free act of revelation, and, for the creature, in the recipient mode of that act — faith. This "correspondence and congruity" takes the form of the *analogia fidei* — analogical intersection given in and to faith. Christ gives himself to believers in a way that "enables us to know him as object in the act and decision of faith," Frei wrote.[54] And yet, though this knowing belongs to the creature, faith's comprehension of Christ cannot reduce him to an object to be known like any other.

How might believers be said to "genuinely know" this object that is unlike any other? And how can it be a believer's positive act of knowing, if such knowledge is available only in virtue of God's miracle? "[O]ur reliance for this similarity is upon [God's] own act in making himself similar to the creature," Frei explained. In other words, God takes up and uses the creature's concepts and basic form. "[A]nd yet," Frei countered, "[God remains] identical with himself in this act" that brings about a radical congruity. In other words, in this act God remains qualitatively distinct from humanity, and the human concepts God uses retain their social and practical identities. There is no "higher synthesis" in the relation; no confusion or change in the parts. Moreover, God's activity in the person of Christ uniquely orders the whole. "In all this, one need hardly add, the customary understanding of analogy is turned about," Frei wrote. "In the relation of faith, it is God who is the analogue and man who is the analogate. In faith and to faith the creature and not the Creator stands in need of explanation, of clarification by analogy."[55]

---

52. This, Frei explains, occurs in virtue of what Barth identified as the *analogia fidei*. Frei locates Barth's account of this in *KD* I/1, 250ff., and II/1, 68-93, 252-67. See Frei, "Niebuhr's Theological Background," 52.

53. Ibid.

54. Ibid., 53.

55. Ibid., 52. It should come as no surprise if Frei's description of the analogical motion reflects a Chalcedonian pattern (without separation and division; without confusion or change; the parts then uniquely ordered in relation to the Person of Christ). Hunsinger credits Frei with having first taught him to see the Chalcedonian affirmation of Christ's incarnation as a heuristic pattern. On these points, see Hunsinger's "Karl Barth's Christology: Its Basic Chalcedonian Character," in *Disruptive Grace*, 131-47. For an overview of the history and character of Barth's use of analogy, see McCormack's *Karl Barth's Critically Realistic Dialectical Theology*, 16-26, 312-14, 367.

At the same time, Frei made quite clear that Barth's increasingly explicit use of an analogical thought form did not mean that he eliminated dialectic from his thinking. He was well aware that Barth had openly expressed concern about his increasingly explicit emphasis upon the possibility of positive speech about God in his lectures on the first volume of the *Church Dogmatics* (1931-32). Clearly, Barth had worried about producing "an all too knowledgeable, 'undialectical posterity.'" He had worried that his students might become "'far too positive' in their enthusiasm over the rediscovery of the 'great concepts of God, Word, Spirit, revelation, faith, church, sacrament, and so on,'" as though "'we speak *of* them because we know how to speak *about* them with such relative freedom,'" Eberhard Busch recounted.[56]

Nonetheless, viewed through the lens of these latter claims, it is no longer tenable to maintain that Frei positioned Barth's Anselm text as a discrete "revolution" in Barth's thought *in abstraction from* the broader development of his thinking over the preceding decade. Clearly, Frei (following Barth's recollection well after the fact)[57] saw the Anselm book as the point at which Barth perhaps most powerfully and succinctly explicated a movement in his thinking that Frei believed to have been completed sometime between the first and second editions of *The Doctrine of the Word of God.* Even so, when read in light of the full breadth of Frei's claims in his dissertation, it is apparent that Frei saw the position that Barth described in the book on Anselm as a culmination of "a steady shift toward a doctrine of analogy."[58] This shift was not an abrupt occurrence. Frei saw distinct reasons to think that it had been occurring in Barth's thought over the preceding decade.

Contrary to how they may appear at first, the apparently opposing characterizations with which Frei accounts for this shift — "gradual" and "revolutionary" — do not present a simple contradiction. In fact, they fit together complementarily in the scheme of the project. Which characterization Frei

---

56. Busch cites Barth's comment to his friend Eduard Thurneysen of January 9, 1931. See Eberhard Busch, *Karl Barth: His Life from Letters and Autobiographical Texts,* trans. John Bowden (Eugene, OR: Wipf & Stock, 2005), 214. Busch also cites *CD* I/1, 162.

57. Barth, "How My Mind Has Changed," *The Christian Century,* September 13 and 20, 1939.

58. Frei, *Barth's Break with Liberalism,* 522. These subtleties of Frei's account contrast with McCormack's characterization of Frei's treatment of this issue. McCormack construes Frei as (1) locating the *Christliche Dogmatik* of 1927 within the so-called "dialectical period" without qualification, (2) characterizing Barth's "turn" to analogy as dramatic ("revolutionary"), and (3) positioning that turn squarely within the Anselm text. See McCormack's *Karl Barth's Critically Realistic Dialectical Theology,* 4.

stresses at a given point depends upon his mode of analysis at the point in question. When laying out the specific milestones of the development in Barth's thought Frei tends to defer to Barth's personal recollections published in the "How My Mind Has Changed" articles. In those moments, he gestures to the Anselm text as a point of "revolutionary" importance in the development of Barth's thought. However, when Frei descends to the level of close textual analysis and criticism of Barth's use of dialectic in the second edition of *Romans* in the final hundred pages of his dissertation, Barth's incipient use of analogy — and the gradual development of those uses in his work throughout the 1920s — become both apparent and important.[59] What is clear is that Frei had a distinct sense that analogy and dialectic coexisted in Barth's thinking throughout the 1920s. Analogy did not appear on the scene in the Anselm book as a distinctively novel element.

Now, even if my excavation of Frei's dissertation brings new insight into his early reading of Barth's development, so what? Aside from a more precise appreciation of the nuances of Frei's thinking on the matter, the fact that he continued to attach considerable importance to Barth's book on Anselm makes even this revised version just another variation on the basically flawed Balthasarian account, does it not?[60] If Frei had a clear sense at this point of the dialectical character of Barth's use of analogical thought form, then where did it go in the work that followed? Did Frei simply forget about it? I submit that he did not. In fact, it is evident throughout his ensuing engagements with Barth's work.

Frei remained attentive to the indirectness entailed in Barth's description of the analogical relation between God's act of revelation and human concepts throughout his career.[61] Scripture and the church speak authentically of God in himself in virtue of God's miracle wrought in the *analogia fidei*. And yet, that

---

59. Frei, *Barth's Break with Liberalism*, 562, 568, 576-77. Frei acknowledges that his comments extending beyond that period present a far too cursory examination of what he takes to be "the later, analogical period of Barth's thought."

60. I am not suggesting that this retrieval and repositioning of Frei's account finally gets the full development of Barth's thought correct. There remain other points of disagreement between other of Frei's claims about Barth's development and McCormack's account. Examples would be Frei's locating Barth's shift to dialectical method as occurring between *Romans I* and *II*, and his claim that Barth did not finally break with "relationalism" until some time between the two editions of *Romans*. See McCormack, *Karl Barth's Critically Realistic Dialectical Theology*, 202, 147.

61. See, for instance, Frei, "Theology and the Interpretation of Narrative," in *TN*, 108; Frei, "Analogy and the Spirit in the Theology of Karl Barth," in *Hans W. Frei: Unpublished Pieces*, ed. Mike Higton, 9-10, 21-23; "Response to 'Narrative Theology,'" 22.

peculiar human speech remains never without qualification. Frei found this "partial correspondence" quite difficult to articulate. Nevertheless, it was on this basis that Frei clearly identifies Barth's reliance upon dialectical thought form reaching well into the *Church Dogmatics.* Explicating a seminal passage in Barth's account of the *analogia fidei* in the *Church Dogmatics* he wrote:

> [T]he fact that God veils himself in his revelation excludes the notion of equality or identity *(Gleichheit)* between God and faith. The fact that he unveils himself in his revelation excludes the notion of total non-correspondence *(Ungleichheit).* Now this mysterious act of veiling and unveiling is not a quantitative balance (as the terms "immanence" and "transcendence" of God are sometimes taken to imply) between two magnitudes in God and *(per analogiam)* in man. "Partial correspondence" means no quantitative division in God or man. The act of veiling and unveiling himself in revelation is a unitary act of the unitary God to unitary man, *though it may only be grasped dialectically. But even the dialectic is teleologically ordered, for the gracious will of God to reveal himself is basic to his veiling as well as his unveiling of himself.* The word "partial" must be introduced then not for reasons of quantitative division in the relation between God and man but in order to grasp that our genuine apprehension and the conformity that takes place in it meet their limit in the very same act of God which enables them to come about in the first place. So the conformity or correspondence of faith-apprehension with its indirect object, God, remains partial.[62]

As these lines demonstrate, Frei understood the indispensability of dialectic to become situated within, and oriented by, the analogical form of God's act of revelation. He understood Barth's account of analogy's relation to dialectic as ordered by "the gracious will of God to reveal himself" and the actuality of his having done so in Jesus the Christ. He takes Barth to have resituated dia-

---

62. Frei, "Analogy and the Spirit in the Theology of Karl Barth," 9-10 (italics added). In this passage, Frei is explicating Barth's claim in *CD* II/1, 190 (Frei's translation). Frei reads this passage as descriptive of the "positive, special presence of God who is invisible and unpronounceable because he is not there in the manner in which the corporeal and spiritual world which he has created is there. Rather, in this . . . world he is there in his revelation, in Jesus Christ, in the proclamation of his name, in his witnesses and sacraments and thus visible only for faith. . . . This means that he is to be seen only as the Invisible one, pronounced as he who cannot be pronounced — and both not as the inclusive concept of limit or as origin of our vision and speech but as the one who orders and permits . . . and in free, gracious decision enables this our hearing and speaking."

lectic within an emphasis upon analogy. In other words, the miraculous possibility of adequate speech about God (predicated as it is on God's miracle of grace) comes to take normative priority to the unqualified need of the creature to negate every human affirmation about God, and follow each denial with an affirmation. And yet, still, for Frei at no point does either work in abstraction from the other.

Frei's claims about the relation of dialectic and analogy in the passage above present a mirror image of his characterization of their relation at the height of Barth's dialectical period. In his dissertation Frei pointed out that analogy occurred entirely on the basis of dialectic in *Romans II*. As Barth's thinking progressed, this relation became in effect reversed. He understood dialectic to be situated within the analogical form of God's act of revelation. The indispensability of dialectic is oriented by the priority of analogy. At no point does either work in *abstraction from the other, even into and throughout the Church Dogmatics*. As such, it is incorrect to ascribe to Frei "the great weakness of the Balthasarian account"[63] after all — that is, the inability to account for the extent to which Barth was a dialectical theologian even into the *Church Dogmatics*. In fact, as the above passage indicates, just the opposite is the case.

Frei continued to refer to the "indirect identity" of God's revelation in biblical witness in virtue of the fact that "[God] did *and does* relate himself to us," as Frei wrote in his 1969 essay commemorating Barth's death.[64] Notice that Frei here suggests that God's self-revelational activity is not simply once for all (there and then). Clearly, relegating God's activity to the miraculous events then and there, and Scripture's reports of those events, would indeed collapse revelation into the biblical text and risk turning theology into biblical positivism, and yet another "bourgeois discipline." However, Frei understands God to continue to relate God's self to believers (again and again, here and now).

Roughly a decade further on, Frei's review of Eberhard Busch's biography of Karl Barth undoubtedly favored the Anselm text. Indeed, he there

---

63. Franke, "Karl Barth, the Postmodern Turn, and Evangelical Theology," 273.

64. Frei, "Karl Barth: Theologian" (1969), in *TN*, 170. In this address, Frei also says things such as "The ground of the actuality of the incarnation, of its ontological possibility, and of our being able to think about it, are one and the same. That God related himself to us means that it was possible, that he must be himself eternally in a way that is congruent with his relating himself to us contingently. . . . The possibility follows from the actuality" (171). McCormack cites these passages, but relegates them to the "early" Frei, a point I deal with below.

identified it as instrumental for understanding Barth's full-fledged use of analogy as a formal "analytical, technical category" in contrast to Barth's "earlier" use of dialectic. And yet, even here the relation between dialectic and analogy remains complex, and more or less consistent with his understanding in the passage just above. Dialectic remains "an important subordinate device (and formal category) in the service of 'analogy.'"[65] Frei ordered both of these devices by the concrete accounts of Jesus' death and resurrection. He understood both dialectic and analogy to be tools in need of proper ordering — each to the other, and both by the identity of Jesus Christ. For Frei, Christ orients not only his predicates, but also any conceptual tools by which we describe and re-describe God's activity in making him present.

Does all this turn engagement with the text into yet another positive science about God's revelatory activity? I do not see how it can. And this for the same reason that Frei's account of historical reference avoids reducing the Gospel accounts of Jesus' resurrection to either a piece of history or to a literary world inside the text, as we saw in his response to Carl Henry. In fact, it is in his exchange with Henry that we see Frei's clear appeals to God's miraculous activity in the present, making scriptural accounts adequate for God's revelatory purposes. The text, as such, is incapable of capturing once for all God's revelation. The adequacy of statements in referring to God finally depends upon the gracious activity of God. As Frei put it, "the message and miracle of faith are accounted for by the very character, and therefore a function of, Jesus' being and his resurrection from the dead; and so Jesus and faith, as well as reality and text, belong together as the miracle of resurrection."[66] For Frei, this miracle occurs again and again, here and now in as far as Christ's "full self-identification with us is perpetual and not temporary."[67]

Conclusion

From the foregoing it should now be clear that Frei accounted for both historical reference and extra-textual reference, and on both points his thinking reflects Barth's influence. He neither reduces scriptural witness to God's "literary presence," nor does he forgo the dialectical character of God's revela-

---

65. Frei, "Eberhard Busch's Biography of Karl Barth" (1978), in *Types of Christian Theology*, 158-59.

66. Frei, "How It All Began," 45.

67. Ibid.

tory activity in and through the Scripture's witness. Of course, if Frei's theological approach does not founder upon questions of historical and textual reference, it may do so nonetheless in virtue of his use of non-foundational philosophical insights for his theological purposes. Here again McCormack articulates concerns shared by others. With Frei's treatment of Barth in *Types of Christian Theology* in his sights, he writes:

> In locating Barth on a spectrum of opinion whose more nearly confessional pole is defined in terms of "Christian *self*-description," Frei opened the door to an understanding of Barth in which questions of reality-reference will be suppressed in favor of a concentration on the internal logic of theological statements. Indeed, the door has even been opened to making an appeal to Barth for a view which would seek the norm(s) governing the Christian language-game in the language itself rather than in the presence of God to the church in Jesus Christ.[68]

Criticisms like this one appear to gain traction against Frei for a couple of reasons. First, indeed, Frei increasingly came to describe the historically situated and socially located practices that constitute the Christian world of discourse as fraught with all the internal tensions, discrepancies, and provisionality characteristic of historical and social processes and culturally situated interpretations. And largely in light of this recognition he came to liken the theologian's task to a sort of "reflexive ethnography" charged with the task of reflecting descriptively and critically explicating these practices and understandings. And yet, Frei was not concerned to be "non-foundational" in his epistemic commitments. "[T]heology cannot even invest so much in the foundational / anti-foundational debate as to come out (*qua* theology) in principle on the anti-foundational side," he wrote.[69] Frei was concerned to be faithful in light of the radical ingression of God's revelation in the person and work of Jesus Christ. If various "non-foundational" philosophical insights proved to be redescriptively helpful in the search for understanding the Word's revelatory activity in and through Scripture, then so much the better for those insights.

In fact, Frei never relinquished the claim that the biblical text is a central normative criterion by which to assess the practices and institutions that constitute this "Christian world of discourse." He did gradually come to an

---

68. McCormack, *Orthodox and Modern*, 123-24.

69. Frei, "Letter to Gary Comstock," November 5, 1984 (YDS 12-184), as quoted by Mike Higton in *Christ, Providence and History* (New York: T. & T. Clark, 2004), 199.

increasingly clear realization that it is not possible to describe the Christian world of discourse as anchored in a static set of representations conveyed in Scripture, and to which all understanding must conform. Rather, the claims and patterns conveyed in Scripture are caught up in the continuing set of cultural and historical practices, and second-order scrutiny, which they orient. Moreover, the tasks of critical reflection upon scriptural understanding are themselves caught up in that search for understanding into which faith impels believers. These precipitate the development, articulation, and self-correction of believers' understandings of the Word's revelatory activity in and through Scripture, as well as their grasp of the implications that extend from it. Frei's construal of the Christian "world of discourse" as sets of linguistic and cultural practices proves to be central to how the biblical witness retains its Christological orientation and theological irreducibility without denying its historical and cultural situatedness.

It is only when certain portions of Frei's work are treated in abstraction from the full scope of his engagement with Barth that charges arise alleging that Frei reduces the theological task to Wittgenstein-flavored reflexive ethnography. When Frei is read in that way, certain passages pertaining to Frei's treatment of Barth in his posthumously published work must be dismissed as either too ambivalent to be accurate, or flatly inconsistent with the allegedly single-minded "concentration on the internal logic of theological statements" ascribed to Frei.

A careful reading of *Types* reveals that Frei explicated the theological task as multidimensional. It is, first of all, "the first-order statements or proclamations made in the course of Christian practice and belief." In its "second-order" level (the level of particular interest to Frei in the *Types* material) it is the Christian community's "appraisal of its own language and actions under a norm or norms internal to the community itself."[70] The latter task has two aspects. The first is the descriptive and redescriptive task of making explicit — bringing to the level of critical reflection — the norms that organize the church and the practices in which the life of faith is embodied. The second aspect, Frei says, is critical examination and correction of those norms and practices. This aspect endeavors to "judge any given articulation of Christian language for its success or failure in adhering to the acknowledged norm or norms governing Christian use of language."[71] What, then, are the "acknowledged norms" to which Christian discourse is

70. Frei, *Types of Christian Theology*, 2.
71. Ibid.

to be held accountable? Frei suggests that these are best articulated in Barth's theology. He identifies them in such phrases as these:

> [T]he Church is accountable to God for its discourse about God. . . . [T]he Church must undertake a critique and correction of her discourse in the light of the norm she sees as the presence of God to the Church, in obedience to God's grace. . . . [T]he criterion of Christian discourse is the being of the Church, and the being of the Church for [Barth] is Jesus Christ, God in his presence or turning to humanity. The question is, Does Christian discourse come from him and move toward him, and is it in accordance with him?[72]

These central claims about the grace-given adequacy of the church's language about God, and the accountability of Christian discourse to God, frequently get overlooked in Frei's thinking.[73] When recognized, they are taken to be quizzical or curious, more or less accurate yet woefully underdeveloped.[74] At worst, they are seen as vestiges of a radically different body of work composed, in effect, by someone else called "the early Frei."[75] On this latter account, "the later Frei" parts company with his earlier self (a "turn" occasionally attributed to the influence of George Lindbeck) and comes to look all too conspicuously like the garden-variety "postliberal" theologian.[76]

---

72. Ibid., 39.

73. Kevin Vanhoozer, for instance, characterizes Frei's later work as a "cultural-linguistic correction" to his earlier work. On this account, Frei's later thinking comes off as textual functionalism that epitomizes what is most erroneous about "cultural-linguistic" approaches. Vanhoozer alleges that Frei confines the theological task to describing the logic implicit in the practices that constitute the church, and thus a task incapable of criticizing and correcting "Christian malpractice." Kevin Vanhoozer, *The Drama of Doctrine* (Louisville, KY: Westminster John Knox Press, 2005), esp. 10-11, 172-73.

74. McCormack recognizes the claims above (Frei, *Types of Christian Theology*, 39) only to set them aside as ambivalently underdeveloped by Frei. He conjectures that Frei was reluctant to be sufficiently forthcoming about Barth's realism because Frei worked as a theologian in a secular, university context. In my judgment, such an explanation is inadequate to the content and motivating concerns of Frei's work from early to late, and is inaccurate when viewed in light of all the examples set forth in the preceding pages. McCormack, *Orthodox and Modern*, 123. I identify and explicate Frei's Christological motivations for his ad hoc uses of Wittgensteinian philosophy and cultural theory in my article, "Between Barth and Wittgenstein: On the Availability of Hans Frei's Later Theology," *Modern Theology* 23, no. 3 (2007): 393-413.

75. McCormack, *Orthodox and Modern*, 160.

76. Kathryn Tanner, for instance, reads *Types* as containing the founding ideas of postliberal theology in as far as Frei develops there an approach in which "theology does

When viewed in concert with Frei's career-long engagement with Barth, and in conjunction with his own account of the literal sense up to the end of his career, the realist claims that appear in his posthumously collected and published fragments cease to be anomalous. In fact, they turn out to be consistent with Frei's characterization of Barth's theology beginning with his dissertation.[77] Moreover, as my parsing of Frei's response to Carl Henry should make clear, they are consistent with his views on the nature of scriptural authority — that "by the miracle of grace . . . the ordinary language in which [scriptural witness] is cast will miraculously suffice."[78] In light of the better situated account I have offered here, "communal self-description" becomes an ecclesially situated and embodied activity that is at once predicated upon and accountable to God's self-revelatory activity in and through Scripture. This is the self-revelatory activity by which God continually gathers the church under the Word. The Word of God is its ground and goal. Not in a "biblically positivist" single act of analogy, but indirectly, again and again.[79]

---

nothing more than uncover a logic internal to those practices themselves." Kathryn Tanner, *Theories of Culture* (Minneapolis: Augsburg Fortress, 1997), 74 (see 184n22). She cites Frei, *Types of Christian Theology*, 2, 20-21, 124.

77. This is not to suggest that Frei's thinking about Barth's work, the nature of the biblical witness, or theology's complex relation to non-theological resources and norms did not develop and mature over his career. Of course they did. For my sustained account of the precise character of the "lengthy and leisurely unfolding" of Frei's thinking on all of these points, see Jason A. Springs, *Toward a Generous Orthodoxy: Prospects for Hans Frei's Theology* (Oxford: Oxford University Press, 2010).

78. Frei, "Response to 'Narrative Theology,'" 24.

79. This essay benefited tremendously from questions and criticisms offered at various points by Todd Cioffi, Katherine Grieb, Kevin Hector, Sam Houston, Keith Johnson, and Paul Dafydd Jones.

No Comprehensive Views, No Final Conclusions: Karl Barth, Open-Ended Dogmatics, and the Emerging Church

John R. Franke

In thinking about the relationship between the thought of Karl Barth and evangelical theology, the discussion often tends to focus on the past history between the two.[1] On the one side are those evangelicals who have viewed Barth with a jaundiced eye for a number of reasons, such as his perceived failure to provide an adequate account of biblical authority, his openness to the possibility of universalism, and the suspicion that in spite of his break with liberalism his thought remained far too much indebted to that theological movement to be of use to those with more evangelical convictions. This has tended to be the majority view among North American evangelicals who have had a long and contentious relationship with Barth. In the midst of this evangelical criticism, a few have defended Barth and insisted that his theology provides a way forward beyond the standard liberal-conservative impasse that shaped so much of evangelical theology in the twentieth century. However, in this narrative both Barth's defenders and his detractors in the evangelical community have generally relied upon and assumed the standard neo-orthodox account of Barth's theological views. The assumption that Barth was a neo-orthodox theologian, indeed the prime exemplar of what came to be called neo-orthodox theology in North America, has had

---

1. For a comprehensive overview of the relationship between Barth and North American evangelicals, see Phillip R. Thorne, *Evangelicalism and Karl Barth: His Reception and Influence in North American Evangelical Theology* (Allison Park, PA: Pickwick Publications, 1995).

the effect of obscuring the ways in which his later theological writings, particularly the *Church Dogmatics,* continued to be shaped by the dialectical patterns that predominated in his early theological thought.[2] This is evidenced in both influential older studies such as those of the highly critical Cornelius Van Til[3] and the more accommodating Bernard Ramm[4] as well as in the presentation of his ideas in more recent evangelical textbooks on theology.[5] Recent work on Barth's thought has suggested that the common conceptions of his work are flawed and do not provide an accurate account of his views.[6]

Another approach to thinking about the relationship between the two, less common in the literature and discussions on the topic, is to consider the future possibilities for fruitful engagement as the evangelical movement continues to reflect on how Barth's work offers fresh perspectives for thinking about the theological task.[7] In this essay, I want to focus on the potential value of Barth's thought for the emerging church conversation as it has been embodied in Emergent Village — an organization spawned among evangelical church leaders, although certainly not limited to them — in conversation with the ideas and thought forms of postmodern theory and the renewal of missional Christianity in the North American setting.[8] It is my belief that the emerging church conversation represents an attempt at the social embodiment and living out of a reading of Barth's theology as the pursuit of an inherently open-ended and pluralist approach to dogmatics.[9] In this con-

2. See Bruce L. McCormack, *Karl Barth's Critically Realistic Dialectical Theology: Its Genesis and Development 1909-1936* (Oxford: Oxford University Press, 1995).

3. Cornelius Van Til, *Christianity and Barthianism* (Philadelphia: Presbyterian and Reformed, 1962).

4. Bernard Ramm, *After Fundamentalism: The Future of Evangelical Theology* (San Francisco: Harper & Row, 1983).

5. See, for instance, Stanley J. Grenz and Roger E. Olson, *20th-Century Theology: God and the World in a Transitional Age* (Downers Grove, IL: InterVarsity, 1992), 65-77.

6. In addition to the work of Bruce McCormack, see George Hunsinger, *How to Read Karl Barth: The Shape of His Theology* (New York: Oxford University Press, 1991); and John Webster, *Barth's Ethics of Reconciliation* (Cambridge: Cambridge University Press, 1995).

7. A recent example of this approach to Barth may be found in Sung Wook Chung, ed., *Karl Barth and Evangelical Theology: Convergences and Divergences* (Grand Rapids, MI: Baker, 2006).

8. For information on Emergent Village, see www.emergentvillage.org.

9. For another interpretation of Barth in relationship to the emerging church, see Chris Erdman, "Digging Up Past: Karl Barth (the Reformed Giant) as Friend to the Emerging Church," in *An Emergent Manifesto of Hope,* ed. Doug Pagitt and Tony Jones (Grand Rapids, MI: Baker, 2007), 235-43.

ception Barth's own material dogmatic constructions represent but one, and only one, particular instantiation and witness to the plurality of the truth revealed in Jesus Christ. They are not intended to be read as a universal dogmatics, nor can they be viewed as such and remain faithful to their formal character as a witness to Jesus Christ.

In order to pursue this line of thought I will begin this essay with a consideration of Barth's conception of revelation and the knowledge of God. This I follow with sections on the plurality of the biblical witness to revelation and open-ended dogmatics. I will conclude with a description of the approach to theology implicitly embodied in the ecclesiology envisioned and articulated by Emergent Village as a practice of the emerging church. In doing so I suggest that Barth's form of open-ended "nondogmatic dogmatics" is a fruitful resource for evangelicals and others who are committed to the emerging church and find in its midst hope for themselves, for others, and for the future of the One Church. Barth's approach to dogmatics provides a formal and material theological context for the intuitions of the emerging church as well as a means of resisting both liberal and conservative positivism in its attempt to move beyond these categories and promote the ecumenical unity of the One Church of Jesus Christ.

Karl Barth, Revelation, and the Knowledge of God

"As [theologians] we ought to speak of God. We are human, however, and so cannot speak of God. We ought therefore to recognize both *our obligation and our inability* and by that very recognition give God the glory."[10] This assertion by Karl Barth provides a concise summary of the situation faced by theology that would seek to bear faithful witness to the living God. In response to these concerns, Barth commends a dialectical approach to theology that acknowledges aspects of the truth found in other methods, but with an awareness of their fragmentary and relative nature. "This way from the outset undertakes seriously and positively to develop the idea of God on the one hand and the criticism of humanity and all things human on the other; but they are not now considered independently but are both referred constantly to their common presupposition, to the living truth which, to be sure, may not be named, but which lies between them and gives to both their

10. Karl Barth, *The Word of God and the Word of Man*, trans. Douglas Horton (New York: Harper, 1957), 186.

meaning and interpretation."[11] However, even in the dialectical approach, it is still the case that human beings are not able to speak of God since they are incapable of relating the affirmations of the dogmatic approach or the negations of the self-critical approach to the reality of the living God at the center of theology since God never enters into the control of human beings. Therefore the only thing that can be properly done is to bear witness to the realities of this situation and to take care to continually relate human affirmations and human negations to each other.

The dialectical theologian knows that this living center cannot be apprehended or beheld and will therefore give direct information and communication about it as seldom as possible in the knowledge "that all such information, whether it be positive or negative, is *not* really information, but always *either* dogma *or* self-criticism. On this narrow ridge of rock one can only walk." If we attempt to stand still we will fall to either the right or the left; hence the only choice is to keep moving forward constantly looking from one side to the other, from positive to negative and from negative to positive.[12] However, while a dialectical method is preferable, this is not because it is more successful than other ways at speaking of God. The fundamental assertion remains that we cannot speak of God. From the standpoint of human beings, theology is an impossibility. Theology becomes possible only where God speaks when God is spoken of. Since human beings have no control over this self-revelatory speech, they are *always* dependent on God in the task of theology. Given the reality of this state of affairs, what humans are able to do is bear witness to their creaturely inadequacy by the continual negation of theological assertions by the affirmation of alternative and opposing assertions. This ongoing practice of setting statement against statement constitutes the shape of Barth's dialectical theological method. But this dialectical method *is not* the means by which humans are able to speak of God. It is rather an emergency measure adopted as the only possible way to bear witness to the impossibility of human speech about God in light of their obligation to bear witness. The dialectical method serves as the means of bearing formal witness to the inadequacy of human beings for the task of theology and their dependence on God.

This follows for Barth out of his conviction that revelation is always an event. In speaking the Word, God is revealed; in sending the Son, God becomes revelation itself; and in sending the Spirit, God effectively is made

---

11. Ibid., 206.
12. Ibid., 207.

known to human beings. In this pattern, God is the subject of revelation. God is *the subject of revelation* in such a way that God *always* remains the subject of revelation. God is *revelation itself,* the "other" in whom God both knows and makes known to creatures. And God is *the historical effectiveness of this revelation,* the very response evoked by this event. In short, God is Father, Son, and Holy Spirit, and only in the actual occurrence of all three taken together does revelation happen. He puts it succinctly at the opening of his discussion of the revelation of God in the *Church Dogmatics:* "God's Word is God Himself in His revelation. For God reveals Himself as the Lord and according to Scripture this signifies for the concept of revelation that God Himself in unimpaired unity yet also in unimpaired distinction is Revealer, Revelation, and Revealedness."[13]

In this understanding of revelation it is important to note the significance of the divine communication of the Word, but also its human reception. On the one hand, we cannot think about the event of revelation without remembering at once those who hear it and receive it. In other words, there is a necessary human dimension that is part of our talk about the Word of God. On the other hand, we must remember that this human dimension is not to be understood as something contributed by the human recipient of revelation independent of the event of the Word. Instead the event of revelation itself creates its own hearers, thus placing those who hear firmly in the event itself. It is because of the very directedness of the Word to human beings that the reception of revelation and the talk of God that it enables must of necessity include the human response.

The actualistic character of revelation means that dogmatics becomes possible only where God speaks when God is spoken of.[14] Since human beings have no control over this self-revelatory speech, they are *always* dependent on God in the task of dogmatics. This does not mean that dogmatics is utterly impossible; it simply means that where it is possible, it is only so as a divine possibility. Only by the grace of God in which God takes up human words and uses them for the purposes of self-revelation, in spite of their inherent inadequacy for the task of genuine self-revelation, does dogmatics become possible by the will of God.[15] In other words, even revelation does

13. *CD* I/1, 295.

14. For a brief description of Barth's actualism, see Hunsinger, *How to Read Karl Barth*, 30-32.

15. On Barth's conception of theological language and its relationship to postmodern thought, see Graham Ward, *Barth, Derrida and the Language of Theology* (Cambridge: Cambridge University Press, 1995).

not provide human beings with a knowledge that exactly corresponds to that of God. The infinite qualitative distinction between God and human beings suggests the accommodated character of all human knowledge of God. For John Calvin, this means that in the process of revelation God "adjusts" and "descends" to the capacities of human beings in order to reveal the infinite mysteries of divine reality, which by their very nature are beyond the capabilities of human creatures to grasp due to the limitations that arise from their finite character.[16] These observations give rise to the theological adage, *finitum non capax infiniti*, the finite cannot comprehend the infinite.

The natural limitations of human beings with respect to the knowledge of God made known in the process of revelation extend not only to the cognitive and imaginative faculties but also to the creaturely mediums by which revelation is communicated. In other words, the very means used by God in revelation — the mediums of human nature, language, and speech — bear the inherent limitations of their creaturely character in spite of the use God makes of them as the bearers of revelation. In Chalcedonian Christology, the divine and human natures of Christ remain distinct and unimpaired even after their union in Jesus of Nazareth. Reformed theological formulations of Christology consistently maintained that one of the implications of the Chalcedonian definition was the denial of the "divinization" of the human nature of Christ in spite of its relationship to the divine nature. With respect to the revelation of God in Christ, this means that the creaturely medium of revelation, in this case the human nature of Christ, is not divinized through union with the divine nature but remains subject to the limitations and contingencies of its creaturely character. Yet in spite of these limitations, God is truly revealed through the appointed creaturely medium.[17]

This dynamic is captured in the dialectic of veiling and unveiling and the notion of indirect identity. This means that in his self-revelation God makes himself to be indirectly identical with the creaturely medium of that revelation. Such revelation is *indirect* because God's use of the creaturely medium entails no "divinization" of the medium; and yet at the same time God is indirectly *identical* with the creaturely medium in that God chooses to truly *reveal* himself through such mediums. This is the dialectic of "veil-

---

16. On Calvin's understanding of the accommodated character of all human knowledge of God, see Edward A. Dowey, Jr., *The Knowledge of God in Calvin's Theology*, 3rd ed. (Grand Rapids, MI: Eerdmans, 1994), 3-24.

17. On the relationship between Barth's Christology and the Chalcedonian formulation, see George Hunsinger, *Disruptive Grace: Studies in the Theology of Karl Barth* (Grand Rapids, MI: Eerdmans, 2000), 131-47.

ing and unveiling" which maintains that God unveils (reveals) himself in and through creaturely veils, and that these veils, although they be used of God for the purposes of unveiling himself, remain veils. Further, the self-revelation of God means that the whole of God, complete and entire, and not simply a part, is made known in revelation, but nevertheless remains hidden within the veil of the creaturely medium through which he chooses to unveil himself. Hence, nothing of God is known directly by natural human perception.

In Christological terms, as Bruce McCormack observes, this means that the process by which God takes on human nature and becomes the subject of a human life in human history entails no impartation or communication of divine attributes and perfections to that human nature. This in turn means that "revelation is not made to be a predicate of the human nature of Jesus; revelation may not be read directly 'off the face of Jesus.' And yet it remains true that God (complete, whole, and entire) is the Subject of this human life. God, without ceasing to be God, becomes human and lives a human life, suffers, and dies."[18] The consequence of this notion of indirect revelation is that it remains hidden to outward, normal, or "natural" human perception and requires that human beings be given "the eyes and ears of faith" in order to perceive the unveiling of God that remains hidden in the creaturely veil. In this conception revelation has both an objective moment, when God reveals himself through the veil of a creaturely medium, and a subjective moment, when God gives human beings the faith to understand what is hidden in the veil. In this instance, the objective moment is Christological while the subjective moment is pneumatological.

In the framework of indirect identity, we are able to affirm God's use of language in the act of revelation without denying our theological and existential awareness of its inherent limitations and contingencies as a contextually situated creaturely medium. Barth secures the divine primacy in God's epistemic relations with human beings by maintaining the "actualistic" character of revelation. In other words, revelation in this conception is not simply a past event that requires nothing further from God. This would imply that God had ceased to act and become directly identical with the medium of revelation. If this were the case, the epistemic relationship between God and human beings would be static rather than dynamic with the result

18. Bruce L. McCormack, "Beyond Nonfoundational and Postmodern Readings of Barth: Critically Realistic Dialectical Theology," in *Orthodox and Modern: Studies in the Theology of Karl Barth* (Grand Rapids, MI: Baker, 2008), 110.

that human beings would be able to move from a position of epistemic dependency to one of epistemic mastery. Instead, God always remains indirectly identical with the creaturely mediums of revelation, thus requiring continual divine action in the knowing process and securing the ongoing epistemic dependency of human beings with respect to the knowledge of God. This epistemic dependency that is the natural outworking of indirect revelation points to the nonfoundational character of theological epistemology. As mentioned previously, where theology becomes possible in spite of its impossibility from the human side, it does so only as a divine possibility. An approach to theology that takes these insights on board will be one that finds its ongoing basis in the dialectic of the divine veiling and unveiling in revelation. This construal of revelation demands a theology that takes seriously the ongoing reality of divine action not only on the level of the theological epistemology it presupposes but also on the level of the theological method it employs. Apart from this, theology is reduced to something that is humanly achievable and subject to human manipulation and control.[19]

A nonfoundationalist approach to theology seeks to respond positively and appropriately to the situatedness of all human thought and therefore to embrace a principled theological pluralism as an appropriate part of a dialectical theology.[20] It also attempts to affirm that the ultimate authority in the church is not a particular source, be it Scripture, tradition, reason, or experience, but only the living God. Therefore, if we must speak of "foundations" for the Christian faith and its theological enterprise, then we must speak only of the triune God who is disclosed in polyphonic fashion through Scripture, the church, and the world, albeit always in accordance with the normative witness to divine self-disclosure in Jesus Christ. It promotes a theology with an inherent commitment to a principle of continual reformation and maintains without reservation that no single human perspective, be it that of an individual or a particular community or theological tradition, is adequate to do full justice to the truth of God's revelation in Christ.[21]

Some fear that a nonfoundationalist approach to theology presupposes a denial of Truth.[22] Now it is certainly correct that some nonfounda-

19. Ibid., 111-12.

20. For a detailed discussion of nonfoundational theology, see Stanley J. Grenz and John R. Franke, *Beyond Foundationalism: Shaping Theology in a Postmodern Context* (Louisville: Westminster John Knox, 2001).

21. John R. Franke, *The Character of Theology: An Introduction to Its Nature, Task, and Purpose* (Grand Rapids, MI: Baker, 2005), 77-81.

22. For instance, among evangelicals see R. Scott Smith, *Truth and the New Kind of*

tionalists move in this direction and express their commitment to the finitude of human knowledge in a statement such as: the truth is that Truth does not exist. Thus, the assertion is made that nonfoundationalism denies the reality of Truth per se. However, Merold Westphal maintains that such a claim "stems not from analyzing the interpretative character of human thought but from placing that analysis in an atheistic context. If our thinking never merits the triumphalist title of Truth *and* there is no other knower whose knowledge is the Truth, then the truth is that there is no Truth. But if the first premise is combined with a theistic premise, the result will be: The truth is that there is Truth, but not for us, only for God."[23] Here, employing the metaphorical language of foundations, an important distinction is made between epistemological and ontological foundations. While nonfoundationalist theology means the end of foundationalism it does not signal the denial of "foundations" or Truth.

However, these "foundations" are not "given" to human beings. As Bruce McCormack notes, they "always elude the grasp of the human attempt to know and establish them from the human side" and they cannot be demonstrated or secured "philosophically or in any other way."[24] Hence, human beings are always in a position of dependence and in need of grace with respect to epistemic relations with God. Attempts on the part of humans to seize control of these relations are all too common throughout the history of the church and, no matter how well intentioned, inevitably lead to forms of oppression and conceptual idolatry. Nonfoundationalist theology seeks to oppose such seizure through the promotion of a form of theology and a theological ethos that humbly acknowledges and bears witness to the human condition of finitude and fallenness and that, by grace if at all, does not belie the subject of theology to which it seeks to bear faithful witness.

The Plurality of the Biblical Witness

In the event of the Word of God, the revelation of truth, Scripture functions as the Spirit-inspired attestation and witness to the self-revelation of God

---

Christian: The Emerging Effects of Postmodernism in the Church (Wheaton, IL: Crossway, 2005).

23. Merold Westphal, *Overcoming Onto-theology: Toward a Postmodern Christian Faith* (New York: Fordham University Press, 2001), xvii.

24. Bruce L. McCormack, "What Has Basel to Do with Berlin? Continuities in the Theologies of Barth and Schleiermacher," in *Orthodox and Modern*, 88.

through the creaturely medium of the words of the prophets and the apostles. These words are embedded in a socially constructed linguistic context. This means that the means used by God in revelation, in this case the medium of human language, continues to bear the inherent limitations of its creaturely and finite character in spite of the use God makes of it as a bearer of truth in its witness to revelation. Hence, while Scripture is inspired by the Spirit and is truth written, it nevertheless remains subject to the historically and culturally conditioned character that attends to all human language.[25]

One of the entailments of the contextual character of the Bible as an inspired and true witness to the event of revelation is its plurality. Canonical Scripture is itself a diverse collection of witnesses or, put another way, a manifold witness to the revelation of divine truth.[26] In fact, the Bible is not so much a single book as it is a collection of authorized texts written from different settings and perspectives. Each of the voices represented in the canonical collection maintains a distinct point of view that emerges from a particular time and place. In other words, the Bible is polyphonic, made up of many voices.

The self-revelatory speech-act of God is received among diverse communities over long periods of time and in a plurality of cultural settings. The human reception and response is shaped by the communal and cultural settings in which revelation occurs. This is part of the act of revelation itself that creates its own hearers and places them and their response firmly in the event itself. Here we remember that it is the directedness of the Word of God to human beings that means the human response must be included in the event of revelation and the talk about God that it enables.

The revelation of the triune God is received in a plurality of cultural settings and is expressed and proclaimed from these diverse contexts to others over the course of history in accordance with the sending of the church into the world as a representative of the image and mission of God. As truth written, Scripture paradigmatically reflects this plurality and diversity. In this way Scripture is the constitutive and normative witness for the formation and proclamation of Christian community. At the same time, it is also the first in an ever-expanding series of presentations of the Christian faith throughout history for which it is paradigmatic.

25. John R. Franke, "The Nature of Theology: Culture, Language, and Truth," in *Christianity and the Postmodern Turn: Six Views,* ed. Myron Penner (Grand Rapids, MI: Brazos, 2005), 201-14.

26. On the plurality of Scripture, see John Goldingay, *Old Testament Theology: Israel's Gospel* (Downers Grove, IL: InterVarsity, 2003); and I. Howard Marshall, *New Testament Theology: Many Witnesses, One Gospel* (Downers Grove, IL: InterVarsity, 2004).

In this polyphonic collection, each voice makes a distinct contribution to the whole and none manifests dominance over the others. The Bible contains a diversity of literary forms such as narrative, law, prophecy, wisdom, parable, epistle as well as others, and within each of these forms we have the expression of numerous canonical perspectives. The presence of four Gospels provides the most obvious and most instructive example of plurality in the biblical canon. It also stands as a paradigmatic affirmation that the witness of the Christian community to the gospel of Jesus Christ, in accordance with the canonical tradition, can never be contained in a single, fixed perspective.

In keeping with this perspective the early church resisted attempts at harmonizing the Gospels into one single account, such as that of the *Diatessaron* of the early church writer Tatian. The fourfold witness of the Gospels of Matthew, Mark, Luke, and John indicates the irreducibility of the gospel of Jesus Christ to a single account. This means that true "catholic" faith is pluralistic. "It is 'according to the whole,' not in the sense that it encompasses the whole in a single, systematic, entirely coherent unit, but rather in the sense that it allows for the openness, for the testimony of plural perspectives and experiences, which is implied in the fourfold canonical witness to the gospel."[27] The multiplicity of the canonical witness to the gospel is not incidental to the shape of the community from which it emerged under the guidance of the Holy Spirit, and which it envisions for the future. Attempts to suppress the plurality of the canonical witness by means of an overarching, universalistic account will lead to serious distortions of the gospel and the community that is called to bear witness to it.

The plurality of forms and perspectives embedded in the biblical witness suggests that no single voice or interpretive approach will be able to do justice to this diversity. Further, it may also be taken to imply that any of the forms and perspectives in the Bible itself will fail to bear adequate witness to the self-revelation of the triune God if they are abstracted from the other forms and perspectives and used in a reductionistic fashion. In relating these diverse forms as the Word of God it is important to envision their plurality-in-unity and unity-in-plurality. As evangelical theologian Kevin Vanhoozer asserts: "strictly speaking, the diverse canonical parts neither contradict nor cohere with one another, for both these notions presuppose either the presence or absence of conceptual consistency. But this is to assume that the various books of the canon are playing the same language game. They are not.

---

27. Justo L. González, *Out of Every Tribe and Nation: Christian Theology at the Ethnic Roundtable* (Nashville: Abingdon Press, 1992), 22.

Two notions that occupy different conceptual systems are nevertheless *compatible* if neither negates the other."[28]

It is worth reminding ourselves at this point that this plurality should not and cannot be construed as leading to an "anything goes" sort of relativism. The Christian conviction that God speaks rules out this sort of approach, and the acknowledgment of diversity and plurality in the Bible must not be used as an attempt to support such a perspective. In addition, as witness to the revelatory speech-act of the triune God, the plurality of Scripture should not be used as a denial of the unity of the canon. In keeping with the conviction that the Bible is inspired by the Spirit for the purpose of bearing witness to the self-revelation of God and guiding the church into truth, we affirm that the Bible constitutes a unity as well as plurality. But this unity is a differentiated unity expressed in plurality.

As such, the Bible has given rise to a variety of meanings and interpretations that are derived from the work of exegesis, theology, and the particular social and historical situations that have shaped its interpreters. In the task of seeking to read the Bible as a unity-in-plurality and plurality-in-unity, we should expect a variety of models and interpretations due to the very nature of the canonical texts themselves. They authorize multiple perspectives within a set of possibilities that are also appropriately circumscribed by the shape and content of the canon. The point here is not that anything goes, but rather that within the context of what "goes" we should expect plurality. Indeed, the plurality of the church is a faithful expression of the plurality of Scripture which is in turn a faithful witness to the plurality of truth lived out in the eternal life of God and expressed in the act of revelation.[29]

As the Word of God and *normative* witness to revelation, Scripture consists of inspired human speech-acts that bear authentic witness to the divine speech-act of the event of revelation. As such, Scripture is truth written and its pages bear manifold witness to the plurality of truth. As the Word of God and *paradigmatic* human and creaturely witness to the event of revelation, Scripture also invites greater plurality than that contained in its pages, in order that, under the guidance of the Holy Spirit, the witness of the church to the truth in the world may be continually expanded to all the nations in keeping with the mission of God.

---

28. Kevin J. Vanhoozer, *The Drama of Doctrine: A Canonical-Linguistic Approach to Christian Theology* (Louisville: Westminster John Knox, 2005), 275.

29. For a more detailed discussion on the plurality of truth, see John R. Franke, *Manifold Witness: The Plurality of Truth* (Nashville: Abingdon, 2009).

John R. Franke

Open-Ended Dogmatics

In light of this, how should we understand the nature and task of dogmatics? If it is something that only becomes possible and actualized by divine initiative, then what are our obligations as human beings and would-be disciples entrusted with the gospel? If our witness to the Word of God and the truth of the gospel will always be characterized by plurality, how should we go about the practice of dogmatics? The answer is that we must be obedient to the task of bearing witness in such a way that both reflects the obligations of gospel witness and does not lose sight of either our inability to do so apart from the ongoing work of God or our dependence on others in the task of bearing this witness.

Dogmatics is an ongoing, second-order, contextual discipline that engages in critical and constructive reflection on the beliefs and practices of the church.[30] In the words of Barth it is "the science in which the Church, in accordance with the state of its knowledge at different times, takes account of the content of its proclamation critically, that is, by the standard of Holy Scripture and under the guidance of its Confessions."[31] It is a human enterprise and as such must not be viewed as "a matter of stating certain old or even new propositions that one can take home in black and white."[32] In keeping with the calling to bear witness to the God revealed in Jesus Christ, it is the perpetual task of theology to continually begin again at the beginning in accordance with the nature of its subject.

A dialectical approach to dogmatics serves as the means of bearing formal witness to the inadequacy of human beings for the task of dogmatics and their dependence on God. In short, it is preferable to other methods as the most effective measure of bearing witness to both our obligation and our inability to speak of God. The notion of dialectical theology as a theological method intended to bear witness to both human obligation as well as human inability with respect to speaking of God is further developed through community and plurality. We have suggested that the event of the Word of God encompasses not only the divine act of revelation, but also its human reception. The socially constructed nature of human communities reminds us that this reception is always a communal and cultural dynamic as people

30. For a discussion of dogmatics (or theology) as an ongoing, second-order, contextual discipline, see Franke, *The Character of Theology*, 83-118.

31. Karl Barth, *Dogmatics in Outline*, trans. G. T. Thomson (New York: Harper & Row, 1959), 9.

32. Ibid., 12.

in different contexts hear and receive, through the action of the Holy Spirit, the revelation of God.

Hence, the dialectical pattern of dogmatics is not ultimately something that is most fully worked out by individuals engaged in the task of theology but rather by communities of theological reflection under the guidance of the Spirit in relation to other communities that make up the Christian church, the one Body of Christ. In other words, the corporate theological reflection of the church, taken as a whole, is necessary to bear proper human witness in a culturally and ethnically diverse world. This is the great theological dialectic of the plurality of truth in the church lived out as the various parts of the Body of Christ are faithful to bear their witness in relation to the whole. No single community, tradition, or perspective can speak for the whole church. Each has its own vocation and calling in relation to the whole as ordered and guided by the Holy Spirit.[33]

One of the implications of the witness to the event of the Word of God expressed in the plurality of the biblical canon is the challenge that this entails for the traditional construal of theology as "systematic" theology. This nomenclature suggests that theology can be conceived as a relatively stable system of truth that is communicated in the act of revelation. It implies that the witness of Scripture may be summarized in the form of the system of theology that it supposedly contains and to which it bears witness. Now without doubt the Bible has been read in such a fashion, with the result that numerous systems of theology have been discerned in its pages and proclaimed to be the one true system of doctrine taught in Scripture. This system then functions as an interpretive guideline for reading the Bible.

A dialectical approach to theology takes into account the plurality that is contained in the biblical canon and provides a coherent means of addressing this situation in the method that it employs. It does not proceed on the assumption that various genres and strands of the canon can be arranged into a uniform system of teaching and therefore does not suppress the plurality of the Bible and its witness to the plurality of truth revealed in the event of the Word of God. As such, it is able to account not only for the diversity of Scripture but also for the diversity of the church throughout history as a manifestation of both canonical plurality as well as the plurality of social and historical situations in which the Christian community has come to expression.

---

33. On the significance of this plurality, see Lamin Sanneh, *Translating the Message: The Missionary Impact on Culture* (Maryknoll, NY: Orbis, 1989).

One of the dangers of the systematic approach to theology is that it quickly leads to sectarianism in the Christian community as different expressions of the church conclude that they have arrived at the one true system of doctrine. Inevitably they find themselves in conflict with other traditions that have come to different conclusions. The resulting fragmentation and divisiveness in the church is in clear contrast to the work of the Spirit in promoting the unity of the church.

Having said this, how are we to account for the clear tendency to systematization that has characterized much of the Western theological tradition, particularly since the development of the scholasticism of the medieval church and the continuance of this approach to theology in the Protestant tradition? In other words, isn't something like systematization inevitable as soon as we start to attempt to do theology with an eye to bearing witness to the truth as something that is definite and coherent in keeping with its relationship to the living God? We have said repeatedly that the plurality of truth is not license for the conclusion that anything goes, but will this pursuit of truth not inevitably lead to a form of systematization, albeit a dialectical one, that is nevertheless similar to the systems that have emerged throughout the history of Christian theological reflection? In other words, is the challenge and danger of systematization not finally inescapable in the witness of theology that takes seriously its obligation to speak of God as a means of bearing witness to the truth of the gospel? Barth addresses this question in the context of his own articulation of dialectical theology in the *Church Dogmatics*:

> In this work — it cannot be otherwise in view of its object — we have to do with the question of truth. It is, therefore, inevitable that as a whole and in detail the aim must be definiteness and coherence, and the hope is that the definiteness and sequence of the truth will actually be disclosed. But this being the case, is it not also inevitable that "something like a system" will assert itself more or less spontaneously in dogmatic work? Why, then, should a "system" be so utterly abhorrent? If it asserts itself spontaneously in this way, can it not be forgiven? And if so, why should we be frightened away by a law forbidding systems? May it not be that a "system" which asserts itself spontaneously (not as a system, but as a striving for definiteness and coherence) signifies obedience and is therefore a shadow of the truth? It may well be so. But even in this case the danger is still there. The fact that unauthorised systematisation may be forgiven does not mean that the tendency to systematisation is authorised. Nor does the

fact that even in the fatal form of an intrinsically unauthorised systematisation true obedience may finally be demonstrated and a shadow of the truth disclosed.[34]

In other words, while the tendency of the discipline of theology to take on the form of "systematic" theology is understandable, perhaps even inevitable as a shadow of the truth, this does not mean that it is ever to be seen as an authorized form of theology. Further, precisely because this systematic form of theology does tend to spontaneously assert itself we must be vigilant in guarding against it through conscious and continual efforts at resisting it and breaking it up when it takes shape. This is part of what we mean when we speak of theology as an activity that must be reformed and always reforming according to the Word of God.

This being said, how should we proceed in bearing the witness of theology? As part of our obligation to speak of God, the church engages in the task of dogmatics through the development and articulation of models of Christian faith. These models should be in keeping with the canonical teachings and narratives of the Bible, appropriate to the particular social and historical context in which they are situated, and informed by the history of the church. This means that the sources for the construction of these models are the Bible, the thought-forms of the contemporary setting, and the traditions that make up the tradition of the church.[35] The intent of this constructive process is to envision all of life in relationship to the living God revealed in Jesus Christ by means of biblically normed, historically informed, and contextually relevant models and articulations of Christian faith that communicate the Christian story and its invitation to participate in the reconciling and liberating mission of God.[36]

Theological models function as heuristic conceptions that enable complex issues and questions to be opened up for reflection and critical scrutiny. A model is "a relatively simple, artificially constructed case which is found to be useful and illuminating for dealing with realities that are more complex and differentiated."[37] And while models are not able to fully capture all the complexities and nuances of the phenomenon under consideration, they are

---

34. *CD* I/2, 868-69.

35. On Scripture, tradition, and culture as sources for theology, see Grenz and Franke, *Beyond Foundationalism*, 57-166.

36. On the nature and significance of models, see Stephen B. Bevans, *Models of Contextual Theology*, rev. ed. (Maryknoll, NY: Orbis, 2002), 28-33.

37. Avery Dulles, *Models of Revelation* (New York: Doubleday, 1983), 30.

able to stimulate engagement and interaction with it. Hence, as Ian Barbour points out, models should be viewed "seriously but not literally."[38]

In this way models are constructions rather than exact representations of phenomena to be studied. For example, the Christian teaching concerning the Trinity provides a model of God and the relationship shared between Father, Son, and Holy Spirit. It is not a direct and literal picture of this relationship; such a depiction is beyond human comprehension. However, in keeping with the self-revelation of God in the event of the Word, the doctrine of the Trinity is intended to communicate actual features of the eternal life and character of God. As such, it is a second-order linguistic depiction that provides genuine comprehension and insight concerning God. Models provide images and symbols that enable us to conceive of the richness and complexity of the divine life and action of God in the world without the claim that they are absolutely literal and precise. As Stephen Bevans puts it, models function like images and symbols and "provide ways through which one knows reality in all its richness and complexity. Models provide knowledge that is always partial and inadequate but never false or merely subjective."[39] Effective and useful models provide genuine insight into theological questions with the understanding that such knowledge is always partial, fragmentary, and provisional.

As analogous and heuristic conceptions of God and the relationship of God to the created order, models facilitate engagement and provide insight and understanding without the claim that they provide an exact and referential representation of God. God is transcendent and unique, and categorically different from anything in creation. As the early church theologian Irenaeus once remarked, God "may most properly be termed Light, but He is nothing like that light with which we are acquainted."[40] In reflecting on this statement, George Hunsinger remarks that "God's cognitive availability through divine revelation allows us, Irenaeus believed, to predicate descriptions of God that are as true as we can make them, while God's irreducible ineffability nonetheless renders even our best predications profoundly inadequate."[41]

---

38. Ian G. Barbour, *Myths, Models, and Paradigms: A Comparative Study in Science and Religion* (New York: Harper & Row, 1974), 7.

39. Bevans, *Models of Contextual Theology*, 30.

40. Irenaeus, *Against Heresies* 2.13.4, in *The Ante-Nicene Fathers*, vol. 1, ed. Alexander Roberts and James Donaldson (Grand Rapids, MI: Eerdmans, 1987).

41. George Hunsinger, "Postliberal Theology," in *The Cambridge Companion to Postmodern Theology*, ed. Kevin J. Vanhoozer (Cambridge: Cambridge University Press, 2003), 47.

Their constructed, contextual, and fragmentary character points to the need for a plurality of models in the task of theology. Bevans comments that due to "the complexity of the reality one is trying to express in terms of models, such a variety of models might even be imperative" and goes on to suggest that "an exclusive use of one model might distort the very reality one is trying to understand."[42] No single model will be adequate to account for the plurality of the biblical witness, the diverse perspectives on it in the tradition of the church, and the complexity entailed in the interaction between the gospel and culture that gives rise to theological reflection.

The distinction between finite creature and infinite Creator and the diversity of human situatedness and experience affirm that a plurality of models in dialectical relation to one another is imperative in the task of bearing faithful witness to the subject of theology. In fact, the exclusive use of one model of theology, even a dialectically conceived model, will lead to a distortion of the very reality which the model is attempting to make better known. The divine subject matter of theology coupled with the limitations of finite human perspectives lead to the conclusion that a proper conception defies a single unique description and *requires a plurality of perspectives in relationship to each other.*

From this perspective, the task of dogmatics will always be characterized by plurality in its continual dependence on God. Because of the subject matter of theology and the situatedness of its practitioners, dogmatics must always be shaped by an intentional commitment to ongoing dialectical engagement, provisionality, and open-endedness in keeping with its calling and intention to bear faithful witness to the God revealed in Jesus Christ. That this is the case is derived from the very character of the Word of God itself as the material principle of dogmatics which "destroys at its root the very notion of a dogmatic system. Where there is no longer a secure platform for thinking and speaking, there is likewise no system."[43]

The Emerging Church

In conclusion we now turn our attention to the emerging church conversation and suggest that Barth's dynamic, actualistic, and open-ended approach to dogmatics is embodied in the intuitions of the emerging church. Since

42. Bevans, *Models of Contextual Theology*, 30.
43. CD I/2, 868.

space does not permit a full discussion in this context I will simply offer a brief description of the movement and illustrate its open-ended plurality through the ecclesiology articulated on the Emergent Village website.[44]

In North America the emerging church has come to be associated with a movement initiated by a group of leaders with roots in evangelical Protestantism through ecclesial and/or academic connections.[45] The most visible and influential leader to this point in time has been Brian McLaren, whose writings in books such as *A New Kind of Christian* and *A Generous Orthodoxy* became an early standard bearer for the movement.[46] In time an organization bearing the name Emergent Village was formed to foster the concerns and values of the emerging church with Tony Jones, named as the national coordinator. Because of the establishment of Emergent Village, the formation of Emergent cohort groups across the country, a strong presence on the Internet, the invitation of the National Council of Churches to Emergent Village to send representatives to participate in the work of its Faith and Order Commission, and the increasing proliferation of books on the emerging church by friend and foe alike, many have formed the impression that the emerging church is something like a new denomination.[47] However, this notion is perceptively refuted by Peter Rollins: "While the term 'emerging Church' is increasingly being employed to describe a well-defined and well-equipped religious movement, in actual fact it is currently little more than a fragile, embryonic, and diverse conversation being held between individuals over the Internet and at various small gatherings. Not only does the elusive nature of the conversation initially make it difficult to describe what, if anything, unifies those involved; the sheer breadth of perspectives held by those within the dialogue makes terms such as 'movement', 'denomination' and 'church' seem somehow inappropriate."[48]

---

44. These connections and the themes of this essay are developed at greater length in John R. Franke, *Beginning Again: Karl Barth, the Emerging Church, and Open-Ended Dogmatics* (Grand Rapids, MI: Eerdmans, forthcoming).

45. On the shape of the movement, see Tony Jones, *The New Christians: Dispatches from the Emergent Frontier* (San Francisco: Jossey-Bass, 2008).

46. Brian D. McLaren, *A New Kind of Christian: A Tale of Two Friends on a Spiritual Journey* (San Francisco: Jossey-Bass, 2001) and *A Generous Orthodoxy* (Grand Rapids, MI: Zondervan, 2004).

47. Among the most influential of the books critical of the emerging church is D. A. Carson, *Becoming Conversant with the Emerging Church: Understanding a Movement and Its Implications* (Grand Rapids, MI: Zondervan, 2005).

48. Peter Rollins, *How (Not) to Speak of God* (Brewster, MA: Paraclete Press, 2006), 5.

How then can we describe the movement?[49] While several trajectories might be helpfully identified, I suggest the common theme is an open-ended plurality framed within the context of a diverse, historic, and global Christian faith. In other words, from my perspective, the story of the emerging church is found in the numerous and multifaceted micro-narratives among the individuals and communities that make up the fabric of the emerging church conversation. This plurality works against the sort of reductions involved in the question, what does the emerging church believe? In a descriptive sense, the situation is similar to the sixteenth-century Protestant Reformation. If you asked a participant in that movement what this diverse collection of so-called Protestant Christians *really* believed you could certainly find someone who would give you an answer, but it would vary greatly from person to person and place to place. However, while the Protestant church was characterized by plurality, this did not mean that Protestants were pluralists. They were not. Instead they were committed to establishing the one true church over against the Roman Catholic Church, which they viewed as a heretical distortion of the one true church. They were committed to one true way to be a Christian, the one right way to read the Bible, the one true system of doctrine, the one right set of practices. In their collective search different groups came up with alternative and competing conclusions on these matters. But these differences did not lead them to embrace plurality. In many ways the situation is quite similar to much contemporary evangelicalism, particularly in its more conservative iterations.

While plurality characterizes the emerging church movement, or better, the emerging church conversation, the movement also *affirms* plurality as an appropriate and necessary manifestation of Christian community. From the perspective of those in the emerging church plurality is not so much a problem to be overcome as it is a manifestation of the blessing and presence of God. It is not to be opposed, but rather something to be sought and celebrated. This openness to plurality is in part the result of on-the-ground realities of rethinking church in a postmodern, post-Christian environment. Emerging churches have been described as communities that seek to practice the way of Jesus in the context of various postmodern cultures.[50] This basic commitment calls forth openness to innovation and a

---

49. For the most helpful overview of the emerging church published to date, see Eddie Gibbs and Ryan K. Bolger, *Emerging Churches: Creating Christian Community in Postmodern Cultures* (Grand Rapids, MI: Baker, 2005).

50. Gibbs and Bolger, *Emerging Churches*, 27-46.

variety of communal forms as the message and entailments of the gospel are proclaimed and socially embodied in new and ever-changing situations. The experience and forms of particular Christian communities emerge in the context of the concrete interaction between the gospel and the particular social, historical, and cultural situations in which these communities are embedded. The concrete social forms and practices of these emergent, missional communities cannot be predetermined apart from this contextual interaction.

From this perspective diversity is to be expected. No single set of assumptions, outlooks, viewpoints, and practices will be appropriate or necessary for every context and situation. And some things that are especially helpful and illuminating in one particular setting may in fact be counterproductive and misleading in another. One size will not fit all. Plurality is desired and required. From this perspective, conversation becomes one of the primary values of the emerging church. It takes the whole church, in all of its diverse manifestations, to teach us about the meaning, scope, and significance of the gospel and to bear faithful witness to it in the world. This ongoing conversation is also the means by which we can be liberated from the hegemony and limitations of the dominant cultural narratives of our time as we listen to the voices of others who have not shared in these narratives.

This affirmation of plurality is reflected in one of the primary values articulated by the Emergent Village community on its website: "We are committed to honor and serve the church in all its forms — Orthodox, Roman Catholic, Protestant, Pentecostal, Anabaptist. We practice 'deep ecclesiology' — rather than favoring some forms of the church and critiquing or rejecting others, we see that every form of the church has both weaknesses and strengths, both liabilities and potential." Out of this commitment comes the desire to be irenic and inclusive with respect to the plurality of traditions that make up the history and present reality of the Christian community and to learn from the church in all its forms. This affirmation of ecclesial plurality leads to the articulation of four specific and concrete practices: (1) "To be actively and positively involved in a local congregation, while maintaining open definitions of 'church' and 'congregation.' We work in and with churches, seeking to live out authentic Christian faith in authentic Christian community"; (2) "To seek peace among followers of Christ, and to offer critique only prayerfully and when necessary, with grace, and without judgment, avoiding rash statements, and repenting when harsh statements are made"; (3) "To speak positively of fellow Christians whenever possible, especially those with whom we may disagree"; and (4) "To build sincere friendship with Christians from other traditions."[51]

The self-understanding of Emergent Village with respect to ecclesiology underscores the earlier point that "emerging church" does not signify anything like a particular denomination. Rather, it is a movement that can be found within the various traditions of the church as well as on the edges of traditional forms of Christian community. Those who identify with the emerging church range from conservative to liberal on the ideological spectrum, although most are interested in moving beyond such labels, and come from both evangelical and mainline denominations as well as from independent churches and those interested in establishing Christian communities outside of these traditional contexts. The open-ended plurality of its ecclesiological intuitions is consonant with the implications of Barth's open-ended dogmatics with its resistance to systematization, comprehensive views, and final conclusions.

At the same time, the emerging church commitment to plurality raises two particular challenges. First, while the Christian faith is properly characterized by multiple expressions, it is also true that not all expressions of Christianity are appropriate. Indeed the history of the church is littered with manifestations of Christian community that are at odds with the message of the gospel. The value of plurality must not lead to an "anything goes" type of mentality in the Christian community. Resisting this possibility is an ongoing challenge for those of us convinced of the importance of affirming and promoting plurality in the church.

Second, while the emerging church is committed in many ways to the plurality of Christian community, for all of its variety of forms it continues to reflect the relative lack of diversity that characterized the traditional ecclesial contexts from which it emerged. For the most part the conversation about the emerging church continues to be shaped primarily by the perspectives and concerns of the dominant social, intellectual, and cultural forms of the North American context. This has meant that, for the most part, the emerging church conversation has attracted very little interest from those who do not share in these assumptions and outlooks and often feel excluded and alienated by them.

In order to address these challenges, the emerging church must be vigilant in the establishment and maintenance of a healthy and robust commitment to the discipline of *self*-criticism. Such a practice provides the context in

51. See www.emergentvillage.com/about-information/values-and-practices.

which we make ourselves open to the work of the Holy Spirit and allow the Word of God to challenge and deconstruct our own assumptions and commitments in order to correct our shortcomings and failures and to broaden the horizons of our vision. This practice of self-criticism must be developed and nurtured in order that inappropriate forms of Christian community can be identified and corrected while at the same time allowing for the continued expansion of appropriate diversity and plurality in the church for the sake of the gospel and our participation in the mission of God. In the cultivation of this habit, the emerging church can benefit from Barth's conclusion:

> There is no point in dogmatic thinking and speaking if in it all systematic clarity and certainty is not challenged by the fact that the content of the Word of God is God's work and activity, and therefore God's free grace, which as such escapes our comprehension and control, upon which, reckoning with it in faith, we can only meditate, and for which we can only hope. It is not from an external attack of doubt or criticism, but from its own very concrete focal point and foundation, from the source of all Christian and therefore dogmatic certitude, that all its insights and first principles, the nexus of its axioms and inferences derive; and even these statements are constantly questioned both as a whole and in detail, and their temporariness and incompleteness exposed. The focal point and foundation themselves determine that in dogmatics strictly speaking there are no comprehensive views, no final conclusions and results. There is only the investigation and teaching which take place in the act of dogmatic work and which, strictly speaking, must continually begin again at the beginning in every point. The best and most significant thing that is done in this matter is that again and again we are directed to look back to the centre and foundation of it all.[52]

This reminds us that our best dogmatic and theological work will always fail to do adequate justice to its subject matter and that we must never grow satisfied and complacent with our findings. Instead, in constant dependence on God and the Word of God, we must cultivate the habit of open-ended dogmatics and begin our work again and again at the beginning. By this form and practice of dogmatics we will bear formal witness to the axiom of the Psalmist (Psalm 127:1, TNIV): "Unless the LORD builds the house, the builders labor in vain. Unless the LORD watches over the city, the guards stand watch in vain." Only in this way can we bear faithful witness to the God revealed in Jesus Christ.

52. *CD* I/2, 868.

Ontological Violence and the Covenant of Grace: An Engagement between Karl Barth and Radical Orthodoxy

Kevin W. Hector

The editors of this volume thought it would be instructive to set Karl Barth in conversation with theological movements that have gained a following among contemporary American evangelicals. In view of the attention that Radical Orthodoxy (RO) has attracted in recent years, I was asked to consider its relative merits vis-à-vis Barth. My argument can be simply stated: on the one hand, RO is attractive to American evangelicals, it seems, because it challenges the taken-for-granted authority of secular and scientific theorists, and advocates an admirably peaceable vision of all creation. On the other hand, RO's approach to "the Other" (when he or she is not a Radically Orthodox Christian) is often characterized by just the sort of totalizing violence that RO opposes. In what follows, I will argue that this totalizing tendency is rooted in RO's ontological commitments, specifically (a) its "abstract" understanding of God and creation and (b) its commitment to an ecclesiomonistic understanding of creatures' "participation" in God.[1] I will then suggest that RO's vision of "ontological harmony" would in fact be

1. Throughout this paper, I use the term "abstract" in a somewhat technical sense, referring to the sort of theologizing which begins with general categories (such as "omnipotence," "absoluteness," "infinitude," etc.) whose content has been fixed apart from their application to the covenant of grace. As Barth remarks, "*latet periculum in generalibus*" (*CD* II/2, 48).

I am grateful to Eric Gregory and Keith L. Johnson for their insightful comments on an earlier draft of this essay.

better supported by some of Barth's theological commitments, specifically, what we might call his "covenant ontology." Finally, in order to address one of the most common criticisms of Barth — and to bring some balance to my treatment of RO — I will suggest that Barth's account of "mediation" (or putative lack thereof) can be helpfully supplemented by a version of RO's historicist-participationist pneumatology. What thus comes into view, I hope, is a more thoroughly peaceable "ontology of peace."

Before proceeding, two clarifications are in order. First, my discussion of "Radical Orthodoxy" focuses mostly on the movement's central figure, John Milbank. While the themes I lift up are vital to the entire movement, my treatment of them will focus on their appearance in Milbank's work.[2] Second, although I think that RO's ontological commitments and Barth's account of mediation are liable to some serious objections, I am not arguing that their views are irremediable, nor that the other's views are alone adequate to address these objections. I am simply arguing that Barth's ontological commitments could contribute something helpful to RO's vision of harmony, just as an RO-friendly understanding of mediation could helpfully elaborate some underdeveloped points in Barth's ontology. Onward, then, to my argument.

I. Radical Orthodoxy and Violence

1.

As many commentators have observed, there seems to be a contradiction at the heart of Radical Orthodoxy: on the one hand, RO is committed to an ontology of peace in which difference is neither totalized nor excluded; and on the other, RO commonly responds to "others" precisely by totalizing *and* excluding them.

We begin with two features that have attracted evangelicals to RO, namely, its particularism and its commitment to ontological harmony. Over against the (putatively) "liberal" tendency to subordinate the meaningfulness and truth of Christian belief to non-Christian authorities such as science or philosophy, RO insists that Christian belief must "provide its own

---

2. The "ontology of participation" upon which this paper focuses has been identified as RO's "central theological framework"; for this, see John Milbank, Graham Ward, and Catherine Pickstock, "Suspending the Material: The Turn of Radical Orthodoxy," in *Radical Orthodoxy: A New Theology*, ed. John Milbank, Catherine Pickstock, and Graham Ward (New York: Routledge, 1999), 3.

account of the final causes at work in human history, on the basis of its own particular, and historically specific faith."[3] Herein lies some of the radical-ness of RO: unlike the sort of theology which seems embarrassed by the par-ticularity of Christian claims — the sort of theology which seeks constantly to make itself palatable to its cultured despisers — RO sticks unabashedly to its particularly Christian guns. There is not even a hint of embarrassment in its commitment to the doctrines of the Trinity, incarnation, resurrection, and so forth; in fact, RO claims that these doctrines are the key to under-standing everything, including secular theories.

This brings us to a second point of attraction: RO is committed to Christian particularity because it is convinced that Christianity provides a uniquely peaceable view of the world. RO insists that, unlike other metanarratives, Christianity "recognizes no ontological violence. It con-strues the infinite not as chaos, but as a harmonic peace which is yet beyond the circumscribing power of any totalizing reason." "Peace," in this view, "no longer depends upon the reduction to the self-identical"; rather, it "harmo-nizes but does not cancel out other differences."[4] RO is thus trying to avoid the sort of violence that one commits when "others" are either marginalized or forced to fit into one's own totalizing thought-world (at the expense of their otherness).[5] Christianity counters this kind of violence, according to RO, by harmonizing difference (rather than totalizing or excluding it), and, controversially, they claim that Christianity *alone* provides such harmony. We will consider the reasoning behind this claim in due course, but for now

3. John Milbank, *Theology and Social Theory: Beyond Secular Reason* (Oxford: Black-well, 1990), 380. Note well that the pagination in the recently released second edition of *The-ology and Social Theory* (Blackwell, 2006) differs from that of the first edition. This paper generally follows the thought (and pagination) of the first edition, both because it was the first edition that spawned Radical Orthodoxy, and because there are few substantive changes in the second edition.

4. Quotations from Milbank, *Theology and Social Theory*, 5; Milbank, "Foreword" to James K. A. Smith, *Introducing Radical Orthodoxy: Mapping a Post-Secular Theology* (Grand Rapids, MI: Baker Academic, 2004), 18.

5. Emmanuel Levinas described this violence as a "neutralizing the existent in order to comprehend or grasp it," an approach which is "not a relation with the other as such but a reduction of the other to the same . . . making them play roles in which they no longer rec-ognize themselves, making them betray not only commitments but their own substance" (*Totality and Infinity: An Essay on Exteriority*, trans. Alphonso Lingis [Pittsburgh, PA: Duquesne University Press, 1969], 45-46, 21). RO shares Levinas's aversion to this sort of on-tological violence, but claims that Levinas's philosophy is unable to overcome it; for this as-sessment, see John Milbank, *Being Reconciled: Ontology and Pardon* (New York: Routledge, 2003), 139ff; *Theology and Social Theory*, 306.

it is important to note that, in RO's view, "only Christian theology now offers a discourse able to position and overcome nihilism itself," because "theology alone remains the discourse of non-mastery."[6] This is the case, RO claims, because Christianity, and Christianity alone, embodies a non-totalizing, non-nihilistic ontology of peace, according to which otherness is harmonized rather than excluded or reduced to sameness.

2.

On the one hand, then, RO advocates a vision according to which differences are neither excluded nor totalized but brought into a musical harmony with one another. On the other hand, RO's critics consistently object that RO responds to non-Radically-Orthodox thinkers precisely by forcing them to choose between assimilation and nothingness. Due to editorial constraints, unfortunately, we cannot elaborate and defend this objection here, though it has been amply treated elsewhere.[7] The objection can be summed up in terms of the strategy it ascribes to RO: RO briefly rehearses some problem which arises in non-Christian discourse, it interprets this problem as evidence that, taken by itself, non-Christian discourse slides into nihilism, and it proposes that Radically Orthodox Christianity alone avoids this result. Because RO has decided, as we shall see in a moment, that non-Christian discourse must either participate in the tradition of the

6. Milbank, *Theology and Social Theory*, 6. As Milbank claims elsewhere, Christianity is "*the* difference from all other cultural systems, which it exposes as threatened by an incipient nihilism" (ibid., 381). James K. A. Smith provides a nice catalogue of some RO "onlies" in his *Introducing Radical Orthodoxy*, 166-67. RO positions itself especially over against secularity, which it sees as "totalizing and terroristic because it acknowledges no suprahuman power beyond itself by which it might be measured and limited" (Milbank, *Being Reconciled*, 5). This is comparable to Milbank's overall argument in *Theology and Social Theory*; see 279-80 and *passim*. Serious doubts have been raised against this account of secularity. Jeffrey Stout's criticism on this score is, I think, decisive; see his *Democracy and Tradition* (Princeton, NJ: Princeton University Press, 2004), 92-117.

7. On this point, see, for instance Stout, *Democracy and Tradition;* Christopher Insole, *The Politics of Human Frailty: A Theological Defense of Political Liberalism* (London: SCM, 2004); Bruce Marshall's review of *Truth in Aquinas* in *The Thomist* 66 (2002): 632-37; as well as the extensive criticisms raised in the following journal issues devoted to Milbank/RO: *Journal of Religious Ethics* 32, no. 3 (June 2004), *Arachne* 2, no. 1 (1995), *Modern Theology* 8, no. 4 (October 1992), *New Blackfriars* 73, no. 861 (June 1992). Milbank responds to some of these criticisms — to my mind unconvincingly — in these same journals as well as in "Between Liberalism and Positivism," the preface to the second edition of *Theology and Social Theory.*

church or collapse into nihilism, its reading of non-Christians is maximally unsympathetic and thus usually a gross *mis*reading, even while RO is by and large uncritical toward its own views; indeed, as RO itself proudly admits, it "engages in no 'dialogues,' because it does not recognize other valid points of view outside the theological."[8] Hence, for all of its talk of a peace which "no longer depends upon the reduction [of the Other] to the self-identical" and of "discover[ing] a difference that yet has a universal claim and that harmonizes but does not cancel out other differences," RO's out-narration campaign "harmonizes" differences precisely *by* canceling them out — quite literally, since RO consistently consigns non-Christian viewpoints to the category of non-being.[9] As Romand Coles sums up this critique, for RO, Others "rarely appear/are reduced to nothing. Of course, if we count their utterly assimilated appearance in a particular type of Christian garb, then one might claim they appear everywhere. Yet whenever they speak a very foreign tongue, they are ignored or labeled nihilist. This, in spite of all the talk of difference."[10] To many of its critics, therefore, it would appear that RO's out-narration campaign commits the very violence which RO denounces in others.

3.

On the one hand, then, RO is committed to the peaceable harmonization of difference, and on the other, RO seems, at least to a legion of critics, to treat non-Christian thought violently. We can make some sense of why RO seems liable to this criticism by taking a closer look at the ontology underlying its "ontology of peace": insofar as RO is "violent" toward non-Christian (and non-RO) thought, this is arguably due to the fact that it roots its ontology of harmony in an abstract, indeterminate God, and locates the mediation of this harmony in an all-too-specific place, namely, the historical church and its hierarchy.

According to RO, Christianity understands all that is in terms of an original ontological harmony, "a real peace which is a state of harmonious agreement, based upon a common love, and a realization of justice for all."[11] This

8. "Radical Orthodoxy: Twenty-four Theses," thesis 5, quoted in Smith, *Introducing Radical Orthodoxy,* 167.

9. Quotations from Milbank, "Foreword" in Smith, *Introducing Radical Orthodoxy,* 18.

10. Romand Coles, "Storied Others and Possibilities of *Caritas:* Milbank and Neo-Nietzschean Ethics," *Modern Theology* 8, no. 4 (1992): 334.

11. Milbank, *Theology and Social Theory,* 390.

harmony is rooted in the eternal harmony which characterizes God's being: the triune life of God, according to RO, is an "infinite series of differences," a movement "from unity to difference, constituting a relation in which unity *is* through its power of generating difference, and difference *is* through its comprehension by unity."[12] In this view, "the harmony of the Trinity is . . . not the harmony of a finished totality but a 'musical' harmony of infinity."[13] God's very being is thus an inexhaustible harmony of difference, and *this* God, according to RO, is the one in whom all creation lives and moves and has its being: God "originates all finite reality in an act of peaceful donation, willing a new fellowship with himself and amongst the beings he has created," which means that "creation is generated within a harmonious order intrinsic to God's own being" and thus "participates in the God who differentiates . . ."[14] Since the Creator-God infinitely harmonizes difference within Godself, and since all that is, is only insofar as it participates in God's being, it follows that creation "is only a finite series which continues indefinitely toward an infinite and unfathomable God."[15] Creation, in this view, is rooted in an original peace, an original harmony of difference within God in which all creation participates. RO thus posits a non-totalizing, non-nihilistic, "original peace" according to which differences are harmonized: God's being is a harmony of difference, and all that is, is by participating in this being.

Of course, RO does not deny that there appears to be a discrepancy between this "original peace" and the *dis*harmony which characterizes so much of creation. It understands this disharmony as a privation of goodness, rather than as a substantial "other" over against the harmony of being. Disharmony, in this view, is explained "in terms of [our will's] failure to be related to God, to infinite peace, and to other finite realities with which it should be connected to form a pattern of true desire."[16] Evil and disharmony, accordingly, have "no ontological purchase," since they are related not to being as such, but "to a free subject who asserts a will that is truly independent of God and of others, and thereby a will to the inhibition and distortion of reality."[17] Insofar as free subjects refer their desires to something

12. Ibid., 423-24.

13. Ibid., 424.

14. Ibid., 391, 429, 424.

15. Ibid., 405.

16. Ibid., 432. As Milbank elsewhere asserts, "no one, as willing, wills anything but the good, and evil only affects the will to the extent that a deficient good is being willed" (*Being Reconciled*, 6).

17. Milbank, *Theology and Social Theory*, 432.

less than God's perfect harmony, their desires become distorted and, in consequence, disharmonious. RO thus explains the "violence" of modern society, not in terms of an original and ultimate violence, but in terms of wrongly directed desire. RO claims, for instance, that secular society directs its desire to a penultimate, temporary peace among otherwise warring individuals, such that it ends up cultivating disharmony: "For the ends sought by the [earthly city] are not merely limited, finite goods, they are those finite goods regarded without 'referral' to the infinite good, and in consequence, they are unconditionally *bad* ends."[18] RO judges that the secular city is characterized by violence and arbitrariness, and this judgment is underwritten by its belief that "the *direction of desire* is the key factor in determining whether or not a community will be truly just and united."[19] For RO, genuine harmony is possible only when one's desires are referred to God, and since secular society refers its desires elsewhere, it is incapable of harmony.

For our purposes, it is crucial to note that RO's particular understanding of disharmony corresponds with a soteriology: given RO's view of disharmony, "salvation from sin must mean 'liberation' from political, economic, and psychic *dominium,* and therefore from all structures belonging to the *saeculum,* or temporal interval between the fall and the final return of Christ."[20] We have referred our desires to penultimate ends, and so fallen out of harmony with God and one another, which means that our salvation depends upon God's restoration of this harmony. Salvation thus "takes the form of a different inauguration of a different kind of community."[21] Jesus is the Savior, in this view, in that he "came to expose the secret of social violence hidden 'since the foundation of the world,' and to preach 'the kingdom,' as the possibility of a life refusing mimetic rivalry, and, in consequence, violence."[22] Jesus re-establishes harmony by referring himself wholly to God and by inaugurating a new community in his Spirit, a community which is in harmony with God and so with the rest of creation. Unlike all other so-called societies, this community is a true society, since "true society implies absolute consensus, agreement in desire, and entire harmony among its members," which is "exactly . . . what the Church provides."[23] The church is, accordingly, "the restoration of being," which is why RO asserts

18. Ibid., 406.
19. Ibid., 400.
20. Ibid., 391.
21. Ibid., 391-92.
22. Ibid., 393-94.
23. Ibid., 403.

that "the unity and inner-communion of Christians is not just a desirable appendage of Christian practice, but is itself at the heart of the actuality of redemption. The Church itself is the *telos* of the salvific process."[24]

RO thus understands salvation as God's act of restoring creaturely harmony, and it understands the community founded by Christ as the mediator of this harmony. A clear grasp of the latter point will go a long way toward explaining RO's apparently "violent" treatment of non-Christian thought, and in order to understand this point, it will help to consider a rather obvious objection: how can RO claim that the church provides "absolute consensus, agreement in desire, and harmony among its members," when there is so much evidence to the contrary? To understand RO's response, it is important to consider, first, that RO espouses a participationist ontology according to which "every higher level until that of Godhead not only cause[s] but also 'g[ives] to be' the lower levels."[25] Second, we need to have in view RO's understanding of ecclesial hierarchy, the goal of which is "a 'co-working' with God" wherein "one starts to transmit the power of divine charity and the light of divine knowledge to those initiates within the churches who have not yet risen so far in the scale."[26] Putting these two pieces together, the picture that emerges looks something like this: at the top of the ecclesial hierarchy are those who stand in continuity with Christ and thus (a) refer their desires to God and (b) agree with one another; these are the Apostles' successors. Not everyone in the church stands in continuity with Christ, though; most have not yet attained this status. Insofar as those at the top of the hierarchy have transmitted their desires to those below them, however — insofar, that is, as those at lower levels of the hierarchy defer to those at the top — they participate in that which is above them, namely, the apostolic successors' participation in Christ's harmony. Hence, there is a sense in which everyone in the church participates in the new being initiated by Christ and therefore stands in harmony with God and others, since they belong in the church only by virtue of their participation in those who stand in continuity with Christ. RO thus claims that, by participating in (those who participate in) Christ, the church's sociality instantiates a renewed, harmonious being.[27]

24. Ibid.

25. Milbank, "Foreword," in Smith, *Introducing Radical Orthodoxy*, 14.

26. Milbank, *Theology and Social Theory*, 404.

27. We cannot deal here with RO's important claims about the relationship between harmony and the forgiveness of sins (for which see *Theology and Social Theory*, 411ff., and *Being Reconciled*).

4.

Briefly stated, then, RO claims that creation harmoniously participates in God's infinite harmony, that creatures bring about disharmony insofar as they desire penultimate goods, and that Christ re-establishes harmony by inaugurating a new community in the Spirit. This brief account begins to shed some light on why RO consistently — and, to its critics, vexingly — insists that Christianity *alone* overcomes violence.[28] If (a) our desires are ontologically harmonized just in case they are referred to God, and (b) this harmony exists in the church alone, because only in the church are everyone's desires harmonized with God and one another, it follows (c) that those outside this community must not be in harmony with God, with their own being, or with one another — it follows, that is, that the Christian community is alone able to avoid sliding into violence and nihilism.

Our account likewise sheds light on why RO responds as it does to those outside the church. Though there are moments when RO appears to think that there is nothing harmonious outside the church — one of the movement's contributors has claimed, for instance, that "morality or authentic virtue is possible only for the community of the redeemed," such that "what appear to be instances of mercy or compassion or justice outside the body of Christ are merely semblances of virtue"[29] — RO usually allows that those outside the church may indeed refer their desires to God and so achieve some degree of harmony. It is crucial to note, however, that on the basis of their collateral commitments, RO has to see such extra-ecclesial harmony as itself strictly dependent upon the historical church. As RO sees it, "if right desiring and openness to revelation have entered the picture . . . this is already a work of grace, and already exists in some typological, *which is to say real historical,* relation to scripture and tradition," such that these right desires "do not stand simply 'outside' Christian tradition"; there is, accordingly, "no grace not mediated by the

28. RO claims, for instance, that "the absolute Christian vision of ontological peace provides the *only* alternative to a nihilistic outlook" (*Theology and Social Theory,* 434), that "theology *alone* remains the discourse of non-mastery" (*Theology and Social Theory,* 6), and that Christianity is "the *only* non-nihilistic perspective, and the *only* perspective able to uphold even finite reality" (Milbank, Ward, and Pickstock, "Suspending the Material," 4) — my emphases.

29. Smith, *Introducing Radical Orthodoxy,* 243. Smith's comments occur in the midst of his discussion of RO's somewhat ambiguous/ambivalent position on this issue; Smith sees *Theology and Social Theory* as agreeing with Smith's own position and *Being Reconciled* as apparently departing from it.

Church."[30] According to this account, even if those outside the church unwittingly refer their desires to God, this reference depends upon a historical connection with the community inaugurated by Christ. To see what this means, consider how RO might interpret the March on Selma: they could affirm that those who marched across Pettus Bridge acted rightly (even those who were not part of the church), but they would have to insist that those outside the church acted rightly only insofar as those inside the church "transmitted" right desires to them — insofar, that is, as those outside the church participated in the being of those "above" them. Since RO maintains that the church alone stands in harmony with God and others, it can account for glimpses of harmony outside the church only in terms of their historical dependence upon the church — in terms, that is, of their "real historical" participation in the new being.

5.

One final point: because, on the one hand, the church is the redeemed community which is alone in harmony with God, and because, on the other, all creation should be in harmony with God, RO insists that the church must universalize its narrative to include all creation: RO "attempts to reclaim the world by resituating its concerns and activities within a theological framework," which means that "every discipline must be framed by a theological perspective"; for "otherwise[,] these disciplines will define a zone apart from God, grounded literally in nothing."[31] In RO's view, every square inch of the universe must be referred explicitly to God, for otherwise disharmony will prevail. RO is thus committed to out-narrating all other viewpoints in order to demonstrate that any narrative that does not refer itself to God will slide into violence, thereby to show that the Christian narrative is alone capable of

---

30. Milbank, *Being Reconciled*, 118, 138; my emphasis. Milbank elsewhere describes his account of "participation" as a kind of "materialism" which should be understood in terms of "the external relation of person to person in the community" (*Theology and Social Theory*, 415), and recommends understanding contemporary culture "in terms of multiple but converging narratives of typological anticipation, unrecognized scattering of the seed sown by the incarnate Logos, and various fallings-away and partial survivals of Christian norms," such that, for instance, "we regard postmodernity, like modernity, as a kind of distorted outcome of energies first unleashed by the Church itself" (*Being Reconciled*, 121, 196). It would thus appear that Milbank's gestures toward a "cosmic Church" ("the Church, like grace, is everywhere" [*Being Reconciled*, 138]) reflect a claim about Christianity's historical influence, and not about God's redemptive work outside the church.

31. Milbank, Ward, and Pickstock, "Suspending the Material," 1, 3.

maintaining harmony. Since RO sees redemption as harmony with God, and since it sees harmony with God in terms of reference *to* God, RO's out-narration campaign plays a *redemptive* role in reclaiming all of creation for God. This being the case, it is not hard to see why RO's universalizing drive is so strong.[32]

This all-or-nothing attitude is reinforced by the abstractness and inde-terminacy of RO's theological ontology. RO describes God as "the infinite series of differences" who is "superabundant Being" and "a power within Be-ing which is more than Being," in view of which they insist that "nothing in God can be unrealized," and that "no actualization, even an infinite one, ex-hausts God's power, for this would render it finite after all."[33] Because RO understands God as an infinite series of differences (without further specifi-cation of these "differences"), and because it sees any unassimilated differ-ence as a threat to God's infinitude (an infinity which is, again, unspecified), we can see why RO *must* take an all-or-nothing attitude toward difference: if anything in all creation were not taken up wholly and immediately into God's uniting-of-difference, this would constitute a limitation on God's Godness; as such, everything in creation must either be taken up into God's harmony or else . . . not be. Hence, for RO, it really is an all-or-nothing mat-ter: a thing either participates directly in God's being, or it is nothing. There is no space in their ontology for anything in between.

*   *   *

In sum, RO sees all of creation as participating in God's harmonious uniting-of-difference (a harmony which characterizes God's very being), and it sees disharmony as arising out of our failure to refer our desires to God. God redeems creation from disharmony, on this account, by inaugu-rating a new, harmonious community, and this community works to weave more and more of creation into harmonious participation in God's being. Yet it seems that this ontology sets RO at odds with its commitment to peaceableness, since it leaves RO with few options for dealing with non-Christian thought: non-Christians must either be assimilated to Christian

---

32. It is instructive to consider the fact that, in order to accommodate RO, Hans Frei would have needed an additional category — call it "Type 6" — within his famous typology: Type 6, the inverse of Type 1, would be characterized by the systematic subordination of non-Christian thought. For the typology itself, see Frei's *Types of Christian Theology,* ed. William Placher and George Hunsinger (New Haven, CT: Yale University Press, 1992).

33. Milbank, *Theology and Social Theory,* 423.

thought or consigned to non-being. In order to preserve its commitment to harmony and difference, therefore, it would appear that RO should revise its ontological views. The rest of this paper suggests some ways in which it might do so.

II. Barth and Covenant

This section argues, simply, that if evangelicals are looking for an ontology which more adequately supports a commitment to harmony, they would do well to consider the one proposed by Karl Barth.

1.

To understand how Barth's ontology enables one to see difference as ultimately harmonious, it is helpful to begin with Barth's scrupulous insistence upon the *particularity* of God and of God's relationship with creation. Barth contends, for instance, that the Creator "is not synonymous with the concept of a world-cause . . . whose being seems to consist decisively in the fact that it is absolutely different from the world," nor is the Creator synonymous with an infinite series of difference.[34] No: according to the Creed, "the God who created heaven and earth is God 'the Father,' i.e., the Father of Jesus Christ."[35] If we want to know who Christians understand the Creator to be, therefore, we must turn to Jesus Christ, for "it is wholly and utterly in [him] that we are to know what really is the good-pleasure of [God's] will, what is, therefore, his being, and the purpose and orientation of his work, as Creator of the world and Controller of history."[36] If we want to know who the Creator God is, we must look to God's revelation in Christ, and when we look to him, we discover "nothing more surely and definitely than this — that in free obedience to his Father he elected to be man, and as man, to do the will of God."[37] Jesus Christ perfectly obeys the Father's will, which means that Jesus Christ's will is the Father's will — and Christ's will is to fulfill God's covenant with humanity. This being the case, we must say that Jesus Christ not only reveals God's will, he is God's will: God eternally wills to become incarnate in order

34. *CD* III/1, 11-12.
35. Ibid., 11.
36. *CD* II/2, 54.
37. Ibid., 105.

to fulfill the covenant with humanity.[38] This fact also tells us something about God's eternal being: God wills (eternally and only) that the Son would bear the name Jesus Christ, that the Father would be the Father of Jesus Christ, and that the Spirit would be the Spirit of Jesus Christ.[39] God's very being is thus determined-for-covenant, and God is in-covenant as Godself precisely by corresponding to Godself: because God's "proper" being is a communion of love, God can determine Godself for covenant without changing Godself.[40] Even apart from the latter determination, God is eternally a Father who begets the Son, the Son who perfectly reflects the Father's love, and the Spirit who bears witness to their love.[41] God's very being is thus a communion of love, and God would enjoy this communion even if God had determined not to be God-with-us. God has determined to be with us, however, which means that God's being-triune is determined-for-covenant: the Father determines to adopt us as God's children by persisting in his love for the Son; the Son determines to supply the objective basis of our adoption by persisting in his reflection of the Father's love; and the Spirit determines to supply adoption's subjective basis by persisting in his witness to this love. In electing to be God-with-us, accordingly, God corresponds to Godself.

---

38. Thus Barth: "We are not thinking or speaking rightly of God himself if we do not take as our starting-point the fact which should be both 'first and last': that from all eternity God elected to bear this name. Over against all that is really outside God, Jesus Christ is the eternal will of God, the eternal decree of God and the eternal beginning of God" (*CD* II/2, 99).

39. *CD* II/2, 115: "There is no such thing as Godhead in itself. Godhead is always the Godhead of the Father, the Son, and the Holy Spirit. But the Father is the Father of Jesus Christ and the Holy Spirit is the Spirit of the Father and the Spirit of Jesus Christ."

40. Barth therefore claims that God's triunity is "the basis of his whole will and action even *ad extra*, as the living act which he directs to us. . . . It is the basis of the election of man to covenant with himself; of the determination of the Son to become man, and therefore to fulfil this covenant. . . . And because he is the God of triune life, he does not will and do anything strange by so doing. In it he lives in the repetition and confirmation of what he is in himself. . . . [I]n all these things he is primarily true to himself, revealing himself as the one he is in himself, as Father, Son and Spirit, in expression and application and exercise of the love in which he is God" (*CD* IV/2, 345-46). It is therefore important to say that God would be triune even if God had not determined to be with us, though it is also important to say that God retains no being-in-Godself which is otherwise than in-covenant: "We cannot speak correctly of God in his being in and for himself without considering him always in this attitude [toward humanity]," such that "that which he is for himself and prior to us he is with a view to us" (*CD* II/2, 6-7; *CD* IV/1, 53).

41. I elaborate and defend this model in "Immutability, Necessity, and the Limits of Inference: Toward a Resolution of the Trinity and Election Controversy," *Scottish Journal of Theology* (forthcoming).

This correspondence is crucial to understanding Barth's doctrine of creation: given that election is the internal basis of creation, it follows that God creates the world by corresponding to Godself, too. Because God is triune, "[God] can become the Creator and therefore have a counterpart outside himself without any contradiction with his own inner essence, but in confirmation and glorification of his inner essence."[42] God creates precisely by corresponding to Godself: the basis of creation is "a divine movement to and from a divine Other; a divine conversation and summons and a divine correspondence to it."[43] The Father eternally begets a counterpart, and God creates the world by repeating this begetting *ad extra*. From this, it follows that creation corresponds to the Son's relationship to the Father: "In God's own being and sphere there is a counterpart: a genuine but harmonious self-encounter and self-discovery," and "man is the repetition of this divine form of life; its copy and reflection."[44] God thus creates the world for the sake of having a covenant-counterpart *ad extra,* which means that creation is for-covenant: "What God created when he created the world and man was not just any place, but that which was foreordained for the establishment and the history of the covenant, nor just any subject, but that which was to become God's partner in this history."[45] Hence, just as God is not God-in-general but the triune God who is determined-for-covenant, so creation is not creation-in-general but creation-for-covenant.[46]

The relationship between God and creation is likewise "particular": Barth insists that "what God does in himself and as the Creator and Governor of man is all aimed at the particular act in which it has its center and meaning" — the particular act, that is, of being God-with-us.[47] God "was satisfied to enter into *this* relationship with *this* reality distinct from himself, to be the Creator of *this* creature, to find in *these* works of his Word the external sphere of his power and grace and the place of his revealed glory. . . ."

---

42. *CD* III/1, 183.

43. Ibid.

44. Ibid., 185.

45. Ibid., 231.

46. The "goodness" of creation, therefore, is not goodness-in-general, but goodness-for-covenant; hence, "'It was very good' means concretely that it was adapted to the purpose which God had in view; adapted to be the external basis of the covenant of grace" (*CD* III/1, 213). Because creation is for the sake of the covenant, the goodness of creation is the fact that it is fit for God's covenant fulfillment, and "its nature is simply its equipment for covenant" (*CD* III/1, 231).

47. *CD* IV/1, 7.

His creative will was divine from the very outset just because it was not infinite but had this specific content and no other."[48] This means, among other things, that God's sovereignty is specific, too: "the true God is the one whose freedom and love have nothing to do with abstract absoluteness or naked sovereignty, but who in his love and freedom has determined and limited himself to be God in particular and not in general, and *only as such* to be omnipotent and sovereign and the possessor of all other perfections."[49] Because God's sovereignty is specific — God is sovereign and omnipotent as the covenant-God and not otherwise — God's sovereignty is not "threatened" if God does not micromanage every detail of the universe's existence. (We will say more in a moment about evil, which Barth defines as that to which God says No, namely, being-apart-from-covenant.)[50] Barth's ontol-

---

48. *CD* III/1, 214-15.

49. *CD* II/2, 49, emphasis added.

50. Like RO, Barth insists that "evil" does not represent a second principle over against God, nor a reserve of territory which is supposed to be "independent" of God's sovereignty. For Barth, "evil" is that which God has rejected — and what God has rejected is being-outside-covenant. Unlike RO, evil here has no "independent" existence precisely because it serves the good; God says No (to being-outside-covenant) *for the sake of* the Yes (to being-in-covenant). In Barth's account, God wills humans as God's covenant partners; God thus wills that we would say Yes to that to which God says Yes, and No to that to which God says No; God says Yes to being-in-covenant, and God wills that we would repeat this Yes. But since God's covenant partner is not God, "it is inevitable that this confrontation with what God repudiates, should mean for man, who is certainly not God and not almighty, that evil confronts him as a hostile power, a power which is, in fact, greater than his own power. In this case, then, the defeat of this evil power cannot be so self-evident as it was in God's case. . . . It must become the content of a history: the history of an obstacle and its removing; the history of a death and a resurrection; the history of a judgment and a pardon; the history of a defeat and a victory" (*CD* II/2, 141). For the sake of the covenant — for the sake, that is, of that to which God says Yes — God wills that humanity should confront that to which God has said No, so that humanity can repeat this No, and God wills that humanity's Yes and No should depend upon God alone, so that humanity would be "thrown wholly and utterly upon the resources of his grace," so that "man should proclaim his glory" (*CD* II/2, 141). God wills, accordingly, to become human in order to reject what God rejects (viz., standing apart from covenant) in order to affirm what God affirms (being-in-covenant). Hence, although there is a sense in which God wills that to which God says No, God does so only for the sake of rejecting this in Christ. Evil has no independent existence, accordingly, but only the limited existence that God has marked out for it in view of the covenant (see *CD* II/2, 142-43). We humans certainly try to affirm that which God has rejected, of course — we try, that is, to live apart from God's covenant with us — but God has rejected our rejection in Christ. Jesus Christ is thus "the only truly rejected man," since God's rejection of sin takes place once and for all in Christ, and in Christ God therefore rejects our being-apart-from-covenant. As

ogy thus loosens the grip of RO's worry about "reserving any territory independent of God": because God is a specific God, it follows that God's lordship — and creation's dependence — are specific, too. If this is the case, it follows that God's lordship is not incompatible with a certain amount of creaturely "independence," as long as this independence falls within God's covenant will. It thus follows that, for Barth, the affirmation of God's lordship is not to be confused with the strenuous assertion that creation is maximally and exhaustively, intensively and extensively, dependent upon God. Barth, no less than RO, would insist that creation depends upon God's preserving grace, but Barth sees this preservation in very specific terms: creation is preserved-for-covenant. This entails, for Barth, that God's providence and omnipotence are not "absolute" in any abstract sense, which entails further that God's omnipotence is not threatened if, for instance, there is a sense in which things hold together under their own steam. (We can see here two very different ways of reading Colossians 1:17.) While there is clearly a sense, therefore, in which RO's ontology is much more radical in its insistence that all creation depends upon God, it is not clear whether this is an unqualified virtue, since there may be reason to worry about paying God whatever compliments we see fit. Like Barth, RO insists that Christian theology must take its bearings from God's revelation in Christ by the power of the Spirit, yet it is precisely by following this principle that Barth's doctrine of creation — and of God's sovereignty over it — departs from RO.

2.

With this account in view, we can see how Barth's ontology provides us with some resources for dealing with the problem outlined above, namely, RO's apparently "violent" treatment of beliefs and actions which do not participate in the historical church. In order to do justice to RO's concerns, a candidate ontology must preserve the integrity of difference even in harmonizing

---

such, the one who rejects God is not rejected *by* God, since "with Jesus Christ the rejected can only *have been* rejected. He cannot *be* rejected any more. Between him and an independent existence of his own as rejected, there stands the death which Jesus Christ has suffered in his place, and the resurrection by which Jesus Christ has opened up for him his own place as elect" (*CD* II/2, 453). Our would-be rejection of God is "null" (*CD* II/2, 316). As such, Barth has not "reserve[d] a territory independent of God," precisely because God's covenant faithfulness overcomes our covenant infidelity. For a fuller treatment of these issues, see my essay on atonement in *The Westminster Handbook to Karl Barth* (Louisville, KY: Westminster John Knox, forthcoming).

it, for otherwise the harmony which results will be totalitarian and violent rather than musical. Barth's ontology satisfies this condition. In Barth's view, recall, God has eternally determined to be in covenant with us, and God creates and governs the world for the sake of this covenant. Just as God has rejected any other way of being God, so God has rejected any other way of creation being creation. This being the case, "*de jure* all men and all creation derive . . . from the reconciliation accomplished in [Christ], and are ordained to be the theater of his glory and therefore the recipients and bearers of his Word."[51] This means, among other things, that "in the world reconciled by God in Jesus Christ there is no secular sphere abandoned by him or withdrawn from his control, even where from the human standpoint it seems to approximate most dangerously to the pure and absolute form of utter godlessness."[52] One consequence of this is that human self-interpretation is not the final word: someone may remain outside the church and "refer" his or her life to something other than God, but since (a) all creation depends upon God, (b) God has determined to be gracious to humanity (and has ruled out any other way of being God), and (c) God's grace does not depend upon our response, it follows (d) that God's grace is active in our lives prior to and apart from our response to it. As Barth explains, "God precedes with his own will and work all other will and work because his decree of grace in Jesus Christ has already preceded the creation of all things and therefore the being and activity of the creature." Hence, "always and everywhere when the creature works, God is there as the one who has already loved it."[53] We should not be surprised, therefore, that a person's life may in fact refer "beyond" what he or she takes it to refer. For this reason, Barth insists that non-Christians (as well as Christians) can speak words which bear witness to God's grace, words which, "whatever their *subjective* presuppositions, stand *objectively* in a supremely direct relationship with the one true Word, which are not exhausted by what they are in themselves, which may even speak against themselves."[54] Because all creation is preceded by the covenant of grace, our words and works stand in an *objective* relationship to God which exceeds whatever we may *take* that relationship to be. Our actions thus outrun our interpretation of them. This means, among other things, that we cannot infer from (a) "This person does not self-consciously

51. *CD* IV/3.1, 117.
52. Ibid., 119.
53. *CD* III/3, 119.
54. *CD* IV/3.1, 125.

refer his or her actions to God" to (b) "This person's actions are not in fact referred to God." As a result, one has no grounds for assuming that non-Christian stories tend toward nihilism; one must take an ad hoc, rather than a priori, stance toward such stories. As Barth concludes, "we must be prepared to hear, even in secular occurrence, not as alien sounds but as segments of that periphery concretely orientated from its center and towards its totality, as signs and attestations of the lordship of the one prophecy of Jesus Christ, true words which we must receive as such even though they come from this source."[55]

This is not to say, of course, that all beliefs and actions bear positive witness to God's grace in Christ, since both within the church and without there are words which bear witness to that which God has not willed, namely, being-apart-from-covenant. But even here, we do not encounter a finally unharmonized difference, since this, too, has a place in God's covenant will — as that to which God has said No. God's rejection of sin takes place once and for all in Jesus Christ, which means that he is "the only truly rejected man"; in Christ, God rejects our being-apart-from-covenant. As such, the one who rejects God is not rejected *by* God, since "with Jesus Christ the rejected can only *have been* rejected. He cannot *be* rejected any more. Between him and an independent existence of his own as rejected, there stands the death which Jesus Christ has suffered in his place, and the resurrection by which Jesus Christ has opened up for him his own place as elect."[56] Our would-be rejection of God is thus outrun by God's rejection of our rejection; hence, even with respect to our rejection of God, the final word is not non-being, but being-in-covenant. As such, Barth's ontology has not "reserved a territory independent of God," because God's covenant faithfulness overcomes our covenant infidelity.

Barth's covenant ontology thus *harmonizes* difference, since there is no difference that stands wholly outside of the covenant. Yet it equally harmonizes *difference,* since the Other maintains its otherness even in being related to the covenant. Given that a person's beliefs and actions can be harmoniously related to God even if they are not explicitly referred to God, it follows that they do not have to become something other than their author takes them to be in order to be good, which means that they can be harmonized *as* difference. We can likewise account not only for those who unwittingly bear witness to God's grace, but for those who explicitly reject God's grace, too.

55. Ibid., 124.
56. *CD* II/2, 453.

On the view under consideration, this rejection stands: we do not twist it into something it is not (such as "anonymous acceptance of God") in order to make it fit into our story. Neither, though, do we simply consign it to non-being, since the final word to be said about such a stance is that God has rejected it: God rejects our rejection and thereby upholds the covenant of grace, which means that rejection, too, is harmonized — as rejection — into a covenant ontology. In this ontology, then, difference remains difference, but it is nevertheless brought into an ultimate harmony. Barth's covenant ontology thus appears better able to harmonize difference than RO's own neo-platonic ontology.

3.

This view does face a few serious objections, however. Some evangelicals may worry, for instance, about the apparently universalistic consequences of Barth's ontological commitments. In response, we should note, first, that Barth maintains that he is *not* a universalist, since "a grace which automatically would ultimately have to embrace each and every one would certainly not be free grace. It surely would not be God's grace."[57] Barth does not, in other words, claim that hell is empty, although he hopes and prays that this would be the case.[58] He does insist, however, that "no eternal covenant of wrath corresponds on the one side to the eternal covenant of grace on the other."[59] God has determined to be God with us and has rejected our rejection of God; this being the case, our rejection cannot make God turn against us. A person "can become a sinner and place himself within the shadow of divine judgment. . . . But he cannot reverse or change the eternal decision of God."[60] It seems to follow, then — although Barth does not spell this out — that *if* anyone suffers eternal condemnation, it must be his or her *self-condemnation*, his or her obstinate persistence in acting as if he or she were rejected by God and outside God's covenant. In any event, he or she cannot finally *be* rejected by God; "he can endure a likeness of the punishment and death that Jesus Christ has suffered in his place, but he cannot — even remotely — endure death itself."[61] Hence, even if those who reject God's grace

57. Barth, "The Proclamation of God's Free Grace," in *God Here and Now,* trans. Paul M. van Buren (New York: Routledge, 1964, 2003), 41. See also *CD* IV/3, 477.
58. For this, see "The Proclamation of God's Free Grace," 42, and *CD* IV/3, 478.
59. *CD* II/2, 450.
60. Ibid., 317.
61. Ibid., 454.

suffer the fruits of their determination, they do not stand like a surd outside God's covenant determination. Moreover, even if such a person were condemned to hell, this would still not mean that he or she represents an unharmonized difference, since this person, too, would join the chorus of witnesses to God's grace by testifying to that to which God has said No; this means that "he is not . . . without a divine determination. And his *ex profundis* — even if they are the *profunda* of hell — becomes *Gloria Deo ex profundis.*"[62] Hence, although Barth's covenant ontology is not necessarily universalistic with respect to eternal salvation, it is universalistic in claiming that there is no height or depth in God or creation which stands outside of God's determination to be God-with-us.

An objector might also wonder whether Barth's account still ends up treating difference "violently," since those whom he sees as witnesses to the covenant of grace might not take themselves to *be* witnesses. In response to this objection, it is important to keep in mind the difference between, on the one hand, identifying someone as beloved of God and an unwitting witness to this fact, and on the other, insisting that the goodness of their actions depends upon their historical relation to the church. Whereas the latter view may suggest that one's identity, beliefs, actions, and so on are "unconditionally bad" insofar as they stand outside the church,[63] the former allows that one's beliefs and actions *as such* can count as good, while quietly insisting that his or her rejection of God does not stand outside of God's love for him or her. It is hard to see how the latter would count as "violence."

Before concluding, one further issue must be addressed: while Barth's ontology may provide us with resources by which to see harmony among differences, one might reasonably wonder whether his ontology appears "peaceable" only because he says so little about how this harmony is historically mediated.[64] Our treatment of this issue must be brief, but in order to

---

62. Ibid., 457.

63. Milbank, *Theology and Social Theory*, 406.

64. This question bears obvious affinities with one of the most common objections to Barth's theology; see, for instance, Nicholas M. Healy, "The Logic of Karl Barth's Ecclesiology: Analysis, Assessment and Proposed Modifications," *Modern Theology* 10, no. 3 (July 1994): 253-70; Robert W. Jenson, "You Wonder Where the Spirit Went," *Pro Ecclesia* 2 (1993): 296-304; Joseph L. Mangina, "Bearing the Marks of Jesus: The Church in the Economy of Salvation in Barth and Hauerwas," *Scottish Journal of Theology* 52, no. 3 (1999): 269-305; John Yocum, *Ecclesial Mediation in Karl Barth* (Aldershot: Ashgate, 2004); and Eugene F. Rogers, *After the Spirit: A Constructive Pneumatology from Resources outside the Modern West* (Grand Rapids, MI: Eerdmans, 2005), 19-32.

see how Barth could address this concern — or to see what Barth might learn from RO on this point[65] — it should suffice to consider five points.[66] First, it is important to distinguish between the mediation, on the one hand, of the ability to recognize how various persons, beliefs, actions, and so forth stand in harmony with God and one another, and, on the other, of the authority to recognize these recognitions.[67] The importance of this distinction will become evident below. Second, we can explain the mediation of both kinds of recognition in intersubjective terms: one learns how various performers and performances harmonize by submitting one's candidate harmonizations to the authority of those whom one recognizes as competent harmonizers, until one is recognized as oneself a competent harmonizer. One learns to recognize harmony, in other words, by trying to go on in the same way as precedent harmonizations which one recognizes as authoritative, and by thus seeking this same status for one's own harmonization. Third, as I have argued elsewhere, insofar as we can trace this chain of precedents back to Christ's own recognition of the disciples, there is good reason to understand this chain as itself the mediation of Christ's normative Spirit.[68] We can thus understand the mediation in question as proceeding along the following lines: during Christ's ministry, he taught his disciples how to follow him by telling them what they should say and do, by correcting their missteps, by affirming their successes, and so forth. Through this process, the disciples began to understand what it meant to follow Jesus, and they did so by internalizing the norms according to which he assessed their performances. Once Jesus recognized them as knowing how to make such assessments, he recognized their authority over others' beliefs and actions: one could now learn how to follow Jesus by submitting one's beliefs and actions to the disciples' normative assessments. Once a person had been recog-

65. Thus RO: "An abstract attachment to non-violence is therefore not enough — we need to practice this as a skill, and to learn its idiom. The idiom is built up in the Bible, and reaches its consummation in Jesus and the emergence of the Church" (*Theology and Social Theory*, 398).

66. I have elaborated accounts along these lines in chapter two of *Theology Without Metaphysics;* "The Mediation of Christ's Normative Spirit," *Modern Theology* 24, no. 1 (January 2008): 1-22; and "The Recognition of Baptism," *Koinonia* 19 (2008): 13-37.

67. The ability to recognize the relevant performers and performances is a necessary, but not sufficient, condition of following Christ: necessary because one can intend the relevant performances only insofar as one knows what would count as such, but not sufficient, since there is a crucial difference between knowing what would count as a proper performance and actually engaging in such performance.

68. I defend this claim especially in "The Mediation of Christ's Normative Spirit."

nized by the disciples as knowing how to go on in the same way, still others could learn how to do so by submitting their beliefs and actions to that person's assessments, and so on. In this way, the norms according to which Christ assessed whether one was following him were passed along to others, and since these norms are the means by which one is conformed to Christ, it follows that this account can help us understand one of the central works traditionally ascribed to the Holy Spirit. Fourth, the fact that this mediation is a work of Christ's Spirit does not entail that the Spirit is at work only in the church, nor that the Spirit's work outside the church is historically dependent upon its work inside it. It would take us too far afield to elaborate this claim here — it has been sufficiently defended elsewhere[69] — but we can understand the Spirit's work outside the church in roughly the following manner: human beings all over the earth — not to mention a significant number of "higher" infralinguals — have developed recognitive practices by which to hold one another accountable, to treat certain performances and performers as correct and others as incorrect, and it would appear that these practices are the site where a community's norms are mediated and contested. Insofar as these norms are themselves in harmony with the Spirit of Christ, they can be recognized as an extra-ecclesial work of the Spirit.[70] Finally, though, there is reason to think that the authoritative status of "recognizing recognizer" lies ultimately with those who have been explicitly taught by the Spirit of Christ within the church, since it makes little sense to think that those not so taught would be the final arbiters of what counts as following Christ.[71] This suggests that the mediation of *this* status depends upon its historical mediation by the ecclesial community. Note well, however, that those who stand in recognizable continuity with Christ's normative Spirit may not themselves stand within the church, as it is not hard to imagine someone who has learned how to recognize what counts as follow-

---

69. In addition to Hegel's *Phenomenology of Spirit,* see Axel Honneth, *The Struggle for Recognition: The Moral Grammar of Social Conflicts* (Cambridge: MIT Press, 1995), and Robert Brandom, "The Structure of Desire and Recognition: Self-Consciousness and Self-Constitution," *Philosophy and Social Criticism* 33, no. 1 (2007): 127-50.

70. In turn, these "extra-ecclesial workings of the Spirit" may themselves depend upon the work of Christ, such that this claim could be taken as an elaboration of Barth's famous discussion of Jesus Christ as the Light of Life in *CD* IV/3.

71. To be sure, there is a further sense in which the final arbiter of whether something counts as following Christ is Christ himself. The present account funds this finality in terms of the objectivity of the normative commitments thus undertaken, but we cannot elaborate this point here; see "The Mediation of Christ's Normative Spirit."

ing Christ, yet who has determined not to do so. That is to say, competence in recognizing these performances and performers is a necessary, but not sufficient, condition of following Christ. These points are, admittedly, merely the outline of a proper treatment of the issue, but given the extent to which each of its elements has been treated elsewhere, it should suffice to demonstrate that Barth's covenant ontology need not depend upon an a-historical, unmediated picture of how differences can be harmonized.

*   *   *

Barth's covenant ontology thus provides a way of harmonizing difference which (a) sees all differences as part of the same story, yet which (b) maintains the integrity of difference as such. On his view, otherness — even non-Christian otherness — does not have to become something other than it is in order to be good, to be positively related to God, or to be part of the Christian story. Barth's ontology appears better suited than RO's, therefore, to uphold a vision of harmony that avoids both totalitarianism and nihilism.

III. Conclusion

By way of conclusion, I want to recap my central arguments and highlight some of their virtues. We began by observing RO's admirable commitment to ontological peace: over against both nihilism and totalitarianism, RO proposes a way of harmonizing difference. We then noted, however, that RO's ontological commitments seem to conflict with this proposal, since those commitments lead RO to decide in advance that non-Christian beliefs and actions are harmonious only insofar as they are historically dependent upon the historical church. This stance ends up violating RO's commitment to peace, since it deals with otherness precisely by reducing it to sameness. In order to avoid this result, we traced an alternative ontology according to which God's determination to be in covenant precedes and so determines all creation. This being the case, Christians are freed (and obligated) to take an ad hoc approach to non-Christian voices, since God has elected them, too, and since they, too, bear witness to this election. Moreover, even those who explicitly reject the covenant do not stand outside of this covenant's harmony, since God persists in being God-with-humans by rejecting their rejection. On the one hand, then, this ontology *harmonizes* difference, since all difference is a part of the same story, and on the other hand, it harmonizes *difference,* since otherness is harmonized without having to become something other than it is. We concluded, therefore, that this covenant ontology is better equipped to achieve RO's goals than RO's own ontology.

One of the virtues of this account, accordingly, is that it upholds a vision of ontological peace on the basis of which difference is genuinely harmonized and which therefore avoids both nihilism and totalitarianism. Because it recommends an ad hoc (rather than a priori) approach to non-Christian voices, this account would help RO to resist a temptation to which it all too often succumbs. RO regularly caricatures its opponents and then hastily dismisses them, and it is not hard to see why: if one knows in advance that all stories degenerate into nihilism if they are not referred explicitly to God, then one may not feel the need to attend carefully to the details of such stories. On the other hand, if the goodness of one's story outruns whatever one might refer it to, then Christians should listen carefully to these stories in order to hear echoes of God's grace in them. RO could resist this temptation without adopting Barth's ontology, of course, but adopting it would make it easier for them to do so — and that, I take it, would be an important contribution to RO's own project.

Stanley Hauerwas and Karl Barth:
Matters of Christology, Church, and State

Todd V. Cioffi

I

In his introduction to the life and work of Stanley Hauerwas in *The Hauerwas Reader*, William Cavanaugh claims that while many evangelicals are repelled by Hauerwas's "colorful" language, they seem to embrace the centrality of Jesus Christ and the critique of secularism in his work.[1] Indeed, Hauerwas's influence can be seen in a recent collection of evangelical reflections on the Christian life, but not exactly as Cavanaugh suggests. While Hauerwas's critique of secularism is in fact taken up by many evangelical theologians, it seems that Hauerwas's emphasis on the role of the *church* as the locus of meaning and activity for the Christian life, and not necessarily the centrality of Jesus Christ, is especially attractive to evangelicals.[2] The re-

---

1. See William Cavanaugh, "Stan the Man: A Thoroughly Biased Account of a Completely Unobjective Person," in *The Hauerwas Reader*, ed. John Berkman and Michael Cartwright (Durham, NC: Duke University Press, 2001), 30.

2. For example, see William Dyrness, "Spaces For An Evangelical Ecclesiology," in *The Community of the Word: Toward an Evangelical Ecclesiology*, ed. Mark Husbands and Daniel J. Treier (Downers Grove, IL: InterVarsity, 2005); Michael Jinkins, "The Gift of the Church: *Ecclesia Crucis, Peccatrixe Maxima*, and the *Missio Dei*," in *Evangelical Ecclesiology: Reality or Illusion?* ed. John C. Stackhouse, Jr. (Grand Rapids, MI: Baker, 2003); James K. A. Smith, "The Church as Social Theory: A Reformed Engagement with Radical Orthodoxy," in

---

I want to thank Matthew Lundberg and Scott Starbuck for reading an earlier draft of this chapter and offering helpful advice on how to improve it.

sult is that some evangelicals appear to be embracing a Hauerwasian staple: contrasting the church and the world such that Christians must choose *either* the church and its distinct way of life *or* the world and its secular forms of life.[3] Moreover, as Hauerwas has argued over the years, one consequence of choosing the church over the world is that the world's politics must be rejected, and so we find Hauerwas repudiating Christians who embrace America's secular liberal democracy. As expected, then, we also find some evangelicals following suit in denouncing significant aspects of American democracy.[4]

My concern, at this point, is that while evangelicals have much to learn from Hauerwas about the significance, and in fact indispensability, of the church and its practices for the Christian life, they may also learn to develop an animus for all that resides outside the walls of the church, especially when it comes to our democratic life in America.[5] But does it have to be that way? I don't think so. That is, I think there is a way to appreciate Hauerwas's emphasis on the significance of the church for the Christian life while avoiding his apparent rejection of the "world" and its politics, and especially democratic life. To see this, I want to take up an important aspect of Hauerwas's

---

The Community of the Word: Toward an Evangelical Ecclesiology, ed. Mark Husbands and Daniel J. Treier (Downers Grove, IL: InterVarsity, 2005); Leanne Van Dyk, "The Church in Evangelical Theology and Practice," in *The Cambridge Companion to Evangelical Theology,* ed. Timothy Larson and Daniel Treier (Cambridge: Cambridge University Press, 2007); D. H. Williams, *Retrieving the Tradition & Renewing Evangelicalism: A Primer for Suspicious Protestants* (Grand Rapids, MI: Eerdmans, 1999).

3. As an example, see David E. Fitch, *The Great Giveaway: Reclaiming the Mission of the Church from Big Business, Parachurch Organizations, Psychotherapy, Consumer Capitalism, and Other Modern Maladies* (Grand Rapids, MI: Baker, 2005).

4. Ibid., 160-68.

5. In commenting on *The Blackwell Companion to Christian Ethics,* which is claimed to be a book that Hauerwas's "friends have written . . . for him," and thus, takes up many of Hauerwas's most prized positions, Romand Coles notes that so many of the authors in this work give the impression that Christians have no need of that which is outside the church, particularly in regard to the non-Christian. Coles writes, "these pages threaten to establish a sense of the church in a manner that may at least vitiate the possibilities for . . . receptivity, and that may possibly steer Christians in markedly different directions — directions that render such relations with others [i.e., non-Christians] less likely and less fruit-bearing." See Romand Coles, "'Gentled Into Being': Vanier and the Border at the Core," in Stanley Hauerwas and Romand Coles, *Christianity, Democracy, and the Radical Ordinary: Conversations between a Radical Democrat and a Christian* (Eugene, OR: Cascade Books, 2008), 211. My concern is that precisely this sort of attitude that seems to stem from Hauerwas's writings is taking root among evangelicals who are engaging Hauerwas's work.

work over the years, namely, his reading and appropriation of Karl Barth's theology. By turning to the work of Karl Barth we will discover a way of maintaining the integrity of the church and engaging the world without losing any ground for the church or Christian life.

The purpose of this paper then is twofold. First, I want to suggest that if evangelicals continue to read Hauerwas for insight into the nature of the church and the Christian life that they do so in conversation with Karl Barth's views on the relationship between the church and the so-called secular world, and especially the secular political realm. On this score, I can only be suggestive, in that I will not put Karl Barth in conversation with evangelical theologians but will limit my treatment to Hauerwas's engagement of Barth with the hope that evangelicals will benefit from listening in on the discussion that follows. Nevertheless, I will return at the end of this chapter to suggest what it is that I think evangelicals can learn from Karl Barth, particularly in dialogue with Hauerwas, on the relationship between the church and the world. Second, I want to offer a reading of Barth that corrects Hauerwas's reading of Barth. Given the influence that Hauerwas has on theological discourse, it is important that those who encounter Barth through Hauerwas's writings have an opportunity to consider alternative readings of Barth, both in terms of what are arguably more accurate readings and in terms of what exactly are the implications of Barth's theology for understanding the church's relationship to the world and its "secular" ways. More specifically, I want to argue that Hauerwas does not fully appreciate, or perhaps even ignores, the centrality of Jesus Christ in Barth's work. In regard to Barth's theology, Hauerwas confuses the proper ordering of the church, the world, and the state to Jesus Christ, ultimately undercutting the lordship of Christ over these realms. From Barth's perspective, Hauerwas gives the *church* priority *over* Jesus Christ and the freedom *Christ* has to be Lord *over* the church, the world, and the political realm. Consequently, I want to suggest that we reconsider Hauerwas's emphasis on the church as seemingly over and against the world and consider Barth's Christological construal of the church-world and church-state relationship, which allows for a more reciprocal relationship between the church and the world while maintaining the integrity of the church. With this, I want to turn to Hauerwas's reading of Barth.[6]

6. Hauerwas's references to Barth span the lengthy body of work that Hauerwas has produced. Consequently, my treatment of Hauerwas's reading of Barth is incomplete at best, and at times may be more impressionistic than systematic. Of course, a systematic comparison of Hauerwas and Barth would be no easy task, especially given the very unsystematic character of Hauerwas's work.

II

There can be no doubt that Karl Barth has been a major influence on Hauerwas's thinking. In recounting his graduate training in theology at Yale, Hauerwas says that it was Barth who taught him "that when all was said and done, it is all about God."[7] And yet, not long after graduate school, it seems that this insight gives way to "it is all about the church." For example, when James Gustafson, one of Hauerwas's teachers at Yale, was asked to say something "theological" he responded with "God." Upon reflection, Hauerwas thinks that instead of saying "God" Christians should say "church," for it is the "significance of the church" that "*determines* the nature and content of Christian . . . reflection." On this point, Hauerwas adds, "what was *most original* about the first Christians was not the peculiarity of their beliefs, even beliefs about Jesus, but *their social inventiveness* in creating a community whose like had not been seen before."[8] While Hauerwas's point is more nuanced in the essay from which these quotations come, his claims nonetheless leave the impression that Christian theology, let alone Christian discipleship, is more about the human enterprise of the church and less about the life of the triune God. In other words, Hauerwas is not incorrect to emphasize the distinctiveness of the early Christian community in regard to the world in which those Christians found themselves. Nor is he incorrect to stress the significance of the church for understanding and appropriating Christian convictions in the world. But Hauerwas's lack of precision in carefully ordering the *priority* of God's activity in Jesus Christ by way of the Holy Spirit in establishing and sustaining the church, including its proclamation and confession, leaves the impression that the point of the Christian life is more nearly the church and not more accurately God and what God is doing in and for the church *and* the world. Indeed, when such emphasis is placed on human efforts to establish the church, there should be no surprise then that Hauerwas concludes that the church, as a distinct association of like-minded persons, can only be fully realized when set apart from the world, or other distinct human associations. It is not long after his Yale days that Hauerwas's ecclesiology will dominate his thinking, and that every so often

7. See Stanley Hauerwas, "Race: The 'More' It is About: Will D. Campbell Lecture," in *Christianity, Democracy, and the Radical Ordinary: Conversations Between a Radical Democrat and a Christian* (Eugene, OR: Cascade Books, 2008), 94.

8. Stanley Hauerwas, "On Keeping Theological Ethics Theological," in *Against the Nations: War and Survival in a Liberal Society* (Minneapolis, MN: Winston Press, 1985), 23 and 43 respectively. Emphasis added.

Barth appears in his work as if to sanction such ecclesial dominance and even Hauerwas's subsequent distaste for the "world" and dismissal of liberal democracy.

Take for example what is perhaps Hauerwas's most "popular" book, *Resident Aliens,* co-written with his former Duke colleague William Willimon. Here Hauerwas contends that, in an American context, *the* "overriding political task of the church . . . is to be the community of the cross," a "radical alternative" to the world, and especially "American democracy."[9] Of these sweeping claims, Hauerwas singles out for criticism more often than not American democracy as the source of many of America's ills and, more troubling, the church's. At core, the issue of American democracy is "political liberalism," i.e., that form of politics which stresses individual freedom, equality, and toleration.[10] The problem, says Hauerwas, is that political liberalism teaches that the "primary entity" of society is "the individual, the individual for whom society exists mainly to assist assertions of individual-ity."[11] In the context of American democracy, the issue is exacerbated in that the American church is often pressed into service (think "God and country") of helping our liberal society prop up and encourage "individual fulfillment."[12] But of course the role of the church in the world is not to support the false notion that the goal of life is individual fulfillment, and consequently, it is hard to see how the church can support such a political vision as promoted by political liberalism and democracy. In the end, for Hauerwas, critiques of both "world" and "democracy" appear to go hand in hand, and both "world" and "democracy" are opposed to the church, which is always and everywhere a contrast community of the cross.

What is curious throughout Hauerwas's critique are clipped references to Karl Barth, giving the impression that Barth, too, would be highly critical of the "world" and American democracy. For instance, according to

9. See Stanley Hauerwas and William H. Willimon, *Resident Aliens* (Nashville: Abingdon, 1989). See 47, 45, and 32f., respectively.

10. For a helpful definition of political liberalism and its American democratic form, and a discussion on the relationship between liberalism and religion in America, see Ronald F. Thiemann, *Religion in Public Life: A Dilemma for Democracy* (Washington, DC: Georgetown University Press, 1996), especially 74-75. On the point that modern liberalism is not devoid of promoting virtue among its citizens, see Peter Berkowitz, *Virtue and the Making of Modern Liberalism* (Princeton: Princeton University Press, 1999), especially 15-22.

11. *Resident Aliens,* 32.

12. Ibid., 33.

Hauerwas, within Barth's early theologically liberal context, "Barth knew that *the* theological problem was the creation of a new and better church."[13] Continuing to ascribe to Barth, Hauerwas adds, "So the theological task is not merely the interpretive matter of translating Jesus into modern categories but rather to translate the world to him. The theologian's job is not to make the gospel credible to the modern world, but *to make the world credible to the gospel*."[14] As we shall see, Hauerwas is not completely out of step in his interpretation of Barth. Barth would agree that we can only make full sense of the world in light of the gospel. And yet, for Barth, to suggest that Jesus and our claims about him cannot make inroads into the language and modes of the world is in fact misguided. Moreover, to suggest further that the theologian is *never* to make the gospel "credible" to the world — indeed that there is never to be a matter of reciprocal interaction between the church and the world — is not only misguided but problematic. It is problematic in that the church is presented as being at constant odds with the world, continually seeking to critique, denounce, and ignore the world for it knows not the church's Lord. But this simply is not the case for Barth, and it is not clear how Hauerwas is drawing from Barth when he appears to be missing some of the more sophisticated and nuanced aspects of Barth's Christological construal of the church-world relationship. Given that his comments about the church-world relationship and Barth come at the onset of *Resident Aliens,* we are left to believe that Barth helps set the stage for the rest of the book and its battle cry for the church to brace itself against the world, and in the American context to brace itself against democratic life. Yet, as I hope to show, we should be wary of Hauerwas's reading of Barth in an effort to distance the church so rigidly from the world, the political realm, and democracy. Of course, Hauerwas wrote *Resident Aliens* as a more popular book and not as a scholarly treatise on major theologians such as Barth. And yet, we find similar misgivings with Hauerwas's reading and use of Barth in his more scholarly engagement with Barth in his Gifford Lectures.

III

In those Gifford Lectures, published in 2001 as *With the Grain of the Universe,* Hauerwas claims that Barth is "the hero" of the story he is trying to tell, and

13. Ibid., 24. Emphasis added.
14. Ibid. Emphasis Hauerwas's.

gives two full chapters to his engagement with Barth's work.[15] Hauerwas's story is that "any attempt to provide an account of how Christian theological claims can tell us the way things are requires a correlative politics. In theological terms, such a politics is called 'church'" (39). In other words, for the Christian story to tell us the truth about the world and our lives we need the church, and without the church the Christian story falls flat. The plot of Hauerwas's story is driven by Barth, and we are led to believe that Barth, too, is trying to tell a story about the church being a counter-politics to the world, and in Hauerwas's terms, once again, this means an antipathy toward secularism, political liberalism, and especially American democracy.

According to Hauerwas, Barth's work is an attempt to provide "confidence in Christian speech" and "exemplifies how Christian language works," allowing the reader to become a more adequate knower of God (143). Such an effort started with Barth's break with theological liberalism and is especially seen in his Romans commentary, where according to Hauerwas, Barth was "reminding us that what is wrong with the world is its failure to acknowledge that God is God," and that this is the same problem that plagued liberal Protestantism and continues to this day (152). For Barth, knowledge about God does not start with self-examination, reflection on the human condition, or even analysis of the religious self; rather, knowledge of God begins and ends with God's self-revelation. As God reveals himself to us, our "knowledge" of God amounts to our "witness" of God. That is, we can only "describe" what God has revealed to us. Knowledge of God, in other words, is the act of confession. In this way, the subject matter of theology is and remains God, and Christians can only testify to the subject that is God. Hauerwas writes, "The *Church Dogmatics* is Barth's attempt to display the language of the faith in such a way that the form of theology does not belie the subject of theology" (174). And to this Hauerwas adds, "The *Church Dogmatics* is Barth's attempt to exhibit the conceptual and moral skills that we must have if we are to be adequate witnesses to the God revealed in the Bible" (176).

Hauerwas's last claim is worth pausing over. According to Hauerwas's reading of Barth, if Christians are to speak truthfully about God, they must exhibit not only the proper conceptual skills, as given and formed by the Bible and the confessions of the church, but the proper "moral skills." We can

---

15. Stanley Hauerwas, *With the Grain of the Universe* (Grand Rapids, MI: Brazos Press, 2001), 206. Hereafter all references to this work will be noted parenthetically in the body of this chapter.

only speak truthfully about God if we are living faithfully before God. Put somewhat differently, Hauerwas contends, "Barth was attempting to show that Christian speech about God requires a transformation not only of speech itself but of the speaker" (176). With this point, we discover why Barth is the pivotal figure in Hauerwas's work, namely, because Barth "was engaged in a massive attempt to overturn the epistemological prejudices of modernity" (190). The appeal for Hauerwas is that Barth did not set out to establish divine revelation as an *epistemological* doctrine, thereby fitting knowledge of God into one of various epistemologies available to the theologian. Rather, Barth shows that knowledge of God is not bound by *our* epistemological doctrines and instead requires the knower to conform to the activity of God. Our knowledge of God, in other words, *presupposes* God's self-revelation and our transformation in order that we can know God. This leads Hauerwas to suggest that "any account of Barth's understanding of the possibility of our knowledge of God must end by attending to his understanding of the church's witness to God, as well as to his understanding of the moral life that the church makes possible" (192). Apparently what Hauerwas finds attractive about Barth, then, is that Barth supposedly provides for the church the moral key with which to unlock the possibility of knowledge of God. The church, in other words, provides the conditions by and under which persons can come to know God. Yet, Barth's breakthrough for Hauerwas stands as worthy of both praise and criticism.

On the positive side, Barth's understanding that God is known only by way of God's self-revelation as discerned in the Christian community is appealing to Hauerwas because it emphasizes the distinctive character of Christian speech and life, and thus the church. In this way, Barth allowed *the church* to break free of Protestant liberalism and any attempt to accommodate the church to non-Christian modes of discourse, moral practices, etc. Along the way, Barth exposed many of the most cherished conceits of modernity and in particular the notion that humans are the measure of all that is. Having said that, we can better see why and how Hauerwas has drawn on Barth to safeguard the American church over the years from allowing itself to be co-opted by various "secular" enterprises that know not the story of God, such as, in Hauerwas's mind, political liberalism and American democracy.

On the negative side, however, Hauerwas claims that Barth did not adequately develop the sort of ecclesiology that allows for the proper maintenance of the distinctiveness of Christian speech and life. In other words, it is not clear that for Barth the church is actually necessary in order for Christians to encounter God and necessary to establish what God is doing in the world. More specifically, Barth did not give sufficient emphasis to the social and moral practices of the church in shaping Christians into the sort of people that are able to know God, establish the true significance of the church, and show the world that it is in fact "the world" and in need of the church for its true identity. Hauerwas writes, "Barth, of course, does not deny that the church is *constituted by* the proclamation of the gospel. What he cannot acknowledge is that the community called the church is *constitutive of* the gospel proclamation" (145, emphasis added). Contrary to Barth, Hauerwas contends — in so doing strengthening his argument by drawing on the work of Joseph Mangina — that the church is the "binding medium" in which Christian faith takes place, and furthermore, that the church "is, if not the message, *the condition* of possibility of grasping the [Christian] message in its truth" (145, emphasis added). The problem with Barth, therefore, is that although he thinks the church's task is to witness to God's self-revelation, Barth cannot show how the church (and here Hauerwas turns to Mangina again) "'*as a configuration of human practices,* makes much difference'" to the task of witnessing to God (192, emphasis Hauerwas's). According to Hauerwas, then, Barth fails to show what difference the church makes in *establishing* the distinctiveness of Christian proclamation of God (i.e., knowledge of God) and the moral life that flows from such proclamation. In Barth's view, the church becomes secondary, and seemingly unnecessary as a set of social and moral practices, to the proclamation of the gospel and indeed knowledge of God. With Barth, the church has lost its savor in the world.

According to Hauerwas, one of the more troubling outcomes of Barth's ecclesiology is that Barth is willing to trade on the church's identity in order to relate the gospel to the world and vice versa. Put bluntly, Barth allows the church to become too worldly at times. For instance, according to Hauerwas, Barth provides two extremes in the church's dealing with the world. First, the church can retreat into a type of monasticism, leaving the world to its own devices, or second, it can take such a positive view of the world as to approximate and assimilate the attitudes and convictions of the world to the detriment of the church (201). In an attempt to avoid both extremes, Barth tries to steer a middle path between the opposing positions. And yet Barth "fails," Hauerwas asserts, "to specify the material conditions that would sustain his 'middle way'" (202). In other words, how can the church be both distinctive and not distinctive in terms of, on the one hand, pulling back from the world and, on the other, embracing the world? What exactly would this look like, or, in Hauerwas's words, what "material conditions" would need to be in place, in terms of social and moral practices, for this to be possible? In the end, Hauerwas thinks that Barth is simply wrong about the church being able to steer a middle course between the extremes of "monasticism and the liberal embrace of the secular" (202). The problem, says Hauerwas, is that Barth's attempt to navigate a middle course for the church is but the other side of his "overly cautious account of the role of the church in the economy of God's salvation. Because the church cannot trust in its calling to be God's witness, Barth seems far too willing to leave the world alone" (202). As an example, Hauerwas holds that Barth gave too much to the secular state in developing his political theology as laid out in one of his more systematic political essays, "Christian Community and Civil Community," published in 1946. In this essay, Barth argues that the secular political realm, especially in the form of a democratic state, has much to offer both the church and the world and can even be a witness to the gospel. To Hauerwas's mind, Barth is simply too willing, as a result of a faulty ecclesiology, to trade on the *true* political character of the church in an effort to say something relevant about secular political life. Hauerwas finally laments that Barth "gave the state far too much independence" (203n67).

And so the story goes. Although Barth is the hero of the tale Hauerwas is telling, he is a hero with an Achilles' heel, weak and vulnerable when it comes to the secular modern state. And yet, there is something not quite right about Hauerwas's description of Barth's political theology, and more basically Barth's construal of the church-world relation. In the next section, I want to address briefly Barth's understanding of the church-world relation and proceed with an account of Barth's political theology, and particularly his view of the secular democratic state, as I think this will most clearly challenge Hauerwas's concerns that Barth has given too much away for the church in trying to navigate a "middle way" between the church and the world.

IV

To begin, I will sketch briefly the relation between the church and the world in Barth's major work, *Church Dogmatics*. While my treatment of this material can only be cursory at best, it nonetheless will provide a basis on which to appreciate more fully Barth's political theology. This sketch will involve three steps.

First, in *Church Dogmatics* II/2 Barth roots both the church and the world in Christology.[16] Both the church and the world are *in* Christ and so their very being is dependent in and on him. As such, Jesus Christ is Lord of both, and any sense of an inflexible precedence of the one over the other is ruled out in principle. What emerges is a patterned relationship between Jesus Christ, the church, and the world. This pattern is a differentiated yet integrated whole. That is, in the same way that the Council of Chalcedon in 451 declared that the two natures of Jesus Christ — divine and human — find union in the person of Jesus Christ, so, too, both the church and the world find union in Jesus Christ. In other words, the church-world relation forms, and here I'm borrowing from George Hunsinger, a "Chalcedonian pattern," a distinction-in-unity and a unity-in-distinction.[17]

Second, turning to Barth's doctrine of the church as it unfolds in *Church Dogmatics* IV/1-3, we find Barth playing out what it means to say that both the church and the world are *in* Christ. Because Jesus is Lord of both church and world, he can call witnesses to himself both inside and outside the church.[18]

As Barth puts it, Jesus is not "idle" in the world, but is Lord of all men and women.[19] As such there can be reciprocity between the church and the world, whether in the form of civil or political life. And this allows what I want to call a *qualified mediation* between the church and the world, suggesting that while the church has a priority in providing a witness to the Word of God, Jesus Christ, in the world, the church is not the sole proprietor

16. *CD* II/2, 566-83, 631-61, 719-26. All references to this volume will be noted parenthetically in the body of the chapter.

17. On Barth's use of a "Chalcedonian pattern" in his *Church Dogmatics*, see George Hunsinger, *How To Read Karl Barth: The Shape of His Theology* (New York: Oxford University Press, 1991), 185-88, 201-18. Thinking along the lines of Chalcedon, it may be thought that the church represents the divine nature and the world the human nature. But this is not quite the case. Rather, for Barth, if a Chalcedonian pattern depicts a relationship between a center and the periphery, or the divine and human, both the church and world constitute the periphery, or the human, and *only* Jesus Christ, the one Word of God, is the center. Hence, the church and world are unified in that they find their center in Jesus Christ, and thus, offer a *differentiated witness* to Jesus Christ. While the church possesses a greater likelihood of offering witness to Jesus Christ, this may not always be the case. In fact, all witness to Jesus Christ short of the Eschaton is provisional, which suggests that the church and world possess a more fluid, complementary relationship in offering witness to Jesus Christ.

18. *CD* IV/1, 650-725, and especially the sort of claim of Jesus Christ as Lord of all made on 661. Along these lines, Barth adds that the church cannot limit God's "hidden ways . . . in which He may put into effect the power of the atonement made in Jesus Christ (Jn 10:16) even *extra ecclesiam*, i.e., other than through [the church's] ministry in the world" (688).

19. *CD* IV/2, 724.

of such witness. For Barth, then, the world can, and does, provide witness to the Word according to the grace of God.[20]

Finally, this is made most clear perhaps in IV/3.1, where this qualified mediation, as I am calling it, is developed by Barth in terms of "secular parables" or "parables of the Kingdom [of God]."[21] The contention is that, because Jesus Christ is Lord of both the church and the world, "true words" can be spoken both inside and outside the church through the agency of Christ in his prophetic office. In other words, Christ at times enables both Christians and non-Christians alike to speak true words about God, humanity, or creation. The way the church identifies these "true words" in the world is by way of analogy. The church compares and contrasts secular words to scripture and dogmatic teaching, and if a legitimate correspondence is discerned, then the church can claim to hear secular words of truth or secular parables of the Kingdom of God. In the end, while the church is a *direct* witness to the Word of God, performing a role not granted to the world, the world's witness is *indirect*, it is parabolic, and yet it nonetheless shares with the church in witnessing to Jesus Christ. What this suggests is the possibility for a mutually edifying relationship between the church and the world. For Barth, one of the better examples of such an edifying relationship is the church-state relation. And with this, we turn to Barth's political theology.

As Hauerwas notes, Barth's political theology is best displayed perhaps in a collection of three essays under the title *Community, State, and Church.* Of the three essays, the one most illuminating for our purposes is "Christian Community and Civil Community," originally published in 1946.[22] In this essay, we discover that for Barth the church and state can inform one another of an "external, relative, and provisional order of law" that reflects "the original and final pattern of . . . the eternal Kingdom of God and the eternal righteousness of His grace" (154). This is possible, Barth claims, because, as we have seen with his understanding of the church-world relation, both church and state share "a common origin and a common center," Jesus Christ (156). Barth illustrates this by way of concentric circles with a common center. Christ is the center of the concentric circles, which represent the Christian and civil communities. Thus, Christ is in the center, the church is the inner circle, and the civil community is the outer circle, and something

---

20. *CD* IV/3.2, 740.

21. *CD* IV/3.1, 38-135.

22. Karl Barth, "Christian Community and Civil Community," in *Community, State, and Church* (Gloucester: Peter Smith, 1968). All references to this essay will be noted parenthetically in the body of the chapter.

of a Chalcedonian pattern emerges. Because both communities find their center in Christ, both communities can witness to and serve Christ and his kingdom.

This point of Christ being the center of both the church and state is one I want to develop a bit further, and here is where I think Barth's political theology is most illuminating. A key to understanding Barth's 1946 essay is the doctrine of divine justification. In section fifteen of the essay Barth writes, "The Church is based on the knowledge of the one eternal God, who as such became man and thereby proved Himself a neighbor to man, by treating him with compassion (Luke 10:35f.)" (171). Barth's reference to God's compassion points back to his work in *Church Dogmatics* II/1, where he notes that God's compassion for humanity is based on God's justification of sinful humanity.[23] Barth adds that God's compassion is a "sympathetic communion" with humanity, an expression of God's mercy for humanity, regardless of whether persons know it or not. In other words, God is "for" humanity whether or not persons are "for" God. What sets the church apart from the state, and indeed the rest of the world, is not that God's compassion has been directed only to the church, but that the church *knows* that God's compassion and reconciliation is effective for all humankind. The state as such remains ignorant of this knowledge and can only be made aware of God's reconciliation of humanity by way of the church and its activity. Thus, the knowledge of God's reconciliation, or divine justification, is what guides the church in its mission in the world, especially in the political realm. The church knows that no human being stands outside of the compassion of God, but in fact stands reconciled to God by way of divine justification in and through Jesus Christ. Barth's reference to God's compassion in the middle of his 1946 essay is an *indirect* but potent reference to God's justification of the ungodly and how this affects the political realm.

God's reconciliation or justification of humanity leads Barth to conclude, in "Christian Community and Civil Community," that the church and the state are able and should pursue the "humanizing," as Barth puts it, of people's lives. That is, the state and the church should never be about abstract causes, whether political or otherwise, but should seek to treat persons with compassion, mercy, and all that allows for human flourishing. To do this, Barth argues, is to provide for a "provisional sanctification" of men and women in the social and political realms (157).

Barth strengthens this claim by providing a *direct* reference to divine

23. *CD* II/1, 371.

justification. He writes, "The Church is the witness of the divine justification, that is, of the act in which God in Jesus Christ established and confirmed His original claim to man and hence man's claim against sin and death" (172). The "original claim" of which Barth speaks is, as laid out in *Church Dogmatics* II/2, God's eternal decree to be humanity's covenant partner. The divine claim on humankind, therefore, refers to the "right" God has on humanity, establishing and confirming the "basis and justice," as Barth puts it, of "man's situation" (561). God's claim on humanity translates politically into notions of human dignity, human rights, and the need for equality under the law within a constitutional state. With this unfolding, we are able to discern an important aspect of the movement from divine justification to the political realm, namely, from God's claim on humanity for its wellbeing to the state's obligation to provide for a humane environment in which human flourishing can occur. As the church and state are "in" Christ — and here we should not lose sight of the importance of the preposition "in" for Barth in this instance — so too, in ways appropriate to their respective vocations, they can and should reflect God's merciful claim on humanity.

While Barth maintains in his 1946 essay that the "concrete attitudes to particular political patterns and realities . . . [should] remain a completely open question" (157) — and that in fact the church should *not* have an "exclusive [political] theory of its own" or "establish one particular [political] doctrine as *the* Christian doctrine of the just State" (160) — he does suggest that democracy, or at least a form of government that has several democratic features, will be more than likely the most attractive to the church (181). What guides the church at this point is that of "analogy" or "correspondence" to the content of the gospel (170). Recall that "true words" or "secular parables" can be spoken in the world, and applied here the idea is that such words can come by way of the state. The state therefore can speak parabolic truth that the church can recognize, affirm, benefit from, and promote in the world as an analogue to the Kingdom of God. It is by way of analogy, then, that the church can move from gospel to democracy.

Barth provides several examples of this. For instance, as the church is the gathering of a free association, so too the state should guarantee the freedom of its citizens to make lawful decisions in regard to certain spheres, such as family, education, culture, and the like (174). Or, as God justifies humanity against sin and death, so too the state should establish equal protection under the law for all persons, which moves in the direction of a constitutional state as opposed to one of anarchy or tyranny (172). Also, as the church seeks to identify and honor the variety of gifts of the Spirit in the church, the political sphere should seek to separate and share the different political functions of the state, such as the legislative, executive, and judicial tasks (175). And finally, as the church believes that the human word is capable of being a vehicle for the Word of God, so too should the state allow for the "free human word in the political sphere" (176-77), for one never knows when true words of Christ will be spoken. These analogies, then, bear a "striking tendency," Barth writes, "to . . . what is generally called the 'democratic' State" (181). As Barth puts it, "the Christian view shows a stronger trend in this direction than in any other" (182).

But it is important to notice that the church's support of democracy is not based on the truth of democracy *as such,* but on the polity of the church — the life of Christians as gathered around the preaching of the Word of God, the sacraments, and the fellowship of the Holy Spirit in their midst. The church, in other words, is the best model of political life and when the church examines the various political polities, agendas, etc., available in the world, it should seek and promote those political arrangements that more nearly reflect the church's polity. That is, the church seeks those political arrangements that more nearly reflect what God has accomplished for the world in Jesus Christ and, in this regard, what God has given the church to know and indeed proclaim. Thus, the church can endorse democracy without giving the heart of the gospel away to liberal democracy. Moreover, the church may affirm democracy, and in fact any political set of arrangements if warranted, on so-called secular grounds knowing that such "grounds" are in fact already claimed by God in Christ and that the connection between the church's life and the political polity under consideration is that of analogy to the church's embrace of the gospel. For Barth, then, the church is free to engage political life, the state, etc., and yet to remain free from the ideological chains of political agendas that demand comprehensive allegiance. Indeed, while Barth embraces democracy, he is clear that democracy is not to be embraced uncritically over all other political polities. Barth claims, "the essence" of Christian politics or political theology is not any one system "but a constant direction, a continuous line of discoveries on both sides of the boundary which separates the political from the spiritual spheres" (180). The "constant direction" is the gospel and lordship of Jesus Christ and the "continuous line" of discovery is the path that both the church and the state should take in more nearly reflecting Jesus Christ and his will for this world.

V

Having laid out briefly what I take to be the salient features of Barth's theology of the "world" and the political realm, I want to offer some general impressions on the relationship between Hauerwas and Barth. First, it seems that there is much in Barth's construal of the church-world and church-state relationships that Hauerwas would find amenable. For Barth, the church is central for knowing God's activity in this world, something that the state or any other institution or human community cannot or should not claim. Indeed, the church is the locus of activity in which the gospel is known and proclaimed. Yet, what Hauerwas emphasizes but Barth is unwilling to add is that the church is *constitutive* of God's activity in the world. What Barth is willing to say is that if human activity is to be deemed reflective of the lordship of Christ in the world, we need the church to point that out, for it is only the church that has been given the calling of knowing what the activity of God looks like in the world. To the degree that explicit knowledge of God and God's activity in the world is the concern, the church is indispensable for such knowledge and consequently indispensable for nurturing that knowledge in persons by way of the church's practices. In this sense, church practices make all the difference in the world in regard to knowing and nurturing knowledge of God and obeying God's will. The church, in other words — and this seems to be Hauerwas's concern — is indispensable for a *direct* witness to God and God's will. But this is not the only witness to God available in the world, for Christ, as Barth puts it, does not sit idle in the world waiting for the church to act.[24] Indeed, because Jesus Christ is active in the world *as Lord,* there can be indirect witnesses to the lordship of Christ. As we have seen, the political activity of the state can be just such a witness. In Barth's terms, Hauerwas's con-

---

24. Interestingly, Hauerwas seems to affirm just this point in his earliest work on Barth, *Character and the Christian Life,* originally published in 1975. Here, Hauerwas seems favorably to quote Barth on Christ's lordship over all women and men, "'If [Jesus Christ] acts *extra nos pro nobis* and to that extent *in nobis,* this necessarily implies that in spite of the unfaithfulness of every man he creates in the history of every man the beginning of his new history, the history of man who has become faithful to God.'" If Christ is the history of every man and woman, then this impact on history would surely affect the political realm and that Christians could engage in "secular" politics knowing that Christ has already affected the history which politics seeks to shape. Unfortunately, to my knowledge, Hauerwas never returns to this claim of Barth, although he seemingly affirms it early on in his career. See Stanley Hauerwas, *Character and the Christian Life: A Study in Theological Ethics* (Notre Dame, IN: University of Notre Dame Press, 2001 [1975]), 140. This work is the published version of Hauerwas's PhD dissertation. On the quotation from Barth, see *CD* IV/4, 30.

cerns to maintain the indispensability and integrity of the church are anything but lost, and so it is hard to see exactly why Hauerwas is so critical of Barth's construal of the church-world and of the church-state.

Second, while the church makes a difference in the world, for Barth, it simply does not, indeed cannot, make *all* the difference. The church is limited in its role as a witness to God. Precisely in its limitation and fallibility as a witness to God the church can benefit from the world's or state's own indirect witness to the lordship of Christ. For example, the church has not always understood what it means to "humanize" life and thereby reflect God's merciful claim on persons. At times, then, the state and other secular institutions have provided the means by which the church can better learn what a more just construal of human life looks like. Insofar as this is the case, the church can learn from the world and indeed the state. In Barth's terms, such turning to the state by the church is hardly giving too much to the state but simply acknowledging that Christ's lordship extends far and wide in the world and that the church is wise to pursue Christ and his influence wherever they are to be found. Hauerwas is right to suggest that in this way Barth is attempting to steer a middle path between a sectarian church and an accommodationist church. But he is wrong to think that Barth does not provide *any* material conditions of how this may work, and hence falls too closely to the accommodationist side. Barth's political theology and its claims of human dignity, rights, and a form of democracy are only some examples of what the material conditions are.

Third, it is hard to see how Hauerwas's criticisms of Barth's view of the so-called secular world and particularly of the secular state gain much traction. It appears that Hauerwas simply misses Barth's rich theological, and indeed *Christological,* description of the church and state and their relationship in light of God's claim on the world in Jesus Christ. It is not the case, as Hauerwas alleges, that Barth gives too much to the state and not enough to the church *on Christological grounds.* Hauerwas would have to show how Barth's Christological construal of the church-world and church-state relationship is problematic, but to my knowledge Hauerwas nowhere does this. In the meantime then, it seems that Hauerwas has either misread Barth or simply ignored the key features of Barth's Christological understanding of the church-world and church-state relationship.

Fourth, this leads me to the conclusion that the main difference between Barth and Hauerwas appears to lie with the former's Christology and the latter's ecclesiology. For Hauerwas, it seems that the church, at least in Barth's view, encroaches on the work of Jesus Christ in securing human salvation, redemption of the world, and the ongoing life of the Christian community. According to Barth, there is a careful ordering of the relationship between Christ and his church. It is, as we have seen, a unity-in-distinction and a distinction-in-unity, or a Chalcedonian pattern. But this pattern, for Barth, must be delineated as a relationship of priority, which is to say, the priority rests on Jesus Christ and his lordship over the church.[25] For Hauerwas, the priority within this pattern seems to rest solely on the church, in that the church contains the person and work of Jesus Christ, his benefits of grace to the world. Consequently, to Hauerwas, the church limits Christ's activity in the world to the practices of the church. According to Jennifer Herdt, one reason this may be the case is that Hauerwas has given himself over to "Wittgensteinian insights" or the idea that truthful description of the world is limited to a community's "language game" and that quite often various language games, indeed various communities' conception of the truth, are incommensurable. In this sense, Hauerwas has limited his treatment of the church to "'traditional particularistic claims'" and consequently built the church upon that which is not distinctively Christian.[26] The outcome, Herdt argues, is that for Hauerwas "the church" becomes the central character of the Christian story he is telling and not God, and indeed not Jesus Christ. If so, says Herdt, then Hauerwas's "starting-point" is no less anthropological than the liberal Protestantism that he is trying to denounce (234), for his interest in the church is more nearly that of concern for the integrity of a Wittgensteinian language game. While Hauerwas worries that Barth may have fallen to one side of the middle path that Barth is attempting to navigate, it seems that in fact Hauerwas has fallen to the accommodationist side in the end.

VI

In sum, because of his ordering of the church, world, and state by way of his Christology, Barth is able to maintain the integrity of the church and its

25. On Barth's understanding of the priority of God's activity in Jesus Christ through the Holy Spirit in regard to the church's life, see Keith Johnson's fine article in this volume, "The Being and Act of the Church: Barth and the Future of Evangelical Ecclesiology," especially section V.

26. Jennifer A. Herdt, "Justification's End: Aquinas and Wittgenstein on Creation and Wonder," in *Grammar and Grace: Reformulations of Aquinas and Wittgenstein,* ed. Jeffrey Stout and Robert MacSwain (London: SCM Press, 2004), 233. All references to this essay will be noted parenthetically in the body of the chapter.

practices while embracing, albeit in an ad hoc manner, the world and state insofar as it indirectly gives witness to the mercy of God and lordship of Christ. How the relationship between the church, world, and state on this score will look is relative to the context and tasks at hand. Of course, analogically speaking, it will ideally look like the life of a faithful church in obedience to God in Christ through the Spirit. Yet, there is no guarantee that the church will be faithful to God, according to Barth, and it is precisely at these moments where the church and indeed the world and the political realm are maintained by the faithfulness of Jesus Christ to secure his earthly body and the world from the chaos of sin and for the hope of redemption.

In the final analysis, while Hauerwas's emphasis on the church has become quite attractive for some evangelicals, even if they bristle at his "colorful" language, they should remain critical of Hauerwas's ecclesiology in terms of how it is employed in the church-world and church-state relationships. My concern is that if evangelicals uncritically embrace Hauerwas's seemingly "rigid dualism," as Jeffrey Stout puts it,[27] between the church and the world, they will run the risk of developing — or continuing, as the case may be — an antagonism and resentment for the so-called secular world and its dealings. Such a stance is all the more disconcerting when we consider that evangelicals may reach these conclusions thinking that Karl Barth supports such a stance, given Hauerwas's repeated references to Barth. Yet, it has been my intention throughout this paper to show (1) that Hauerwas's reading and criticism of Barth is off the mark when it comes to Barth's understanding of the Christological construal of the church-world and church-state relationship and (2) that evangelicals would do well to consider Barth's views on these matters. For, in the end, Barth provides us with a theologically rich and profound understanding of Jesus Christ's lordship over both the church and the world, one that allows us, and in fact obligates us, to embrace the world in seeking a more merciful and just social and political order precisely because we are to embrace the proclamation and life of the church as Christ's witness in the world.

---

27. Jeffrey Stout, *Democracy and Tradition* (Princeton: Princeton University Press, 2004), 148-49.

Afterword: Reflections on Van Til's Critique of Barth

Bruce L. McCormack

Cornelius Van Til's engagement with Karl Barth's theology was extensive and lifelong. It is not possible to treat every one of his writings on Barth here; an examination of the critique in its originating forms will be sufficient, since that critique changed little over time. My goal is simply to clear the ground of some basic misunderstandings. And so in this chapter I concentrate my attention, first, on Barth's use of Kant's epistemology and, second, on the relation of revelation to history.

Preliminary Observations

The first thing that needs to be said about Van Til's critique is that it was born at a time when Barth studies were still very much in their infancy. *The New Modernism* appeared in 1946, five years before Hans Urs von Balthasar's landmark study and eight years before the German and Dutch editions of G. C. Berkouwer's careful study. For that reason, Van Til cannot be expected to know what scholars know today (with the benefit of decades of scholarly conversation, not to mention the forty-seven volumes of the critical edition of Barth's collected works). But it also has to be said that Van Til showed little inclination to make use of the secondary literature that was in existence when producing this work.[1]

---

1. He refers one time each to books by Peter Monsma, Th. L. Haitjema, Hans Wilhelm Schmidt, Theodore Siegfried, and to a single essay by Erich Przywara. See Cornelius Van Til,

A second observation: Van Til is not given to extended analysis of primary source material. His citations from Barth's writings are usually limited to a phrase or a single sentence — with the exception of *The Epistle to the Romans,* where his quotations are at times lengthier. For the most part though, he simply paraphrased — often adopting Barth's voice, speaking in Barth's persona. By any measure, this was a virtuoso performance. Van Til was operating largely in a vacuum of his own creation, with no conversation partners whose readings might challenge his own.

Third: Van Til did not believe that any fundamental changes took place in Barth's thinking from his earliest pre-war years on up through the early volumes of the *Church Dogmatics.* The so-called "break" with liberal theology is a matter of appearance only. Allegiance to Immanuel Kant's epistemology was something Van Til thought to be basic to Barth's thinking both before and after the shift to dialectical theology.[2] He thus saw no reason not to draw freely from Barth's writings from any phase of his theological development in order to produce a smooth synthetic picture. Moreover, his study of the *Church Dogmatics* in this book stops with II/1.[3] So the last phase of

---

The New Modernism: An Appraisal of the Theology of Barth and Brunner (Philadelphia: Presbyterian and Reformed Publishing Company, 1946), 67, 89, 192, and 193.

2. Van Til, *The New Modernism,* 73.

3. Van Til tells us that "When this section [i.e., the section on "Election" in his own book] was written, the second half of the second volume of Barth's *Kirchliche Dogmatik* had not yet appeared. Subsequent reading of that volume has convinced the writer that Barth's treatment of the doctrine of election in it is essentially the same as in the works discussed in this section." See Van Til, *The New Modernism,* 276n1. "Subsequent reading" did not, however, give Van Til an accurate understanding of Barth's new doctrine of election — nor an understanding of how it differed from his earlier version. Van Til seems to have been under the impression that Barth still taught the "activistic" doctrine which one finds in second *Romans.* "The true doctrine [i.e., Barth's view] cannot even appear upon the scene till we clear the ground of the idea of an eternal counsel according to which it takes place. . . . Election must not be thought of as a finished something at any point. It is not finished either in God or in man." That would be a seriously misleading statement if applied to the doctrine of election elaborated in *CD* II/2. It is true that Barth had *earlier* affirmed that election and reprobation *happen* when a person comes up against the creaturely veil of God's self-revelation and, in that situation, is either given or refused by God the eyes of faith to see what lies hidden beneath the veil. Election in this earlier account (which one finds spelled out most clearly in §18 of the *Göttingen Dogmatics*) is virtually synonymous with what the older Reformed theologians referred to as "effectual calling" — with the one important exception that Barth understands such "calling" in that phase to be ongoing. And so Barth can still speak of an *electio continua* in *CD* I/2 (a phrase which Van Til takes up in support of his reading, *The New Modernism,* 277) because I/2 is a work which belongs to the same phase of Barth's development as the *Göttingen Dogmatics.* See *CD* I/2, 349. But in *CD* II/2, Barth rejects the "activistic" view by

Bruce L. McCormack

Barth's development — initiated by revision of his earlier doctrine of election in CD II/2 — would have remained unavailable to him even if he had possessed an eye for developmental problems.

Van Til's Reading of Kant and its Impact on his Critique of Barth

We turn then more directly to the content of Van Til's critique. The foundation for that critique was laid in Van Til's interpretation of Kant's epistemology. And here already, serious questions arise. Van Til understood quite well that Kant had restricted human theoretical knowledge to the phenomenal world. The human knower is, as it were, cut off from the "object" (understood as the noumenal "thing-in-itself"). What we know are things as they appear to us. But the conclusions Van Til then drew from this state of affairs

name. See *CD* II/2, 188-94. And he can do so because he has now shifted the center of gravity in his doctrine of election from the believer's here and now to pre-temporal eternity. For the Barth of II/1 and II/2 (as for the old Reformed theologians), election is a decision that takes place before the world was created. Of that there can be no question. But, even on the basis of Barth's earlier doctrine it would not have been true to say (as Van Til does): "That God's potentiality is identical with his actuality means for Barth the reverse of what it means in the Reformed Faith. In the latter it indicates the doctrine of the ontological trinity, God's complete self-sufficiency apart from the process of time-created existence. For Barth it means God's freedom to grow through identification with the process of time-existence. God is said to be exhaustively revealed in history. By that Barth would have us see that there is no logical necessity inherent in reality that would keep it from developing. *God can wholly deny Himself as a transcendent being in order that, through this denial, He may add to His being.*" Van Til, *The New Modernism*, 278 (emphasis mine). Against this reading it has to be said that Barth's overwhelming concern throughout the phase that stretched from 1924 to 1936 (or so) was with the God-ness of God in His self-revelation. How can God reveal Himself to human beings, how can God assume a human nature and live a human life *without undergoing change?* That was Barth's leading question. No doctrine was more important to him than that of divine immutability. And that certainly does not change in *CD* II/1 and II/2. What does change is that the election is now made to be descriptive of an *eternal* decision. And while the ontological significance of that decision where the being of God is concerned is currently under debate among Barth specialists, all participants in this debate agree that Barth understood the ontological Trinity to be complete in protology (before the world was made) and that God is free in electing to be God for us in Jesus Christ (in the sense of "freedom from external compulsion" as well as "freedom from need arising out of internal deficiency). For that reason, Barth's God, too, is self-sufficient. For a thorough contrast of Barth's understanding of God's being as "in becoming" — as opposed to the idea that God's being "becomes," see Eberhard Jüngel, *God's Being Is in Becoming: The Trinitarian Being of God in the Theology of Karl Barth*, trans. John Webster (Grand Rapids, MI: Eerdmans, 2001).

showed that he had not fully grasped how Kant's epistemology actually worked. He thought, for example, that a Kantian should not be able to tell the difference between an orange and a snowball.[4] In saying this, he showed that he had not understood that Kant was an empirical realist in the precise sense of holding that the content of our knowledge comes to us entirely from without. Kant did not believe that knowledge is simply constructed by the human mind through the use of the "categories of the understanding." The "categories" simply provide the forms of knowing which help us to order sensible experience. Considered as pure forms (in abstraction from time), they include: unity, plurality, totality, reality, negation, limitation, inherence and subsistence, causality and dependence, community, possibility and impossibility, existence and non-existence, necessity and contingency.[5] At the end of the day, the Kantian is no different than the Platonist or Van Til's "historic" Christian in sensing that a snowball is white, that it is wet and melts in warm hands, etc., and in sensing that an orange is, well, orange, that its skin can be removed, and that it is good to eat. The content of the knowledge for all three is the same. And since the categories are thought by Kant to be universally valid and a priori in nature, there is no reason why it should be otherwise.[6] Kant was anything but a skeptic.

Van Til also failed to understand that Kant did not think it was the categories themselves that produced "antinomies." What creates antinomies is the *misuse* of the categories to posit the existence of something for which sense data is lacking (as happens, for example, in relation to talk of a "First Cause" in the old cosmological arguments for the existence of God). So Van Til is wrong to suggest that the Kantian "must keep up the fiction that these categories are means by which facts that are independent of them can be found.

---

4. Van Til, *The New Modernism*, 18: "We have argued that, on the Critical view of fact, no fact can ever be distinguished from another fact; snowballs might be taken for oranges."

5. A. C. Ewing, *A Short Commentary on Kant's Critique of Pure Reason* (Chicago: University of Chicago Press, 1974), 134-35.

6. Van Til also treats the categories as tools that are employed volitionally, through an act of will. Consider for example the following statement: ". . . we have reached an all-time high of nominalistic assertion. It is man's will to believe which is made his right to believe on the ground that one guess is as good as another." To illustrate, Van Til suggests that the Kantians are like castaways floating on a vast sea. They may *want* to believe that they are not surrounded by sharks. But the truth is that they are only staying alive by eating shark meat. How then do they cope with their fear of sharks? They give them another, arbitrarily chosen name. "They are called beefsteak and pork chops *by us,* and that is all that matters *for us.* They are what we call them." Van Til, *The New Modernism,* 25. But, of course, this is not Kant. The categories are not volitionally employed. They are a priori forms of knowing.

Without that fiction we should not look for anything new. Yet the fiction must be known to us to be no more than a fiction. If it were taken as truth, we should once more be lost in the mazes of our mutually contradictory affirmations and negations. We might, for instance, with equal justice both affirm and deny that God has made the world. Knowing it to be a fiction, we can apply logically contradictory affirmations to the buzzing, blooming confusion before us and make a path for ourselves in the jungle of Chance."[7] Van Til is wrong to draw this conclusion from Kant because the categories do not help us to "find" anything; they simply order intuited sense data. If anything, things give themselves to us through sensation. So the fiction described does not exist for Kant. Again: the correct employment of the categories will certainly bring order into the "buzzing, blooming confusion before us" but it will *not* create antinomies. Kant was anything but an irrationalist.

These mistakes aside, it is clear what Van Til himself believed (as an alternative to his picture of Kant) and why he thought Kant to be such a great threat to the Christian faith. Van Til held that there is no such thing as a "brute fact" which requires first to be interpreted by human beings in order to be given meaning. Everything that exists has been created by God; everything that happens has been ordered by God's providence. The true meaning of every "fact" is the meaning it is given in the eternal counsel or plan.[8] "God does not meet facts at second-hand. He meets them before they exist. His interpretation of them is prior to their very being."[9] So God has made a world that reflects the rationality of God's plan. Our acts of "discovery" presuppose a rational order which is embedded in God's world and maintained by His providential rule. For Van Til, the elimination of these basic beliefs would mean that the world was no longer governed by God but by chance. Such order and meaning as could still be "found" in it would actually be the creation of the autonomous human knower, who has usurped the place of God.

Seen in the light of this basic conviction, Van Til's concerns become a bit more comprehensible. He understood the whole of modern theology to be a single hymn of praise to Kant. All modern philosophers and theologians were, in his view, "phenomenalists." Barth was no exception. Indeed, Barth's use of "orthodox" language made him worse than others, since such use enabled him to conceal his debt to Kant. At the end of the day, the "new modernism" was no

7. Ibid., 16.

8. Ibid., 78: in classical Reformed theology, Van Til says, "the idea of a self-existent and self-contained God" comes to expression, "whose plan serves as the principle of individuation of whatsoever comes to pass."

9. Ibid., 14.

different than the old. Van Til's judgment on both was finally the same. "There is perhaps no instance of greater intellectual confusion found in the annals of human error than that of the retention of orthodox Christian forms by a purely naturalistic theology such as Modernism is. It is as though carbolic acid were poured into water bottles without a change of label."[10]

So what, if anything, did Van Til get right here? Well, he was certainly not wrong in thinking that a revolution had occurred in Kant. I would myself describe that revolution in the following way. What took place as a result of Kant's epistemology was the demise of the belief that order and rationality are simply embedded in the world and that knowledge takes place when human rationality is conformed to the rationality of the real. The human mind plays a role in the construction of knowledge; it is not merely passive. And with that loss of confidence in an evident providence, classical metaphysics (which was rooted in a cosmology that drew its life from that belief) also collapsed. Philosophers not happy with Kant's subject-object split were left to find a new basis for metaphysics — as occurred in differing ways in the thought of Johann Gottlieb Fichte, Friedrich von Schelling, and G. W. F. Hegel. And theologians could, if they chose, try to build upon the philosophical theologies of one or the other of these philosophers. Or they could, as Barth would later do, adopt a more nearly anti-metaphysical stance, thereby keeping a measured distance from all metaphysical schemes (old and new) while seeking to find a ground for Christian theology in God's self-revelation in Christ alone. They could then treat the problems dealt with by Idealists and Romantics alike as "parables" of subject-matters and questions dealt with by Christian theologians; as projects which could shed light on the theological problems they treated; as auxiliary aids and nothing more. As for Barth, he continued to believe with classical Reformed theology that God has an eternal will for the world. To that extent, he agreed with Van Til. But he did not believe that the content of that eternal will could be read from the face of nature or history. To be known, it had to be revealed — and was in Jesus Christ.

Van Til was also right to insist that Barth was indebted to Kant for helping him to articulate the structural features of his doctrine of revelation in the early years of his dialectical phase.[11] His conception of the *Realdialektik*

---

10. Ibid., 371.

11. See Bruce L. McCormack, *Karl Barth's Critically Realistic Dialectical Theology: Its Genesis and Development, 1909-1936* (Oxford: Clarendon Press, 1995), 130-31, 218-26, 245-62, 269-70.

of veiling and unveiling was first teased out with considerable help from Kant's phenomenal-noumenal distinction. But, as I have argued previously, Barth did not need Kant any longer once he discovered the ancient anhypostatic-enhypostatic Christology in the spring of 1924 and began to absorb the lessons of the traditionally Reformed understanding of the *indirect* relation of the two natures in Christ to each other (as mediated through the "person of the union").[12] The old Reformed theologians rejected the "divinization" of the human nature of Christ through its union with the divine Logos that was taught by the Lutherans — and in doing so established the material *ontological* conditions Barth needed to explain why it is that the Subject of revelation (viz. God the Logos) remains hidden to view precisely in revealing Himself. So after 1924, the claim that revelation is indirect was no longer a Kantian claim; it was a distinctively Reformed claim.

Either way, of course, Barth is still a "phenomenalist" in Van Til's sense. That is to say, Barth rejected the idea that revelation is *directly* given to the human knower — whether in nature, or history, or Scripture, or even in Christ. Indeed, it is finally because he believes revelation not to be directly given in Christ that Barth does not believe that it is directly given in nature, history, or Scripture. And *that* is the real sticking point between Barth and Van Til — the water's edge where the whale and the elephant meet in mutual incomprehension, each of them unable to enter the other's world and dwell there. *It is in the realm of Christology that all of the issues between them come to a head.* Van Til's preoccupation with philosophical issues only distracts our attention from what is truly important.

The Problem of Revelation and History

Van Til's efforts to understand Barth's Christology through the years would always be influenced by his initial study of the second commentary on Romans especially. The problem he grappled with there — and it is by no means an easy one to solve — was the relation of revelation to history.

---

12. Bruce L. McCormack, "Revelation and History in Transfoundationalist Perspective: Karl Barth's Theological Epistemology in Conversation with a Schleiermacherian Tradition," *Journal of Religion* 78 (1998): 18-37; reprinted in idem, *Orthodox and Modern: Studies in the Theology of Karl Barth* (Grand Rapids, MI: Baker, 2008), 21-39; idem, "Der theologiegeschichtliche Ort Karl Barths," in *Karl Barth in Deutschland (1921-1935): Aufbruch — Klärung — Widerstand,* ed. Michael Beintker, Christian Link, and Michael Trowitzsch (Zürich: TVZ, 2005), 15-40.

Again, Van Til believed that revelation is always directly given to the human knower. "The real issue is that of direct historical revelation. Calvin and the other Reformers, no less than later orthodoxy, with one voice affirm the direct revelation of God in history. Calvin, in particular, finds man surrounded by the direct revelation of God. For him nature and history alike speak with such perspicacity of the God who made them that only a blinded sinner can fail to see this point."[13] Whether Calvin actually taught any of this in quite so unguarded a fashion is a separate issue. Certainly Calvin's belief that revelation in nature will lead only to idolatry and superstition if not read with the "spectacles" of Scripture, his doctrine of accommodation in relation to God's speech in Scripture, and, above all, his emphasis upon the distinction of the two natures of Christ (over against the Lutheran idea of an interpenetration of the natures) all serve to qualify the idea of a *direct* revelation.[14] Be that as it may, Barth was struggling in his commentary to express the idea that God is the *subject* of revelation not just before He reveals Himself, but during the revelation event and even after it. Revelation, Barth insisted, does not become a predicate of history in that God reveals Himself through the medium of history. God remains ontologically distinct (or "other") than the various media He takes up in revealing Himself; therefore, though revelation makes its impact felt precisely *in* history, what is "left behind" after a "revelation event" (let us say, after Jesus ascended into heaven) are the "effects," so to speak, of a divine act which has taken place in the past. In themselves and as such, these "effects" do not reveal. But they can be taken up by God again — in and through a renewed activity — and once again become the vehicles of God's self-revelation. In and of themselves, the media of God's self-revelation are not revelatory — that is the key point.[15]

In order to make this point, Barth developed a rich battery of images. One of these was "primal history" *(Urgeschichte)* — a term which he adopted from the writings of Franz Overbeck but whose meaning he dramatically altered.[16]

---

13. Van Til, *The New Modernism*, 140. See ibid., 105: "For Calvin, nature and history directly display the thoughts of God. . . . [T]here is, accordingly, a direct revelation of God in history."

14. John Calvin, *Institutes of the Christian Religion* (Philadelphia: The Westminster Press, 1960), I.v.11-15 (on why the revelation in nature is not of profit to us); I.vi.1 (on the Scriptures as "spectacles); I.xiii.1 (on "accommodation"); and II.xiv.1-3 (on the "communication of attributes").

15. For the textual basis in Barth's Romans commentary for these claims, see McCormack, *Karl Barth's Critically Realistic Dialectical Theology*, 245-66.

16. Ibid., 226-35.

"Primal history" is used to suggest that revelation occurs in a "moment without before or after."[17] Revelation thus has no extension in time. It does not stretch out, so to speak, on the plane of history. Why this complex and convoluted way of speaking? The answer is far more pedestrian than is often imagined. Barth simply wanted to say that while revelation occurs *in* history, it is not *of* history. That is to say, the forces operative in history do not produce revelation. Revelation must come to history from without. Here again: revelation is not a predicate of history.

Now these are, admittedly, conceptually demanding ideas. Van Til was not the first to misunderstand them and he would not be the last. Van Til understood well enough that Barth was saying that revelation is not a predicate of history. But he took "primal history" to be a *region* located somewhere beyond ordinary history without any clear relation to ordinary history. "Primal history is a dimension that lies as it were between super-history and ordinary or surface history, while yet it impinges on both. Revelation is super-history in the sense that there is eternal happening in God himself. On the other hand, revelation is also ordinary history. Yet it is neither in super-history nor in ordinary history that God meets man. It is in the tension between the two that revelation takes place, and it is this tension that constitutes the realm of primal history."[18] It is clear in this passage that Van Til thinks that Barth is finally incoherent. Barth would like to be able to say that revelation occurs in ordinary history, but he cannot. His idealistic commitments will not, in Van Til's view, allow him to do so. And so Barth finally locates revelation in a realm beyond history. But that is a one-sided picture of what Barth is saying. Revelation does indeed occur in history but it does so in such a way that it does not become a predicate of history. That is the point.

Having located revelation in a realm beyond history, however, Van Til was ill prepared to understand Barth's Christology when it finally began to be elaborated (in 1924f.). I have already noted that Van Til did not lend any credence to Barth's claims to have distanced himself from many of the perspectives found in the second Romans commentary. That conviction had to mean that the location of revelation beyond history would remain a controlling idea for Van Til's reception of Barth's Christology — and it did. In the

---

17. See Eberhard Jüngel, "Einführung in Leben und Werk Karl Barths," in idem, *Barth-Studien* (Zürich/Köln and Gütersloh: Benziger Verlag and Gütersloher Verlagshaus Gerd Mohn, 1982), 38.

18. Van Til, *The New Modernism*, 154.

three brief pages which he devoted to a discussion of the Christology of *Church Dogmatics* I/2, Van Til says: "Suffice it to note that, as in the [Christian] *Dogmatics* so in the *Church Dogmatics,* it is, in effect by the idea of primal history that Barth does away, on the one hand, with the orthodox idea of God's eternity and, on the other hand, with the orthodox idea of God's direct revelation in history."[19] Clearly Van Til failed to notice that Barth had explicitly abandoned the term "primal history" in I/2 — and criticized himself for retaining it in *Die christliche Dogmatik im Entwurf.* The reason is that he now judged the term itself to be guilty of introducing the very thing he wished to avoid — making revelation a predicate of history (albeit a "special" kind of history). "Writers have called it 'redemption history' (like the earlier Erlangen school), or 'superhistory' (like M. Kähler, *Wissenschaft der christlichen Lehre,* 2nd ed. 1893, p. 12f., and, after him, P. Althaus), or 'primal history' or 'qualified history' (as I did myself, unfortunately, in reference to F. Overbeck, in the first volume of this book, p. 230f.). *Revelation is not a predicate of history, but history is a predicate of revelation.*"[20] Once Barth began to develop a concept of the incarnation in 1924, he could no longer make the medium of revelation to be anything other than ordinary history. No one who takes seriously the lived existence of the incarnate God through time can do that. That he did not abandon the term "primal history" right away (it still appears obviously in *Die christliche Dogmatik im Entwurf*) suggests only that his learning process was at times a slow and painful one. But the death knell had already been sounded for "primal history" in 1924.

The crucial question, then, is how Barth understands the two natures of Christ to be related to each other and to what the ancients called the "person of the union." On his answer to that question, virtually the whole of his concept of revelation in the *Church Dogmatics* would depend. Van Til, however, has little real interest in this question.[21] He only has eyes for "primal history"

---

19. Ibid., 227.

20. *CD* I/2, 58.

21. It is interesting that Van Til understands Barth to have held that what happens in the incarnation is that God changes "His being into the being of man" — interesting because, if true, it would collide so very sharply with Barth's repeated emphasis upon the hiddenness of revelation. After all, a God who simply morphed into a human being would, by doing so, make Himself directly available. See on this point Van Til, *The New Modernism,* 215-16. So how does Van Til come to this remarkable conclusion? How is it that he can say "Not needing His own being, God can change wholly or in part to the opposite of Himself. God's absoluteness consists in freedom to become the opposite of Himself and to take into Himself that which is opposite to Himself" (ibid., 226)? The first thing to be said is that the

and therefore he thinks that Barth continues to secure the hiddenness of God in His self-revelation through this device. In truth, Barth had been basing the hiddenness of God for quite some time on the old Reformed belief that the relation of the natures is mediated through the "person of the union" — a person (or "subject") which remains hidden to view within the veil of creaturely flesh.[22] It is not an idealistic understanding of history which is controlling his thinking but Reformed Christology.

In Van Til's later writings on Barth, the category of "primal history" receded in importance, but his concerns over Barth's rejection of a direct revelation did not. The focal point of those concerns was now to be found in a terminological distinction between *Historie* and *Geschichte* with which Barth is alleged to have worked.[23] But as before with "primal history," the terms in question are treated much of the time as referring to a distinction of *realms*. Certainly, whatever else *Geschichte* is, in Barth's hands, it is not "ordinary history," according to Van Til: "the real resurrection took place in *Geschichte* rather than in ordinary history."[24] Thus the *effect* of the distinction is the

---

last clause in this last statement has in it more than a grain of truth; the rest of it, however, rests on a misunderstanding — as becomes clear when Van Til returns to the point in a later essay and, thankfully, provides a reference so that one can test the basis of his judgment (no textual basis for the claim is offered here). The text in question is found in *CD* I/1 and reads as follows: ". . . the lordship discernible in the biblical revelation consists in the freedom of God to difference Himself from Himself, to become unlike Himself and yet to remain the same, to be indeed the one God like Himself and to exist as the one sole God in the fact that in this way that is so inconceivably profound He differentiates Himself from Himself, being not only God the Father but also . . . God the Son." See Van Til, "Has Karl Barth Become Orthodox?" *Westminster Theological Journal* 16 (1954): 161-62n90; here citing *CD* I/1, 320. Now Van Til is absolutely right to see in this passage a reference to the incarnation. God becoming "unlike" Himself refers to becoming human — and this becoming human is made to stand in an intimate relationship to the eternal act of self-differentiation which is constitutive of the triune life of God. Yet what he misses and simply cannot take seriously, is Barth's insistence that, in becoming unlike Himself in becoming incarnate, God *remains the same*. What is clear here is that Van Til has not understood the Christology which provides the basis for Barth's doctrine of God (and the becoming human while remaining the same). Barth does not believe that God becomes His opposite, but he does believe that a *relation* to the human Jesus belongs to the essence of God (so that the human experience of suffering and death can reasonably be said to be an event that God takes into His own life in order there to take away their power).

22. See McCormack, *Karl Barth's Critically Realistic Dialectical Theology*, 358-67.

23. Van Til, *Christianity and Barthianism* (Nutley, NJ: Presbyterian and Reformed Publishing Co., 1962), 13-16.

24. Van Til, "Has Karl Barth Become Orthodox?" *Westminster Theological Journal* 16 (1954): 135-81, 175.

same as the earlier use of "primal history": it secures the existence of a realm in which things are said to happen in a time that is other than calendar time.

The problem is that the distinction is largely one of Van Til's own creation. To the extent that it finds a root in Barth's writings at all, it is a distinction between two quite different hermeneutical approaches to the study of events which have not been caused by the forces operative in history; it is not a distinction in realms. The word *Historie,* when it is not used simply as a synonym for *Geschichte,* refers in Barth's vocabulary to the writing done by modern historians about historical events — the writing of or about history, in other words. It does not refer to a special realm related in some indefinite way to *Geschichte.*

This emerges clearly in Barth's treatment of the creation narrative in Genesis as "saga." Barth clearly holds that "the fact that creation encloses in itself the commencement of all time does not alter in the very slightest the fact that it is itself real history and that as such takes its place in time. But it cannot be overlooked that this fact gives this history a supremely distinctive and exceptional character in relation to all others. Its distinction obviously consists objectively in the fact that it has no pre-history with which to stand in a retrospective connexion or relationship, but that it consists in an absolutely new event which seen from the standpoint of the creature begins with itself."[25] Moreover, this objective distinctiveness of the creation event must give rise to a distinctiveness on the subjective side as well. There were no eyewitnesses to this event. So the biblical narratives that relate the history of creation have a different character than do those that relate events for which there were eyewitnesses. And that fact alone "has often led to a denial of the historicity and temporality of creation and the reinterpretation of the biblical witness as a declaration which really aims at an unhistorical and timeless relationship between the Creator and the creature."[26] Against this tendency, Barth says two things. The first is that "the biblical witness must oppose such a reinterpretation. Even here it can only recount history and it can be understood and evaluated as historical narration. It has to say what it does in fact say — that creation was the commencement of time but that it has also taken place in this commencing time."[27] The second is that the difficulties facing a historian do not simply disappear where this is recognized. There is a real problem here. The problem is that "history which we cannot see and compre-

25. *CD* III/1, 76.
26. Ibid., 77.
27. Ibid.

hend is not history in the historicist sense [*Geschichte, die wir nicht zu sehen and zu begreifen vermögen, is aber jedenfalls keine historische Geschichte*]."²⁸

What Barth is getting at here is quite easily explained by reference to a well-known historicist, Ernst Troeltsch. In a groundbreaking essay published in 1898, Troeltsch set forth three postulates that, he thought, must always govern historical investigation. The first of these is that historical judgment is, at best, probable in nature — which necessitates a critical testing of all historical claims with regard to the degree of their probability. The second postulate is that "analogy" provides the criterion for making judgments concerning probability.²⁹ The third postulate is that "all historical happening is knit together in a permanent relationship of correlation."³⁰ That is to say, the forces at work in nature and history today are the forces which have always been at work in nature and history. There are no others. Therefore, any attempt to explain what happened in the past can only make appeal to the forces known to be operative in nature and history. Now in response to this, Barth would likely have said that the third postulate is actually metaphysical in character. Certainly, it cannot be defended by historical method alone. The historian *as historian* must indeed limit herself to historical explanation — and that means that she must limit herself to those explanations which can be defended by means of appeal to analogies to events known to be caused by the forces operative in nature and history. What she cannot do, however, is claim that the kind of explanation she is able to offer is the only possible explanation there can be. She ceases to be a historian when she does that — and becomes a philosopher or theologian. So when confronted by ancient reports of an unusual event then (one without a pre-history and for which an appeal is made to divine causality in the reports themselves), she can try to assess their probability on the basis of tools available here. But she must also exercise a certain humility with regard to the limits of her method and tools.

So when Barth says that creation is not the kind of history that we can see and comprehend "in the historicist sense," he is simply saying that the

---

28. Ibid., 78.

29. Ernst Troeltsch, "Historical and Dogmatic Method in Theology," in idem, *Religion in History*, trans. James Luther Adams (Minneapolis: Fortress Press, 1991), 13-14: "The illusions, distortions, deceptions, myths, and partisanships we see with our own eyes enable us to recognize similar features in the materials of tradition. Agreement with normal, customary, or at least frequently attested happenings and conditions as we have experienced them is the criterion of probability for all events that historical criticism can recognize as actually having happened."

30. Ibid., 14.

historian as historian is not qualified to render a final judgment upon it. He is saying that there will be cases where she must say "I can neither confirm nor deny that this happened, functioning strictly as a historian." He is, in effect, granting to Troeltsch that historians must operate on the basis of analogy in order to do history at all and that they must make appeal only to the forces to which they, as historians, have access. But he is not granting the historicist reduction of all explanation to historical explanation of this kind.

The same thing is true of the resurrection. The resurrection is an event in space and time. Already in his second commentary on Romans Barth had said that the resurrection is "bodily"[31] — which has to mean an event in space and time. But the issue is: what is a historian to do with reports of post-resurrection appearances? The explanation offered for these appearances in the New Testament writings is that the God and Father of our Lord Jesus Christ raised Him from the dead. Confronted by such an explanation, the best the historian can do (from the standpoint of Christian theology) is to leave some room for it by saying that the tools she uses are not adequate for eliminating that explanation from consideration. But functioning strictly as a historian, neither can she confirm that explanation — for the simple reason that historians interpret events *historically,* meaning in terms of forces operative in nature and history.

Now one might have thought that such reflections are pretty straightforward and unexceptional — and they are. But Van Til tried to understand what Barth was saying *not* in relation to the historicism against which Barth was protesting but rather in relation to Barth's claim that revelation is not direct. In doing so, he wound up with a distinction of realms — and with that, the evacuation of all of Barth's doctrinal affirmations (the Virgin Birth, the sinlessness of Jesus, His substitutionary atonement, His resurrection) of their contact with real historical events.[32] This is the explanation for his otherwise incomprehensible claim that Barth's theology "is calculated to lead men to think that they are not sinners, that they are not subject to the wrath of God, that their sins need not be washed away through the blood of the Son of God and the Son of man, Jesus of Nazareth who was born of the virgin Mary, died and rose again with the same body with which he was laid in the tomb."[33] Every student of Barth knows that the only item in this list

31. Barth, *Der Römerbrief (1922)* (Zürich: TVZ, 1940), 183.

32. Van Til, "Has Karl Barth Become Orthodox?" 173. Van Til was also misled by Barth's rather complicated account of the relation of the time of Jesus Christ to ordinary time in *CD* I/2 — but that must remain a story for another day. See ibid., 138n9.

33. Ibid., 181.

which has even a grain of truth in it is the second ("that they are not subject to the wrath of God"). All the others are constructs of Van Til's imagination.

Conclusion

The preceding explanations do not, by any stretch of the imagination, address all of Van Til's objections to Barth. What they do succeed in doing is clearing the ground of two basic misunderstandings — one in relation to Kant's influence on Barth and one in relation to Barth's understanding of history. What remains are the differences that will not go away between Van Til's version of "historic Christianity" and Barth's reconstruction of Christian doctrines. These differences are rooted finally in the fact that Barth's doctrine of God is Christologically controlled while Van Til's doctrine of God controls his Christology[34] — though this is just the tip of the iceberg. Van Til had a pre-modernist sense of confidence that the rationality that is proper to God's eternal counsel and plan was somehow embedded in the natural order as well as in the flow of history. Barth regarded such confidence as belonging to a world which no longer existed; hence, his massive assault on natural theology and the need to ground knowledge of God differently than it had been in the past.

Which of these approaches is to be preferred is not self-evident. So the choice between them must not be casually or reflexively made. It must be made only after careful testing in the light of the witness of Scripture and the engagement with the Christian tradition in all of its breadth. Anything less will serve neither the cause of truth nor the well-being of the evangelical churches.

34. That Van Til's Christology is controlled by his doctrine of God is clear when he says, for example, that in becoming incarnate, the second person of the Trinity "does not give Himself wholly. He retains His aloofness from man. His divine nature keeps itself in self-contained isolation from his human nature. It retains its own incommunicable attributes in splendid isolation from man even in the incarnation. Thus Jesus Christ cannot as God be said to be very man." Ibid., 160. Seen in the light of statements like these, it is understandable that G. C. Berkouwer would wonder whether Van Til was sufficiently attuned to the dangers of Nestorianism. See Berkouwer, *The Triumph of Grace in the Theology of Karl Barth* (Grand Rapids, MI: Eerdmans, 1956), 391. Be that as it may, one wonders how it is possible to have *direct* revelation of God in Christ on the basis of a Christology that tilts so dramatically in the direction of Nestorius. One might be forgiven for thinking that an indirect revelation is all you could get.

Contributors

Clifford B. Anderson
Curator of Special Collections
Princeton Theological Seminary

Kimlyn J. Bender
Associate Professor of Theology and Philosophy
University of Sioux Falls

Todd V. Cioffi
Assistant Professor of Congregational and Ministry Studies
Calvin College

John R. Franke
Theologian in Residence
First Presbyterian Church (Allentown, PA)

John E. Hare
Noah Porter Professor of Philosophical Theology
Yale Divinity School

George Harinck
Professor of the History of Neo-Calvinism
Vrije Universiteit Amsterdam

Contributors

D. G. HART
Visiting Professor of History
Hillsdale College

KEVIN W. HECTOR
Assistant Professor of Theology and of the Philosophy of Religions
University of Chicago

MICHAEL S. HORTON
J. Gresham Machen Professor of Systematic Theology and Apologetics
Westminster Seminary, California

KEITH L. JOHNSON
Assistant Professor of Theology
Wheaton College

BRUCE L. MCCORMACK
Charles Hodge Professor of Systematic Theology
Princeton Theological Seminary

SUZANNE MCDONALD
Assistant Professor of Theology
Calvin College

ADAM NEDER
Associate Professor of Theology
Whitworth University

JASON A. SPRINGS
Assistant Professor of Religion, Ethics and Peace Studies
Kroc Institute of International Peace Studies
University of Notre Dame

Index

American Presbyterianism, 44-45, 52-66. *See also* "Auburn Affirmation"; Orthodox Presbyterian Church (OPC); Presbyterian Church (U.S.A.)

Analogy: as *analogia fidei*, 286-95; as correspondence between divine and human action, 167, 215-16, 225-26; and parable, 289; as witness (indirect or parabolic), 358, 360-63

Arminianism, 228-30, 235, 263, 266n.48

Atonement: Barth on, 132, 138-42; limited, 235, 240-41; Paul on, 231-33; penal substitutionary, 228; universal, 228-29, 239-40, 242-43. *See also* Universalism

"Auburn Affirmation," 55, 64

Augustine, 83, 143n.136, 196n.69

Balthasar, Hans Urs von, 14, 140, 146, 246-48, 284

Baptism, 218-23

Barth, Karl: on church, 194-98, 204-5, 356-61; and criticism of his "Christomonism," 144, 146; and dialectic of veiling and unveiling, 284, 293-94, 305-7, 371-72; and Dutch neo-Calvinism, 19-22, 24, 33, 36-41; evan-gelical reception of, 45-52, 65-66, 69-70; and federal theology, 120-21, 133-36; Hauerwas on, 350-56; as neo-orthodox, 15, 31, 46, 52-53, 92, 300-301; problems in his Christology, 171-76; on religious experience, 106-10; on theological knowledge, 104-6; turn from liberalism, 46, 92, 106, 353

Bavinck, Herman, 17-19, 26, 28, 34, 37

Beckwith, Francis, 202, 207

Berkouwer, Gerrit Cornelis: Barth on, 15n.10, 178n.3; criticism of Barth on history and eternity, 130, 133-34, 137; criticism of Barth on law and gospel, 142-43; criticism of Barth's universalism, 145, 253, 264, 266; on Schilder, 35; on Van Til, 28, 380n.34

Bonhoeffer, Dietrich, 91, 147

Boring, Eugene, 233-35

Bromiley, Geoffrey, 48-49, 62, 177, 179n.5

Brunner, Emil: and dialectical theology, 13-14, 23, 30, 56, 59; and criticism of Barth, 121, 130, 137-38, 144-45

Bultmann, Rudolf, 47, 51, 77

Busch, Eberhard, 103-4, 291, 294

Buswell, James, 79-80